CW00828567

ZANZIBAR

ZANZIBAR

Its History and Its People

W. H. INGRAMS

STACEY INTERNATIONAL

First published in 1931 by H. F. G. Witherby, London

Zanzibar

This edition published by
STACEY INTERNATIONAL
128 Kensington Church Street
London W8 4BH
Telephone: +44 (0)20 7221 7166 Fax: +44 (0)20 7792 9288
Email: info@stacey-international.co.uk
www.stacey-international.co.uk

ISBN: 978-1-905299-44-7

Printing and binding: Oriental Press, Dubai

CONTENTS

The plate section appears between pages 210-211
The maps appear between pages 30-31 and 62-63

FOREWORD

The republication of W.H. Ingrams's compendium on *Zanzibar, Its History and Its People*, seventy-six years since its original publication in 1931 and 40 years after its reprint in 1967, shows the renewed fascination with these Isles of Cloves, and the continuing relevance of Ingrams's work. Since it has remained rare despite being reprinted, I was very happy to accept the invitation from Leila Ingrams to write the Foreword in this valuable book.

Given the inevitable shortcomings of colonial scholarship, considering the times and purposes for which such books were written, it is nevertheless remarkable that colonial civil servants found the time and energy to collect and preserve for posterity such important information about the territories under their control. That modern scholars have to start with a critique of such writings does not detract from their value without which we would have little to check and compare what can still be gathered from oral research in these very rapidly changing times.

Reading the Table of Contents of Ingrams's volume, one is impressed by the breadth of his investigations, from the Stone Age fossils found at Chukwani, about which we are only beginning to get archaeological confirmation, to the early twentieth century, from political history to the ethnography of the indigenous people of Zanzibar, not forgetting their production systems, social organization, beliefs and traditional medical practices.

In his 1931 Preface, Ingrams mentions that the manuscript had reached 'impossible proportions' and had to undergo 'various surgical operations designed to reduce its bulk.' One can only hope that the excised parts still survive in the Ingrams Papers which could constitute an additional source of information on the history and ethnography of Zanzibar. He also mentions that he was forced to omit much that had appeared in two previous works on Zanzibar: *Zanzibar, an Account of Its People,*

Industries and History, and *School History of Zanzibar* which he wrote with Mr. Hollingsworth in 1925. These works have become extremely rare even in Zanzibar, and their republication in some form should prove to be extremely useful to those undertaking new research on these islands.

Abdul Sheriff

Former Professor of History at the University of Dar es-Salaam and Advisor and Principal Curator, Zanzibar Museums, Zanzibar

PREFACE

I am delighted to write this preface to *Zanzibar, Its History and Its People* which has given me the opportunity to reacquaint myself with this great tome of Zanzibari ethnography. It was one of those huge and formidable looking books that I used to see as a school child in Stonetown in the 1970s in a glass case during my frequent visits to the library housed at what is locally referred to as *Makumbusho Ndogo*, the Museum of Natural History in Zanzibar. However, it was not until I was a student that I had the opportunity to explore its pages as part of a literature review for my anthropology assignment at Brunel University. I read it avidly and thoroughly enjoyed it, particularly the details of Zanzibari arts and crafts.

The book is essentially an historical ethnography of Zanzibar. Although aimed at a specialist audience, it is also accessible to the general reader. The extensive and thorough review of written historical evidence, mainly from secondary sources in the first section of the book is enlightening and provides good reference material. The author also describes local legends, and their important social function in recording and constituting the oral history of the island. However, as is the case with many writings of the time, the emphasis is on 'Great Men' of the past. Zanzibar has also produced women who were notable in their contribution to Zanzibari notoriety. For example, Princess Salme bint Said bin Sultan, the first Zanzibari published woman writer and the first Arab writer of an autobiography, and Siti bint Saad, a celebrated classical musician.

The author's extensive observations and lived experiences

– both on the main island of Unguja and Pemba and the smaller islands which make up Zanzibar – provide a detailed and lively account of society at the time and make engaging reading.

Ingrams was not a typical anthropologist or historian with a dry academic approach. He went out to Zanzibar in 1919 as Assistant District Commissioner. In his last posting in Zanzibar, he served as Private Secretary both for the British Resident, and for the Sultan of Zanzibar. His various professional hats or turbans, and his fluent Kiswahili, facilitated entry into the island's cultural life and gave him additional insights. I believe this work was also inspired by his love and appreciation of the islands and its people. Leila Ingrams, his daughter, has sustained these sentiments by agreeing to republish this tome (although it has been reprinted), for the *Wananchi,* local people, and those encountering the islands for the first time.

Zanzibar, Its History and Its People, a comprehensive work, perhaps daunting on account of its size, is a joy to read, and is a rich resource for scholars and general readers alike.

Said el-Gheithy
Sayyida Salme Foundation

INTRODUCTION

My father, the author of this work, was appointed Assistant District Commissioner in Zanzibar on 4 July 1919 – he was 22 years old. He started to collect material for this book in 1921 and continued until he left in 1927. During those years he gathered an enormous amount of material from the inhabitants themselves. The first part is a thorough review of the history of Zanzibar and the second is ethnological – covering a wealth of subjects and detailed vignettes of everyday life of individuals.

On my own visits to Zanzibar I have been approached on several occasions concerning the reprinting/republication of this work. I have sought advice from authorities whose knowledge of Zanzibar is far greater than mine to ask if the work was worthy to be republished. I was told researchers and scholars find it an important source. Much of the material contained in the book is still relevant to the Zanzibar of today. A new index replaces the old.

Contemporary readers may find that the vivid tone of the book is in contrast to modern scholarship. My father was a direct person – he called a spade a spade and would have been equally direct about himself and his country, England! I appreciate all the advice and comments I have been given concerning how to present the work – perhaps a smaller publication that would include theoretical and practical aspects? My own feeling is that I have no right to shorten and change somebody else's work – therefore I have left it 'warts and all'. This is absolutely irrespective of the author being my father. I would feel the same about another's work.

I think it is appropriate to add Sir Claud Hollis's testimonial on William Harold Ingrams:

'Mr Ingrams is an industrious and conscientious officer, possessing self-reliance, initiative and general administrative ability. He is tactful and sympathetic in his dealings with all classes. He probably knows more about the Arabs and natives of Zanzibar and Pemba than any other European, and has written some very useful papers on their history and customs and on the dialects in use in the Protectorate.

'His social and moral qualities are excellent and he has much personality and charm of manner.

A. C. Hollis *(Signed)*

Acting High Commissioner, Zanzibar, June 23 1925'

I would like to extend my special thanks to Professor Abdul Sheriff, Said Al-Gheithy, Dr Madeleine Gantley, Elizabeth Ingrams, Zainab-Lila Mohammed and Laura Marziale who have assisted me with this work by their kind help and support and welcome advice. My thanks are also due to those who have suggested that *Zanzibar, Its History and Its People* should be republished.

I will leave the last part of this Introduction to my father and copy here extracts from his classic book, *Arabia and the Isles*, first published in 1942 – fifteen years after he left Zanzibar, which capture his love of the islands and the people and his friendships with the then rulers of the island.

'There are places where one instinctively feels at home. I did in Zanzibar and in the Hadhramaut … As I go to each new place I make a habit of watching it draw nearer, and I always hope it will be the dawn that gives me the first glimpse of a new home. So far I have been lucky and the impression left on me with the sun rising on the shores of Zanzibar on the morning of August 25, 1919, is ineffaceable.

'As we drew near, and as the sun rose, feathery palms appeared standing amid a vivid green of grass and undergrowth. A coral shore of dazzling whiteness and a sea shaded from pale green to dark blue made an unforgettable foreground. The tall white houses of Zanzibar town, standing high and square, reached almost to the water front, dominated by the verandaed palace with high clock tower called the Beit al-Ajaib – the House of Wonders. Its clock seems always six hours wrong to the newcomer, for it keeps – and may it always keep – Arab or Biblical time and is set at sunset each day. There is but one minaret on Zanzibar's waterfront, at its northern end, Malindi, where the dhows congregate. It is a minaret of Hadhramaut pattern and was built by a man from Shihr …

'… I soon found that that Colonial Office pamphlet had described the duties of District Officers with extreme economy of words …

'But I had many other jobs: I was the local Pooh Bah [in Pemba]. I was Port Officer, Collector of Customs, Postmaster, Registrar of Births, Deaths and Marriages, Probate Agent, Registrar of Documents, Sub-Treasurer and I dare say other things as well …

'Back in Zanzibar I left the country districts for good and in 1925 held several posts in addition to my new work in the Secretariat. Amongst other jobs I was Private Secretary to the Sultan [Seyyid Sir Khalifa bin Harub] and to the Resident [Sir Claud Hollis] at the same time. But apart from occasionally writing letters for the Resident to the Sultan and answering them for the Sultan to the Resident, the double role did not worry me much except during the naval visit, when day after day I would see the Admiral off from a Residency party and, very often with a hasty change of uniform, make my way as fast as possible to one of the palaces to receive him on behalf of the Sultan. They were the most considerate masters. I owe much to Sir Claud Hollis and so does Zanzibar. For his Highness [Seyyid Sir Khalifa bin Harub], he would always say: "I must consult Her Highness first." They were an affectionate couple and after the Sultan took to a motor-car they were often to be seen driving out together. I never knew a man in a position such as his with more natural dignity and charm. On State occasions no country could have had a fitter representative, and in matters of State concern he had a surer instinct for what was right than many of those who advised him.'

Leila Ingrams

PREFACE

THOUGH the modern city of Zanzibar is at the most two hundred years old, it has a fascination usually attributed only to much older foundations. The impression it makes on the casual visitor is a distinct one, that is not eclipsed, much less effaced, by sojourns in other and better known Eastern cities. It is generally admitted that one can recapture more of the atmosphere of *The Thousand Nights and a Night* in Zanzibar than in the modern City of the Caliphs, and I know of no other town where in a few short hours one can see such a pageant of history as is paraded before one's eyes in Zanzibar in the early months of the year. At this season one sees anchored in the harbour those strange crafts whose prototypes for years untold have brought traders and colonizers from all parts of the East, and one encounters in the streets representatives of all the many races that have helped to make the island's history.

But the fascination of Zanzibar extends beyond the confines of the city. The island cannot aspire to majestic scenery, but there is beauty to be found all round its coral shores and in the waving palm and scented clove groves of the interior.

The interest and the influence of Zanzibar, however, reaches far beyond its own borders. For centuries it was the principal emporium of the eastern seaboard of Africa.

I have written at length of the countries that traded with Zanzibar and the east coast from the earliest times in the historical chapters of this book, but I had not thought it possible that those who traded there could have dealt with the city of London in early days. However, it seems likely that produce from Eastern Africa reached London long before the merchants of Mincing Lane traded in its cloves, for, delving into the history of Smithfield, I found in Fitzstephen the following lines on London's foreign trade, written in the twelfth century:

> "Aurum mittit Arabs: species et thura Sabæus:
> Arma Scythes: oleum palmarum divite sylva
> Pingue solum Babylon: Nilus lapides pretiosos."

At one time the Zanzibar Empire stretched from Guardafui to the Rovuma River, and inland beyond the great lakes. In addition, its ruler held sway over all the south-eastern corner of Arabia, and his influence stretched beyond even these extensive borders. At this time, the heyday of the Zanzibari-Omani Empire, the island became celebrated in the well-known saying, " When you play the flute at Zanzibar, all Africa, as far as the Lakes, dances." This empire has passed, but much of its influence remains. Swahili is one of the principal languages of the world, and it has been spread far and wide from Zanzibar. From Port Said to Durban, from Zanzibar across the Congo to the west coast, in Southern Arabia, Western India and in Madagascar, there will be found men who speak it. Many of the Creoles of Mauritius and Réunion are of Zanzibar origin, and the Creole language, though French in its vocabulary, is Bantu in its grammar. You may hear in the Creole of Mauritius the folk-lore that you have heard in the Swahili of Zanzibar.

As for the Island of Pemba, though it is somewhat overshadowed by the glory of Zanzibar, it is not without its fame. It has been described as the " Pearl of the Indian Ocean," and to the Arabs it is known as Jezirat al Khuthra, or the Green Island. It is certainly one of the beauty spots of the world. In East Africa and Madagascar it has a more sinister fame, as it is looked on as the very University of Witchcraft.

From the Colonial Civil Servant's point of view, I suspect that there is but one Zanzibar and that one is rather spoilt by starting a career in the Protectorate, but none the less I count myself very fortunate to have spent the years from 1919-1927 there. Nearly all the material in this book was collected during that time from the inhabitants themselves. Certain of the history has been gleaned from other authorities, but as regards the ethnographical part, I found an unexplored field and therefore, despite its shortcomings, I hope the book will be of use to those whose study lies in this subject, and also to those who come to the island to help its people to achieve their destiny.

I think it is true to say that Zanzibar until recently has been only dimly aware of its earlier history, and barely conscious of the fact that it is the mother of the other dependencies of Eastern Africa. Some of this history I have already published in work derived from the historical chapters in this book and from others that from considerations of space have had to be omitted. An abstract of it first appeared, together with a résumé of the Ethnography, in *Zanzibar, an Account of its People, Industries, and History*, and in the *School History of Zanzibar*, which Mr. Hollingsworth, of the Zanzibar Education Department, and I wrote in 1925. Some of it has reappeared in Mr. Hollingsworth's *Short History of the East Coast of Africa*, and the children of Zanzibar and the east coast are therefore now enabled to learn something of the story of their own country. No country can afford to neglect its history, and it is my hope that lessons may be gained from this story which may be of value in the making of future history.

It is possible that Zanzibar history may yet be taken much farther back. In 1927 I took to the South Kensington Museum some fossils obtained in blasting operations at Chukwani, six miles south of Zanzibar town, and was informed that they had the appearance of being a typical Pleistocene stone *breccia*. It has yet to be proved that they are what they seem, namely the remnants of the meals of Stone Age men, from the bottom of a collapsed cave.

As regards the ethnography, nothing beyond the résumé referred to above and a few articles in *Man* and the *Zanzibar Gazette* has appeared before. The only safe foundation for any civilization is that built on the traditions and life of a people, and so I hope that this record of the manners and customs of the Zanzibaris will be of use to them and those who are called on to administer them. I have included in the book a good deal of the magic practised in both islands, and I hope that an understanding of it will help, with patience and sympathy, to its elimination as education progresses.

I have given an extensive bibliography of Zanzibar literature in *Zanzibar, an Account of its People, Industries, and History*. Space forbids the reproduction in this book of the names of any books not actually used.

I have to acknowledge the help and encouragement given to me by Mr. T. A. Joyce, M.A., O.B.E., Deputy Keeper of the Department of Ceramics and Ethnography in the British Museum. It was he who first instigated me to write the book, and he has given me every help possible towards getting it published. He has very kindly read it and made suggestions for its improvement, which I have endeavoured to carry out. I owe quite an especial debt of gratitude to Sir Claud Hollis, K.C.M.G., C.B.E., now Governor of Trinidad, not only for reading the book and giving me much help, but for the opportunities he made for me while he was British Resident at Zanzibar, to get material and to improve the book in different ways. To many other individuals who have helped me I can only extend a collective expression of gratitude, for their name is legion.

Some of the photographs have been taken by myself, but for others I am indebted to Mr. A. C. Gomes of Zanzibar. The photos of native handicraft were taken by the late Mr. John Heath, of Shrewsbury, and the objects portrayed are either on loan to the Shrewsbury School museum or deposited in the Museum at Zanzibar.

The book has been through many vicissitudes before seeing the light of day. It was started in 1921, and gradually grew till it had reached impossible proportions in 1927; since then it has undergone various surgical operations designed to reduce its bulk, but I doubt whether it would have emerged finally into printed form if it had not been for my wife, who rescued it from the oblivion of a dusty shelf, read it, made further suggestions for its improvement and finally herself bearded the publisher in his den.

The actual publication of the book has been made possible by the generosity of the Zanzibar Government who, with the consent of the Colonial Office, have subsidized the work in a very substantial fashion, and I wish therefore to take this opportunity of tendering my very sincere thanks for their most practical assistance.

W. H. I.

Port Said,
October, 1930.

DEDICATED
(BY GRACIOUS PERMISSION)

TO
HIS HIGHNESS SEYYID SIR KHALIFA BIN HARUB,
K.C.M.G., K.B.E.,
SULTAN OF ZANZIBAR

AND TO
HIS SUBJECTS,
ESPECIALLY THOSE WHO,
EITHER DIRECTLY OR INDIRECTLY,
HAVE ASSISTED IN THE
COMPILATION OF THIS BOOK.

CONTENTS

MOSQUE WITH MINARET, MALINDI, ZANZIBAR

(Built late 19th century. Shape of Minaret and pattern of chevron very similar to those used by the builders of Zimbabwe.)

INTRODUCTORY

CHAPTER I

INTRODUCTION

In the first introductory and historical chapters of this book I have endeavoured to give a perspective to the main part of the book, namely, the ethnology of Zanzibar. In the ordinary way, when writing of the life and customs of a primitive people, the historical introduction can be dismissed in a few pages, but in Zanzibar circumstances are different, and owing to a variety of reasons which will be found outlined, its history is long and complicated, and the customs of the people are coloured, to a large extent, by external influences, as throughout the centuries the Zanzibaris have absorbed the manners of the various civilizations that have been imposed upon them.

The book is concerned in the main with the native inhabitants of the Islands of Zanzibar and Pemba. In the historical portion it has been impossible to avoid dealing, to a large extent—at any rate in the earlier part—with the adjacent African coast. The islands and the coast have been intimately connected—historically, politically and ethnologically—for a very long period.

GEOGRAPHICAL DELIMITATIONS

The Zanzibar Protectorate, as defined by the Zanzibar Order-in-Council 1924, comprises the Islands of Zanzibar and Pemba and islands within the territorial waters thereof. This definition is somewhat smaller than that in the *procès-verbal* of the 9th of June, 1886, defining the territories of the Sultan of Zanzibar, which includes all islets within a 12-miles radius of Zanzibar and Pemba. The

Zanzibar Sultanate includes not only Zanzibar and Pemba and islands geographically dependent on them and Latham Island, but also the 10-mile wide coast strip of Kenya Protectorate.

The Island of Zanzibar is situated in 6° S. latitude, and is separated from the mainland by a channel 22½ miles across at its narrowest part. It is the largest coralline island on the African coast, being 54 miles long by 24 broad (maximum measurement), and having an area of 640 square miles. To the north-west of Zanzibar, separated by a channel about a mile wide, is the Island of Tumbatu, which is of ethnological importance, as it is the headquarters of one of the three tribes of the protectorate. It is administratively included with Zanzibar Island. It is 6 miles long and one wide, and is 3,619 acres in extent.

Some 25 miles to the north-east of Zanzibar, athwart the 5th degree of South Latitude, lies the Island of Pemba. It is smaller than Zanzibar, being 42 miles long by 14 broad (maximum measurement), and having an area of 380 square miles.

The annual rain-fall amounts approximately in Zanzibar to 56 inches, and in Pemba to 75 inches. The rainy seasons are well defined; the heavy rains occur in April and May, previous to the setting in of the south-west monsoon, the light rains in November and December, before the recurrence of the north-east monsoon. The mean maximum temperature in Zanzibar is 84·9, and the mean minimum 76·6. The corresponding figures for Pemba are 83·6 and 73·2 respectively.

Thirty-five miles to the south of Zanzibar lies Latham Island. It is a small island inhabited only by vast numbers of sea-birds utterly fearless of man. Known to the natives as Shan Jove or Fungu Kizimkazi, it was probably originally discovered by the Portuguese, but named after the East Indiaman *Latham*, which rediscovered it in 1758. It was annexed to Zanzibar in the nineties.

GEOLOGICAL HISTORY

Recent research by Mr. G. M. Stockley has entirely altered the ideas previously held as to the geological history of Zanzibar and Pemba.

It was not until the Miocene that Pemba—the older of the two islands—emerged from the sea. Contrary to what was previously believed, Pemba emerged not joined to the mainland, but as an island separated from the mainland and from Zanzibar by a rift fault. During this period Zanzibar was still beneath the sea.

The beginning of the Pliocene found Zanzibar still submerged, and the present topography of Pemba being gradually determined. At the end of the Pliocene and the beginning of the Pleistocene, Zanzibar was connected with the mainland as an arm which formed a promontory. Later the advance of the sea destroyed the connection with the mainland, and a small archipelago of three islands developed.

The retreat of the sea in late Pleistocene times gave it its present outline, and decided the terraces of Zanzibar and Pemba.

At the beginning of the Holocene, the present geological age, Zanzibar and Pemba were densely forested islands, but they are now practically denuded of forest. During this age Pemba has been subsiding a little, and the valleys of both the islands, and of the coast, have been drowned by the present advance of the ocean, which forms them into creeks.

VEGETATION

The native vegetation of Zanzibar can be divided into five zones, the first of which are the mangrove swamps.

The mangrove seed is peculiarly adapted for travelling by sea, and for taking root in the sea; that species which germinates on the tree and drops with a pointed weighted end into the mud, and is thus planted by the parent tree, being to my mind one of the most remarkable provisions of nature.

The second zone is that of the beaches and rocks, which support the Euphorbia, the wild date palm (*Phœnix reclinata*), some other species, and also certain Asiatic species like the Casuarina, indigenous to the South Sea Islands and the India Archipelago, and brought thence by the great current that sweeps across the South Indian Ocean from Asia to Africa. The Screw pine is also another of these Asiatic immigrants. I think the Borassus palm should also be included in this zone; of this there are two species —that of Asia without a bulge, and that of Africa with one. These are generally confined to the coast region, the former to the east facing the Indian Ocean, and the latter to the west facing the mainland of Africa.

The third zone consists of the scrub bush, and is mainly of one species, *Psiadia dodaneifolia*, which emits a peculiar odour well known to those who have travelled across this zone on hot days.

The fourth is the Bush savannah, which includes that peculiar monstrosity, the baobab tree. This tree, I believe, is generally considered indigenous to Africa as well as Asia, though no doubt some of those on the east coast of the island made the long journey across the Indian Ocean in the seed stage.

The fifth and most interesting zone is a part of the great tropical forest of Africa, and includes several species peculiar to Zanzibar.

The chief species are *Landolphia kirkii*, the rubber vine, and peculiar to the Island of Pemba; *Typha latifolia*, the tree bamboo; *Elæis guineinsis*, the oil palm; *Raphia ruffia*, the raffia palm, and also several good timber trees, including a cassia, called by the natives "Mvule." The chief remaining example of this forest is the Ngezi forest in the north of Pemba.

FAUNA

The chief animals of Pemba are: Mammals—the Mozambique or grey monkey (*Cercopithecus rufoviridis*), a small gazelle (*Cephalophus pembæ*), galago (*Galago crassicaudatus*), the black pig (*Sus scrofa*), genett (*Viverra megaspila*), and a tree coney (*Dendrohyrax adersi*). Reptiles include sternnotheres (*Sternothærus sinuatus* and *S niger*), the black-necked cobra (*Naia nigricollis*), the Egyptian cobra (*Naia haje*), and the boomslang. Pemba also boasts a species of cat-fish (*Clarias*), found in the fresh-water ponds.

Zanzibar animals include most of the above, except the grey monkey, the black pig, the sternnotheres and the poisonous snakes.

But in addition Zanzibar has the leopard, the civet cat (*V. orientalis*), the slender mongoose (*Mungos gracilis*), the blue or Syke's monkey (*C. albigularis*), and the red bush pig (*Potamochœrus africanus*).

It has also four mammals peculiar to itself, the Zanzibar Guereza (*Colobus kirkii*), the Zanzibar Duiker (*Cephalophus adersi*), the Giant Elephant Shrew (*Rhyncocyon adersi*), and a squirrel (*Paraxerus palliatus lastii*).

Among reptiles it has the python, the Nile monitor (*Varanus niloticus*), and a large burrowing vegetable-eating skink.

It should be remarked that the black pig of Pemba is a relic only of Portuguese times, and that the tree coney is mainly confined to Tumbatu Island, which it shares chiefly with *Nesotragus moschatus*.

Zanzibar no doubt owes its mammalian fauna to the fact that it was, until well on in Pleistocene times, connected with the mainland. Those species which are now peculiar to the island must have developed since that date. How Pemba, which, according to recent ideas, was never joined to the mainland, succeeded in obtaining its terrestrial fauna is a problem that must at present remain unsolved. It is to be noted, however, that its mammalian fauna is far more scanty than that of Zanzibar.

DERIVATION OF THE NAME OF ZANZIBAR

The ancient name for Zanzibar and its people is the Zinj, and it is of interest and importance here to explain its origin, history and use.

Major Pearce says: "It is generally accepted that the name 'Zanzibar' is derived from the Persian word 'Zangh,' meaning a negro, and 'bar,' a coast. Thus the name, in its widest sense, signifies 'The Negro Coast.'"

The *Periplus* does not mention the word, but speaks of the "Continent of Azania," which Burton says "is probably an adaptation like Azan and even Ajan of the Arabic Barr el Khazain, or the land of the tanks, the coast below Ras Hafun and Ras el Khayl."

Pliny also speaks of the Azanian sea. Ptolemy states that immediately after Opone is another bay where Azania begins. "At this beginning are promontories, Zingis (*Zingina promontorium*), and the tree-topped Mount Phalangis." Azania appears to contain the element Zenj, as does possibly Unguja, the native name, first recorded by Yakut (Lenguja) in the thirteenth century.

The Adulis inscription of the fourth century gives Zingabena, and Cosmas Indicopleustes speaks of the Sea of Zenj and Zingium.

Abu Zayd Hasan, Masudi, Albiruni and Idris all mention it, as do Ibn Batuta, el Nowayn and Abulfeda.

The word Zanj, says Burton, is a corruption of Zinj (whence the plural Zunuj, evidently the Persian Zang or Zangi = the black) by the Arabs, who ignore the hard "gaf." "In modern Persian 'Zangi' still means the negro, and D'herbelot says of the Zenghis that they are properly those called Zingari, and by some Egyptians and Bohemians." Dr. R. S. Charnock derives from Zangi the racial gipsy names Czingany. It., Zingari, Var. Cingani, Zingara, Cingari, Port., Ciganos, German, Zigeuner.

The Arabs, Burton states again, like to derive the word Zanzibar from Zayn Za'l Barr = "Fair is this land." The original derivation of the word "Zang" is a matter for some speculation; the earliest use of the word appears to be that of Ptolemy. The ancient Egyptians called the people "Nehesi," and the Arabs the "Sudan."

It seems possible that the Persian word is a derivation from the natives' name for themselves; it may be connected with Zimba, cf. Vazimba, Zimbabwe, Agysimba, etc. "Barr" is the modern Persian word for "the coast," the old Persian being "Para," and the Arabic "Sahil."

The word Barra in Swahili, as used in Zanzibar, means the mainland; the Arabic "Barr" is also used for "country," i.e., Bar arab = Arabia, and Bar ajam = Persia. They also use the word Bilad (in Hindustani Bilati, whence, of course, the word coined in the late war, "Blighty").

Cosmas Indicopleustes has the following remarks: "Beyond Barbaria there stretches an ocean which has there the name of Zingion. Bordering on the same sea is the land called Sasos, which possesses abundant gold mines. Barbaria is also called Troglodytyca."

Zinj was one of the three old Persian and Arabian sections of the world, namely, Hind, Sind, and Zinj referred to by the mediæval European geographers as India Major, Minor and Tertia. It must be remembered that from ancient times to well on in the Christian era, Asia and Africa were confused, and East Africa considered as one of the East Indies.

Another form of Zinj is the Japanese *Tsengu*, and of Zanzibar the Chinese *Tsengpat*.

In early maps and voyages the word *Zanzibar* appears under a variety of different forms, of which

Zanzibar, Zanjibar, Chancibar and Xengibar are examples.

In Vasco da Gama's voyage the island is called Jamgiber, and down to quite recently, after the modern name Zanzibar was adopted, the mainland opposite was called Zanguebar. The length over which Zanguebar extended has been variously shown by different geographers, Arabian and otherwise. It should extend from about the Juba River down to at least Mozambique Island, though in early days it was usually protracted as far as Sofala.

CHAPTER II

The People

POPULATION

In a dispatch to Lord Lansdowne in 1901, Mr. Cave, the Consul-General, recapitulated the various estimates that had been made of the population of Zanzibar as follows:

"The earliest estimate that we have is that of Captain Smee of the Indian Navy, who reported in 1811 that the population of these islands amounted to 200,000, of whom two-thirds, or 133,000, were slaves. The population of Zanzibar Island was estimated by Dr. Ruschenberger in 1835 at 150,000, by Dr. Krapf in 1844 at 100,000, and by M. Guillain in 1846 at 60,000 to 200,000. Then, in 1858, Sir Richard Burton gave the number of residents in both islands as 400,000, of whom two-thirds, or 266,000, were slaves, and a similar estimate was made by the Sultan, Seyyid Barghash, in 1873. These figures were considerably reduced by Mr. Consul Smith, who believed that twenty years later, in 1894, the number of inhabitants did not exceed 150,000, and that this number did not include more than 75,000 slaves. And, lastly, in February, 1895, Sir Lloyd Matthews gave it as his opinion that the population of the Sultanate amounted to about 208,700 souls, of whom 140,000 were slaves."

The first actual census was taken in 1910, but the methods used were rough and ready, and it is generally regarded as having been only approximate. The population was returned as being 114,000 souls in Zanzibar Island and 83,000 in Pemba, a total of 197,000, which included 230 Europeans and about

9,000 other non-natives, mainly Indians, and not including Arabs.

In 1921 a non-native census was taken which showed 260 Europeans and a total of about 14,000 non-natives.

A native census was taken in 1924 which showed that that section of the population numbered about 186,000, of whom 16,000 were Arabs. The total population at that date was about 202,000, since when it has considerably increased, chiefly owing to immigration.

Further detailed information can be obtained from the census report of 1921 and 1924.

INHABITANTS

The population of Zanzibar is one of the most cosmopolitan in the world. In the census of 1910 and 1921 the non-African population has been shown as belonging to the following peoples: British, French, German, Portuguese, American, Norwegian, Italian, Greek, Dutch, Hebrew, Swedish, Goan, Indian, Cingalese, Parsee, Arab, Baluchi, Japanese, Chinese, Armenian, Seychellian and Mauritian, and others could no doubt be added to this list. The African element includes a diversity of tribes too numerous to attempt to catalogue in full. Besides Abyssinians, Egyptians, Nubians and Moors, it includes a number of representatives of the Hamitic peoples, mostly Somalis but a few Masai, and a large number of Bantu tribes. But for ordinary purposes the population is divided into (1) Europeans, (2) Indians, (3) Arabs, and (4) Africans, and from the viewpoint of Zanzibar history and ethnology, these peoples may be classified as follows:

(1) Europeans.

(*a*) British. Have been the paramount power since 1890, and have exercised an influence totally out of proportion to their numerical strength owing to their political position.

(*b*) Others. Of no ethnological or historical significance.

(2) Indians—mainly.

(*a*) Mohammedans. Mostly of Shia sects. Important commercially.

(*b*) Hindus. Have been longest connected with the coast. Important commercially.

(*c*) Parsees. Of no historical or ethnological importance.

(3) Arabs.

(*a*) Omani. The ruling race. Of principal importance since the early nineteenth century.

(*b*) Shihiris. Hardy people from the Hathramaut. Small traders and water-carriers, etc., for the most part. Of no importance ethnologically.

(4) Africans.

(*a*) The native tribes of the Protectorate—the Wahadimu, Wapemba and Watumbatu, to whom the major part of this book is dedicated and on whom it is focused.

(*b*) The Comorians — natives of the Comoro Islands, who consider themselves as Arabs but are Bantu in speech. They are of no ethnological importance.

(*c*) The freed slaves. Descendants of slaves brought to Zanzibar mainly during the nineteenth century, and who still call themselves by the names of the mainland tribes from whom they are descended.

(*d*) Mainland immigrants, chiefly Wanyamwezi.

The ethnological influence of the Europeans is sufficiently indicated in the chapter on the Swahilis and Freed Slaves. The influence of the Indians—practically negligible—is dealt with in the Introduction to the ethnological portion, and I append here a short account of their connection with the coast.

The customs of the Omani Arabs I have briefly described in the ethnological portion.

The freed slaves are dealt with in a chapter in the ethnological section.

THE NATIVE TRIBES

The whole of these peoples of Zanzibar and Pemba who have an African origin, together with those on the opposite coast, are generally referred to as Waswahili.

The word Swahili is Arabic in origin and derived from the plural of Sahil—Sawahil, which means coasts. The word therefore means the people of the coast. Dr. Steere, at the end of the preface of his hand-book, says: "The natives themselves jestingly derive it from Sawa Hila, which a Zanzibar interpreter would explain as 'All same cheat.'"

Nowadays the word is generally accepted to mean the mixed race, a blend of the aboriginal coast natives, slaves brought from the up-country region and Arabs, which lives in most of the towns on the coast and in Zanzibar.

However, in the remote parts of the island, where there is not much attraction for Arabs and Indians to go, the natives are left more or less as aboriginal as they ever were; in Zanzibar they are generally accepted as being of three tribes, namely:

(1) The Wahadimu, the people who inhabit the eastern coast of Zanzibar from north to south and much of the southern region where it is habitable.

(2) The Wapemba, or original inhabitants of Pemba Island.

(3) The Watumbatu, who are the purest bred of the three and live on the Island of Tumbatu.

Hadimu means in the usual way a slave, a freed slave, a servant, a dependant, but the Wahadimu have always been a free people, and Archdeacon Dale, in the *Peoples of Zanzibar*, gives the meaning as the Manumitted. Certainly the title is always regarded as honourable, and they themselves derive it from *Ahadi*, "a promise," as they say they made

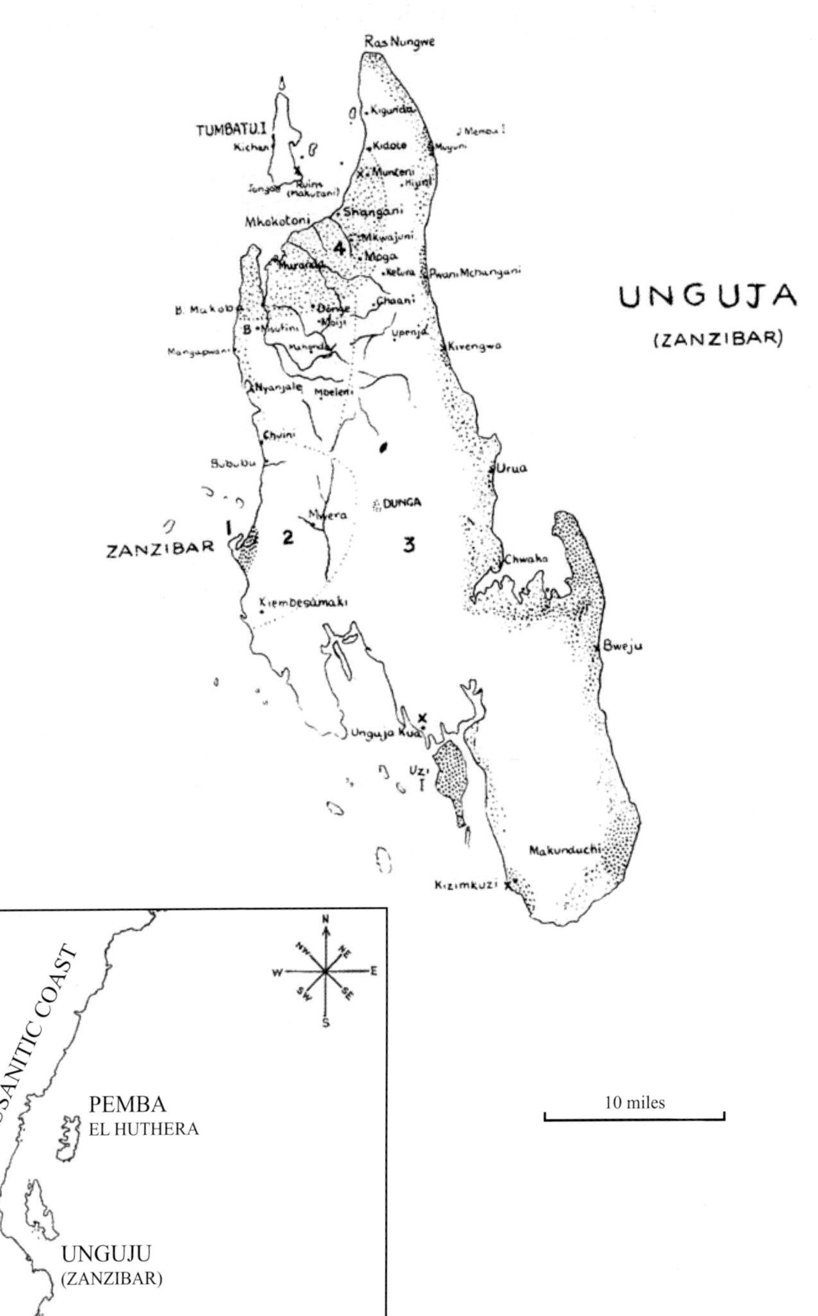
UNGUJA
(ZANZIBAR)
Ras Nungwe
TUMBATU.I
Mkokotoni
Shangani
Mkwajuni
Moga
Pwani Mchangani
Chaani
Kivengwa
B. Makoba
Nyanjale
Chuini
Bububu
DUNGA
Mwera
ZANZIBAR
1
2
3
4
Urua
Chwaka
Kiembesamaki
Bweju
Unguja Kua
Uzi I
Makunduchi
Kizimkuzi
10 miles
N
NE
E
SE
S
SW
W
NW
AUSANITIC COAST
PEMBA
EL HUTHERA
UNGUJU
(ZANZIBAR)

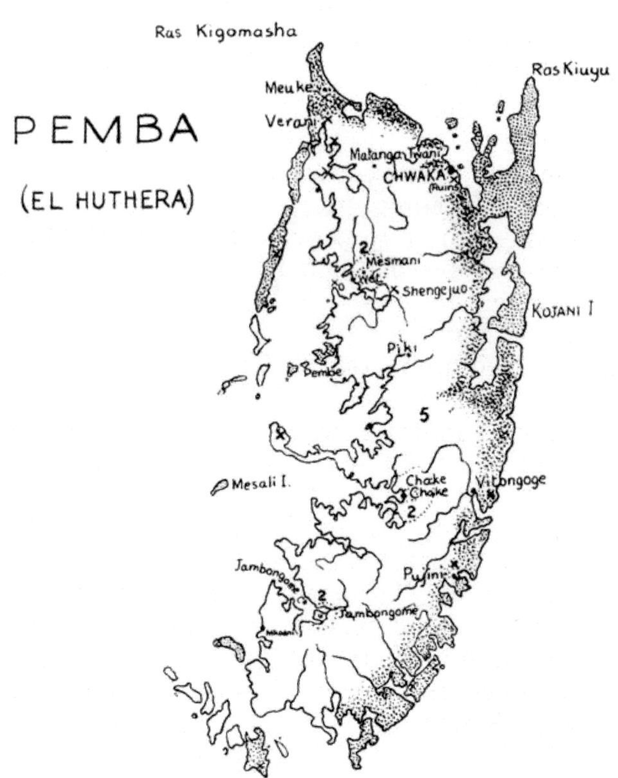
PEMBA
(EL HUTHERA)
Ras Kigomasha
Ras Kiuyu
Meuke
Verani
Matanga
CHWAKA
Mesmani
Shengejuo
Kojani I
Piki
Pembe
Mesali I.
Chake Chake
Vitongoge
Jambangome
Pujini
10 miles

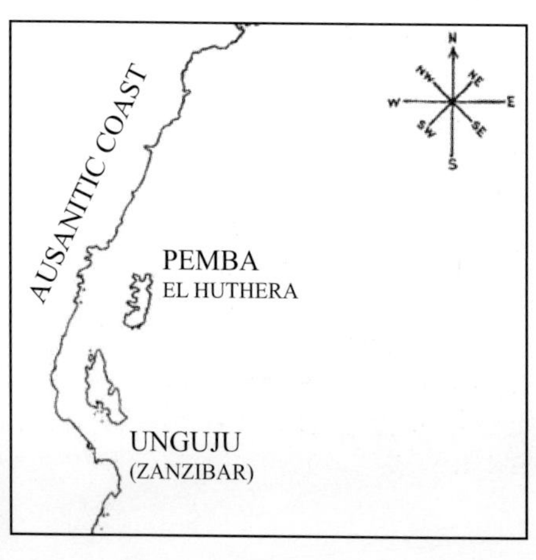
AUSANITIC COAST
PEMBA
EL HUTHERA
UNGUJU
(ZANZIBAR)
N
NE
E
SE
S
SW
W
NW

promises and agreements with the successive conquerors of the country to do work and pay taxes on condition of otherwise being left to themselves.

In the map facing this page, I have endeavoured by means of hatching to show the strongholds and distribution of the tribes. It is impossible to claim any exactness for this, but I have made it as accurate as possible, and I think it is not far out.

The dark hatching in each case represents the localities where the purest of each tribe live, and the light shading represents the less pure. The thickness of hatching must not be taken to mean thickness of population in any way; in fact, some of the places thickest hatched are more sparsely populated and vice versa.

The figure 1 indicates where the foreign element—white and Indian—chiefly reside. Figure 2 represents the Swahilis, and must also be taken as being included in figure 1; figure 3 is the Wahadimu; figure 4 the Watumbatu, and figure 5 the Wapemba. The region above figure 2 in Zanzibar Island is too mixed to give any idea of what section predominates, and is a mixture of Swahili, Tumbatu and Hadimu people.

The peoples of Nungwe, Kijini, Muyuni, Pwani Mchangani, Kiwengwa, Chwaka, Bwejuu, Makunduchi, Kizimkazi and Uzi Island are pure, or almost pure, Wahadimu, and Dunga was formerly their capital. The district round Unguja Kuu is now, I think, fairly evenly Hadimu and Swahili, and is so indicated. The only absolutely certain place is Tumbatu Island, where I think one can guarantee that, except for two policemen, there is no one who is not an Mtumbatu. The non-stippled portion on the main island is largely Tumbatu in influence. Most of the men I know in Mvuleni and Shangani are of Tumbatu origin. Ketwa recently refused to amalgamate with Moga, as they said they were Wahadimu and Moga was Tumbatu. Mwanda has a lot of Tumbatu fishermen. Donge and Mbiji, Bumbwini Makoba (whose sheha is head of all

Tumbatu people) and Bumbwini Msufini, quarrelled and separated under different shehas, for the same reason that Moga and Ketwa would not unite.

And so I think my demarcation is fairly correct.

Pemba is, of course, much purer, but there again the purest is on the east coast.

I have omitted to mark the Island of Kojani in a slightly different manner, not because I think the inhabitants are anything but Wapemba, but because I believe them to be older and purer still. In fact, there are a few words that are only used in Kojani, and not even in the Pemba dialect.

There are small settlements of Watumbatu on the south-east coast of Pemba.

The people of Makunduchi are so unlike any other section of the population that I have devoted a special chapter to describe the customs peculiar to them.

MAINLAND TRIBES

Of the mainland and other semi-African tribes, members of the following nineteen are most numerous, though the names of over fifty others have been recorded in abstracting census figures:

Kamba	Songosongo	Sukuma	Bajuns
Comoro	Nyamwezi	Nyassa	Manyema
Kikuyu	Dengereko	Bisa	Zaramu
Makua	Ganda	Zigua	Yao
Gindo	Sagara	Digo	

Of these the Wanyamwezi, the Akamba and the Wakikuyu are the most important in the economic life of the country.

The Zanzibar and Pemba natives do not take kindly to the heavy manual labour involved in the performance of work as paid labourers for cleaning and weeding shambas, and such work as road-making, and the Wanyamwezi particularly do this work well.

They are hard workers and thrifty (which is more

than Zanzibaris are), but they rarely take up shambas themselves, though they would probably do well if they could be encouraged to do so.

Many of them cannot be regarded as permanent settlers, as they only come to make money and return to the mainland. Few bring their wives, and this, and the fact that they have no headmen of their own in this country, sometimes causes friction with the local natives.

Many were brought over as clove-pickers in 1922-1923, but their employment on this form of labour was not a success, owing to their being strange to this kind of work, though they worked hard.

In religion they are generally pagan, though they readily embrace Christianity or Islam. If they remain pagan, they build their little devil-houses (called Kinyimanyera) in front of their huts and retain the practices of their tribe.

CONNECTION OF THE INDIANS WITH THE COAST FROM THE EARLIEST TIMES TO THE PRESENT DAY

Despite the fact that the Hindus appear to have been trading with the east coast of Africa from very early times, they can never, until possibly the last year or two, be considered to have had any political influence on it. As in early times, so to-day the Hindus and most of the Indians come to Zanzibar or to the coast as visitors, and, having made their money, return to their homes. During all the time they are in Zanzibar the money they make is sent home.

It is considered that the earliest sea-going trade in the Indian Ocean started in the time of that enlightened ruler, Nabonidus, the last of the Chaldean kings of Babylon, and a man far in advance of his times. For a couple of centuries following his reign it is probable that sea trade between India and Babylon flourished, and even in his time ships are known to have come to Babylon from India and from China.

These traders were mainly Dravidians, but partly Aryan, and their explorations led to the settlement of Indian traders in Arabia, East Africa, Babylon and China. Not only did the Hindus make trading settlements on the coast of East Africa, but they appear also to have penetrated well inland. Indeed, it is recognized that they had considerable intercourse with the Abyssinians.

It is an interesting fact that Speke, when laying his plans for his expedition to discover the source of the Nile, secured his best information from a map reconstructed from the Puranas. This showed the great Krishna River running through Cush-ndipa, the great lake in Chandristhan, the country of the moon, which gave the correct position in relation to the Zanzibar Island. This country they gave the name of the moon, because of the people who lived in it, namely, the Nyamwezi tribe. *Wanyamwezi* means " the men of the moon."

This trade of the Hindus must have been going on long before the birth of Christ, and the mention of the word *Nauplios* or *Nargilios* (an Indian word for coco-nut) in the *Periplus* is a confirmation of the trade of the Indians on the Zanzibar coast round about Rhapta, near Zanzibar, in the first century A.D. Almost every traveller who has visited the coast has mentioned the Indians there, and Vasco da Gama found Indians, especially men of Calicut, at Mozambique, Kilwa, Mombasa and Malindi, at which latter place he obtained a Gujerati pilot who conducted him across to Calicut.

There is no need to dwell long on this trade. Everyone who visits Zanzibar knows the Indian traders, and it may be presumed that they and their methods have been the same since first they visited the island or the coast, though doubtless they feel more secure nowadays than they did in bygone times.

Since very early the Banyans have formed the customs at Muscat, Zanzibar and Chake Chake, and indeed at most places on the coast. A harmless and inoffensive people, they probably did little to upset the susceptibilities of the inhabitants of the country, though, from all accounts, in the nineteenth century it was considered an easy way of settling debts to cut the throat of the Indian to whom they were owed.

The Indians in Zanzibar are both Moslems and Hindus. The former comprise the Ismailia Khojas, the Ithnasheri Khojas, the Bohoras, the Memons and the Sindhis. In addition there are a few Sikhs, who cannot be classified either as Moslems or Hindus.

Of the Hindus there are of the higher class the Brahmins, the Bhatiyas, the Jains; of the middle class the Luwanas and the Kumbis; and of the menials the Kumbhars, the Meghwars and the Chamars.

POLITICAL AND ECONOMICAL

The three tribes, most of the Swahilis and many of the Arabs, are subjects of His Highness the Sultan (and I believe officially designated "natives," though I shall not use this interpretation in this book), but abroad, i.e., out of the island dominions and on the mainland territory, they are considered "British Protected Persons." They are chiefly Mohammedans of the Sunni (Shafi), Hanafi and Ibathi sects.

The fundamental law of the land in civil matters is the law of Islam, and native custom is administered when it is not repugnant to moral justice.

Formerly, when there were consular courts, there was great confusion, and even now that the German, French, Austrian, American, Belgian, Italian and Portuguese systems have been eliminated, there is still a mixture of English, Indian, various kinds of Mohammedan, and Hindu law administered, as well as the native customs I have referred to. In addition there are two separate judicatures, that of His Highness, dealing with only His Highness's subjects, and that of His Britannic Majesty, which deals with British and foreign subjects and mixed cases. Some natives practise as Vakils (pleaders) in the subordinate courts.

The Mohammedan law and religion is, I think, pretty well recognized as being the most suitable for the natives in their present conditions and mode of living. Certainly the Holy Sharia seems much fairer than even the English system as far as distribution of property goes. In Zanzibar (and of course among all Mohammedan people) there is no such thing as being "cut off with a shilling"; in any case, only a small proportion may be willed away, and the rest must be divided in certain fixed proportions. Very few natives do make wills, and so it is all divided, except a small percentage and certain fees which are paid to the government, who in turn take the responsibility of the correct division.

It would be impossible, and out of place, to give a table of inheritance, but I will give a few instances, roughly correct, of some of the shares.

One daughter or sister when alone gets half; if there are two or more daughters or sisters, they get two-thirds between them, and a mother gets one-third. A son when alone gets all, but if there is a daughter, he gets double her share. If his parent leaves a mother, grandmother, husband or wife, father or grandfather, he gets the residue. With certain more distant relations he gets all, and they are excluded. Father, grandfather, brother, nephew and uncle may, if alone, get all, but with other heirs they get what is left after the others have had their share, but with the exception of father and grandfather, they get none if there is a son. A wife or wives get a quarter.

It is interesting to note that parents are never excluded from inheritance, and must always, if incapable, be supported.

If a native dies without heirs at all, his money goes to the Bel-el-mal or native treasury, and after a lapse of years, if no one turns up, it is credited to revenue, and so spent on the upkeep of the country.

Slavery having been abolished, labour has now

to be paid for, though many of the freed slaves still live on their former owners' plantations and refer to themselves as slaves, and are often proud of their title. In this way Arabs who were kind to their slaves now reap the benefit of it; as a matter of fact, I believe slaves did not undergo much hardship once they had been purchased and installed on their owner's plantation. Poor people who live rent free on plantations are called *Maskini wa Muungu* (God's poor).

The clove industry, which I refer to briefly here and not under the chapter on industry (for it is not really interesting from an anthropological point of view), is the one in which most natives are engaged during the time of picking. Many are employed at it all their lives, as they *lima* or weed and cultivate in the shambas, though nowadays many labourers of mainland tribes (chiefly Wanyamwezi and Wakikuyu) are employed on this work, for a clove plantation needs most careful nursing and cleaning, or it will not bear.

Many of the Arabs are seriously in debt to money-lenders, who, even if they are followers of the Prophet, find some way of getting round the prohibition as to usury, and in many cases make the Arabs and natives sign for much more than they actually receive. A native is so simple that if he sees, say Rs. 200, he will willingly sign for double that amount, recking naught of the day of settlement. I remember the case of a poor fisherman who received Rs. 45, and undertook to pay back 16 fraslas of cloves, of which the market value would probably be at least Rs. 320, and might be a great deal more.

The price of picking a pishi (kibaba = 1½ lb., pishi = 6 lb., frasla = 35 lb.) of cloves varies from 4 to 5 pice at the beginning of a season, and in some seasons has actually risen to 16 pice per pishi (64 pice = 100 cents = R. 1 = 1s. 4d. at par). A labourer gets about 12 annas a day (4 pice = 1 anna), and a craftsman Rs. 2 to 3.

PART I

HISTORICAL

A. EARLY HISTORY AND EXTERNAL INFLUENCES

CHAPTER III

INTRODUCTORY

UNTIL recent times very little of the history of Zanzibar has been chronicled in writing, and, with the exception of occasional glimpses vouchsafed to us in the writings of ancient and mediæval authors, the history is largely a matter of conjecture, to be drawn from comparison of customs, etc., with those of other peoples. The history of Zanzibar is therefore to be compiled from the following sources:

(*a*) Speech, (*b*) customs, (*c*) archæological remains and antiquities, (*d*) legend and tradition, (*e*) the writings of various historians and travellers, (*f*) native written records where such exist, and, in the case of the latest period, (*g*) official documents and printed books.

Zanzibar owes its history mainly to its insularity, to its convenience as a jumping-off place for the east coast of Africa, to its proximity to Asia, and to the trade winds or monsoons, which account to a large extent for its close political and commercial connection from the earliest times with India, the countries bordering on the Persian Gulf, and the Red Sea.

THE STONE AGE

There is no trace of Zanzibar or Pemba having been inhabited during either Stone Age.

The early Bantu people were formed by an admixture of Hamites, who came across India and Arabia and mixed with the negro people whose cradle was probably in the region of the great lakes. Passing over the "Horn of Africa," where they met and mixed with negroes, the Hamites found their way down south and mixed with the Bushmen to form the Hottentots. This southern way was soon closed by the negroes and mixed tribes. Unrecognized by the pure Hamites, to whom purity of breed was of importance, these mixed tribes were forced more and more to the society of the negroes, and thus the early Bantu tribes were formed of negro people with a smattering of Hamite blood.

THE FIRST INHABITANTS OF ZANZIBAR

At what date men first came it is impossible to say, but that they were firmly established before the beginning of the Christian era, and before the Bantu invasion, can hardly be doubted. It is even possible that they were there during neolithic times, though no trace of stone implements has yet been found.

They were no doubt negroes, and of a stature taller than that of Zanzibar's inhabitants to-day. We may say with certainty that they were fishermen and sailors, and they used dug-out canoes and wicker fish-traps. They ate at least turtle and fish. They may have lived in caves; they certainly worshipped at them and at trees. Their gods were tree spirits, and perhaps later the sun.

Early Influences on Zanzibar Civilization

THE HELIOLITHIC CULTURE

The use of this term requires a little explanation. The time of this culture extended from about fifteen thousand to three thousand years ago. The term is derived from the outstanding feature of the age, the erection of sun-stones. It would be unwise to say that the cult, which spread over the coasts of India, Africa and Arabia, touched Zanzibar itself at the time it flourished, but there is no doubt that certain of the practices of the age affected the people who were afterwards to colonize the islands.

They include the following: (1) Circumcision. (2) The couvade, sending the father to bed at the birth of a child. (3) Massage. (4) Making of mummies. (5) Megalithic monuments. (6) Artificial deformation of the heads of the young by bandages. (7) Tattooing. (8) Religious association of the sun and the serpent. (9) Swastika.

Of these customs (1) and (3) definitely obtain in Zanzibar; as regards (4), mummified blood is used in magic; as regards (5), several customs connected with dolmen worship obtain; (7) a debased form of tattooing is known; (8) occurs in the Nature myth common in Zanzibar, that eclipses of the solar orb are due to the sun being attacked by a snake; and (9) occurs, though no meaning is attached to it. It is often used in decorations. The dug-out canoe, which has been a feature of Zanzibar for thousands of years, was also an integral part of the heliolithic cult.

Sir Norman Lockyer states that the geographical distribution of rag offerings coincides with the existence of monoliths and dolmens. Rag offerings are made in Zanzibar at wells, caves and prominent thickets of trees, and, of course, on the shore and on prominent rocks. These rocks, some of which I have seen, are the nearest thing to menhirs in the island, some of them being in pillar form. There are no true menhirs, for the all-sufficient reason that there is no suitable stone with which to make them.

The originators of this cult were brown-skinned men, and it reached over the Mediterranean, through India, up the Pacific coast of China, and spread across to Mexico and Peru. The practices referred to spread all over that region, but did not get far north, nor farther south than Equatorial Africa. It was a coastal cult, not reaching deeply inland.

THE SUMERIANS

From about 6000 to 3000 B.C. flourished a wonderful civilization in the region of the Euphrates and the Tigris, and during this long period came probably the first forerunners of those yearly visitors to Zanzibar from the shores of the Persian Gulf.

These Sumerians were not the Semites of to-day, nor were they Aryans, though they were possibly of

Iberian or Dravidian affinities. There are traces of their language and magic on the coast of East Africa to-day. The affinities of Sumerian with Bantu were first suggested by Burton in 1885, and more have been shown by Mr. Crabtree in *Primitive Speech*. In addition to similarities of words, there are also peculiarities of grammar and construction common to both.

The following examples of Sumerian and Swahili words show such a similarity that it seems almost certain the Swahili is derived from the Sumerian.

Sumerian.	*Swahili.*	*English.*
ZI	—ZIMU	Spirit
—MU	M(U)—	Indicates life
UZ	(M—)BUZI	Goat
EME	ULIMI	Tongue
DU	DOMO	Mouth
MULU	M(U)TU	Man
TAM, GAN, GA, CHA	MCHANA, MTANA	Day

R and L are often interchangeable in the two languages.

As regards the grammar and construction of the language, the following parallels are worthy of note:

(1) Almost universal thematic harmony of the vowels.

(2) Formation of the greater number of derivatives by means of suffixes.

(3) System of declension by means of casual suffixes to the root word without affecting any change in it.

(4) Absence of any distinction between masculine and feminine genders.

(5) Existence of a negative conjugation.

(6) The use of verbal forms instead of conjunctions.

"They developed their civilization, their writing and their shipping, through a period that may be twice as long as the whole period from the Christian era to the present time" (Wells).

At Nippur the Sumerians built a temple to their

god, while at Eridu they had their seaport from which the first ships sailed and ventured on the Persian Gulf, to come afterwards farther afield, and possibly to visit Zanzibar on the wings of the north-east monsoon. Eridu is now miles from the sea, and but five miles from Ur of the Chaldees, but it remained the seaport down to not later than 5000 B.C. These Sumerians appear to have developed from an agricultural into a nautical people. This seems the more apparent as they had in their language no true word for *river*, which they represented by two ideographs meaning the *watery deep*, and the spirit of the deep must have been a chief object of worship at the time when the primitive hieroglyphs were first formed. The "ship, too, played a prominent part in the life of their inventors, and the picture of it represented it as moved not by oars, but by a sail" (Sayce). It may be noted here that the primitive Babylonian picture of a boat is strikingly like that of Egypt.

THE ASSYRIANS

About the year 2750 B.C. there arose among the Semitic peoples to the west of Babylon a great leader, Sargon I, who united them, conquered the Sumerians, and extended his rule from beyond the Persian Gulf on the east as far westward as the Mediterranean. This empire lasted for two hundred years, but while they were soldiers these Semites were barbarians, and therefore became absorbed in the Sumerian civilization. "This Sumerian learning had a very great vitality" (Wells). It survived many vicissitudes, and through the medium of many who absorbed it or who were absorbed by it, passed its traces on to many lands.

As the Akkadian Empire of Sargon lost its pristine vigour, two other peoples rose in power: first the Amorites and then the Elamites. These gave way before the Assyrians, who came from higher up the Tigris, and took Babylon about 1100 B.C. under Tiglath Pileser I.

A Babylonian cylinder shows the Assyrian Hercules, Nin, wrestling with an ox, and then, crowned with the horns of the ox, wrestling with a lion, and it is generally considered that this is the origin of the horn as a sign of chieftainship. As such a symbol the horn is common in East Africa among the descendants of the Persian Zinj Empire.

The Assyrian Empire lasted for about five hundred years, and under Sennacherib extended its conquests considerably, until the career of his army was cut short by pestilence in Egypt.

THE CHALDEANS, MEDES AND PERSIANS

The Assyrian Empire was brought to a close by its defeat at the hands of the Chaldeans, who, with the Medes and Persians, took Nineveh in 606 B.C. This Chaldean Empire did not last long; its great figure was Nebuchadnezzar the Great.

The last Chaldean king was Nabonidus, who was remarkable for the impetus he gave to sea-going trade. In his time dhows traded between Babylon, India and China, and the encouragement he gave to this led to further explorations, so that it was not long before there were settlements of Hindus in Arabia, East Africa and China. The Hindus not only made trade settlements on the coast, dating from the seventh century B.C., but apparently, as has already been related, penetrated inland towards the region of the great lakes.

Nabonidus was defeated by Cyrus in 539 B.C.

There are many striking similarities between the magic of the Chaldeans and that practised in Zanzibar to-day.

Having traced the history of the Persian Gulf and its influence on the history of East Africa down to the time of its conquest by the Chaldeans, we must now go back some centuries to the head of the Red Sea in order to trace the connection of ancient Egypt with the coast.

CHAPTER IV

Early Influences on Zanzibar Civilization—*continued*

THE ANCIENT EGYPTIANS

The time of the Pharaohs of Egypt must be especially interesting to the historian of Zanzibar, not only because of the fact that they too brought their customs and magic to Eastern Africa, but also because under their auspices were made the first voyages as far as Zanzibar of which there are historic accounts.

The ancient Egyptians had a very important trading mart at a place called Punt, which has been identified as probably being in the modern Somaliland. This Punt is frequently mentioned in the history of Egypt, and seems to have been a place much of the same kind as the Zanzibar of to-day, where the goods of the Orient and of Africa were brought to be sent to Egypt. Vessels from Arabia, Persia and even India probably traded there, and possibly also from the Zanzibar coast, so that it is conceivable that the Egyptians called at Zanzibar in very early times indeed.

As far back as the VIth Dynasty an expedition to Punt is recorded, and Sankkhara, who flourished in the XIth Dynasty, traded there. During this period of the Middle Kingdom (3358-1703 B.C.), three dynasties of Hyksos or Shepherd kings flourished from 2214 B.C. to 1703 B.C. These Hyksos who conquered Egypt were probably Semitic, speaking a language of the Western Semitic type. They came from Canaan. These migrants were first called Aamu, and latterly

Arapin, though at what date they obtained the latter appellation has not been stated. Arapin, of course, means Arabs, and Arabs were first spoken of in the reign of Solomon, about 1000 B.C. "*The Kings of Arabia* controlled the trade of the old world much as does the Seyyid of to-day" (Crabtree). Some of these people wandered into the interior and some followed the coast. Those that went into the interior lost their nationality and became, claims Mr. Crabtree, the origin of the Hamites. The remainder were called Arabs. The reign of the Hyksos kings, he says, marks the zenith of their migration, and its close marks the point where the racial history of Eastern and Central Africa become more or less fixed.

During the Empire (Dynasties XVIII to XX) 1703 B.C. to 1110 much foreign trade and conquest took place. Queen Hatasu of the XVIIIth Dynasty had relations with Punt, and Seti of the XIXth (1400-1280 B.C.) boasted at Sesibi, in the modern Abyssinia, that his dominions reached southward "to the arms of the winds."

Herodotus records that Rameses II (Sesostris) dispatched an expedition about 1400 B.C., which perhaps reached Madagascar. Rameses III was also a great imperialist. But the crowning feat of navigation was achieved when Neco of the XXVIth Dynasty (630-527 B.C.) dispatched a fleet of Phœnicians from the Gulf of Suez with abundant supplies, which sailed southward till they had the sun at noontide upon their starboard, i.e., rounded the Cape of Good Hope, and sailed back northward by the Atlantic, the Straits of Gibraltar and the Mediterranean, till they reached Egypt again. They took three years to do it, and landed each year long enough to sow a crop of wheat and harvest it.

"The importance of these expeditions to Punt cannot be over-estimated. They are the earliest attempt at organizing a fleet of powerful ships to voyage far away from home waters" (Keble Chatterton). A picture of a Punt expedition is preserved in Queen Hatshop-situ's temple, and a description of it will be of interest. There are five ships arriving, two of which are moored. The first has sent out a small boat, which is fastened by ropes to a tree on the shore, and bags and amphoræ, probably containing food and drink as presents to the chief, are being unloaded. Then the produce of Punt can be seen being loaded on. There are bags of incense and gold, ebony, ivory tusks, leopard skins, and trees of frankincense piled upon the decks. These were probably not all domestic produce, but represented goods brought from other ports.

We have seen above that these ancient Egyptians were great navigators. Their ships were in all probability derived, as we have seen, from the Sumerians, who were the first to use sails. The square sail of the Egyptians became the lateen of to-day, and the dhow has its progenitor in the square-sailed ship of the Egyptians. Its appearance and the part of the world in which it is found suggest this. The lateen sail was probably evolved when the necessity of having a sail that could easily allow of tacking was realized; it is of great antiquity, and has been the same since about 360 B.C.

A comparison of Egyptian magic with the magic and some of the native dances performed in East Africa shows many striking similarities. It is probable, too, that the language of East Africa owes words to them. As an example the Egyptian word for "black," *Nehesi*, may be quoted, for surely the Swahili *Nyeusi* is derived therefrom.

Sir Charles Eliot mentions an Egyptian idol as having been found at Mogadisho, but inquiries have failed to elicit any certain information as to its present whereabouts. It is said to be in Germany.

The chevron pattern—a favourite of the Sabæan builders, and much used in Zanzibar—is probably in origin the Egyptian symbol for water, and indicates prosperity. The royal house of Malindi claims to be descended from the ancient Egyptians.

THE PHŒNICIANS

Among all the people of old none were greater sailors than the Phœnicians. Unlike some of the peoples we have been considering, they did not last long as an independent nation, but performed much of their voyaging under the auspices of foreign powers. Phœnicia was under the suzerainty of Egypt from about the sixteenth century B.C., and suffered from invasions of Hittites in the fifteenth and fourteenth centuries. In the latter century Egyptian rule began to decline, and for the next five centuries Phœnicia was an independent and flourishing country, though it was associated with the Jews in about the tenth century B.C. Tyre and Sidon were its great strongholds, and from these places the Phœnicians sallied forth to found new towns. The great Carthage was founded from Tyre before 800 B.C.

Phœnicia was invaded by Assurbanipal in the ninth century B.C., and from that time till the seventh century it was a dependency of Assyria. The Phœnicians at first pursued their peaceful callings, but the eighth and seventh centuries were marked by many revolts, and about 630 Phœnicia again became practically independent. Nebuchadnezzar conquered it about 605 and it became part of Babylonia, and when Cyrus conquered Babylonia in 539 B.C., Phœnicia also fell to him. Then there was another period of prosperity lasting for two centuries until Alexander the Great conquered it. After this time (333 B.C.) Phœnician trade began to decline. Subsequently Phœnicia passed to Egypt, and in 64 to Rome, when its history as a separate entity ended.

The Phœnicians were Semites: the word is derived from *Φοενι κοί*, which means red men; the Romans call them Pœni or Punici, but their own name seems to have been Khna or Kina'an (Canaan). Like the Semites of to-day, the Phœnicians were chiefly traders. The early trade that was going on in the world before about the seventh century B.C.

was almost entirely a barter trade. This barter trade, of course, has existed on the coast of Africa practically down to the present day. "But," says Mr. Keble Chatterton, "the Phœnicians were more than mere traders or fighters; they were the world's greatest explorers—until the fifteenth and sixteenth centuries of our era." It was the Phœnicians who made that trip round Africa in the sixth century B.C. at the bidding of Pharaoh Neco; it was the Phœnicians who visited Eastern Africa even earlier with the Jews in the time of Solomon. The Phœnicians also visited Cornwall for tin, and in 520 B.C. Hanno reached Liberia and brought back chimpanzees.

"Either from the Egyptians or the Phœnicians —but almost certainly from the latter—the people down the east coast of Africa learned the art of navigation pretty thoroughly, for we know from Hakluyt that when, at the end of the fifteenth century of our era, Vasco da Gama doubled the Cape of Good Hope and called at the East African ports, he found that the arts of navigation were as well understood by the Eastern seamen as by himself. This would seem to imply that these Africans had years ago reached the state of advancement in sailing a ship already possessed by the more civilized parts of the world" (Keble Chatterton).

THE JEWS

Another people who left some mark behind them in the regions of Azania were the Jews, and we have already noticed that they came down with the Phœnicians about a thousand years before Christ.

King David formed an alliance with King Hiram of Tyre, and it is perhaps to that alliance that their settlements in Eastern Africa were due.

Solomon continued his father's alliance, and his kingdom was used by the Phœnicians as a high road to the Red Sea, where they built ships. As a result of this partnership, untold wealth was accumulated in Jerusalem.

Solomon built his fleet at Ezion Geber, " which is beside Eloth on the shore of the Red Sea." Hiram supplied the sailors, " shipmen that had knowledge of the sea," and they went to Ophir and brought back gold and almug trees and precious stones. And he " had at sea a navy of Tharshish with the navy of Hiram; once in three years came the navy of Tharshish, bringing gold and silver, ivory (elephants' teeth) and apes and peacocks."

The land of Ophir was most likely in the region of the Zambezi, though the actual name was probably applied by the Hebrews to a coast town of Southern Arabia which was a great centre of East African trade, and was to the Phœnicians and Jews as Punt was to the ancient Egyptians. It was, in fact, another forerunner of Zanzibar. It has been suggested that the Havilah of the Scriptures was probably this region between the Zambezi and the Limpopo, and that the ancient gold workings there were opened by the Himyarites, who were followed by the Jews and Phœnicians. The produce of the mines was carried down to the coast and shipped at Tharshish, which may have been somewhere by the modern Sofala. It has also been supposed that peacocks were not really intended, but parrots, as peacocks were probably kept in Palestine long before, and as they breed freely in captivity, there would be nothing very remarkable in them.

The Queen of Sheba or Saba in South Arabia also visited Solomon, having heard of his glory, and tradition has it that she formed a matrimonial alliance with him. In fact, the Abyssinian monarchs claim descent from this union. Saba had trade with the coast before Solomon, and no doubt the queen would be surprised at the number and size of consignments passing through her ports and warehouses for Solomon, and hearing much of his glory from his ships' captains, would wish to see his state.

The Kebra Negast which relates the story of the Queen of Sheba and her son, by Solomon, Menyelek, says in describing her wealth and trade: "And moreover, she was exceedingly rich, for God had given her glory and riches and gold and silver and splendid apparel and camels and slaves and trading men (or merchants). And they carried on her business and trafficked for her by sea and by land and in India and in 'Asivàn (Syene)." She claimed that her southern boundary stretched "to the Sea of Blacks and Naked Men."

There was apparently much social and commercial relation between Palestine and Madagascar during Solomon's reign, and possibly in David's. Jews had intercourse with the natives of Madagascar even in pre-Solomonic days. In Solomon's time colonies of Idumæan Jews from the Red Sea peopled the Comoro Islands. The people of the Grand Comoro preserve many Israelitic rites and customs. They cherish the memory of Adam, Abraham, Lot, Moses and Gideon, but have no knowledge of the Prophets after David, which seems to show that the Jewish immigrants left their home at a very early date.

It would be surprising, therefore, if the Jews had not touched at Pemba or Zanzibar, especially as there was a well established settlement there at the beginning of the Christian era. There are certainly traces of Hebrew magic in the magic of the natives, and the fact that there are not more definite traces is probably due to the fact that any traces of Jewish prophets, etc., would have long ago been swamped in Islamic teaching.[1]

The great intercourse of the Jews with East Africa was interrupted because the ships of Jehosaphat were broken at Ezion Geber, but as coins of the Maccabees dating from more than a century B.C. have been found in Natal and Zululand, it is probable that some slight intercourse was kept up almost to the time of the Christian era.

[1] But a charm quoted by Beech (*Aids to the Study of Kiswahili*) mentions Moses and the Psalms, and is very like one given by Gaster (*The Sword of Moses*, p. 62).

THE GREEKS

Herodotus (484-428), in his history, makes several references of interest about East Africa. Two of them (Melpomene, 42, and Euterpe, 102), describing the circumnavigation of Africa by Neco and the expedition of Sesostris, have already been mentioned, and it is probable that the passage (Thalia, 102), which describes natives collecting gold dust by means of ants, refers to East Africa.

Xerxes (*ob.* 465) is said to have sent Sataspes to circumnavigate Africa, and to have executed him because he failed. Heraclides is also said to have journeyed round Africa, but there is little foundation for it.

Aristotle (384 B.C.) was a noted geographer, in addition to being a philosopher, and conceived the idea that the earth was round. He mentions Taprobane (Ceylon) as being off the east coast of Africa.

Mention must be made of Alexander the Great not only on account of his Eastern empire, which would be bound to affect to some extent trade in East Africa, but because he either directly or indirectly put an end to the empires we have been previously considering. In 334 he crossed the Hellespont and defeated the Persians at the River Granicus. He then overthrew Darius at Issus in 333, and after that subdued Syria, overran Palestine and Egypt and founded Alexandria in 331. Soon after he again defeated Darius and routed him at Arbela. Babylon, Susa and Persepolis all fell to him, and in 326 he invaded India and conquered the Punjab. He had to return owing to the home-sickness of his troops. He died at Babylon of fever in 323 when only thirty-three years of age. He was buried in a golden coffin at Alexandria.

Abu Zeid Hassan states that Alexander the Great sent Greeks to occupy Socotra, and that they settled there and subsequently became Christians. It is also stated that Alexander, who, of course, must have heard of East Africa, wished to make a journey there, but that he had no opportunity. Possibly had it not been for his untimely death, East African history might have been better defined for us in these early days.

It is well known that the Greeks knew and travelled along the east coast of Africa, and the *Periplus* written in Greek gives us our first description of the coast. This book we shall examine in detail in a future chapter, but mention may here be made of the lost town of Rhapta, mentioned in it as the "very last market town of the continent of Azania." Pangani has been suggested as the site of this lost town, but the discovery in 1907 of a coin of Ptolemy X Soter (151-80 B.C.) at Msasani, north of Dar-es-Salaam suggests another situation. The description of Msasani Bay and Harbour in the *African Pilot* shows it to be just such a place as would have been a pleasing harbour to the ancients. Msasani is but a short distance from Konduchi, and it is from this latter place that the people of Makunduchi in Zanzibar claim origin. The people of Makunduchi still perform a dance with tridents (described elsewhere in the book), which is distinctly reminiscent of the worship of Poseidon. It is extremely probable that at this last town on the coast on some suitable promontory the Greek sailors would have erected a temple to the presiding god of the sea in his capacity of Soter, the Saviour, to whom they owed their safety for their voyage outwards and to whom they would pray for a safe journey home. In addition to this custom, that of placing the Zanzibar baby in a winnowing fan is in origin Greek, and appertains to the worship of Dionysus. It cannot be said for certain, however, that the Swahili adopted this custom direct from the Greek. The word *tufani*, a strong wind, common at Makunduchi, though used elsewhere, seems to be derived from τυφῶν.

THE SABÆANS AND HIMYARITES

Of these two peoples of South Arabia the Sabæans were the earliest, and Saba was a flourishing commercial state many centuries before the birth of Christ. Our information concerning them is derived from the Himyaritic inscriptions which have been deciphered comparatively recently (and of which probably many remain to be found), traditions of a legendary nature preserved in Mohammedan literature, and information from outside sources. Sea traffic between South Arabia and India, and, of course, between South Arabia and East and South-East Africa, was established very early. From India the spices of the East came by sea as far as the coast of Oman, and from there they went overland to the Arabian Gulf to be shipped to Egypt. The caravan route went from Shabwat (Subota in the Hadramaut) to Marib (Mariaba), the capital of Saba. It then diverged north-west to Macoraba (the modern Mecca) and by way of Pietra to Gaza on the Mediterranean. The trade from Sofala came by sea up the east coast of Africa. The prosperity of the Sabæans lasted until the Indian trade went by sea. This seems to have happened in the first century A.D., when their power declined.

After the decline of the Sabæans the balance of power in Southern Arabia fell to the Himyarites. Their country lay between Saba and the sea. Except in Arabia, the Himyarites were not a great power, though no doubt they did a great deal of trade by sea. In Arabia their kings, known as Tubba's, made them dominant in the south, and they even exercised sway over the northern tribes until the fifth century A.D., when the latter revolted and became independent. Their maritime situation exposed them to attack and the population decreased. The Himyaritic Empire ceased to exist as a power about the sixth century A.D.

The trade of the Sabæans and the Himyarites with the coast of Africa was continuous from before the time of Solomon right down to the first century A.D. They set forth from the great trading cities of Yemen, Aden and the Hadramaut, along the east coast of Africa. "They must have made an emporium of Zanzibar, and possibly they occupied the little Island of Mozambique" (Johnston). It was probably they who opened up the gold workings of Zimbabwe, though it has recently been settled that the buildings there, of which the ruins exist to-day, were not built by them. There are, however, in East Africa many features in architecture which may have been derived from early South Arabians. The use of the chevron pattern has been mentioned, and there are phalli in Zanzibar. At Mambrui in East Africa there are phalli which are quite unmodified. Both these features occur also at Zimbabwe, and though the buildings there are mediæval, such characteristics were probably derived from early visitors, and it is very probable that these early visitors from Saba and Himyar were the founders of what came to be known as the "land of Ophir." It has indeed been asserted with some degree of probability that Ophir and Sofala are different forms of the same word.

The Queen of Sheba was but one of the long line of monarchs who ruled over these hardy sea-going peoples. Later Moslem historians identified her with Bilqis, the daughter of Sharahil.

Thirty-three names of Sabæan kings have been collected, and it is interesting to note that Sargon, in 715 B.C., recorded that he had received tribute from Pharaoh, the King of Egypt, "of Shamsiyya, the Queen of Arabia, of Ithamar (Yathaamar) the Sabæan, gold, spices, slaves, horses and camels." This gold was the gold of Sofala, and may not the slaves have been from the same place as those slaves of Zinj which we shall hear of later at the time of the Baghdad Caliphate?

The end of the early South Arabian States was hastened by an event that is known to all Arabs and

Moslems. This was the bursting of the dyke of Marib.

This dyke was apparently built by Abdi Shams Saba, the guardian of Yaarub, some few miles south-west of Marib, in a gap in the mountains through which the River Adanu flows. The dyke was built in order to prevent floods and partly also for purposes of irrigation. At about the end of the third century A.D., the wife of the reigning king of Marib, by name Zarifa, dreamt she saw a rat digging holes in the dyke and removing huge boulders with his hind legs. As a result the peoples of Saba departed. Gradually the waters broached the dyke and spread over the country, leaving it desolate. So the Sabæans disappeared for ever, though for a short while the Himyarites lingered on.

CHAPTER V

THE BEGINNING OF THE CHRISTIAN ERA

For the period comprised in the last two or three centuries B.C. and the first century or so A.D. our authorities are Eratosthenes (*c.* 276-194 B.C.), Strabo (born about 63 B.C.), Mela (about A.D. 43), Pliny (A.D. 23-79), the *Periplus* (about A.D. 60) and Ptolemy (about A.D. 127-151).

Eratosthenes, astronomer and geographer, was born at Cyrene. In his time it was thought in the West that the Southern Ocean began below Cape Guardafui. Little else which concerns us is to be gleaned from his writings, except that he testified to the great trade of the Southern Arabian States.

Strabo, another Greek geographer, travelled in Asia, Africa, and other places about 24 B.C., and wrote a geography in seventeen books. He described Egypt pretty extensively, and was aware of Somaliland, which he thought was a cinnamon-bearing country. He thought also that Cape Guardafui (Notu Ceras) was the last promontory of Africa on the east.

Mela, a Roman geographer and a native of Spain, wrote a book in three parts called *De Situ Orbis*. He, too, showed the Ethiopian Sea as below the horn of Africa, but the vague ideas and rumours of another country beyond he embodied in a shadowy continent of the Antœci, showing Taprobane at its eastern extremity, and describing it either as a great island or the first part of another world.

Hippalus, a Roman navigator, in about A.D. 45, observed the changes of the monsoon in the Indian Ocean. Doubtless this had long been known to the Arabs, Phœnicians and Hindus, but they very probably kept it to themselves for their own purposes, and for the same reason that the Phœnicians concealed their tin mines in Spain and Cornwall, i.e., that they alone might make profit of it. This discovery was of immense importance, as it meant that the Romans sent their shipping into the Indian Ocean. Hippalus's discovery is described in the *Periplus* and referred to by Pliny.

Pliny was more of a naturalist than a geographer, and his *Historia Naturalis* is more valuable in its descriptions of the products of countries than in its geography. He thought that the Atlantic Ocean began at Messylum (probably Ras Hantare, latitude 11° 28′ N.), so that his geography was even vaguer than that of his contemporaries.

The evidence of the early geographers shows that but little about Eastern Africa was known in the West, and practically nothing at all about that part of it which includes Zanzibar. It was Hippalus who showed the way to the East, and Western knowledge of the Indian Ocean dates from that discovery.

The most important authority for this period is the *Periplus*, to the unknown author of which we must be exceedingly grateful, for, except Neco's voyage, we have no other written mention of a voyage to Zinj until the flight of Suleiman and Said six centuries after, and but little after that for another three or four hundred years.

But the *Periplus* is of particular importance, because not only does it give us a description, however brief, of these countries in the first century, but it confirms our deductions regarding their early history.

It will be convenient to give in full that part of the *Periplus* which concerns the Zanzibar coast.

The author informs us that from Cape Guardafui to Opone (Ras Hafun) the coast was not subject to a king, but that each market-town was ruled by a separate chief.

He then goes on to say: "Beyond Opone, the shore trending more towards the south, first there are the small and great bluffs of Azania; this coast is destitute of harbours, but there are places where ships can lie at anchor, the shore being abrupt; and this course is of six days, the direction being south-west. Then come the small and great beach for another six days' course, and after that in order, the Courses of Azania, the first being called Sarapion and the next Nicon; and after that several rivers and other anchorages, one after the other, separately a rest and a run for each day, seven in all, until the Pyralaæ Islands and what is called the channel; beyond which, a little to the south of south-west, after two courses of a day and night along the Ausanitic coast, is the island Menuthias, about three hundred stadia from the mainland, low and wooded, in which there are rivers and many kinds of birds and the mountain-tortoise. There are no wild beasts except the crocodiles; but there they do not attack men. In this place there are sewed boats, and canoes hollowed from single logs, which they use for fishing, and catching tortoise. In this island they also catch them in a peculiar way, in wicker baskets, which they fasten across the channel-opening between the breakers.

"Two days' sail beyond, there lies the very last market-town of the continent of Azania, which is called Rhapta; which has its name from the sewed boats (πλοιάρια ῥαπτά) already mentioned; in which there is ivory in great quantity, and tortoise-shell. Along this coast live men of piratical habits, very great in stature, and under separate chiefs for each place. The Mapharitic chief governs it under some ancient right that subjects it to the sovereignty of the state that is become first in Arabia. And the people of Muza now hold it under his authority, and send thither many large ships; using Arab captains and agents, who are familiar with the natives and intermarry with them, and who know the whole coast and understand the language.

"There are imported into these markets the lances made at Muza especially for this trade, and hatchets and daggers and awls, and various kinds of glass; and at some places a little wine, and wheat, not for trade, but to serve for getting the good-will of the savages. There are exported from these places a great quantity of ivory, but inferior to that of Adulis, and rhinoceros-horn and tortoise-shell (which is in the best demand after that from India), and a little palm-oil.

"And these markets of Azania are the very last of the continent that stretches down on the right hand from Berenice; for beyond these places the unexplored ocean curves around towards the west, and running along by the regions to the south of Ethiopia and Libya and Africa, it mingles with the western sea."

The "Bluffs of Azania" and the small and great beach are respectively El Hazin and Sif El Tanil, and the "Courses of Azania" are the Barr Ajjan and Benadir coast of the Arabs. The Pyralaæ Islands are undoubtedly Pate, Manda and Lamu.

It is interesting to note that at this date the Pyralaæ Islands were of no importance, for beyond the name no note is given of them. It is just possible that Πυραλάαι is a corruption of Kipungani, for the channel referred to behind Lamu is called Mlango Kipungani by the natives, and is said by the *African Pilot* to be deep enough for large boats at low water.

The expression "Ausanitic coast" is interesting, as it shows that dominion over the coast by the South Arabians was well recognized. Ausan was a state of Arabia, independent about the seventh century B.C. Later Ausan was absorbed by another state, Kataban, and the coast became Katabanic. When Kataban fell to Saba, the Zanzibar coast passed with it too to the Sabæans, who in turn surrendered it to the Himyarites on their access to power.

We now come to Menuthias, which is generally identified with Pemba, Zanzibar or Mafia (in which it is supposed that the name is still perpetuated—till recently Mafia was called Monfiyeh, though the native name is Chole). I prefer an identification with

Palta I
Munda I
Lamu
Pyralaœ Is.
N
NE
E
SE
S
SW
W
NW
AUSANITIC COAST
AZANIAN
OCEAN
Chwaka
Menuthias
Rhapta
Monfia
"....until the Pyralaœ islands and what is called the channel; beyond which, a little to the south of south west, after two courses of a day and night along the Ausanitic coast, is the ISLAND of MENUTHIAS about 300 stadia from the mainland....."
Statute Miles
0 20 35 40 60 80 90 100

Pemba, briefly for the following reasons: (*a*) because of the distance from Lamu to North Pemba, two δρόμοι νυχθήμεροι, which is correct for a dhow to-day, though rather fast; (*b*) because of the sailing directions—a little to the south of south-west—which is also more correct for Pemba; (*c*) because of the distance from the mainland, given as three hundred stadia. The early stade of Herodotus, the Olympic or standard Greek stade, was 606¾ English feet. The stade of Eratosthenes was 520 feet, and that of Dio Cassius (about A.D. 180) was 647 feet. Any one of these may be meant. The distance would therefore be 34 miles 836 yards, 29 miles and 960 yards, or 36 miles and 486 yards. Whichever stade is meant, the distance given is only an approximation, but it was something over 30 miles, and that is a better guess at the distance from Pemba (35 miles) than Zanzibar (25 miles). (*d*) Pemba was more colonized than Zanzibar in mediæval times, and these settlements were probably the result of earlier occupation. (*e*) It is the first island one gets to, and the bay in the north is very inviting to ships and dhows from the north. (*f*) Pemba, though hilly, is low, and the forests, which were of long standing, still survive in the north. Zanzibar in the north and Tumbatu are more scrubby than wooded, and, owing to the shallow soil on the coral rag, could never have been "wooded." (*g*) There is a good river in the north of Pemba. Nothing much can be adduced from the description of fauna given, though of the two islands Pemba is the only one that to-day boasts a tortoise, even though it be small and aquatic. That there are no wild beasts is also truer of Pemba than Zanzibar. Pemba's fauna is less varied than that of Zanzibar.

The note about the sewed boats, canoes from single logs, and wicker fish-traps is extraordinarily interesting. It shows that natives were well established on the island, and were pursuing the trade which they still pursue, and with the methods they still use. It may be mentioned here that the

"Mgono" fish-trap, peculiar to Pemba, is fixed as described in the *Periplus*.

Rhapta is probably Msasani, where presumably the sewed boats used to be made, as the town was called after them (ῥαπτά). Nowadays these "Mitepe," as they are called, are made at Lamu. The question arises "from what trees were the canoes hollowed and from what wicker were the fish baskets made?" Nowadays the former are made from mango trunks and the latter from coco-nut mid-ribs. It is probable that coco-nuts may have been already introduced, but the mango possibly not. There is, however, a good hardwood tree, a species of cassia, called mvule, the wood of which is now used, amongst other purposes, for making planks for dhows, and that may have been the wood used, for it grows wild.

We next learn that even at this date tribes were formed along the coast, of men very great in stature and under separate chiefs. One gathers from this description that they were probably negroes and that the Bantu invasion had not yet started. The East African coast Bantu of to-day is not a man of such stature as to strike one as being particularly tall. Ivory was plentiful, and tortoise-shell. The former we have remarked before, and it was one of the reasons for all this ancient trade. Tortoise-shell was mentioned by Masudi at a later time and is still exported.

The reference to the Mapharitic chief who governed the coast "under some ancient right that subjects it to the sovereignty of the State that is become first in Arabia" is of the first importance, as it is a first-century confirmation of all that we have seen before of the hold of ancient peoples over the coast. Later on this chief's name is given as Charibael, an Arabic title (Kariba-Il), which means "God blessed him."

This king, Kariba-Il Watar Yuhanim (Great, Beneficent), was one of the Sabæan kings whose names have been collected from the South Arabian inscriptions, and as we may imagine, was a person of some considerable importance. He lived at Saphar (the modern Zafar), and the *Periplus* mentions that he was the king of the Homerites and Sabaites (Himyarites and Sabæans). He ruled about A.D. 40-70. The Mapharites (Maafir), a tribe located in the southern Tehama, owned a kind of allegiance to him, as do tribes to-day in Oman (and Arabia generally) to settled kings. The chief of the Maafir was Cholaebus (Kulaib). The people of Muza (the modern Mocha) held it under his authority and sent ships there as they do to-day. It is to be noted that the author was aware that the Arab captains knew the whole coast, and then as now intermarried with the natives. This intermarriage had been going on for centuries before, and accounts for the presence of the customs of these ancient peoples mixed up in the customs of to-day, for the presence of their words in the language of the Swahili and for the very formation of the Swahili people themselves. The next items of information as to imports and exports are also important, and show that the barter trade of two thousand years ago was just the same as it has been till very recent days.

So much for the *Periplus* as far as it concerns Zanzibar. Claudius Ptolemæus, our last authority for this period, was a native of Egypt and worked at Alexandria. His date of birth and death are unknown, but his first known astronomical observation was made in A.D. 127 and his last in A.D. 151. His work is known as *Geographike*, and was compiled from other works and not from personal observation. It was derived from astronomical data, travellers' hearsay as to distances, and, of course, previous researches. His chief errors as regards the parts of the world that interest us here were that India is not shown as peninsular, Ceylon (Taprobane) is too large, and Asia is extended too far southwards and joined to the south of Africa. But this is an advance on Pomponius Mela, and Ptolemy continued the map of Africa to Cape Delgado, known to him as Prasum

Promontorium. His knowledge was not improved on for many years to come.

RÉSUMÉ OF THE EARLY TRADE ON THE ZANZIBAR COAST

All the evidence we have considered goes to show that sea-going trade had its birthplace in the Persian Gulf; that its childhood was spent there, on the coast of Arabia and in the Red Sea, and that possibly one of the first areas in which it developed was the east coast of Africa. The canoe, the first serious sea-going vessel, was an integral part of the heliolithic culture which spread very early by sea-going canoes, though the process took a long time. "There were not only canoes, but Sumerian boats and ships upon the Euphrates and the Tigris, when these rivers, in 7000 B.C., fell by separate mouths into the Persian Gulf. There are pre-dynastic neolithic Egyptian representations of Nile ships of a fair size capable of carrying elephants. The earliest ships on the seas were either Sumerian or Hamitic; the Semitic peoples followed close on these pioneers" (Wells).

The Semitic peoples' trade we have seen in brief. It was entirely a barter trade on the coast from the earliest times until quite recently. As far as East Africa is concerned it was a sea-borne trade. And not only did it result in colonizing, it resulted in the development of shipping.

"Sailing ships are the links which bind country to country, continent to continent. They have been at once the means of spreading civilization and war. It is a fact that the number of ships to be built increases proportionately as the trade of a country prospers. There will always be a summons in the sea which cannot be resisted. It summoned the Egyptians to sail to the land of Punt to fetch incense and gold. It summoned the Phœnicians across the Bay of Biscay to the tin mines of Cornwall. It called the Vikings to coast along the Baltic shores for pillage and piracy" (Chatterton), and it summoned these peoples of old to the land of Zinj to fetch gold and silver, slaves, " ivory, apes and peacocks."

So far we have only considered the sea-borne trade, but all these products referred to were generally obtainable only in the interior, so that even in early times there must have been caravan routes which were more fraught with danger and hardship than sea routes, owing to the risk of attack by hostile tribes and other dangers that have lasted down to our own times. There are records of early caravan routes in Egypt, and there were very early caravan routes from the far west through Abyssinia to Zeila (the Avalitis of the *Periplus*).

The gold that was mined in Rhodesia perhaps four thousand years ago was man-borne to the coast. In the times of the *Periplus* there must have been routes to coast towns, such as Rhapta, and probably for centuries before, ivory and slaves and other goods had been brought from the interior to the coast ports and carried thence to Menuthias for reshipment, as they are to-day. Sir R. Burton mentions that in early times there was a caravan route open from the Zanzibar coast to Benguela.

The *Periplus* mentions that ivory in great quantity, rhinoceros-horn, tortoise-shell and palm-oil were exported from Menuthias and Rhapta. Slaves it reports from Malao (Berbera) and Opone (Ras Hafun), whence at that time they were required in increasing numbers for Egypt. Gold it does not report, but the author does not describe the coast as far south as Sofala.

It is needless to stress the antiquity of these products: ivory is recorded as a commercial article in Egypt about 2600 B.C. (VIth Dynasty), and there are numerous and ever-increasing records of it in later dynasties. The use of ivory was known to nearly all these old peoples. The use of gold as an article of commerce is as old or older than history. Africa and Asia both yielded this product, while the history of slave-hunting, slave-driving and the slave trade is bounded only by the time during which there have been strong men and weaker for them to prey on. Tortoise-shell, rhinoceros-horn and palm-oil are still articles of export from Zanzibar. The imports—lances, hatchets, daggers, awls, glass, wine and wheat—are still much the same if brought up to date. In these days the most notable addition is clothing. The natives of Zanzibar wore their own vegetable-cloth clothing in those days, if indeed they wore anything at all.

Mr. Wells has picturesquely summed up the trade of this period thus: "Galleys and lateen-sailed ships entered and left crowded harbours, and made their careful way from headland to headland, and from headland to island, keeping always close to the land. Phœnician shipping under Egyptian owners was making its way into the East Indies and perhaps even farther into the Pacific. Across the deserts of Africa and Arabia, and through Turkestan, toiled the caravans with their remote trade; silk was already coming from China, ivory from Central Africa, and tin from Britain, to the centres of this new life in the world." From the emporia of Punt, of Ophir, and of Azania, these luxuries came to deck the temples and adorn the women of Babylon, of Nineveh, of Egypt, of Tyre and Sidon, of Jerusalem, of Greece and of Rome.

CHAPTER VI

REASONS FOR PAUCITY OF INFORMATION ABOUT EAST AFRICA FROM SECOND CENTURY TO SEVENTH CENTURY

FROM the time of Ptolemy to the time of the birth of Islam, information as to what was happening in Zanzibar is of the scantiest. In fact, during the whole of this time, we have not one single date on which to hang a narrative. The reason for this is that Europe and the Near East, from which alone any information concerning the coast could have been obtained, were far too occupied with their own troubles to give any attention to those of an outpost of the Himyaritic Empire, which was itself decaying.

During the second and third centuries A.D., the Roman Empire steadily declined, and, in the fourth and fifth centuries, the western part of it was overrun and destroyed by the Goths, the Vandals, the Huns and other barbarians. Though Constantinople was well placed to exercise dominion in any direction, the ineptitude of Constantine's successors, and the lack of spirit and sea craft are sufficient reasons for the fact that no advantage was taken of its favourable position.

BANTU INVASION

The cradle of negroes in Africa was probably somewhere in the neighbourhood of the great lakes, where they pursued their agricultural calling, and expanded rapidly without interference, until a pastoral people, the Hamites, crossed over from Arabia into Africa.

The original home of the Bantu race is supposed to have been somewhere in the south-western basin of the Nile, possibly the southern part of the Bahr-al-Ghazal province.

About a hundred years before the beginning of the Christian era, the Bantu peoples who had been forming for about a thousand years before, started off from the Nile direction on their great career of conquest. The aborigines were still in the neolithic age, but the Bantus were armed with weapons of copper and iron, which no doubt considerably facilitated their progress. Guided possibly not only by tribal pressure, but by the desire for salt, these hordes swept down southwards and made for the coasts. They penetrated to the coast of the Indian Ocean somewhere opposite Zanzibar, and after occupying these islands, where they no doubt found negroes of the type described in the *Periplus*, spread northwards up the east coast until checked by the Gallas on the Tana River. This description rather gives the idea that this second Bantu invasion happened in a few years, but it was really a gradual process lasting probably about six hundred years, i.e., from about 100 B.C. to A.D. 500.

It must be remembered that once Africans started coming to Zanzibar and Pemba they never left off. Despite all the digressions we may make, and different times and peoples we may consider, the colonization of Zanzibar is bound up in this fact, and in the fact that once traders from the north and east started coming they too always came, whatever change of fortune made or upset different empires and principalities. These Bantus were very impressionable people; they had their own magic and culture, and they easily absorbed that of their visitors who stayed long enough to impart it to them.

In addition to the events in the West already referred to as contributing to the paucity of information regarding Zanzibar during the first six centuries A.D., this invasion of the Bantus must be considered also as an important contributory cause, for these Bantus were comparatively well armed, and the

Eastern voyagers were but little better equipped, so that the natives were altogether a different proposition to the negroes living in Zanzibar before. It was not till the Arabs took to the use of better weapons and firearms that they recovered their superiority.

THE COAST FROM THE SECOND TO SEVENTH CENTURIES A.D.

Although we hear practically nothing at all of the coast during this period, it must not be supposed that nothing was going on there. As I have before pointed out, once Africans began to settle in Zanzibar, and once Asiatics began to trade and found colonies there, they never stopped, and it is important to remember this, whatever vicissitudes of fortune may have visited peoples and countries.

Our only geographer in this period is Cosmas Indicopleustes of Alexandria, who travelled and wrote a book in the sixth century called *Christian Topography*. Cosmas cannot be said to have largely extended geographical knowledge of Africa. To begin with he took a step backwards in refuting the idea of the ancients that the world was round. He made a journey as far as the Gulf of Aden, but in view of the storms raging at that time of the year, returned and reported that the end of the world was close there.

It remains to chronicle the passing of the suzerainty of the coast from the Himyarites to the Abyssinians in the third century. Cosmas Indicopleustes indicates that the whole Zinj coast during the third to sixth centuries, to a point almost certainly below Mogadisho, was subject to the Negus of Abyssinia.

During the dynasty of Tubba's, the Abyssinians conquered some parts of the Yemen, and Christian governors were sent by the Negus of Abyssinia to rule it in his name. Then a descendant of the Tubba's and a Jew, Dhuhawas, determined to stamp out

Christianity, and summoned the Himyarites to his aid. They, desiring to be rid of the Abyssinians, flocked to his standard, and for a short time he triumphed over and massacred the Christians. This, however, came to the ears of the Emperor Justinian (A.D. 527-565), who requested the Negus to take action. The latter sent an army of 70,000 under the command of Aryat to subdue the Yemen. Aryat soon defeated Dhuhawas, who is said to have committed suicide, and laid waste the land and sent many of the women and children to the Negus as slaves. Aryat became Viceroy, but mutiny soon broke out in his army, and Abraha, the head of the rival faction, disposed of him and was confirmed in his appointment. He built a church at Sanaa, which was defiled by one of the pagan Arabs belonging to Mecca. Abraha therefore led an expedition in the year of the Elephant (A.D. 570) against Mecca which failed disastrously, but the Abyssinian suzerainty was not ended until a Himyarite, Seif bin Dhi Yasgan, determined to seek the aid of the Turks. They, however, at that time did not wish to undertake the care of South Arabia, so he proceeded to the Court of Nushirwan the Just of Persia, who assisted him with a small force, and Yemen became a satrapy of Persia.

After this the balance of power in Arabia went to the northern Arabs welded together by Mohammed, and the care of the East African coast passed gradually to the Persians, who were destined to play a great part in East African history and who brought, in time, many of their Zoroastrian customs to Zanzibar and Pemba.

The seventh century was marked by the rise of Mohammed, an event which was destined to have far-reaching results on the east coast of Africa.

CHAPTER VII

Early Modern Visitors from the Near East

THE FIRST EMIGRATION FROM OMAN TO ZANZIBAR

During the reign of the Caliph Abdul Malik, when el-Hajjaj was Governor in El Irak and reducing that realm to the sway of the Umaiyades, he determined also to reduce Oman, which still kept its allegiance to the Arabian Caliphate. His attempts were stoutly withstood by the two chiefs of Oman, brothers, by name Suleiman and Said, the sons of Abbad. These two belonged to the great family of El Azd, and were probably grandsons of a former Chieftain Abdel Julanda, who ruled over Oman in the time of the Prophet. The brothers repeatedly drove back the invaders, and it was only a subsequent expedition under Mujjaah, who, already defeated once, came a second time with 5,000 cavalry, that reduced the gallant country and made it a province of Damascus. Suleiman and Said escaped, and emigrated to the "land of the Zinj," taking their families and a number of their tribes with them. This would be about the year 695, for el-Hajjaj reduced Mecca in 692, and became Governor of Irak in 694.

This is an important date in the history of the coast, as it shows that for a long period in the times of darkness before referred to, the Omanis were still voyaging to East Africa, and that it was well known and subject to them to some extent. At any rate the brothers would not have gone there had they not been assured of a better reception than they would have met with in any part of Arabia.

Oman had accepted the mission of Amr, dispatched

by the Prophet in 630, and embraced Islam, so that without doubt the two princes of the ruling house were of that faith.

This piece of history is recorded by Ahmed bin Yahya el Baladzory in his book *Futuh-el-Buldan*.

Another piece of information concerning the reign of Abdul Malik is recorded by Captain Stigand in *The Land of Zinj*. It was related to him at Pate, near Lamu, by Bwana Kitini, apparently an authority on Pate history, as he also wrote the "History of Pate," published in the *Journal of the African Society*. I will quote it in the original words:

"The beginning of these coast towns, he who first made them was a ruler called Abdul Malik bin Muriani (i.e., the Caliph Marwan). The date was the 77th year of the Hejira. He heard of this country, and his soul longed to found a new kingdom. So he brought Syrians, and they built the cities of Pate, Malindi, Zanzibar, Mombasa, Lamu and Kilwa." In a footnote it is stated (the information is probably traditional) that the following towns were built by Abdul Malik, and that in each town, or group of towns, he had a Liwali or Governor: Mukadisho (*mui wa mwisho* = the end city), Marika, Barawa, Tula, Twavae, Koyama, Vumbi, Kismayu, Omwi, Ndao, Kiwayu, Pate, Faza, Shanga, Emezi (Wangi), Magagoni (Tukutu), Amu (Lamu), Manda, Taka, Kitao, Komona, Uziwa, Shaka (said to be from Shah), Mea, Ozi, Malindi, Watamu, Mvita, Wasin, Kilwa, Tungi and Ngazija (the Comoros).

In favour of this statement being literally true is the date A.D. 701, which was in the reign of Abdul Malik, the fact that Syrians would naturally be employed by him as he lived at Damascus, and the obvious truth it recognizes that all the groups of ruins on the coast are clearly connected in origin. It may be taken as a confirmation of the piece of history we have just been considering, namely, that some of the coast settlements were first founded by exiles from Oman. In an indirect way, of course, the credit may be given to Abdul Malik, as he drove them from their native land.

Captain Stigand also says that Abdul Malik's son Hamza is said to have brought the Holy Koran to the east coast, and there is also a legend which says that another son, Jafar, ruled on the coast and died at Kiwayu. He married Mwana Manubi of Shanja. Abdul Malik is known on the coast as Mangi Mangi, but the meaning of this complimentary name has been lost.

OTHER EARLY EMIGRATIONS FROM ASIA

On the death of the fourth Shia Imam Ali, surnamed Zain-ul-Abidin, the son of Al-Hussain, who was the grandson of the Prophet and the second son of Ali and Fatima, there occurred a great schism in the ranks of the Shiites, one part following his son Mohammed Baqir, and the other his son Zaid. These latter were called Zaidiyah, or Ammu Zaid, which has been corrupted to Emozaid.

It is related by Joao de Barros that after the death of Zaid, who was conquered and slain by Hisham bin Abdul Malik, the Umaiyade Caliph, in 739, Zaid's son Yahya fled to Khorasan, and the tenets of the Zaidiyah spread throughout Yemen. Some of the Zaidiyah fled to East Africa, and, fortifying themselves on the coast about Shangaya, soon achieved some power.

Some generations after this the same historian relates that seven brothers fled from El Hasa (which was either in the Persian Gulf or in Central Arabia), being driven out by the oppression of a neighbouring sheikh. In three vessels they are said to have crossed over to the African coast, and about A.D. 908 founded Mogadisho and Brava, which became capitals of important states.

The Emozaid were regarded as heretics by these orthodox Sunni people of El Hasa, and, being driven inland, formed a close connection with the negroes. They became, in fact, the wandering traders of the interior, collecting the products of the country and conveying them to the coast for sale. It is conceivable that the *El Hasa* people were of the *El Harth* tribe of Arabs, who are known to have settled on the Zanzibar coast very early (Colonel Rigby states A.D. 924).

The next immigration to the coast was that of Ali, son of Sultan Hassan of Shiraz by an Abyssinian slave. Presumably on this account he could not get on with his six brothers, and so set out to seek his fortunes in East Africa. Passing Mogadisho and Brava, where he found previous immigrants, he arrived at Kilwa, where he founded what was to become the capital of the Zinj Empire in the year 975.

Mention may here be made of another early immigration, which was that of the Nebhan Maliks, who were turned out of Oman and Pate. It is said that shortly after the death of Hussan, son of Ali, one Isafah of Benu Omaya, belonging to the tribe of al Quraish, killed most of the nobles of Medina and drove out the Benu Uni. This would probably be about the year 50 of the Hejira.

The name of Bajuni is said to be derived from Benu Juni or Bani Juni, the children of Juni, and the tribe is supposed to have sprung from one Juni Katada. The descendants of this man left Arabia, and passing through the Straits of Bab al Mandeb, settled at Mogadisho, spreading thence down the coast to Birikau. After this they met and fought with the Vutila and Wakilo of the Somalis. Some time after they spread farther down the coast, and about three hundred years ago settled in Faza by permission of the King of Pate.

These peoples are called there the Watikuu, but in Zanzibar and Pemba, where they frequently come and generally follow the calling of hawkers, they are known as Wagunya.

THE CONVERSION OF THE COAST TO ISLAM

We have now to estimate from the data given above the approximate date of the conversion of the coast to Islam. We must remember that the natives of the Zanzibar coast are mostly Shafite Sunnis, the Sultan and the chief Arabs alone being Ibathi. Mohammed bin Idris Es-Shafi, the founder of the Shafite school, lived from A.D. 767 to 822, and started his mission in 813. Abdulla bin Ibadh is known to have been living in 744-749. Legends on the coast say that Jafar, son of Abdul Malik, was the first to bring Islam to the coast at Faza, and that he lived there and died at Kiwayu; his other son, Hamza, is also credited with this mission. But, in any case, it was not Hamza or Suleiman and Said (who were driven to the land of Zinj by the instrumentality of Abdul Malik) who caused any extensive conversion of the coast, for Abdul Malik reigned from A.D. 684 to 705, and Es-Shafi's mission did not take place till 813; neither were Suleiman and Said Ibathis, though they came from Oman, as they fled to the coast in A.D. 695, prior to the mission of Abdulla bin Ibadh.

The Ammu Zaid were Shiites, and we know also that Shiraz was Shia in 952, so that Hassan bin Ali (975) was probably a Shia, and if the coast had not been converted in his time it would have become Shia, as the power of Kilwa reached far. We can therefore safely say that the coast became followers of the Shafite school between A.D. 813 and 975. It is probable that the El Hasa or El Harth people brought the doctrines to the coast, for they were Sunnis, and, whether El Hasa was in the Persian Gulf or Central Arabia, Es-Shafi preached both in the Hedjaz and in Baghdad.

Ibn Batuta tells us that the people of Mogadisho, Mombasa and Kilwa were Shafites in the thirteenth century. The earliest records of mosques in the Zanzibar Sultanate are, Kizimkazi A.D. 1107, and Msuka (already ruined) A.D. 1414.

RECORDS OF THE ARABIAN GEOGRAPHERS

However scanty may be the references to the coast during the period of the Abbaside Caliphs of Zinj, yet there must have been considerable intercourse between the coast and the Persian Gulf. Several times during this period are Zinj slaves spoken of as in Irak.

In the reign of the first Abbaside Caliph, in the year 749, his brother, Abul Abbas, massacred 11,000 souls, including men, women and children, and had in his army 400 men of Zinj. In the following year they took an important part in the wars of South Arabia.

That these Zinj increased in number and became a power in the land is shown by the fact that in 850 they revolted, under the leadership of a negro styled Lord of the Blacks. This revolt was felt all over Arabia.

Again in the year 869, a Persian, who claimed to be a descendant of Ali, and styled himself Alid Messiah, but earned the cognomen of Al Khabith (the reprobate), raised at Basra his banner inscribed with a text (Sura IX, 112), promising freedom to all the slaves. The Zinj or Zanzibar slaves, particularly those employed in the saltpetre industry, swarmed to his side, and during the two years following, they spread themselves all over the Euphrates delta, and on the Karun as far as Al Ahwaz. For some considerable period they met with no reverse, and in 871 they captured and sacked Basra, and annihilated its inhabitants.

The Caliph Al Motamid, a weak monarch, was then compelled to call his brother, Al Muwaffak, the real mainstay of the empire, to his aid, and though he had other engagements, he was able from time to time to defeat the negro rebels.

Despite this, however, the insurgents were able at

different periods to invade Irak, Khuzistan and Bahreim, Alwaz was sacked, and they established a capital at Wasit.

Al Khabith even asked one Yakut, the coppersmith, another rebel, to join him in an attack on Baghdad. For ten years the country suffered under his pillages, and it is said that his force numbered 300,000. While this is certainly exaggerated, it is an indication of the large number of slaves from East Africa in Arabia in the ninth century, and of their eagerness for freedom. The rebels were finally defeated in 883.

In the native history related by Captain Stigand, it is recorded that Haroun al-Raschid sent Persians to the coast to continue the work begun by Abdul Malik.

We have already seen that the Emozaids early emigrated to the east coast, and there were successive emigrations from Central Arabia, Oman (the Benu Nebhan), and Shiraz during this period. Each set up different states on the coast, and when the Portuguese came, most of them were each other's enemies, and so fell an easy prey to the Europeans.

Before going on to consider the information provided by Arabian geographers in this period, I must refer to a find of coins recorded in the *Zanzibar Gazette* of September 10th, 1900. A short time previously a native, while digging up cassava in a shamba at Khwarara, found an earthen vessel full of copper coins. The Government broker, Nassor of Lamu, took pains to decipher them, and professed to read them as belonging to the reigns of Sultan Sajaluki (613), Yazid bin Muawiyen (760), and Haroun al-Raschid (686). The dates are wrong, Yazid I having begun to reign in 679, and Haroun al-Raschid in 786. The decipherment may also be incorrect, but as I can find no other record of these coins, I give the information for what it is worth.

Let us now turn our attention to the Arabian geographers and historians, Masudi, Idris, Yakut, Ibn

Said and Ibn Batuta. As belonging to this period, we must also consider Marco Polo's description of Zanzibar.

Masudi (*ob.* A.D. 956), whose full name was Abdul Hassan Ali bin Hussein bin Ali, was a native of Baghdad, and was called Masudi, after Abdulla bin Masud, a companion of the Prophet, from whom Masudi traced his descent. He wrote a history of the world, from the creation to the Caliphate of Muti in 947. He was a great traveller, and visited Armenia, India, Ceylon, Zanzibar, Madagascar, the Chinese Sea and the Caspian Sea. (This from Nicholson, but an actual visit to Zanzibar Island is doubtful, and perhaps for Madagascar read the Comoros.) His book is called *Muruju 'l Dhahab* or *The Meadows of Gold.* He has been described as the Arabian Herodotus. Masudi makes some very interesting observations on the origin of the Zinj. He says when " Noah's posterity began to spread all over the earth, the children of Kush, the son of Canaan (Cham), followed a westerly direction and crossed the Nile. There they formed new groups; some of them, the Nubians, Beeljah and the Zinj, turned to the right between east and west. The others, in great numbers, went westward in the direction of Zagawah, Canem, Makah, Ghanah, and other parts of the land of the Blacks and the Dendemeh. Those who had taken the right between east and west soon separated again, thus forming several tribes of the Zinj such as the Makir, Maskar, the Marira and others. . . . The Zinj, with other Abyssinian tribes, spread themselves to the right of the Nile, down to the extremity of the Sea of Abyssinia. Of all the Abyssinian tribes the Zinj were the only ones who crossed the canal which comes out of the Upper Nile. They established themselves in this country and spread themselves as far as Sufalah, which is on the Sea of Zinj, the farthest limit where the ships sail from Oman and Siraj, for as the Chinese Sea ends at the land of Sirla, so the limits of the Sea of Zinj are near the land of the

Sufalah and that of the Wak Wak country, which yields gold in abundance with other marvels.

"There the Zinj built their chief town, then they elected a king which they called 'Falime.' This has been at all times the name of their paramount chief. The Falime has in his dependency all the other Zinjan kings, and commands 300,000 mounted men.

"The Zinj use the ox as their beast of burden, for in their country is neither mules nor horses nor camels. They do not even know these beasts.

"There are among them tribes which have very large teeth and are cannibals. The territory of the Zinj begins at the canal derived from the Upper Nile, and extends to the land of Sufalah and the Wak Wak."

The word *Falime* is extraordinarily interesting, as it is, of course, the Swahili *mfalme*. The tribes which have very sharp teeth may be the Masai, who file their teeth.

Masudi speaks as follows on the conditions of these lands in his time. He travelled, he says, several times from Sinja (Sohar) the chief town of Oman, to Kambalu, and never did he know a more dangerous sea than the sea of Zinj. Kambalu is generally identified with the Comoro, though I prefer an identification with Mkumbuu in Pemba, for the reason that when written in Arabic the words Kambalu and Mkumbuu are very much alike (كمبلو and كمبو). The "M" of Mkumbuu disappears when the word is written in Arabic, and Mkumbuu was undoubtedly Mkumbulu in old days. "l" is frequently elided, e.g., Muungu for Mulungu. Masudi says that the Arabs colonized this island at the time of the conquest of Crete by the Moslems (in about 730), and that there were there both Moslems and unconverted Zinj. They reduced the Zinj to slavery, but adopted their language. He also states that the Shirazis and the Azdis (Omanis) had all the trade in his days, and mentions that ivory and tortoise-shell and other things were exported. Gold he does not mention. The country abounded in elephants, and the tusks were exported to China via Oman. The Bilad es-Sudan, or country of the blacks, was bounded by Sofala of the Zinj, and the land of the Wak Wak (bushmen).

The time of this description is generally placed about 915, as Masudi left Baghdad on his voyage in 912. Masudi's description of Kambalu applies very closely to what Pemba must have been like in his day.

Idris, who was born at Ceuta, studied at Cordova, and found a patron in King Roger of Sicily. Writing about 1154, he describes the dealings of the Arabs with the Zinj. He says that the ruler of Keish, opposite Muscat, had 505 ships, with which he used to raid the Zanzibar coast for slaves, and that the Zinj, having great respect for the Arabs, used to let them take these people without trouble. He states that the King of Zinj lived at Manisa (? Mombasa), where there were iron mines, and that the inhabitants of Mogadisho, Marka and Brava were Moslems but the rest infidels. He also mentions Malindi and Mombasa, which latter place he records as having a good harbour. He says that Sufalah of the Zinj borders on the land of the Wak Wak, hideous aborigines whose speech resembles whistling (i.e., the clicks of the Zulus). He speaks also of the gold products of this Sufalah, or lowland. He mentions also the Island of Al Komor (? Comoro or Madagascar).

Our next geographer is Yakut bin Abdulla (1179-1229), who was a Greek by birth, enslaved in childhood and sold to a merchant of Baghdad, who gave him a good education, and frequently sent him on trading expeditions to the Persian Gulf and elsewhere. He was subsequently freed, and wrote his book called *Mu'jamu 'l Buldan*. Besides telling us that the people of Tumbatu were Moslems in his time, he mentions also Sufalah as being the most remote town of Zinj, and El Jub as a town of Zinj which exported giraffe skins. El Jub can, of course, be placed on the Juba River. He mentions the trade in gold, and Arab methods of barter.

After Yakut comes Ibn Said, who lived in the thirteenth century, and whose remarks, gathered from hearsay, are as vague as those of Cosmas Indicopleustes. For instance, he confounds Madagascar and the Comoros as one island, and says that north-east of Mombasa was a mountain extending 100 miles into the sea, half iron mines and half magnetic, and that west of Mombasa was a gulf 300 miles long. The King of Zinj lived at Mombasa, and between that place and Sufalah was a great desert (Suffalah = lowland). In his time the inhabitants of Berbera and Marka were Mohammedans. He speaks also of the mountains of the moon.

Our last geographer and historian is the famous Ibn Batuta, whose full name was Abu Abdulla Muhammed bin Abdulla bin Muhammed bin Ibrahim El Zawati El-Tunji, who was born in 1304 at Tangier, and travelled extensively during many years, in which he visited Egypt, Palestine, Persia, Mesopotamia, Arabia, Asia Minor, Russia, India, China and Spain. On one occasion he was Kadhi of Debbi, and he performed the Haj four times. On the first of these pilgrimages he left his native town in 1324, and afterwards visited Mogadisho, Mombasa and Kilwa. At Mombasa, where, like many a modern traveller, he only spent one night, he says there are plentiful bananas, lemons and citrons, but no grain, which was brought from other places. The people were religious, chaste and honest. Of Zanzibar Island he makes no mention at all. Ibn Batuta died in 1378.

Let us now consider Marco Polo's description of Zanzibar. Marco Polo was born at Venice in 1254, the son of Nicolo Polo. In 1271 Nicolo (and his brother Maffeo) set out on his record journey to the East, taking the young Marco with him. After living for twenty years or so in the service of Kubla Khan, they set back on their voyage home from a Chinese port, and arrived safely in Venice three years later (1295). Thereafter Marco took part, in command of a galley, in the fleet of Andrea Dandolo, in the wars against the Genoese, and was captured off Cuyola on September 7th, 1296. For three years he was kept captive, and it appears that during this time he dictated his book, while in prison, to a fellow captive, one Rustician of Pisa. He died about 1324.

The following is his account of Zanzibar:

"This is a very great and noble island, about two thousand miles in circuit. The people are all idolaters, have languages and a king of their own, and are subject to no other power. They are not very tall, but so broad and thick, that in this respect they appear like giants; and they are likewise immensely strong, bearing as large a burden as four other men, which is really no wonder, for they eat as much as five. They are perfectly black and go naked, with the exception of a cloth round the waist. Their mouth is so wide, their nose so turned up, their lips and eyes so big, that they are horrible to behold, and anyone meeting them in another country would believe them devils. Elephants abound, and a great traffic is carried on in their teeth; likewise lions of a peculiar species, with ounces and leopards. In short, they have all kinds of beasts different from others in the world; including sheep entirely white, with only the head black, and none of any other colour.

"Here, too, is the giraffe, a most beautiful creature, whose shape I will describe. Behind, it is low, and the legs very short, while those before and the neck, are very large, so that its head rises three paces from the ground. The animal is small, and is quite harmless; and its colour being red and white, in circles, it is very beautiful. But there is a thing which I had forgotten about the elephant, that it caresses the female in the same manner as the human species. I must say the women of this island are most ugly objects, with large mouth, eyes, and nose, and their breasts four times the ordinary size; in short, they are hideous. The people live on rice, flesh, milk, and dates, and though they have no vines, make a very good liquor of rice, sugar, and spices. There is a great trade, particularly in elephants' teeth; and a good quantity of amber. The men are very brave in combat, and have little fear of death. They have no horses, but fight upon camels and elephants, placing on them castles well covered, with sixteen or twenty men mounted on them bearing lances, swords, and staves, and making a very powerful force in battle. They have no arms except leathern shields, lances, and swords, with which they fight well. When leading the elephant to the combat, they give him to drink of their wine or liquor, which renders him more fierce and effective."

Marco Polo never visited Zanzibar, and his account therefore lacks historical value, but it is interesting as showing what European ideas of the island were in the Middle Ages.

Before we close this period it is well to refer to an event in it, namely, the first crossing of the African continent by a European. This was achieved by a Genoese, called Leone Vivaldi, who crossed from the West, reaching Mogadisho about the end of the eleventh century. It is just possible that some of Marco Polo's information was derived either directly or indirectly from this source.

CHAPTER VIII

Visitors from the Far East

THE MALAYS ON THE COAST

There is definite historical evidence for the visit of Malays to the coast.

The Malays used to be a great seafaring people; their piracies were notorious, and they were very adventurous, and found their way, if not by design, then accidentally over a much larger field than has been supposed. At an early date they dominated the Bay of Bengal, and had settlements and colonies in Java, Sumatra, Borneo and other islands, to the very borders even of Australia. The rig of their ships seems to have been indirectly influenced by the Egyptians. Boats very similar and rig almost identical can be seen to-day on the ships of the Orang Laut of the Malay west coast.

The pure Malays are nowadays a quiet race of sailors and traders, and mostly Mohammedans. At one time they attained a very high degree of civilization, and invented a system of writing, and discovered gunpowder for themselves.

It is generally accepted on account of strong linguistic affinities that Malayo-Polynesian peoples spread to Madagascar at a very early time. The Antimerina, a Madagascar tribe, are also of undoubted Malay or Javanese origin. They apparently landed on the east coast about four centuries ago, and afterwards moved inland.

But it seems probable that Malays came to East Africa before; indeed, in the time of Idris and Ibn Said, they are said to have already come to Madagascar and Sofala.

Idris refers to an empire, which probably had its seat in Java, as the Empire of the Mihradj; and says that its traders used to come to Sofala, were well received by the inhabitants, and had many dealings with them.

Father Torrend has made some observations of interest with regard to the relations of the Malays and Javanese with the Bantus. After referring to Bleek's comparison of the Fiji and Bantu language, which have many similarities in common, Father Torrend says that he notices according to Idris that it was the southern part of Sofala which was mostly frequented by the Mihradj (Malay) traders, close to what he calls the Island of Djalous or Djulus; and that considering that the Zulus in customs closely resemble the Borneans, that the Zulus who have removed to Nyasaland are called Maviti (viti being the proper pronunciation of Fiji), and that Zulu, which he renders "children of the deep or sky," reminds one of the Zulu Sea and Archipelago, he is led to suspect that the first Zulus who organized the Zulu nation were men who came from Mihradj.

It is also probable that many slaves were carried off by the Mihradj from Sofala at times, and this may have been the channel through which the similarities in custom and language were communicated.

The customs observed at the birth of a child among the natives of Zanzibar are almost precisely similar to those observed in Malay, and much of the magic has strong affinities. This would seem to indicate a prolonged and early residence in these islands, and confirms the Pemba legends of "the people of Jawa (Java)."

Areca, betel and sugar-cane are indigenous to Malay; and it is possible that they were brought to the east coast by the Malays; possibly they inculcated the habit of betel-chewing.

Captain Stigand states there used to be ancient pottery on the coast said to have come from Malay. A family at Lamu (the Famao) claim descent from some Chinese or Malayans who were wrecked there at an unknown date.

RELATIONS OF THE CHINESE WITH THE EAST COAST OF AFRICA

The Chinese and Japanese were notable seamen from early times, and built large sailing ships, "Their junks found their way far afield in the Indian Ocean and its borders" (Sir H. Howorth). How early they did fare afield may be gathered from Mr. Chatterton, who says, "Between the Chinese and Burmese junks of to-day, and the Egyptian ships of about six thousand years ago, there are so many points of similarity that we are not surprised when we remember that the Chinese, like the Egyptians, derived their earliest culture from Babylonia, and that India (including Burma) is mainly, as to its culture at least, an offshoot from the Chinese. Until quite recently China remained in the same state of development for four thousand years. If that was so with her arts and life generally, it has been especially so in the case of her sailing craft."

The dealings of what we may call the earlier Chinese with the east coast of Africa extended probably over the period covered by four separate dynasties, from A.D. 619-1644.

The first of these was the greatest national dynasty of China, the Tang dynasty, which lasted from 619 to 960. Some of the numerous coins found at Mogadisho, Kilwa and Mafia have been identified with the K'ai Yuan from A.D. 713-742, and others date from 845. It is also recorded that Abu Zeyd Hassan returned from China via East Africa some time after 851. It is obvious therefore that there was intercourse with China from an early date.

Nevertheless the Tang dynasty intercourse with the outside world was not much encouraged. During the succeeding dynasty, that of the Sungs (960-1279), there was far more intercourse.

Bretschneider made considerable researches into the mediæval trade of the Chinese with the Arabs, and his pamphlet on the subject is interesting reading. On page 13 he states that in 976 an envoy from Tashi brought a negro slave from K'un lun to China, and he created much sensation at court. In a note he says that K'un lun here probably denotes Pulu Condore near Cambodia, but goes on: "In the *San ts'ai hula* (1607) is an article dedicated to the Ts'eng Ssu of K'un lun. (I cannot explain the characters Ts'eng Ssu.) It is said that this land lies in the south-western sea. There is found a large bird p'eng, which obscures the sun in flying, and can swallow a camel. The body of the inhabitants of K'un lun is black, as if covered with black varnish. They make slaves from amidst their own people and sell them to foreign merchants, receiving in exchange dresses and other articles."

The *p'eng* or *pheng* is the rukh. I have discussed the occurrence of this bird in a pamphlet called *Sindbad the Sailor in East Africa*. Ta'shi is the Chinese for the Arabs, K'un lun is here, as elsewhere, Kambalu, and Kambalu probably Mkumbuu, the ruined city in Pemba. Ts'eng Ssu is the Chinese form of Zenj, of which Bretschneider was not aware. A coin found at Mafia in 1916 has been identified as a cash of the Emperor Shan Tsung (1068-1086), and other coins have been found dating from the reign of Shauking (1131-1163). Idris remarks that, when great troubles arose in China, the Chinese transferred their trade to islands which he calls Zaledj or Zanedj, facing the coast of Zinj, where they came to intimate relations with the inhabitants on account of their mildness and accommodating ways. It is possible that one of the islands he refers to was Mafia, where many Chinese coins have been found. Some of the fragmentary china found in Pemba has been identified as cream-coloured Ting ware of this dynasty.

The next dynasty, lasting from 1280-1360, was that of the Mongolians, called Yuan. To this dynasty belonged the celebrated Kubla Khan. Marco Polo relates that he sent messengers to the southern part of Madagascar "on the pretext of demanding the release of one of his servants who have been detained there (this shows prior intercourse), but in reality to examine into the circumstances of the country and the truths of the wonderful things told of it. When they returned to the presence of his majesty, they brought with them a feather of the rukh, positively affirmed to have measured ninety spans, and the quill part to have two palms in circumference. They were also the bearers of the tusk of a wild boar, an animal that grows there to the size of a buffalo, and it was found to weigh fourteen pounds."

The date of this excursion was before A.D. 1292.

The last of these four dynasties is the cultured Ming dynasty (1358-1644). The greater part of the china fragments found in the ruins of Pemba and other parts of East Africa belong to this period. There is also a record of a Chinese fleet visiting Mogadisho for purposes of trade in A.D. 1430.

On page 21 of his pamphlet referred to, Bretschneider gives some interesting extracts from the records of the Ming dynasty (*Ming shi*, Chapter 326).

"Mu ku tu su lies in the sea, distant from Siao po lan (probably a place on the Malabar coast or an island) twenty days' journey. It is a barren country of wide extent, very mountainous. It sometimes does not rain for years. The houses are built of stone. In 1427 an envoy arrived at the Chinese Court from Mukutusu." Mukutusu is Mogadisho, founded, says Bretschneider (probably on the authority of Rigby), in 924 by Arabs.

"Pulawa adjoins Mukutusu, and is likewise on the sea—has little grass and few trees, but produces plenty of salt. There are rhinoceros, elephants, camels, an animal *Ma ha shou* which resembles the chang (antelope), and another animal, resembling the ass, is called *hua fu lu*. Among products are mentioned *ju siang, mo yao, lung sien siang*."

Hua means spotted, and *hua fulu* may refer to the zebra. *Ju* means milk, and *siang* perfume. *Ju siang* is incense (olibanum), *mo yao* is myrrh, and *lung sien siang*, meaning literally "dragon's saliva perfume," is ambergris.

"Chupu lies not far from Mukutusu. During the reign of Yung lo (1403-1425) an envoy came to China from Chupu. The country produces gold, iron, *lung sien siang ju siang*, *hu tsiao* (pepper). There are also lions, ostriches and leopards." Chupu means almost certainly Juba. Yakut speaks of El Jub and its export of giraffe skins. It may be that the particular town referred to is Kismayu.

Traces of the Chinese remaining in East Africa are but few. Professor Schwartz of South Africa dealt with them in 1926 in an article in the *Nation* of South Africa. In Zanzibar it is probable that the conical hat worn by the Wahadimu fishermen was derived from them.

From these facts it will be seen that during the Middle Ages, trade between the Far East and the land of Zinj was no uncommon thing. Masudi himself refers to ivory being sent to China, and it is therefore probable that trade began much earlier, and was well established in his time. Nankin china was traded for gold by the early coast Arabs, and no doubt that is the reason for it being so plentiful in Zanzibar.

The word Zanzibar was by the Chinese adapted to Tseng-pat or Tseng-po, and the Japanese, who may also have come to the coast, called the Zinj, Tsengu. Yule, in his edition of *Marco Polo*, notes that the Japanese Encyclopædia, referring to the east coast, says that there is a bird called pheng, which in its flight eclipses the sun. It can swallow a camel, and its quills are used for water-casks. The pheng is no doubt the same as the rukh.

Concerning the Japanese, Father Torrend says: "If it be true that the Japanese are called Wak Wak, exactly as the Hottentots by some Arab writers, it would appear from a passage in the book of the *Marvels of India* that A.D. 945, they sent a fleet numbering a thousand ships to conquer that Island of Cambalu (probably Pemba) in which the Arabs had established themselves two centuries earlier, with the intention of procuring for themselves and the Chinese, ivory, tortoise-shell, leopard skins, amber and slaves. They would not have succeeded in their main object, but by way of consolation, they would have carried fire and sword into many towns of the land of Sofala. It must be added, however, that the author of the book of *Marvels* seems not to have believed altogether the man who gave this information."

The Chinese records yield a fair amount of information which gives an idea of the knowledge they had of the coast. One of the most important books is that of Chau ju k'ua, entitled *Chu-fan, chi*, which deals with the Chinese and Arab trade in the twelfth and thirteenth centuries.

Of Zanzibar Chau ju k'ua speaks as follows:

"*Ts'ong-pa*

"The Ts'ong-pa country is on an island of the sea south of Hu-ch'a-la.

"To the west it reaches to a great mountain. The inhabitants are of Ta'shi stock and follow the Ta'shi religion. They wrap themselves in blue foreign cotton stuffs, and wear red leather shoes.

"Their daily food consists of meal, baked cakes and mutton.

"There are many villages, and a succession of wooded hills and terraced rocks.

"The climate is warm, and there is no cold season.

"The products of the country consist of elephants' tusks, native gold, ambergris and yellow sandal-wood. Every year Hu-ch'a-la and the Ta'shi localities along the sea coast send ships to this country, with white cotton cloths, porcelain, copper and red cotton to trade."

Ts'ong-pa is the Chinese form of Zanzibar. Here the author means not only the island, but the whole of the territory formerly known as Zanguebar.

Hu-ch'a-la is Gujerat, and the Ta'shi are Arabs.

The great mountain is probably Kilimanjaro.

As regards Pemba, the following item which appears in Probsthain's *Catalogue of Chinese Art*, is of interest.

"*The K'un lun Ts'eng K'i country* [*the Zandj* (*or blacks*) *of K'un lun* (*Madagascar or Pemba*)]

"In the south-west parts adjoining is an island in the sea. This land possesses a huge bird. (The ruc of Arab writers; see *Marco Polo*, Book III, Chapter XXXVII, on Madagascar and Zanzibar.)

"You may cut the quills of their wings to make water-carrying utensils out of them (meaning: carrying on each end of a shoulder-pole). Moreover, they are black-bodied wild men; if you entice them with food you barter as many as you like to do work (as slaves) for the foreign (i.e., Arab) trader."

This painting is numbered as Item IV in a list of six pictures of the Sung dynasty attributed to Li Lung Mien, one of the most famous artists of the world, and the first among all the painters of the Sung dynasty. The set represents scenes from "Foreign and Strange Lands"; opposite each picture there is a Chinese explanation. The English translation in this particular case is given above.

The parentheses are those of Professor Parker who identifies K'un lun as Madagascar or Pemba. This identification, I believe, rests on a note in Yule's *Marco Polo*. Yule says, "Barbier de Meynard (in his edition of Masudi's *Meadows of Gold*) thinks this (Kambalu—of which K'un lun is the Chinese form) may be Madagascar. I suspect it rather to be Pemba.'' Yule gives neither here nor elsewhere any reason for his supposition, but his alternative identification has been quoted by several authorities.

In the chapter dealing with the records of the Arabian geographers, Kambalu has been identified with Mkumbuu in Pemba, and the reasons there given for this identification make it tolerably sure that in the above picture we have a representation of the Chinese idea of Pemba at some time during the period A.D. 960-1280.

Chau ju k'ua has the following chapter in the section of his book called " Countries in the Sea.''

" *K'un lun-ts'öng-K'i*

" This country is in the south-west. It is adjacent to a large island.

" There are usually there (i.e., on the island) great p'öng birds which so mask the sun in their flight that the shade on the sundial is shifted.

" If the great p'öng bird finds a wild camel it swallows it, and if one should chance to find a p'öng's feather, he can make a water-butt of it, after cutting off the hollow quill.

" The products of the country are big elephants' tusks, and rhinoceros' horns.

" In the west there is an island in the sea on which there are many savages, with bodies as black as lacquer and with frizzled hair.

" They are enticed by (offers of) food, then caught and carried off for slaves to the Ta'shi countries where they fetch a high price.

" They are used as gate-keepers (lit. to look after the gate bolts). It is said that they do not long for their kinfolk.''

The large island is probably Madagascar, and the p'öng or pheng, as the Japanese called it, is the rukh of the *Arabian Nights*.

Madagascar was considered adjacent to the Zanzibar coast. The method of enticing children with sweetmeats, and then capturing them as slaves, is an old one, used successfully until the abolition of slavery. The natives of Tumbatu still refer to its use on that island, while Idris (I. 58) says that the Arabs of Oman kidnapped children on the Zanzibar coast by this means. This was in the twelfth century.

In these days then, especially those of the Ming dynasty, Chinese shipping reached far over the seas, and they had a considerable overseas trade; as this was so, and as their descendants are still trading here to-day, it may be wondered why they have not developed their sea trade more.

Mr. Wells has admirably summed up the reasons in his *Outline of History*, and traces them without doubt to the difficulties of writing, speaking and learning Chinese, which even to this day makes Chinese history and the general study of China a closed book to all but the few. Such a drawback cannot but have acted adversely on their relations with Bantu peoples. Other languages they could, and did assimilate, but Chinese would offer almost insuperable difficulties.

CHAPTER IX

The Rise and Fall of the Portuguese

RISE OF THE PORTUGUESE

It is not necessary here to go into the causes which led the nations of Europe to take an interest in the Empire of the East, but after Bartholomew Dias had rounded the Cape of Good Hope, stimulated with the desire to forestall the Spaniards who had dispatched Columbus in 149? to discover the East, the Portuguese sent an expedition under Vasco da Gama with the same object.

Columbus, of course, discovered the New World, though such was far from being his object, but Vasco da Gama, in reaching India, laid the foundation of the trade of the Portuguese in that quarter, which lasted for several centuries, but which has now dwindled till they hold but a few insignificant possessions in East Africa and India. Dominion in East Africa was never the ultimate object of Portugal, but was only looked on as a stepping-stone to India, and their footholds in Eastern Africa, however interesting they may be to the historians of the country, were only incidental (except in so far as the gold trade of Sofala was concerned) to the former object.

Vasco da Gama sailed from the Tagus on the 8th July, 1497, with three ships, of which the *Sao Gabriel* was his flagship, while his brother, Paula da Gama, commanded the *Sao Raphael*, and one Jose de Coimbra commanded the *Birrio*, the third ship of the fleet.

On the 1st March in the following year, he anchored off St. George Island, near Mozambique, where the Governor was one Zakoeja. On the 4th of April he sighted Mafia Island, and on the 5th again "beheld the land," probably the northern portion of Zanzibar Island. About four a.m. on the 6th the *Sao Raphael* ran ashore on the Karanga reef, opposite Mtangata, due west of Chake Chake. While waiting for the high tide to get the ship off, "two canoes approached loaded with fine oranges better than those of Portugal." On the next day, Saturday, 7th April, "they ran along the coast," and "they saw some islands about fifteen leagues from the mainland and about six leagues in extent. They supply the vessels of the country with masts; all are inhabited by Moors." The "islands" were Pemba, which, owing to the many indentations on the west coast, appears in the distance to be several islands, particularly from the north.

On the same day Vasco da Gama arrived at Mombasa, whence he proceeded to Malindi, where the Portuguese formed a friendship never afterwards broken. Here he obtained a pilot, called Cana, who was a Gujerati, and with whom he sailed for Calicut. On his way back to Lisbon, which he reached on the 29th August, 1499, he called first at Mogadisho, which he wantonly bombarded, and then again at Malindi.

After this his personnel was so short that he determined to burn the *Sao Raphael*, which was down on Mtangata reef. "On Sunday, 27th (January, 1499), we left the place with a fair wind. During the following night we lay to, and in the morning we came close to a large island called Jamgiber, which is peopled with Moors and is quite ten leagues from the mainland."

After this they called at St. George and proceeded home.

According to this account Vasco da Gama did not stop at Zanzibar, but Burton says: "Goes declares that Da Gama, after touching Makdishu, arrived at Zanzibar on February 28th (presumably January 28th), and was supplied by its ruler with provisions, presents and specimens of country produce. The island is described as large and fertile, with groves of fine trees producing good fruit, two others Pomba (Pemba) and Mofia (Mafia) lying in its vicinity. These settlements were governed by Moorish princes of the same caste as the King of Melinde, doubtless hereditary Moslem sheikhs and seyyids. The population is represented as being in no great force, but carrying on a good trade with Mombasa for Guzerat calicoes, and with Sofala for gold."

He goes on to say that the historian, Joao de Barros, states that the King of Zanzibar was "of the line of the kings of Mombasa, our enemies." The inhabitants were white Moors and black Moors, the former being a slight people, scantily armed, but clad in fine cottons of Cambaya brought from Mombasa. Their women were adorned with jewels, with Sofala gold and silver, obtained from Mombasa in barter with good stuffs.

On the 9th March, 1500, another fleet of much larger ships, under the command of Pedro Alvares Cabral, set sail, but after heavy losses, and incidentally discovering Brazil, it broke up and proceeded in parties. One ship under Pedro Dias got to Mogadisho, and then returned to Lisbon. The other survivors, numbering six, on the 16th July, collected at Sofala, where they captured a dhow commanded by Foteima, uncle of the ruler of Malindi, who was therefore released. They then called at Mozambique on the 20th July, and afterwards at Kilwa and Malindi, whence they proceeded to Calicut.

On the return voyage they called at Malindi, where they lost the ship commanded by Sancho de Toar, which was wrecked, though the guns were afterwards salved and mounted by the ruler of Mombasa. Passing Zanzibar by, they called at Mozambique, and reached Lisbon on the 31st July, 1501. On the 10th February of the next year, Vasco da Gama set forth on his way to Calicut, and touching only at Mozambique on his way back, arrived at Lisbon on the 1st September, 1503.

The Portuguese now began to send many ships to the East, though it would be out of place here to touch on them, except where their activities concerned Zanzibar or Pemba.

One of the ships that had left Lisbon in the year 1503 became separated from the remainder of the fleet, and, after waiting for the rest at Mozambique and Kilwa, sailed for Zanzibar. This ship was commanded by Ruy Lorenço Ravasco Marques, and in two months' time, cruising off the islands, which he called "Zemzibar," he captured in a real piratical fashion twenty rich ships laden with ambergris, ivory, tortoise-shell, wax, honey, rice, coir, silk and cotton. The king sent a remonstrance, but receiving no satisfaction, manned all his canoes with 4,000 men. Ravasco, however, well-armed two boats with cannon, and, killing 34 men at the first discharge, put the rest to flight, among those killed being the son of the king. After this the Portuguese landed, and were met with resistance, which they soon overcame, and the king sued for peace, which was granted on an agreement to pay tribute. Ravasco found four ships in the harbour, of which he gave two to the son of the King of Malindi. One paid ransom, and the fourth was taken with its cargo as a prize to Portugal.

It appears, therefore, from this, that Zanzibar became definitely subject to Portugal in the year 1503 or 1504. During the next three or four years we hear nothing of Zanzibar. In 1504 a fleet of thirteen of the largest ships built in Portugal touched Mozambique and Malindi on the outward trip, and Kilwa and Mozambique on the return.

On the 22nd July, 1505, Dom Francisco d'Almeida arrived at Kilwa and made a settlement there. He built a fort and deposed Emir Abraham, setting up in his place one Mohammed Ankoni. He preserved the native form of government, but installed Pedro Ferreira Fogaça as captain, and Francisco Coutinho as magistrate. This form of government seems to have been in principle very like that adopted by the European nations to-day in their African and other possessions. Kilwa remained the headquarters of the Portuguese until 1509, when it was determined to transfer the garrison to Sofala. In 1508 a governor-general was appointed to reside at Mozambique. In 1508 Dom Duarte de Lemos was appointed governor of the provinces of Ethiopia and Arabia, and set out on tour to collect the tribute from Mafia, Zanzibar and Pemba, which was in arrears. Mafia submitted, and the people of Pemba escaped to Mombasa, leaving nothing in their houses.

Zanzibar, however, resisted, but the town was captured and given over to looting. The Mwenyi Mkuu retired towards the north, and the rest of the people fled to the bush, "after being well pierced in the flesh with the sharp points and sword-blades of our men."

In the year 1512 Duarte Barbosa wrote his book, which be brought to a close in the year 1516. Under the heading "Pemba, Mamfia and Zinzibar" (which in the Spanish version are called Penda, Manfia and Zanzibar), he writes:

"Between this island of Sao Lourenco and the mainland (not very far therefrom) are three islands, one called Mamfia, another Pemba, another Zinzibar; which are inhabited by Moors. They have great store of food, for in there are found rice, millet, flesh-meat in great quantity, oranges, limes and citrons (of which the woods are full), and every other kind of fruit.

"There is a great plenty of sugar-cane, but they know not how to make the sugar. These islands have Moorish kings. Some of them deal in their stock of flesh and fruit with the mainland, and in very small, weak, ill-found and undecked boats, having but one mast. The planks are bound and sewn together with a cord they call 'cairo' (coco-nut fibre), and their sails are palm-leaf mats. They are a feeble folk, and have but few weapons. The kings of these islands live in great luxury; they are clad in very fine silk and cotton garments, which they purchase at Mombasa from the Cambaya merchants. The women of these Moors go bravely decked, they wear many jewels of fine Çofala gold, silver too in plenty, ear-rings, necklaces, bracelets, and bangles, and they go clad in good silk garments. They have many mosques, and honour greatly the Alcoran of Mafamede."

In the year 1519 the Arabs of Zanzibar captured and massacred certain shipwrecked sailors belonging to the expedition of Don Gorge d'Albuquerque, and three years later the king complained to the Portuguese of the revolt of the Kirimba Islands, which were under his domination, and refused to pay tribute to him. The Portuguese therefore duly reduced the islands to subjection to the Island of Zanzibar again.

In 1528 Mombasa also became unruly, and as Nuno da Cunha called at Zanzibar on his way to assume the Governor-Generalship of India, the king approached him, and he determined to subdue Mombasa with the aid of armies from Zanzibar, Malindi and other places. He took the town and reduced it to entire subjection, causing the inhabitants to pay tribute. With this victory the Portuguese rule of the whole of the coast was consolidated, and became one of four governments depending on a vice-royalty, the others being Malacca, Ormuz and Ceylon. After these events Zanzibar remained in alliance with the Portuguese, and ceased to be tributary.

Many of the Portuguese occupied plantations, and a church was established in which a Brother of the Order of St. Augustine officiated.

This period which we have considered, up to the events just described, covers the rise and stabilization of Portuguese rule on the east coast of Africa.

THE ZIMBA INVASION OF EAST AFRICA

About the year 1570, two hordes of barbarians appeared opposite Tete, north-east of the Zambesi; they came from South Africa, and were of the same origin as the Zulus. The second of these hordes reached the coast in 1585, and ravaged the country from opposite Mozambique to the north. In 1587 they invaded Kilwa, where they ruined the town and killed and ate 3,000 Arabs. Passing northwards, they attacked Mombasa, where the people, oppressed by the Portuguese from the sea, made an ill-advised alliance with the Wazimba, who turned on them and again killed and ate a large number. About 1589 these hordes reached Malindi, where they were defeated by the Portuguese in co-operation with the inhabitants of the town, and a force of 3,000 Wasegeju. Our two islands, and that of Mozambique, were safe from the ravages of these people, who were not provided with transport, but they were a considerable thorn in the side of the Portuguese.

BRIEF TURKISH DOMINATION OF THE COAST

In 1585 Ali Bey, claiming the authority of Murad III, Sultan of Turkey, made piratical progress down the east coast, where, being a Moslem, he received in many places enthusiastic welcome from the inhabitants, who were being oppressed by the Portuguese. He captured a Portuguese vessel, and after Mogadisho, Brava, Kismayu, Faza, Kilifi and Lamu, had readily agreed to submit to the Turks, returned to the Red Sea in April, 1586, with rich plunder of about £600,000 in value, together with fifty Portuguese prisoners.

Dom Duarte de Menezes, Viceroy of India, wishing to restore the authority of the Portuguese, then dispatched from Goa a fleet of eighteen ships, which burnt the town of Mombasa and again reduced it to subjection. In 1589 Ali Bey again set sail from

Mocha with a fleet of five ships, wishing to subdue Malindi, which had always sided with the Portuguese. In this he was unsuccessful, but was again warmly welcomed at Mombasa. He was defeated on 5th March, 1589, by Thomas de Souza Coutinho, brother of the Viceroy of India, with a fleet of twenty ships. The Zimbas also attacked the Turks, and Ali Bey was captured and taken to Lisbon, where he became a Christian.

THE FIRST ENGLISH VISITORS

This section must of necessity somewhat overlap in time some of the period we have considered before, and some of that we shall consider after.

The reason is that these first Englishmen to come to Zanzibar came only as tourists. The all too brief accounts they give us are interesting, but they had no real influence, save in the indirect way that they opened up new places, over the history of the country.

In dealing with these voyagers, therefore, I shall not dwell more than is absolutely necessary on any part of the voyages save those that directly concern the Islands of Zanzibar and Pemba.

The first of these visits occurred in 1591, in which year Sir James Lancaster set forth in the *Edward Bonadventure* from "Plimmouth" to the East Indies . . . to the Isles of Comoro and Zanzibar "on the backeside of Africa," and to other places. At Comoro thirty-two of the crew and the master, William Mace of Ratcliffe, were betrayed by the "perfidious moors, and as the boats were ashore could not be assisted and were for the most part slain. From hence with heauie hearts we shaped our course for Zanzibar, the 7 of November, where shortly after wee arriued, and made us a new boat of such boards as we had within boord, and rid in the road untill the 15 of February, where, during our aboad, we sawe diuers pangaias or boats, which are pinned with woodden pinnes, and sowed together with palmito cordes, and calked with the huskes of cocos shels beaten, whereof they make occam. At length a Portugal pangaia comming out of the harborow of Zanzibar, where they haue a small Factorie, sent a canoa with a Moore which had bene christened, who brought us a letter wherein they desired to know what wee were, and what we sought. We sent them word we were Englishmen come from Don Antonio upon businesse to his friends in the Indies; with which answere they returned, and would not any more come at us. Whereupon not long after we manned out our boat and tooke a *pangaia* of the Moores, which had a priest of theirs in it, which in their language they called a sherife; whom we used very curteously; which the king tooke in very good part, hauing his priests in great estimation, and for his deliuerance furnished us with two moneths victuals, during all which time we detained him with us. These Moores informed us of the false and spitefull dealing of the Portugals towards us, which made them beleeve that we were cruell people and men-eaters, and willed them if they loued their safetie in no case to come neere us. Which they did onely to cut us off from all knowledge of the state and traffique of the countrey. While we road from the end of November until the middle of February in this harborough, which is sufficient for a ship of 500 tuns to ride in, we set upon a Portugal *pangaia* with our boat, but because it was very little, and our men not able to stirre in it, we were not able to take the sayd pangaia, which was armed with 10 good shot like our long fouling pieces. This place for the goodnesse of the harborough and watering, and plentifull refreshing with fish, whereof we took great store with our nets, and for sundry sorts of fruits of the countrey, as cocos and others which were brought us by the Moores, as also for oxen and hennes, is carefully to be sought for by such of our ships as shall hereafter passe that way. But our men had need to take good heed of the Portugals; for while we lay here the Portugal admiral of the coast from Melinda to Mozambique, came to view and to betray our boat if he could haue taken at any time advantage, in a gallie frigate of ten tunnes, with 8 or 9 oares on a side. Of the strength of which frigate and their trecherous meaning we were advertised by an Arabian Moore, which came from the King of Zanzibar diuers times about the deliuerie of the priest aforesayd, and afterward by another which we caried thence along with vs; for wheresoeuer we came, our care was to get into our hands some one or two of the countreys to learne the languages and states of those partes where we touched. Moreover, here againe we had another clap of thunder which did shake our foremast very much, which wee fisht and repaired with timber from the shore, whereof there is good store thereabout of a kind of trees some fortie foote high, which is red and tough wood, and as, I suppose, a kind of cedar. Here our surgeon, Arnold, negligently catching a great heate in his head, being on land with the master to seeke oxen, fell sicke and shortly died, which might haue bene cured by letting of blood before it had bin setled. Before our departure we had in this place some thousand weight of pitch, or rather a kind of gray and white gumme like vnto frankincense, as clammie as turpentine, which in melting groweth as black as pitch, and is very brittle of it selfe, but we mingled it with oile, whereof wee had 300 iarres in the prize which we tooke to the northward of the equinoctiall, not farre from Guinie, bound for Brasil. Sixe dayes before wee departed hence, the Cape marchant of the factorie wrote a letter vnto our capitaine in the way of friendship, as he pretended, requesting a iarre of wine and a iarre of oyle, and two or three pounds of gunpowder, which letter hee sent by a Negro, his man, and a Moore in a canoa; we sent him his demands by the Moore, but tooke the Negro along with vs, because we vnderstood he had bene in the East Indies and knew somewhat of the countrey. By this Negro we were advertised of a small barke of some thirtie tunnes (which the Moores called a junco), which was come from Goa thither, laden with pepper for the Factorie and seruice of that kingdome. Thus hauing trimmed our shippe as we lay in this road, in the end we set forward for the coast of the East India, the 15 of February aforesayd." Comment on this passage is not necessary here, but a few explanatory notes are desirable on some of the words.

Firstly, the "pangaias or boats," which were obviously our old friend, the Mtepe or πλοιαριον ῥαπτον. It is interesting to note that nearly every traveller makes mention of these craft. Further information will be found under "Sailing" in the ethnological part.

Don Antonio was one of the claimants to the throne of Portugal in 1580, when King Henry the Cardinal died. He was the Prior of Crato, and illegitimate son of Luis, younger brother of John III and Henry. There was another brother called Duarte, from a daughter of whom the Braganzas descend. King Philip II, who actually seized the throne, claimed descent from a sister, and the English supported the claim of Antonio.

"Sherife," in the ordinary way, means a descendant of the Prophet, but the Ma Sherifu of Zanzibar and Pemba, though claiming to be so descended, are generally considered rather as a tribe, and are said to have come hither from Wasin Island. We shall come across them again.

The "harborough" in which the *Edward Bonaventure* wintered, or rather "summered," waiting for the monsoon, was almost certainly that of Kizimkazi.

A kind of cedar could only have been the casuarina, which is still used for mast-making, and is plentiful on the shores of Zanzibar and Pemba.

The "pitch" was apparently gum copal.

The "barke" from Goa, which the Moors called a junco, is very interesting. The word junco does not now occur in Swahili, but almost certainly got into the language at that time from the Chinese, who, as we have seen, visited the coast during five centuries. As they came no more the word dropped out, and nowadays we have *manowari* and *meli*, words which need no explanation.

Another account of the voyage by Henry May merely says, "from hence we went for the Isle of Zanzibar, on the coast of Melinde; whereas, wee stayed and wintered vntil the beginning of February following."

The next visit of an English ship to the islands was in 1608.

"On the 28th of February (of that year) the fleet (*The Dragon*, whereof Captain William Keeling was general, and the *Hector*, Captain Hawkins) left the bay of St. Augustine, and having on the passage sighted the Island of Pemba, Cape Dorfu, and the Islands of Abbu de Curia and Dos Tomoas, arrived in April at the Island of Zokotora."

The bay of St. Augustine is in Madagascar, Cape Dorfu, Cape Guardafui, Abbu de Curia, Abd-el-Kuri, between Guardafui and Socotra and Dos Tomoas, the Brothers, two islands south-west of Socotra.

On the 25th of November of that year, the *Ascension*, of which Captain Alexander Sharpeigh was general, anchored off the Island of Comoro, and found the natives there faithful and courteous, a different experience to that of the *Edward Bonaventure*. I here quote the India Office manuscript: "The Island of Pemba was next touched at. At first the people seemed friendly, but afterwards they made a treacherous attack on a party engaged in filling the water-casks, when one man was killed, another wounded, and a third was missing, of whom no tidings could be obtained, when a force landed on the following day to seek for him. On the return of this party the *Ascension* put to sea. During the night the vessel touched ground, but fortunately floated off without having suffered any damage.

"Next day three small ships, 'pangaias,' were

captured. Some of their company were brought on board, and kindly treated, but suddenly they, with their knives, attacked the crew: 'upon this occasyon wee made with them shorte worke, and brought most part of them by sundry wayes to their last home; giving thankes to God for this last deliverye, wherein the owld proverbe was verrefyed, That one Myscheife comes syldome alone.' The goods found in these ships, consisting principally of coarse calicoes of no great value, were transferred to the *Ascension*.

"On the night of the 9th of January (1608-9) there was 'an eclipse of the moone wch. was very fayre, and continewed one hower and 30 minutes.'

"A supply of fresh water was obtained from some uninhabited islands in latitude 4° 10′ S.; there many 'lande turtles of a hudge bignes' were found, also much goodly ship timber grew on the islands."

Mombasa lies in 4° 5′ S., but was certainly not uninhabited. Chale Island, 4° 27′, might have been meant, but there is only one island there. I think that the two islets of Pungutiachi, the Island of Pungutiayu and that of Kisiti, off Wasin Island, and between 4° 30′ and 4° 35′ are probably meant. Of these the *African Pilot* says: "Kisiti, nearly 4 miles eastward of Mwamba Midira, is a small islet near the western end of the reef about one mile long, and having on it a few weather-beaten bushes about 12 feet high; between it and Mwamba Midira is Mako Kokwe, drying 3 feet, and in the channels on either side of that reef are reefs and shoals.

"Pungutiayu, a wooded island 54 feet high, stands on a reef about 1½ miles in length in a north-east and opposite direction, which dries 6 feet; the island is situated 1¾ miles southward of the south-east point of Wasin Island, and nearly midway between is Pungutiachi, a group of wooded islets, 55 feet high, and lying on a reef three-quarters of a mile long east and west. This group, with Pungutiayu and Kisiti, are distinct features in making the land in this locality."

In Captain Sharpeigh's own account of this visit he says: "Having failed to obtain a supply of water at Comoro, Captain Sharpeigh touched at the Island of Pemba, the natives of which place treacherously attacked his men, who were engaged in filling the water-casks. On the day after this attack he put to sea; during the night the *Ascension* touched the ground, but fortunately floated off without sustaining any damage. Next day three small native ships were captured, and some thirty men of their crews were brought on board the ship. These men were seemingly unarmed, but suddenly they, with their knives, attacked the *Ascension's* crew, for which they were either put to the sword or thrown overboard.

"A further supply of fresh water was obtained at some islands in latitude four degrees ten minutes south."

The next visit we have to record is that of the *Union* to Zanzibar in 1609. The *Union* was companion ship to the *Ascension*, and sailed with her from Woolwich on the 14th March (1607-8), but was separated from her after leaving Saldanha (Table) Bay. An account of the voyage of the *Union* was written shortly by Samuel Bradshaw, a merchant aboard her. The accounts of what happened to her at Zanzibar are given in the journals written by people on the *Trade's Increase*, of which Sir Henry Middleton was general, who found her in St. Augustine's Bay at Madagascar, in September, 1610. When the vessels entered the Bay of St. Augustine, the *Union* was found lying at anchor, "for shee had road there six weekes. And she was in great distresse for want of vittles; so wee releved hir, for shee was homward bound, laden with peper, having in hir one merchante whose name was Mr. Bradshew, for the reste of the merchantes with the Captayne was betrayed at a place caled Zensebar." A fuller account is recorded by Nicholas Downton, second in command to Sir Henry Middleton, who says: "The island of 'Madagasker or St. Lawrence' was sighted on the sixth of September, on which day the fleet anchored in the Bay of St. Augustine, where we found the *Union* of London, and the Vice-Admirall of the 4th voyage, whose people was distressed, wanting victuals for to carye them home: who related unto my Genn there infortunate loosing companye wth there Admirall and pinnance betweene Saldania and the Cape Bona Speranza, and never since heard of them: how they put into this baye (outwards bound) to seeke them, also followed after them and put into Zanzibar, an iland bordering of the Abexin coast, where the Portugals made shew of favour and trade, inticing them to land wth there boat, where they betrayed and tooke 3 of there men; the rest seeing there dainger fled wth the boat unto the ship, who proceeded on there journey till, wth contrarye windes before they could recover anye fitt port, for want of water were forced to retourne towards the Bay of Antongill on the E.S.E. side of Madagaskar, but the wind or there course not suiting there determination, they put into a good harbor or Bay of Gungomar, on the north-west corner of Madagaskar, where they were awhile fed wth good words and faire promises and kind entertainment by the king."

These accounts were all from hearsay, and a third one is so imperfectly reported that the incident is placed in Madagascar. It says: "From Saldanha they sailed to the Bay of St. Augustine, where the *Union* was found at anchor. She was homeward bound, and had lost her captain and chief merchants at 'Conggomare,' in the north-east part of the Island of St. Lawrence."

All these voyages were made under the auspices of the East India Company, and many ships were dispatched to the Indies from England in the seventeenth century, which caused the Portuguese to be considerably alarmed as to their monopoly of trade and suzerainty in the East. But it must be remembered that it was not the English but the Omani Arabs, the present rulers of Zanzibar, who drove the

Portuguese from these seas towards the end of that same century.

We have now to jump ninety years to the year of grace 1698, and consider the evidence for the supposed visit of the much maligned Captain Kidd to Pemba, where Burton and legend say he buried treasure.

Captain Kidd sailed from New York in September, 1696, in the *Adventure Galley*. In October he arrived at Madeira, with a brig, the master of whom was one Joynter. Then to Bonavista, where they took in salt, and to St. Jago where they watered.

Afterwards they visited the Cape of Good Hope, and on 12th December, in latitude 32° S., met five English men-of-war and sailed a week in their company, and after parting went to Telere, a port of Madagascar. Kidd, who was not a pirate himself, was sent to catch pirates, who were generally to be found at Madagascar, but finding none there and supposing them to be at their nefarious work farther eastward, sailed in pursuit. In company with a Barbadoes Sloop he next arrived at Johanna, which is not "an island off the Malabar coast" (Dalton), but one of the Comoros. Here he found four East India merchantmen (which may have included any of the ships *Charles II*, *Sidney*, *Sampson* or *Madras*, which sailed from India in the years 1695 and 1696). On March 22nd, 1697, he sailed to another of the Comoros, where he lost about fifty men in a week's time. He therefore left, and after cruising about in the open sea for some time, took up his station at Bob's Key, now called Bab or Pars Islet (latitude 11° 35′ N., longitude 42° 41′ E.), to wait for the Mecca fleet. Up to this time he had in the course of a year captured no prize, but in November, 1697, he met a Moorish ship with a French pass coming from Surat, which being lawful prize he took, and also a lesser prize, and sailed with both of them to Ste. Marie in Madagascar. Here he had a mutiny, and on the 15th June, 1689, most of his men sailed away in the *Mocha* frigate, leaving Captain Kidd with only thirteen men. With these and the Moors he pumped the *Adventure Galley*, but as she sank they all got on board the *Adventure Prize*. For five months he had to wait, and then, taking some passengers, he sailed for Aquilla, in the West Indies, where he arrived in April, 1699, and learnt that they were regarded as pirates.

Now it is obvious from the above that Captain Kidd passed Zanzibar and Pemba on his way north from Mohilla to Bab Islet, and also on his way south from the coast of India to Ste. Marie.

Either of these times he might have stopped at Mesale, but on the way up he had no prize, so presumably if he did bury anything he did it on the way down. Presumably also it would be coin, as most other things would perish. Presumably also he would not be likely to mention he had called there if he wanted to bury treasure. Neither he nor his crew would be likely to say so if they hoped to have any profit out of it.

Our evidence that he did call there is, however, slight, except that there is generally truth behind most traditions.

THE DECLINE OF THE PORTUGUESE

Shortly after Ali Bey had conquered the coast, in about the year 1587, the people of Pemba determined to rebel and rid themselves, as their friends had done at Mombasa, of the Portuguese yoke. They therefore massacred, one night, the Portuguese settlers, men, women and children, and as the Diwani, the chieftain of Pemba, was very pro-Portuguese, they attempted to murder him too, but accompanied by a few Portuguese, he got away to Malindi. However, he was soon afterwards restored by Captain-Major Thomé de Sousa Coutinho, the brother of the Viceroy of India.

He was again expelled shortly after 1594, and this time was deposed and went to Mombasa, where he married a Portuguese woman and became Christian. He afterwards visited India with Dom Francisco da Gama, who also promised to restore him, and the promise seems to have been kept. After this, Portuguese influence appears to have shown signs of decay. The first English ships arrived on the coast on their way to India, thereby threatening the Portuguese monopoly, and in 1622 they lost Ormuz, which was taken by a Persian force assisted by English ships. In 1650 they were driven from Muscat.

In 1627 a serious insurrection took place among the Moslem states, and though the Portuguese were victorious, this rebellion, in which at first the coastal states had some success, must have shaken the foundations of their rule. Yusuf bin Ahmad, Sultan of Mombasa, who had apostasized to Christianity and been afterwards re-converted to Islam, was responsible for a massacre at Mombasa, after which there was a general rising in which Pemba was deeply involved.

The result of this rebellion is recorded in the lengthy Portuguese inscription over a gateway of Mombasa fort:

"In 1635 Captain-Major Francisco da Seixas and Cabreira was commander of this fortress for four years, he being 27 years of age: he rebuilt it and constructed this Guard House. He again subdued to His Majesty the coast of Melinde, which had rebelled in favour of the tyrant: and he made the kings of Otondo, Mandra, Luzwa and Jasa tributary; he personally inflicted on Patta and Siu a punishment hitherto unknown in India, even to the razing of their walls: he punished the Muzumbulos (a negro race), chastised Pemba and its rebellious people, putting to death on his own responsibility the rebel kings and all the principal chiefs: he caused to be paid the tribute which all had refused to His Majesty. For all these services he was made Gentleman of the Royal Household, having already been rewarded for former services, by the decoration of the Order of Christ, with a pension of 50,000 reis, six years' government of Jafampatao, and four years of Biligao with authority of being empowered to fill all the posts during his lifetime.

"Pedro da Silva was Viceroy A.D. 1639."

The orders from Francisco da Gama, Viceroy of India, to Ruy Soares de Mello on his appointment as Captain of Mombasa in 1598, are as follows:

"I order you to put down the insurrection in Pemba, as it is from this island that all movements are made against the fortress (Mombasa). You must arrange that the new king is placed on the throne and supported in everything. This I expect from you."

In 1635 a Portuguese named Barreto de Rezende wrote an account of the Portuguese possessions in Africa, from which we learn that at this time Zanzibar had ceased to be tributary, and several Portuguese with their families owned plantations in the island. With regard to Pemba it was thickly populated and contained fourteen villages, being able to provide at least five thousand fighting men. The natives supplied the Portuguese with 600 makanda (large plaited matting bags) of rice annually, which Rezende says was of a better quality than that received from India. Besides rice, simsim and many other fruits and vegetables were cultivated, and there were large herds of cattle, and much butter (probably ghi) was manufactured. Wild pigs, a legacy of the first Portuguese inhabitants, were already plentiful.

Soon after these things, about 1652, a force of Arabs arrived from Oman and attacked Zanzibar, killing a large number of Portuguese, including one of the Augustine Brothers. This again spread into a serious revolt, so that Francisco da Seixas and Cabreira was again sent to subdue the rebels.

In his report of August 30th, 1653, he states that the ruler of Zanzibar, Pemba and Otondo, had asked for help for Muscat. He gathered together a force of 120 Portuguese, 40 Indians, and 120 natives from Malindi and attacked Zanzibar, reporting he had driven out the queen of the island and her son Otondo, and released 400 Christians from captivity who had been forced to become Moslems. In 1697 the pro-Portuguese Queen Fatima of Zanzibar addressed a letter, dated March 30th, to the authorities at Goa, and in the following year the Imam Seif bin Sultan of Oman, known to the natives as Keid el-Ardhi (lord of the world), drove the Portuguese from Kilwa, Mombasa and Pemba, failing only the fortress of Mozambique, which has remained in Portuguese hands until this day.

Zanzibar and Malindi apparently at this time still adhered to their alliance with the Portuguese, but the power of the Portuguese was now broken for ever.

In 1699, 1703 and 1710, expeditions were organized in Lisbon and Goa to recapture Mombasa, but without success. However, in 1727 an opportunity occurred when the governors of Mombasa and Zanzibar quarrelled and the latter fled to Pate, the king of which place, not wishing to be involved in a war with the Omani Arabs, dispatched a message to Goa and placed himself under the protection of Portugal. General Luiz de Mello Sampayo therefore set forth from Goa with six ships on December 24th to resubdue East Africa. The Portuguese flag was hoisted at Pate and Siu, and the general sailed to Mombasa, where, on March 11th, he bombarded Fort St. Joseph and entered Kilindini harbour.

On the 12th the Liwali surrendered, and within a few weeks the whole of the coast was again under Portuguese rule. This reconquest, however, was of very short duration, the administration of Portugal taking little care to win the affection of the natives and generally making itself oppressive.

In 1729 the Arabs were invited to return to Mombasa, and on August 14th of that year the Portuguese were driven from Pate and on November 29th from Mombasa.

It would appear from local records that the Portuguese had probably retained some half-hearted hold on Pemba when they recovered their domination on the coast in 1728, as we read of tribute being paid; but Pemba always resisted any overlordship, and indeed to some extent passively resents it to-day. Zanzibar, however, has always soon adapted itself to a new form of government, and as in the records of Oman there is no mention of the expulsion of the Portuguese from Zanzibar, it may be presumed that the island remained faithful to the Christians.

Indeed, from the remark in Portuguese records in the year 1728, it would appear that this was so, as the Mwenyi Mkuu in that year received an order from the Portuguese to report himself to them at Mombasa.

The Portuguese made one last effort to regain their supremacy, and another fleet of five ships and a force of over 1,200 men were dispatched, under the same General Luiz de Mello Sampayo, to Mombasa. The fates, however, could not be resisted, for they had decreed that the Portuguese should fail. The ships all foundered, and all on board were drowned in a great storm in the Indian Ocean.

It is a remarkable thing and a significant one that legend and tradition in Zanzibar and Pemba have comparatively little to say about the Portuguese. It is said that they built the fort at Funzi Island, off the west coast of Pemba, which island is now a leper settlement, and has a British Naval cemetery on it. The chief of the Portuguese was called by the natives "Afriti," a title by no means complimentary, as it means a devil.

One of the native written histories in Pemba says that after the Shirazian emigration had taken place the Portuguese came and wanted to make an alliance. The Diwani agreed to this on condition that the Portuguese brought to Pemba all their men who were of seven tribes. These were duly brought and the Portuguese were allowed to stay in the country, the concession being granted for twenty-five years. After this they did evil and were turned out by the Mazrui.

Later on the history states that on Monday morning, the 4th el Haj, 1014 (Sunday, April 24th, 1606) at seven a.m., thirty Frankish ships full of Shirazians with their slaves were seen in the harbour at Pemba. In command of the fleet was a Frank named Johon (John). In 1608 Johon Francisco (? John the Frank) came again and stayed a week, returning with three ships in 1612, bringing presents to the Shirazis. He returned again in 1637 to claim tribute. There was some argument about this payment, and eventually the Shirazis paid a commuted payment. In 1639 he came again, and on this occasion he received a written agreement of a bond he had entered into the time before. In 1641 he came and collected tribute. He died in 1642.

In 1643 his son, Captain John, came to Pemba with five ships, giving many presents and collecting the duty of the year, after which he also died.

Another member of the family, Kison John, appeared in the year 1645 and demanded tribute, which, however, the Shirazians refused to pay. Kison left, but two months later came with a fleet of fifteen ships. The Shirazians, however, were not intimidated by this action, and Kison waged war with them without success for a month, returning in 1652 with a large fleet of sixty-five ships full of European soldiers. Another war now ensued which lasted a few months, and the Portuguese lost over 1,300 men, the Shirazians only about 350.

In 1656 Kison returned with seventy ships, and landing at Mkobwa, stayed there seven days, while the Shirazians prepared again for war. Negotiations were again entered into, but the Shirazians still declined to pay duty on the ground that they did not know if he was the son of Johon. He was able to prove his identity by showing them a particular red seal known to have been his father's. The Shirazians now agreed to pay tribute, and Kison claimed over £1,000 as the annual payment, eventually agreeing to accept less than £100. The agreement was reduced to writing, and Kison, son of Johon, left for home, but on his way home he was lost at sea, and the Shirazians "thanked God for that."

It would seem improbable that this story could be true in all its details; the size of the forces given and the lateness of the dates make it somewhat unlikely. Such a large expedition would surely be beyond the power of the Portuguese to have dispatched at such a time. It is probable, however, that there is some substratum of truth in it, as tradition says that the people of Pemba paid tribute to the Portuguese for a very long time. But little relics of the Portuguese are left in Pemba and Zanzibar to-day. A few words in the language, bull-fighting and wild pigs in Pemba are practically all that remain of their semi-civilized, semi-barbarian rule.

Sheikh Ali bin Mohammed, an old Arab resident of Pemba, also attributed to them the whistling propensities of the Wapemba, and the hats which up to recently used to be worn by the same people. These hats were known in Kipemba as "Shumburere" and were made of the leaves of the wild date palm.

Relics of the Portuguese in Zanzibar consist of a Madonna found at Walezo and a church bell, both of which are in the possession of the Roman Catholic Mission. Portuguese relics at Mombasa and up the coast are far more plentiful.

ESTABLISHMENT OF OMANI DOMINATION ON THE COAST

About a thousand years after the emigration of Suleiman and Said to the land of Zinj, Oman again took a serious interest in the coast. There is, of course, no doubt that communication during this time had been continuous, but the reason for the Omanis coming to the help of the coast people can only have been, that the states of the coast considered that it was from that quarter that help was most likely to be forthcoming to rid the Moslems of the "Polytheists."

It will be remembered that the people of Mombasa

eagerly clutched at any straw that might help them to shake off the bonds of the infidel Christians. Thus when Ali Bey arrived he was welcomed with open arms, and even the Zimbas were preferred to the Portuguese. There can be little doubt that had the Emir Husain, with his Egyptian fleet, made his way to the east coast of Africa instead of to India in 1508, he would have met with an enthusiastic welcome, and the whole course of the history of the coast might have been altered. When the Imam Sultan bin Seif defeated the Portuguese at Muscat in 1650, the chiefs of Mombasa appealed to him for aid, as the Zanorin of Calicut and the Mohammedans of India had appealed to the Mameluke Sultan of India, about a century and a half ago.

Therefore in 1652 an Arab expedition from Oman attacked Zanzibar, killing a large number of Portuguese, including an Augustine priest. This encouraged a general insurrection which, however, the Portuguese, as we have seen, succeeded in quelling, destroying in the process the old capital, probably Kizimkazi. This was quite a minor affair on the part of the Omanis, and eight years later the Imam Sultan bin Seif I, having created a navy, besieged Mombasa and defeated the Portuguese. He had other signal successes over the Portuguese soon, as we have seen, but unfortunately, owing to dissension at home, could not keep up his hold, so that it was left to his son, Seif bin Sultan, whose name is still famous in Pemba legend as Keid el-Ardhi, to drive the Portuguese from all their possessions north of Mozambique. Salilibn Razik gives us but little information about the life of this noteworthy prince, though he remarks that he captured Mombasa, the Green Isle (Pemba), Kilwa and other places from them. He had a great deal of property (one-third of all the date palms in Oman), and undertook a great deal of what in these days would be called Public Works Extraordinary. He had a fleet of twenty-eight ships, the names of some being given. The largest was the *El Falak* of eighty guns, each measuring three spans at the breach. Three of these guns are still in Zanzibar. Legend in Pemba credits him with appearing on the coast when he was known to be in Oman, and says that the Mazrui scaled the fort of Mombasa by using his right arm as a ladder. One of my informants told me that the limits of his conquest southwards was Tungi, and another that in the north they extended to Pate and Lamu. It is said also that he made a Nebhani Liwali at Pate, a Mazrui at Mombasa, and an El Harthi at Zanzibar. Pemba was placed under the Liwali of Mombasa.

Seif bin Sultan established garrisons in Zanzibar and Pemba, and we learn that in 1710 there was a garrison of fifty under one Said in Zanzibar and of thirty in Pemba. He died on Thursday night, 4th October, 1711. Sometime shortly before 1718, Seif bin Sultan II was appointed Imam, but being under age was deposed and another appointed, but he was restored in 1728. Internal dissension was so great that the Imam resorted to the aid of the Persians who, however, assumed a good deal more than they were expected to, and the Portuguese, taking advantage of the weakness of Oman, recaptured Mombasa.

In 1739 the Mazrui governor there threw off his allegiance to the Imam Sultan bin Murshid and declared his independence, an example which was followed by Pate and other states. Sultan bin Murshid, the last of the Yaarubi dynasty, was followed by the great Ahmed bin Said bin Ahmed bin Mohammed Es Saidy, el Azdy, el Omany, the founder of the present Albusaid dynasty of Oman and Zanzibar. In 1746 he appointed Abdulla bin Djad as Liwali of Zanzibar, with a garrison to protect it against the turbulent Mazruis. In 1753 the Mazruis under Ali bin Otham sent a force to Zanzibar, which, however, came to nothing, as Ali bin Othman had been assassinated.

It will be seen, therefore, that Seif bin Sultan I should be regarded as the first joint Imam of Oman and Zanzibar, as Zanzibar never threw off her allegiance to the Omani dynasty. Seif bin Sultan was also the first Omani ruler of Pemba, but this latter place followed Mombasa in 1739, and did not again come under the Omani sceptre till 1822, when, as we shall see, Seyyid Said turned the Mazrui out.

B. LATER HISTORY OF THE NATIVE TRIBES

CHAPTER X

THE ORIGIN OF THE NATIVE TRIBES IN ZANZIBAR AND PEMBA

THE aboriginal tribes of Zanzibar are, as has already been stated, mainly three, the Wahadimu, the Watumbatu, and the Wapemba.

The Wahadimu do very little travelling about, as they are purely agricultural people, except for a few who fish; the only big exception to this is when they visit Pemba at the time of a large crop, to pick cloves. The Watumbatu, on the other hand, are great sailors, and most of the dhows plying in Zanzibar waters are manned by these people. The *African Pilot* says: "Tumbatu has the reputation of supplying the best sailors and pilots for the Zanzibar seas."

The Wapemba are a race of cultivators and fishermen, and are not quite so exclusive in some ways as the Wahadimu, as they sometimes enter into business, and some of them have large plantations. On the other hand, witchcraft and magic are more ingrained in them than in the other people.

The culture of the Africans can be divided into three groups: the desert, the parkland and the forest. In the desert man is nomadic; in the forest he is agricultural and settled; in the parkland he adds the care of cattle to that of his friends.

Among the parkland peoples, clothing is made of skins; basket-work is of the coiled type, the houses are circular, and the food is maize or millet.

In the forest, clothing is of vegetable material; basket-work is of the woven type, and the houses are rectangular. The food is chiefly manioc.

The native inhabitants of Zanzibar and Pemba are of forest origin, as their houses are rectangular and their basket-work is woven. It is probable that they are descended from the forest people who lived in the wooded countries opposite the islands and chiefly to the south. They have used cloth for a long time now, owing to trade with the outside world, but it is probable that they had vegetable clothing before, as the use of skin clothing has generally endured longer than the use of vegetable clothing. Their main crop is manioc, called muhogo; millet is also planted, though not nearly so extensively; maize is a comparatively recent introduction.

Some notes as to the method of cultivation of crops may not be out of place here, as they may help more definitely to define the area from which these people sprang.

In Pemba manioc is planted in small hoed-up patches. In Zanzibar it is planted in long heaped-up ridges. In both islands the manioc is planted on end; in Zanzibar all leaning one way, in Pemba anyhow. The natives of Zanzibar transplant their rice, and those of Pemba do not. (Rice is a comparatively late introduction.) Maize and millet are planted two or three seeds at a time, in small holes in broken-up ground. It may also be noted here that the Pemba houses have no ends to their roofs, but only back and front slopes.

The natives of the Sultanate are fisher-folk and agriculturalists, and it is almost certain that they first came to Zanzibar and Pemba in the former capacity.

Even in these days outlying islands are temporarily inhabited by fishermen who build small bandas, and these little settlements often grow into permanent villages. No doubt this was the way the first Africans came to Zanzibar and Pemba on their own, unless some were brought as slaves.

Zanzibar and Pemba are not far from the mainland, and not too far to preclude these temporary inhabitants from making settlements. As the fishermen, impressed with the good fishing round the shores, stayed longer, their settlements grew into permanent villages, and the men brought their women-folk, who would also bring their manioc to plant.

An article by Miss Werner in the *Journal of the African Society* for 1916 records a story of the Wahadimu, having originally come from Windi, on the coast between Saadani and Bagamoyo. In their own accounts of their origin some of them state that they are derived from the Wasegeju, who now live near Dar-es-Salaam, but stories of the Wasegeju are more common in Pemba than Zanzibar.

In the course of prolonged questioning of Arabs and natives as to the history of the islands, I obtained a number of stories as to early colonizers of the islands, and I propose to give extracts from their tales as they were told to me.

The first extract is from the story of a middle-aged Arab who has travelled a good deal and is interested in such matters. Many of the stories he has given me as true are obviously hearsay, and read more like the *Arabian Nights* than anything else. They are interesting, as it is possible to see the grain of truth from which they sprang, and also they show how many of the stories of the *Arabian Nights* and other romances come to their present form in just such a way, by means of travellers' tales; few people are so credulous of wonders as the Arab. He says:

"At the very beginning, the Wasakalava of Madagascar came to Pemba. They were beaten by the Portuguese. They went to Diba, a country of Persia, where the inhabitants chew tobacco and betel as here, and brought the Washirazi, who were really the first inhabitants, but were beaten by the Wasakalava."

The next is a single sentence from the story of an old man, an Arab, but born in Pemba, "The

Madubwana came from the mainland and lived in Pemba before the Washirazi." The next from an old Sheha, an Mpemba, and proud of it. "The first inhabitants of Pemba were the Madiba; they were the owners of the country, the Washirazi were their Khadim (dependants), they came from the north. The Wadiba are the origin of the Wapemba."

My next historian is probably the oldest Arab in the Protectorate, Sheikh Ali bin Mohammed El Rubhki. He says: "In India are Diba and Jawa. From thence came men and opened up the country of the Sawahil. They made a town at Mkumbuu. In India, as here, are coco-nuts, mangoes, pine-apples, durians. They lived here, and they owned Pate and Mombasa, but their Sultan lived at Mkumbuu, his liwali lived at Pujini. The Portuguese came and turned them out, and stayed here. Then came Seif bin Sultan." Sheikh Ali Mohammed is looked on as a great authority on this history, and I took the opportunity to endeavour to gain confirmation or otherwise of other stories from him. He told me that the people of Diba and Jawa met no one here, except natives. The men of the mainland, of the tribes Digo and Segeju, crossed over. He claims that the ruins of Pemba were built by Indians. "You have only got to look at the customs of the natives," he said, "to see that what I say is true. Kiumbizi (a dance or rather fight with sticks), and Ugoe (a kind of wrestling including a clever throw) are Indian in origin. The Kipemba for Viazi (sweet potatoes) is Madiba. When I was young the Wapemba wore hats like Europeans made from grass, and, as you know, they are much addicted to whistling and bull-fights. These customs they got from the Portuguese." The Wasakalava, he said, never came to Pemba or Zanzibar, though they came to Mafia.

These stories of the Wadigo and Wasegeju are everywhere current in Pemba.

The Wasegeju and the Wadigo look on the Diwan of the Wavumba tribe with peculiar reverence, and as there is a great similarity between the way the Wavumba regarded their chieftain and the way the Wapemba and Wahadimu regarded their Diwani and Mwenyi Mkuu, it is quite possible that there is truth in the tradition that some of them settled in the islands.

These Wavumba are said to have been the descendants of a party of Persians who migrated from Shirazi about A.D. 1200, and settled on the delta of the Umba River, the boundary between Kenya Colony and Tanganyika Territory. The town they founded was called Vumba Kuu, and they appear to have been a people of considerable importance. Their regalia consisted of drums and horns; from the illustrations I have seen of these (20 Man., 1921), the drums appear to be almost identical with those that belonged to the Mwenyi Mkuu (see Chapter XII), while of the horns, one is of a similar pattern to that carved on the tomb of Haruni at Chwaka in Pemba, and to that carved on the Diwani's well at Pujini, while the second, a straight one, is exactly similar to that of the Mwenyi Mkuu.

Apart from the similarity of the regalia, similarity of customs may also be mentioned. Drums and horns were used by both the Wavumba and the Wahadimu at the enthronement of the chieftain, at marriages and deaths of important persons, and also in connection with religious services for rain, victory in warfare, etc.

One of the newer drums of the Wavumba is of the pattern called Tutu, a drum which, if beaten any day in Zanzibar or Pemba, will soon result in the collection of a large number of natives. Two other customs of the Wavumba may be noted; the first, an unusual one in a Mohammedan country, is uncovering the head in the presence of a person of any importance. This originated in the custom of appearing bareheaded before the chieftain. It also occurs among the Wahadimu of Zanzibar, and no native might appear before the Mwenyi Mkuu with his head covered.

The second custom is that of going about bare-headed after the death of the Sultan, but this custom, if it ever was observed in Pemba or Zanzibar, has now fallen into desuetude.

Though the Wasegeju are spoken of in Zanzibar, stories are more frequent of a people called Wadebuli, who are probably the same as the Wadiba of Pemba tradition. In the south of Zanzibar it is invariably of the Wadebuli that the people speak. Archdeacon Dale says: "There arrived off the coast a people called Wadebuli. They came in sailing vessels, and possessed cannon. Their sails were made of some kind of leaf. They had towns on the coast, planted coco-nuts, and sank wells. They also built places for worship, the ruins of which are to be seen all over Zanzibar and Pemba. They treated the Wahadimu most cruelly, until at last they (the Wahadimu) could bear it no longer and appealed to the Arabs of Muscat."

The principal ruins credited to the Wadebuli are a well at Chwaka, an inscribed well at Paje, a mosque at Makunduchi, and a well and some mounds at Unguja Kuu.

About all we can definitely accept of these legends is that "the Wadibu or Wadebuli came, they were a seafaring people, they were here before the Persians, they were cruel to the aborigines, and they left."

Were they the Malays? Jawa, in the Pemba stories, suggests it, and the Malays did come. Or did they come from Diu (pronounced Deev), in Western India?

This latter is a possible explanation, as Deev and Deeb are very similar. Diu is possibly the Bassones of the *Periplus*. Trade has from ages come from Cambay, and I am informed that the natives of Diu are noteworthy sailors, and that many dhows set forth from there. It fell to the Portuguese in 1535, was fortified, and stood a famous siege ten years later. It reached a high degree of prosperity, there being at one time about 50,000 inhabitants. Known as ed-

Diyul to the Arabs, who sacked it in 1668, it never recovered its former prosperity, but is still a Portuguese possession.

More probable, however, than Diu as the original home of the Wadebuli is Dabhol, and some interesting notes by Mr. Löngworth Dames in his edition of *Duarte Barbosa*, in my opinion, practically fix the origin of the name of Wa diba or Wa debuli as, if not Diu, then what Barbosa called the Kingdom of Diul, or possibly the modern Dabhol.

Of Diu he says: "Its name, properly Div, is according to the accepted derivation from the Sanskrit Dvipa 'an island,' like the similar termination in Anchediva, Laccadive and Maldive." Barbosa says also of Diu: "It is on a small island hard by the main, and has a right good harbour, a trading port used by many ships, with exceeding great traffic and commerce with Malabar, Baticala, Guoa, Chaul and Dabul. Ships also sail hence to Meca, Adem, Zeila, Barbora, Magadoxo, Melinde, Brava, Mombasa and Ormus, with the kingdoms thereof."

The articles of trade Barbosa mentions are very numerous, though he does not mention specifically what comes from Africa, and says that the town now (previous to 1516) "has the greatest trade of any found in these regions."

Diul is not so likely, for Barbosa says, "they navigate but little." Mr. Dames says, "The port here called Diul is Deval in Sindh (from the Sanskrit Dēvalā—Abode of the Gods), from the Sindhi form arose the Arabic Day-bul, the name by which the place was known to the Arab chronicles. In the Hindi language the V of Dēval is replaced by W, and it is from the (modern) form Dewal that the Portuguese got their Diul." Dewal was on the western bank of the western boundary in the Indus Delta. Its ruins are now twenty miles inland owing to the silt brought down by the river.

Dabul is more likely than Diul for the Wadebuli. Barbosa says that "it has a very good harbour, whither sail many ships of the Moors from divers lands, to wit, from Meca, Adem and Ormus, and from Cambaya, Dio and Malabar, which constantly deal here in goods of every kind." Dabul is the modern Dābhōl (17° 35′ N., 73° 10′ E.). It is a port of considerable historical importance and great antiquity. It was probably the Palæpatmæ of the *Periplus*, and the Baltipatma of Ptolemy (Sanskrit Dabhileshwar). From the tenth to the fourteenth centuries it had much trade with the Persian Gulf, the Red Sea and East Africa.

To summarize, therefore, the native tribes of Zanzibar and Pemba as they have existed for the past few hundred years have an Asiatic as well as an African origin.

In addition to the Wapemba, Wahadimu and Watumbatu, there are certain families in Pemba which call themselves Mashirazi, or Washirazi, and deny belonging to the Wapemba tribe. The Wahadimu also claim Shirazi origin, but adhere to their tribal name. Of the Watumbatu only the ruling house claim this origin. In view of a claim made by certain families to which I shall refer shortly, it is important to emphasize that these people claim descent from Shiraz in Persia. Burton says: "The Shirazi or nobles derive themselves from the Shangaya settlement, also called Shiraz, on the coast north of Lamu in about South latitude 2°, whence they extended to Tungi, four days sail south of the Rovuma River."

I do not know if Burton is correct in saying that Shingwaya is called Shiraz, but I know that such an origin is vigorously denied by this people, although most of them claim affiliation with the people of Kilwa, who came from Persia. There are also a number of natives who are called Masherifu, and are said to have come from Wasin Island, on which a fraction of the Wavumba also settled. Burton visited the island, but mentions but little of its history. He says that it belonged to Zanzibar, and that he could hear nothing of the tribe called Mazimba stated to have been found there.

Graves recently exposed by the sea at Mkokotoni in Zanzibar are said to have been of Masherifu from Bumbwi on Wasin Island, and there are many Masherifu in Pemba claiming origin from this place. Although nowadays the word Masherifu used in connection with these people in Zanzibar and Pemba does not mean the "descendants of the Prophet," nevertheless it is highly probable that such was the original meaning of the word on the coast. Indeed these Masherifu may be the descendants of Zayd bin Ali bin Hassan bin Ali, the son-in-law of the Prophet, who are known to have migrated to the coast about the 740th year of our era. Native histories at Tumbatu and Kizimkazi give genealogies deriving the Tumbatu and Hadimu notables from the Prophet's family.

Some mention must here be made of certain native families who have taken to themselves the dignity of the appellation "Arab," though it is by no means allowed or accorded to them by the true Arabs. They reside chiefly in Pemba, and claim to be of several well-known Arab tribes, such as the Ghassani and Nebhani, though large groups call themselves Esh-Shirazi.

Until recently these families have been considered as being the ordinary Persian Shirazi of Pemba, but I had the opportunity of investigating their stories and the written documents they have. From these it appears that they claim descent from one Shiraz, whom they allege to have been a son of Malik bin Fahm, well known in Omani history, and say that he emigrated from Jedda. This claim appears to be as much a fiction as that of the Titchbourne claimant.

CHAPTER XI

PERIOD OF THE ZINJ EMPIRE

From time to time during its history the coast has been either collectively under the rule of some Asiatic or European power, or welded together by some outstanding personage as a separate empire. In both cases the whole has in the end dissolved into small parts, generally due to the rise of some petty chief, whom the parent state could not keep in check, owing to the scattered nature of its dominion, and the lack of speedy and efficient transport and communications.

But the building up of the first coastal empire is of considerable interest, both on account of the early date at which it was achieved, and the fact that so many of the ruins of its towns are to be found to-day up and down the coast, and that so many of the inhabitants still strongly claim descent from the Persians.

Our authority for this period is, first and chiefly, *The History of Kilwa*, a document which was known to the Portuguese, and has been preserved for us by Seyyid Barghash and Sir John Kirk, to whom he gave a copy. In addition, there are local histories among the natives of the Islands of Zanzibar and Pemba, and a number of traditions, as well as ruins and other antiquities.

The History of Kilwa describes the founding of the Zinj Empire as follows: "There was a Sultan of Shiraz named Hassan bin Ali, who saw a vision of a rat with an iron snout gnawing at his walls. He foreboded the ruin of his country from this, and communicated it to his six sons. They therefore sailed away in a fleet of seven ships, which stopped at as many different places down the east coast. The first stopped at Mundakha, the second Shoughu, the third Yunbu, the fourth Munfisa, the fifth Jazira el Khathra, the sixth Kulwa, and the seventh Henzwan."

This expedition took place in A.D. 975. Mundakha and Shoughu it is impossible to trace with any degree of accuracy. They might be Mogadisho and Kismayu. The third is probably Yambe Island; the fourth sounds like Mafia, but it has been supposed that it is probably Mombasa, as the native name of Mafia is Chole, and the name Mafia was given by the Portuguese. If it is Mombasa it is a slight argument for that island having been Menuthias. The fifth is Pemba, and the seventh Johanna, one of the Comoro Islands.

A manuscript extant in Pemba says the vision was of a rat crossing a cat, and that Ali bin Hassan and his followers went from island to island, leaving settlers as far as Pemba. Another manuscript says that the Sultan of Shiraz was Darhash bin Shaha, and that he left with his three brothers, his sister and three nephews, and that they and their families landed at Shehiri, Pate, Mombasa, Bayai (?), Pemba, Zanzibar and Kilwa, the Mainland and Tumbatu.

The history of the Zanzibar settlements through this period, which lasted roughly from the year 975 to the coming of the Portuguese to Kilwa in 1501, must now be described. The most important of the states of the Zinj Empire were Kilwa, Zanzibar, Pemba, Tumbatu, Vumba, Utondwe and Mombasa. During the greater part of the period the states were probably more or less independent, though there no doubt existed a form of alliance among them.

HISTORY OF ZANZIBAR

We have seen that Kilwa was founded in the year 975, and its prosperity lasted until the advent of the Portuguese, which date we may conveniently fix here as 1498, the time of the arrival of Vasco da Gama on the coast.

The first we hear of Zanzibar during this period

is that Hasan bin Suleyman bin Ali, Sultan of Kilwa, fled there to avoid the attacks on Kilwa of some Bantu savages. These savages were repelled by the people of Kilwa who recalled their Sultan, and he reigned thereafter for fourteen years. This event probably took place in the eleventh century.

The next date we have is the founding of the Kizimkazi mosque in A.H. 500 or A.D. 1107.

M. Patricolo deciphered the Cufic inscription in this mosque as follows:

"Ordered El Sheikh, el Seyyid Abi Amram, Mfaume El Hassan bin Mohammed may God grant him long life and destroy his enemy, the building of this mosque, on the day of Sunday in the month of El Kada in the year 500 H."

Professor Flury instead of Mfaume prefers "Musa bin." If the former is correct, it would mean the King El Hassan, surnamed father of Amram (it being a Mohammedan custom to name a man by the name of his son, even before the latter appears, and Mfaume being Mfalme, Swahili for king.) If the latter is the right transliteration, the king's name is "Musa, son of El Hassan."

Unfortunately nothing more is known of this prince, though probably he was one of the Shirazian rulers of Zanzibar, and possibly a descendant of that Ali bin Hassan who founded Kilwa. The establishment of a mosque, which is even to-day the most ornamental in Zanzibar, cannot have been a first venture by early colonizers, and seems to indicate that at that time they were well settled. Probably Kizimkazi, the most southerly point of Zanzibar, was the island's earliest capital.

The Shirazians who built these coast towns were of the Shia sect, and therefore, as I have shown, it is probable that Zanzibar was Islamized, if not before their advent at any rate before they made their power felt, because the Zanzibar natives were Sunnis.

We learn from the chronicles of Kilwa that in the thirteenth century the King of Zanzibar was one

Hassan bin Abubakr, and that he undertook to aid the pretender, Said bin Hassan, in his designs on the throne of Kilwa. He is said to have dispatched an army to Kilwa with Said, under one of his Amirs named Zubayr, in order to assist him, but that the army afterwards abandoned Said's cause. It may be inferred from this that at that time Zanzibar was independent and of some importance, but this cannot have lasted long, as we read in the history of Pate that, in the reign of Sultan Omar (1331-1348), Zanzibar was too unimportant to have a king. In the next century Zanzibar seems to have recovered her influence, for the Kilwa chronicles state that an ambassador was sent from Zanzibar in 901 H. (1495) to make peace between the Kilwa rivals, Hassan and Fudayl. This ambassador met the wazir Mohammed of Kilwa and discussed the matter with him, without much result, as it was only finally settled by the death of Mohammed and an appeal to arms, which ended in the favour of Fudayl, the rightful claimant. In 1503 very small tribute was exacted by the Portuguese from Zanzibar. It would therefore appear that from the fourteenth to the sixteenth or seventeenth centuries, the importance of Zanzibar as a power in East Africa was waning. Indeed, from other facts we shall consider later on, there is but little doubt on the point. Probably the island became a mere dependency of Kilwa, and was governed from Tumbatu.

In 1866 gold coins were found at Unguja Kuu with Cufic inscriptions six hundred years old, i.e., dating from the thirteenth century. To-day nothing remains of Unguja Kuu except a few stones, a well, and some earthen mounds, which once were possibly buildings. The inhabitants say that there was once a mosque there.

Such, then, are the brief historical records we have of Zanzibar Island in the time of the great Zinj Empire.

Legend is not entirely silent as to this period in Zanzibar history. As regards Kizimkazi, it is said that the name is derived as follows: Kizi m Kazi, i.e., Kizi is a worker—Kizi knows his work. Kizi was the slave of Mfaume Kiza, first king and founder of Kizimkazi, which was built under his direction by Kizi. So well was the work done that a neighbouring chieftain desired to possess Kizi himself and asked Kiza for him. Kiza, however, refused, so the other chieftain prepared for war. Embarking his troops in dhows, he came and anchored under the lee of Ras Masoni, south of Vundwe Island. Kiza was occupied in building operations on the shore at Kizimkazi at the time, and saw them and understood their purpose.

He therefore prayed two rekaas and asked the Almighty for help. There came clouds of bees which drove the invaders away. Later on the hostile chieftain prepared a second expedition. Marching overland he took the road via Muyuni to Kizimkazi, and got as far as Kiji without the knowledge of Kiza. At this point, however, an outpost gave Kiza information, but it was too late for the latter to prepare. Prescient of defeat, he therefore cut off the right hand of Kizi, and going to the shore prayed the Deity to be removed himself. His prayers were answered; the rock opened, he entered and was no more seen. The spot and crevice in the rock are shown to this day. It is regarded as a holy place, and flags are hung outside it.

When the invaders came they saw Kizi with his hand cut off and that Kiza had vanished, so they returned.

The ruins of Kizimkazi, probably contemporary with the mosque, consist of high walls which at one time apparently cut off a semi-circle of land on the shore. There are small posts or forts at each end.

There are also a number of graves of some interest round the mosque, which, however, may belong to a later period. These graves were described to me as being of the following people:

(1) Mwana Mwatima binti Mfaume Madi Shiraziyeh.

(2) Her son, Mfaume Ali Sherifu.
(3) Sheikh Ali bin Omar Sherifu, a carpenter, one-armed, one-legged, but pious withal, and endowed with legendary powers.
(4) Seyyid Abdulla bin Seyyid Almad Sherifu, who was given a drum and a milk-gourd by the sovereign of Kilwa to whom he was related. (The drum is still in existence, and shown at Kizimkazi.)
(5) Sherif Hassan.

As regards Unguja Kuu, it is curious that native tradition is entirely silent as to its ever having been a town of importance. In fact, apart from the name and the ruins, there is little evidence of its ever having been a capital. Local legends derive the name from the following story.

Two fishermen, Shirazis, by name Pururu, or Mfururu, and Bangalishewa, arrived at Zanzibar town, the one at the Malindi quarter and the other at Shangani. They journeyed north and south respectively searching for each other, and finally met at the present Unguja Kuu. Bangalishewa said: " Zanzibar is great (Unguja Kuu). I have searched for you in each of its harbours and only found you here; indeed Zanzibar is great."

HISTORY OF PEMBA

The history of Pemba during these periods is written all over the island from north to south, in twenty ruins, or groups of ruins, discovered up to date.

As yet no written history of this period has been discovered. Those histories that have been discovered are of a later date, and we shall refer to them later on. We have therefore to depend on legend, which tells us that in the times of the Shirazis, and before the Portuguese, Pemba was divided into five districts, each under a chief and each containing seven towns. These districts were Chwaka (then called Twaka), Mkumbuu, Utenzi, Ngwane and Pokomo. Another informant says that Utenzi and Ngwane are the same, and that the fifth district was Ukoma. There are now no places corresponding with the last three names. The names of the towns, as far as I have been able to get them, were Vitongoje, Mkumbuu, Kichokochwe, Ole, Kojani, Utembwe, Wingwi, Michiweni, Shumba, Mjini Kiuyu, Mjini Ukoma (Chwaka), Kwale, Chambani (by the Wapemba called Kiambani), Msuka, Mbelengwa, Kinowe, Sizini, Kiungoni, Chwale, Kambini, Kangagani, Mvumoni, Pujini, Ukutini, Kiwani, Makongwe, Kiweni and Mtambwe.

At Vitongoje, Mkumbuu, Kichokochwe, Ole, Kojani, Chwaka, Chambani, Msuka, Pujini, Kiwani, Makongwe, Kiweni and Mtambwe ruins have been discovered. In all cases these ruins are mosques, except at Ndagoni and Chwaka, where there are ruins of towns. At Pujini there is a fortress, at Vitongoje, a well and a tomb (though Sheikh Ali Mohammed tells me it is a house), and at Makongwe an unidentified building. There are also ruined mosques at Chaoni, Verani, Kijiweni, Shengejuu and Mtangani; some of these places were no doubt among the number of the towns. There is another mosque on Fundo Island (which is rather an unlikely site for one of the towns), and a ruin at Bogoa.

Fifteen of these Pemba ruins, or groups of ruins, have been investigated by Major Pearce, and he considers that Ndagoni or Mkumbuu is the earliest, dating probably from the tenth to fourteenth centuries. These ruins show far the finest workmanship. They are remarkable chiefly for what was a group of thirteen pillared tombs, though now only four pillars remain standing. From one of them Major Pearce extracted a piece of cream-coloured Ting work of the Sung dynasty (960-1279). One of these pillars has panels on the top decorated with small recesses, and with the rope and chevron patterns.

These pillared tombs are typical of the Zinj Empire period. They are certainly phallic in origin, and there are some undoubted phalli at Mambrui.

Mammæ also appear on some of the tombs, and there are still legends of the worship of the female organs of sex. Burton saw and described a pillared tomb at Tongoni, south of Tanga, and the nearest spot on the mainland to Mkumbuu. In one of these was a glazed tile, bearing the words *Shid-i raushan*, the Persian for "the Bright Sun," which was regarded by the natives with superstitious awe, but which Burton had no qualms about removing and sending to the Royal Geographical Society. Here, too, the natives claimed Shirazian ancestry. Mosques similar to that at Mkumbuu have also been found at Kilwa, built with columns in the same way, and there are many others, chiefly in the neighbourhood of Lamu.

Major Pearce's dating of the Pujini ruins rests on more shaky evidence; he places them round about 1500, a date fixed roughly from the fact that he surmises the loopholes in the citadel walls were used for firearms, and that he picked from the mortar of an interior wall a piece of china, "dating probably from the sixteenth or seventeenth centuries."

The use of gunpowder was known to the Chinese and Malays from a very early date, but apparently it was not used for projectile throwing till about the fourteenth century. It is quite possible also that the loopholes were used for cross-bows—a weapon that seems to have been used from an early date in East Africa, and which is perhaps of Persian introduction. The cross-bow still exists in a rat-trap which is described in the ethnological portion of this book. Fixing the date from a piece of fragment china in mortar is also unsafe. It would almost certainly be in such a position from having been used for restoration or repairs.

But the Pujini ruins, look at them how one will, are a puzzle.

Why is the workmanship in general more inferior to that of other groups? Why a fortress? Why on the east coast? Why with a channel cut up the creek to the sea, where it is so boisterous? Why the loopholes? Why an underground chamber with a horn on the wall and much decorated? These are the questions which we must endeavour to answer when we come to consider the native accounts.

From the pottery discovered, which had been used to ornament the mosque at Chwaka, Major Pearce puts the age of the ruins there, at from possibly the tenth to fifteenth centuries. Here is the pillared tomb of Haruni, whom we shall hear of again. It is interesting, as there are portrayed on it a sun-disc, a relic of the so-called sun-worship of the Zoroastrians and the undoubted sun-worship of the Sabæans, a horn derived, as we have seen, in the first place from the Assyrians, and what is probably a crown derived from the same source. Both these are emblems of royalty in East Africa. Legend has it that Chwaka was a walled town, and traces of the walls are still to be found in the woods.

These three groups are the only big remains of towns in Pemba; the remainder of the ruins are chiefly mosques. From the point of view of dates, it is well to mention some here.

The mosque at Msuka has scratched on the inside of the kibla: "In the name of God, He is all living. The Lord of those who have passed before and of those who are to come—and peace, the year 816." This date corresponds to A.D. 1414, and from several considerations it appears that the mosque was already a ruin when it was written.

The mosques of Chaoni, Mtangani and Kiwani, Major Pearce considers as belonging to the thirteenth or fourteenth centuries.

Captain Cooper rediscovered a mosque on Kiweni Island which had the remains of a plate embedded in the wall. This plate was pronounced by the authorities of the Victoria and Albert Museum, to whom I took it, to be Chinese and of about the date 1750, which is considerably later than other china found. As, however, it was pointed out to me there, it is unsafe to deduce from that that the mosque was not standing before. The same remarks apply to a mosque I myself rediscovered at Chambani, where I got from the wall a cup, which appears to me to be of the later variety. This last mosque was far from the present settlement, and I only found it by asking at Chambani, which I knew was one of the old towns, whether there were any ruins there.

While, as I have said, there is no written history of Pemba during this period, tradition is by no means silent concerning it, though it mostly centres round the name of one man, still used as a bogey with which to frighten children.

There is no doubt that this chief belonged to this period; all the natives are very emphatic about his having lived and ruled long before the advent of the Portuguese.

He is generally known under the sobriquet of *Mkame Mdume* ("he who draws milk from a male"), a nickname given to him on account of his cruelty, and the fact that he apparently squeezed the uttermost ounce of strength, property, or whatever he could, from anyone he could lay hands on.

Under this name he is known to each and every one of the inhabitants of Pemba; what his real name was is more difficult; if pressed to answer, a native will generally say *Mfaume Mshirazi* (a Persian prince), but as several better informed people have told me it was Mohammed bin Abdulrehman, and as no one has disputed it, I see no reason for it not being correct.

Where he came from and where he went to are also matters of doubt; he is generally described as an Mshirazi, but I have heard him spoken of as *Ajjemi* (also a Persian), an *Msegeju*, a man of Mombasa, and by one man as an *Mdiba*. I consider the first is more probable and, as I say, it is generally accepted that that is what he was.

Everyone agrees he built and lived at the fortress of Pujini, and the building of, or dominion over, the following towns is attributed, though by no means with certainty, by various people to him: Ndagoni (Mkumbuu), Chwaka, Vitongoje, Mtangani, Michiweni and Kichokochwe.

Some say that he brought Islam to the island, but this is distinctly doubtful, though from all accounts he was a stickler for the forms of worship.

Hearing that a book written by him was still extant, and in use at Pujini, I got the sheha to let me see it, but I was greatly disappointed, as it contains only *khutbehs* (sermons) and an apparently later insertion of two magical formulæ (translation of which I give elsewhere). There is no date, though it is very well written, and the initial letters of each *khutbeh* are in red.

Besides being a great builder of towns, Mkame Mdume is credited with proficiency at the building of Mitepe (sewed boats), other forms of carpentry and at shooting with a bow.

But of all things he is best remembered for his inhuman cruelties. Those that I have recorded in my notes are the following. He forced men to swim on dry land, and he forced them to shout through their noses! He pricked people with needles till they bled all over. He gave toothless old people *michikiti* (oil palm) nuts to crack with their gums. He banged heads together till the owners became unconscious. He used to cut open pregnant women to see the fœtus inside, and when one of his own wives was pregnant and wanted some ox liver to eat, he gave it her and cut her open to see if the fœtus ate it. It is said that he found the liver on the head of the unborn child, and then said that a pregnant woman should always be given what she asked for, as it was the child that got it! He got stone to build Pujini from a place called Chama Nangwe near Msuka, and would not allow the porters to carry it in the ordinary way, but made them shuffle along on their buttocks with the stones on their heads. It is said that if he did not hear the noise of the crowds of porters shuffling from afar he would go out from Pujini and beat them severely. The mosque at Kichokochwe he built also, and the people carried a stone there, each of them, every Friday after prayer. Woe betided those who failed to carry out his preposterous commands.

Mkame Mdume's authority is said to have extended over all Pemba, and some say beyond even Mombasa. Zanzibar and Ngazija (the Comoros) are said by a few to have owned allegiance to him, but all place his capital at Pujini, where he had a large palace in the citadel. Goods and troops arrived in dhows up the narrow channel he dug behind the ruins, and were brought up the bank and down the steps into the fort.

The situation of the fortress tells us that it is probable that whoever lived there were foreigners, and that they built it as a protection from the islanders. All the loopholes point to the island, and as the creek was fortified and the fort built alongside it, we assume the garrison was dependent, to a large extent, on supplies from the sea.

One legend I have recorded in my notes says that at the time of Mkame Mdume, another chief and his tribe who were called the Magenge disputed with him for mastery. They are said to have been gigantic in stature, and to have also built mosques; Kichokochwe, Michiweni, the Miskiti Shooko at Chwaka and Ole are attributed to them.

Mkame Mdume's end, as I have said, is like his origin, wrapt in mystery. Some say he was killed by the Portuguese. Others say that he died and that his grave was kept secret, but that so great was the power of his name that men worked for forty years after his death, when ordered in his name to do so.

He had two wives, and both were so jealous of each other that they were kept apart at Pujini by a high wall, and a well was dug for each of them. The well of the principal wife is described by Major Pearce as an underground shrine. It has steps leading down to it, and is the one with a horn on the wall. The well of the other wife is described by the same author as an underground chamber, but when I excavated it, it turned out to be a well with steps leading down in the same way.

Mkame Mdume left three children, two sons and a daughter; of the former one was a holy man, and the other Mkame Mdume's viceroy at Chwaka.

The eldest son's name was Mjawili. He is buried at Kidonge, near Chonga, in a spot called after him, Mjawili. The grave is difficult of access, being buried in the depths of forest and bush, but it has never been forgotten, and people still go there to make offerings and pray for children, etc. It is surrounded with many fragments of pottery, etc., left as offerings. There are another six or seven graves near, one of which bears the inscription, "There is no God except God, Mohammed God's apostle. This is the grave of Bana Musa (who) died in the month of Moharram, A.H. 1233." This, of course, is a much later date, but all these graves are those of Sherifs who wished to be buried near such a holy man.

The second son's name was Haruni, and his grave, which we have already noticed, is still pointed out at Chwaka. Of him it is related that he had a jealous wife who, noticing his predilection for another fair lady in the same town of Chwaka, whom he used daily to see when he went to the great mosque, called the Meskiti Jumaa, to pray, determined to put a stop to these clandestine meetings, so she built a small mosque near the palace where she herself could superintend his devotions. This mosque is known as the Meskiti Shooko (Shooko (Kipemba) = Chooko = Chiroko, which is a small kind of pea). The mason she employed to do this was a mainland native from a place near Tanga, and he made it so beautiful (the name signifies that ground peas were mixed up in the mortar to make it hard)[1] that the lady, lest her husband ever should wish to make another like it, cut the mason's right hand off and drove him away.

[1] An analysis I have since had made of the mortar shows no trace of vegetable substance.

Legend then has it that he went back to the mainland and brought an army of his tribe, who destroyed Chwaka town by fire in a night.

Before we leave Chwaka let me take you to a gruesome spot on the Nyambwi creek, where is said to have been a wall called the *Ukuta wa Damu* (the bloody wall). Above here the victims of Mkame Mdume and his son were beheaded, and the blood flowed in such streams that the natives say that even now it has not dried up, and that a patch of red sand in the middle of the surrounding white sand is from the staining of the soil by their blood. A final holocaust took place here when the invaders from Tanga put the population to the sword.

The third of Mkame Mdume's children was a lady named Mwana Mtoto who, like her elder brother, was noted for piety. She outlived them both, and thinking that the glory of Pemba had passed away and that her day had gone, she prayed God to take her and that her grave might not be known. On this the ground before her opened, she entered, and was no more seen. On the approximate place a mosque was built many years after, which has only of late years fallen to ruins. It was built by one of the Mazrui, and the spot is known as Mwana Mtoto to this day.

HISTORY OF TUMBATU

A manuscript history of Tumbatu gives the date of its foundation as 600 H. (1204), the same year as the founding of Pate. This history relates that Sultan Yusuf bin Alawi of the Ahdali, or Alawi tribe, (it is not clear which), a descendant of an illustrious personage, Ali bin Hussein (? Hassan, possibly the founder of Kilwa), came from Tusi, in the county of Basra, a twelve days' journey from Bushire, in the 600th year of the Hejira. Sultan Yusuf had three sons, Abdulla, Bwana Pati and Ibrahim. Abdulla had a son called Ismaili, who is described as the Sultan of Kilwa. He married, it is said, the daughter of Koronda, chief of the Muhiyao tribe who held sway in the Kilwa country. Abdulla was the first Sultan of Tumbatu, and he was succeeded by his brother, Ali bin Alawi. This is all the information the history of Tumbatu gives us about the island.

For the rest we only know that when Yakut visited it, the city of Timbat was a powerful town to which the inhabitants of Lenguja (El Unguja) fled at times when they were in danger. This was in the thirteenth century.

When the Portuguese visited Zanzibar about 1500, they made no mention of Tumbatu, which by that time had apparently faded into insignificance. Thus the rise and fall of Tumbatu occupied approximately three hundred years, and that period apparently also represents the period of the genesis of the Watumbatu tribe of to-day.

The city of Timbat was apparently contemporaneous with that of Unguja Kuu, and far outshone the latter in strength and stability. We have seen that, but little is left of Unguja Kuu, but at Tumbatu very extensive ruins are still standing of stone buildings, including a mosque with a women's chapel attached. Not only did the people hold the island but also, undoubtedly, they had a garrison on the main island facing their city. There is no water on Tumbatu Island, but an excellent spring at Mkokotoni (referred to by Burton), from which the Watumbatu have always drawn their water; there is a port near the spring called Shangani ("where the beads are") where large quantities of beads may still be picked up, and which was probably a bead depot, or trading treasury. Graves are often washed out by the sea, which, while it causes no erosion on Tumbatu, does most decidedly do so at Mkokotoni. Heavy stones of the kind obtainable on Tumbatu lie scattered on the shore, and I have little doubt that these relics are the remains of a garrison that lived at Mkokotoni, dealt with the dhow traffic and guarded the water supply. But only one grave has yet been discovered on Tumbatu, and as the coral there is so hard and there is practically no soft ground, it is but reasonable to suppose that the dead were buried on what is now the foreshore of Mkokotoni. The channel is too deep for large quantities of beads, bones and heavy stones to have been washed over. Legend has it that the Watumbatu are also descended from the Wasegeju. They may be, but in all probability they are the descendants of the Persians by their black concubines, brought by the Persians, from time to time during those three hundred years, to Tumbatu. The Watumbatu on Tumbatu Island are settled on either side of the old and now deserted ruins. It seems to me probable that this is where they have always lived. As the old town became too big, these half Africans would build their mud huts on its outskirts, and when their masters went away, they were left behind inheriting from them a love of the sea, for which they are even now famous. They are the best pilots in Zanzibar waters, but they are poor husbandmen, probably owing to poor opportunities, though being Bantus they make the best of it.

In support of the length of time they have lived in their present villages, it may be mentioned that at Kichangani, the northern village of Tumbatu, there is a mosque, which, while not as old as that in the ruins, is still of a respectable age, and older than the other two stone mosques in use there to-day.

Besides their home on the island, the Watumbatu have settlements over a large part of the north-west of Zanzibar, and a few on the south-east of Pemba. They are a very exclusive people, and dislike outside interference, thus, unfortunately, they are very largely inbred. They have a great pride of race. Many of them are fair, and most are better featured than negroes. They deny ever having been slaves, though they say that the Arab slave traders used to raid their northern shore in days gone past.

CHAPTER XII

NATIVE DYNASTIES OF ZANZIBAR

THE MWENYI MKUU OF ZANZIBAR ISLAND

IN each of the separate principalities of the coast the chieftains had different titles. Those in Kilwa were called kings, or Maliks; in Pate, they were called Sultani; in many coast places they were probably called Jumbe, a title which is said to have been derived from the chief placed by the Sultan of Pate in towns on the mainland. The native chieftains of Pemba Island were called Diwanis, a title obviously derived from the Persian *Diwan*.

From A.D. 1204 to 1554 the chiefs of Vumba were known as Mwana Chambi, from 1554 to 1700 they were called Mwana Chambe Chande, and from 1700 onwards Diwan.

The word *Sheha* is also a title of authority, said by some to be derived from the Persian *Shah*, but it seems to be more likely a modification of the Arab *Sheikh*, to which it approximates in pronunciation.

In Mombasa I have been told the chieftain was called *Binda*, and in Zanzibar the word used was *Mwenyi Mkuu*.

The word *Mwenyi* probably means "holder" or "possessor," and *Mkuu* means "great." Like the kingdoms of Pemba and Tumbatu, that of Zanzibar was also an offshoot of the great Zinj Empire, and as far as it can be traced we have seen its history during that time. Whereas in Tumbatu all natives claim Shirazian descent, and in Pemba there are large clans who do so, it does not appear that in Zanzibar anyone except the old ruling house did so.

Unfortunately as yet no written history of the Wahadimu has come to light, nor do their traditions appear to have been systematically collected.

We have seen several references to these Mwenyi Mkuu's during the period of the Portuguese occupation, but it is not until the end of that period that any of their names are ascertainable. It will be remembered that in August, 1653, Cabreira had reported to Goa that the rulers of Zanzibar, Pemba and Otondo had asked for help from Muscat, and Cabreira, having collected a force locally, drove out the Queen of Zanzibar and her son, the King of Otondo.

Otondo is the modern Utondwe, now an unimportant fishing village due west of Zanzibar town, situated up a salt-water creek two and a half miles long, at the head of a small bay north of Ras Utondwe.

Apparently, though, in bygone days it was a state of some importance locally, and probably also an offshoot of the Empire of Kilwa.

We learn from this statement that in 1653 the island was governed by a queen. What the name of the lady was is difficult to ascertain, as there appear at different times to have been two queens of Zanzibar, Fatima and Mwana Mwema. It is more than probable that the queen who was expelled in 1653 was the latter of the two, as Queen Fatima is spoken of later on.

There are two stories of queens of Zanzibar which may refer to Mwana Mwema, as it appears probable that they do not refer to the later Queen Fatima.

The first of these is that she was married to an Arab from Yemen, and the second one is that she was the elder sister of two brothers, and was eventually persuaded by them to abdicate. The Mwenyi Mkuu who succeeded this queen appears to have been called Yusuf, and at his death he divided the kingdom into two portions; the southern one, with the capital at Kizimkazi, he allotted to his son Bakiri, while the northern portion, including the city of the modern town of Zanzibar, was inherited by his daughter Fatima.

In the year 1697 Queen Fatima of Zanzibar addressed a letter to the Governor-General at Goa. This lady, it appears, had married Abdulla, King of Otondo. Whether this Abdulla was the same person referred to previously as the son of Queen Mwana Mwema cannot be stated with any degree of certainty, as we do not know if the queens of Zanzibar were any relation. Abdulla, King of Otondo, and Fatima, the Queen of Zanzibar, had a son called Hasan.

Hasan succeeded to the throne on the death of his mother, and his name is in Portuguese records in the year 1728, when he was ordered to report himself to the Portuguese at Mombasa on their returning to power in that city. He was apparently excused from a personal appearance, and sent his son Moçu instead. This son must have been his second son. (Moçu is perhaps "Musa." In the Portuguese the phrase *Muinha Mocu* is used. There is some doubt as to whether there should be a cedilla under the "c"; if not it is probably *Mwenyi Mkuu*. Hasan is called "Mfalume Hasan.")

The Mwenyi Mkuu Hasan started to build the present city of Zanzibar, leaving the fisher-folk settled at Shangani, the present European quarter.

Other people, such as the Mafaza, who were settled in the Mwavi quarter, were given different sites to settle on. When King Hasan died he was succeeded by his elder son, Sultan, about whom nothing is known. Sultan was succeeded by his son Ahmed, who flourished before the Arab conquest in 1744, and was the last independent Sultan of the Wahadimu. After his death his son Hasan succeeded him.

Hasan II, not caring to live with his Omani overlord, made his capital at a village called Bweni. He came from the coast near Pagani in the time of Seyyid Said. He does not appear to have been a person of any great importance, but was given a limited authority over the Wahadimu. The ruins of his house at Bweni are still to be seen. He married

Mwana wa Mwana, Queen of Tumbatu. After his death he was succeeded by Mohammed bin Ahmed, said by some to have been his brother, but it appears more probable that he was in the direct line. Burton says, "when the former died, Muigni Mkuu, his Wazir, or brother—here all fellow-countrymen are brothers — succeeded, in default of other heirs, to the position of monarch retired from business. He is a common-looking negroid who lives upon the proceeds of the plantation and periodical presents; he is not permitted to appear as an equal at the Seyyid's durbar, and it is highly improbable that he would ever come into his own again." It is doubtful, therefore, whether this man, whose fame is still great in Zanzibar, belonged to the Alawi clan, to which Queen Fatima and her descendants belonged. Alawi is the name of the descendants of the Khalifa Ali.

The Mwenyi Mkuu at the time of his succession (about 1845) was living with the chief Sheha at Dunga, Kiriemeta bin Ngwamchenga, the best known Sheha of the Wachengani.

The Mwenyi Mkuu was a person of considerable power, although tributary to Seyyid Said and afterwards to Seyyid Majid, and he used to receive large presents from the Seyyid. There was a poll tax of two dollars a head on the Wahadimu, of which one went to the Seyyid and the other was retained by the Mwenyi Mkuu, although Burton remarks that he only received two thousand dollars.

His name used to be mentioned in the Friday Khutbeh, and he was regarded with peculiar veneration by his subjects, over whom he had supreme control. If he went out, any person up a clove tree or coco-nut tree would climb down, as it was improper for anyone to be higher than he, and when people came into his presence they might only do so on their knees with uncovered heads, exclaiming *Shikamu* ("I clasp your legs"). He is credited with all kinds of supernatural powers, and it is related that on one occasion Seyyid

Said quarrelled with him and imprisoned him in the fort at Zanzibar. During the same night, however, the Mwenyi Mkuu disappeared from prison, and was soon after heard of on the mainland. During his absence from Zanzibar Island, which lasted for three years, no rain fell, and Seyyid Said, being petitioned by his people, had to pardon the old ruler and permit him to return to Zanzibar. On his return the rain fell again. So runs the local legend.

The Mwenyi Mkuu, who was born in 1785, set himself, about the year 1845, to build a palace suitable to his dignity, and for ten years the hum of myriads of workers never ceased. Many slaves are said to have been slaughtered to consecrate the foundations, for this was the old custom, the relic of which is still to be seen in the custom prevalent in Zanzibar of sacrificing a fowl or goat before and after a house is built.

About the year 1856 his palace was ready, though the Mwenyi Mkuu did not at once occupy it. It was a magnificent palace with a mosque, bathrooms, and houses for his retainers, and at each of the many doors fifty armed slaves kept guard. In its walls is said to have been buried the sacred horn of the Swahilis, the spot being known only by one man, who kept the secret until on the point of death, when he handed it down to another man. The last time it was blown was three days after the death of the Mwenyi Mkuu. It was said that when it was sounded all the Wahadimu would rally to the call.

By those who remember him, the great lord is said to have borne a certain kingly air, and he was rather a tall man with a fringe of white beard.

A portrait of him, which can be recognized by those who have seen him, is still extant in Zanzibar.

The Mwenyi Mkuu only lived to enjoy his palace for four years, and died in the year 1865, being succeeded by his son, Sultan Ahmed. This Mwenyi Mkuu received the same respect that his father enjoyed, but exercised no power over the people, as he lived in town. He reigned only for eight years, and after his death three of his sisters came into possession and lived together at Dunga.

Three or four years after this one of these sisters died, and about 1871 another died, leaving a daughter called Mwana Nguja (known as Mwana binti Kuu) who married one, Mohammed bin Seif, about the year 1890; one of the other sisters had married a man named Mohammed bin Ali.

Many stories of ghosts are told about the palace at Dunga, probably emanating from all the atrocities that were committed there; in fact, Dunga seems to be a place like Pujini in Pemba, and the Mwenyi Mkuu, like Mkame Mdume, to have been a person with miraculous powers.

So bad was his reputation that when the estate passed into the hands of Mohammed bin Seif, who married into the family and died in 1899, he would never live there, but had to build another house.

Dunga was the last of the native capitals of Zanzibar, and, as we have seen, of recent foundation. The capitals before that seem to have been Bweni for a short time, Zanzibar which was founded by Hasan I, and Kizimkazi.

The regalia of the Mwenyi Mkuu are still in existence, and consist of two beautiful carved drums and two wooden horns called *Siwa*, which are now housed in the Zanzibar Museum. After the death of the Mwenyi Mkuu in 1865, and until that of Mohammed bin Seif in 1899, the drums had been kept locked up in a house near the palace, and no one was allowed in except their custodians. On the death of Mohammed bin Seif they were brought into Zanzibar town, but in 1906 were returned to Dunga, though when the palace was gutted they were taken to the Residency. They are said to have come from Otondo (Utondwe), and were very possibly brought over by Abdulla, the consort of Queen Fatima.

I have said that the title *Mwenyi Mkuu* was always that of the native chiefs of Zanzibar, but there seems to be some controversy on the question, as before the succession of the Mwenyi Mkuu Mohammed bin Ahmed, these rulers of the Alawi tribe are also said to have been called Sultani; but the point is not one of great importance, and both titles seem to be used indiscriminately by the Wahadimu. It may be mentioned that the Portuguese referred to these old rulers as *El Rey*. *Mfalme* was no doubt used, but it cannot be said with certainty that it was more than a generic term. It appears on the Kizimkazi inscription, and, as I have noted above, it is possible that in Portuguese times the king was called *Mfalme* and his son *Mwenyi Mkuu*.

It may be noted that the succession in the case of the Mwenyi Mkuu was hereditary and not lateral, as in the case of the Omani dynasty. The Imams of Oman were, of course, appointed on the elective principle, though Seyyid Barghash, when consulted on the question, said that the law of succession was the law of the keenest blade. It is not possible to say what the rule was in the case of the Diwanis of Pemba; although three brothers appear to have succeeded, the later dynasty did not last long enough for one to observe any particular rule; it may be noted, however, that in deciding headships of families both principles, hereditary and lateral, seem to be considered, whilst in the case of Masheha if a suitable son or brother is not available, someone else is elected.

THE DIWANIS OF PEMBA

In an earlier chapter we have read of the great chief of Pemba, Mkame Mdume, and it will be remembered that he lived in the hey-day of the Shirazis—the time of the Zinj Empire. It seems from legend that he died shortly before or after the advent of the Portuguese. The power of these chiefs was then broken, but the policy of the Portuguese was to keep the native form of government, though the people were tributary to them. As long as the chiefs did as they were told all went well, though, as we have seen, in Pemba the people rebelled more than once.

The chiefs in Pemba were termed Diwanis, but how many of them there were and how far back they arose is difficult to say, as legend, which says that Mkame Mdume was the first, is silent about the names of the others until about probably the end of the eighteenth century.

Our sources of information on these chiefs are the written records and traditions.

We have already seen that Pemba was early divided into five districts, over which there appear to have been separate chiefs called first *Shehas*, though afterwards the authority of these minor chieftains was reduced (as separate clans and families grew up) to the thirty-five towns and other surrounding villages. Over the whole of Pemba appear to have reigned dynasties of paramount chiefs who were Diwanis. The names of these chiefs prior to a hundred and fifty years ago have been lost, though the "King" of Pemba ordered by the Portuguese to report at Mombasa, with other coastal monarchs, in 1728, is called in Portuguese records Ben Sultan Manya, and other references to Pemba princes from the same source have been made in Chapter XI.

About the time of the expulsion of the Portuguese from the coast and the arrival of the Mazrui, there came to the country a fresh dynasty, which, however, apparently had relatives and friends in the island. One of the written histories states that this family came from a place called Pagi, during the first dominion of the Diwanis. It was the family of one Makame bin Abubakar bin Salim. Although Pagi is stated as having been their home town in this history, tradition credits them with various homes, though they are generally called Washirazi.

Sometimes they are referred to by the Wapemba and other people as Masherifu. When used in connection with the natives in Pemba the word *sherifu* does not mean " the descendant of the Prophet," but is the name given by the natives to the immigrants which originated according to tradition from Wasin Island. Whether Makame bin Abubakar ever ruled as the Diwani of Pemba, is a matter of doubt. Apparently the first of this family to hold supreme power was his son Ngwachani, though he apparently was not the eldest.

During his reign the Mazrui Arabs made themselves oppressive. Many stories are told of the Diwani, and he is credited with the same sort of cruelties as Mkame Mdume, who apparently held the affections of the people more than this chieftain. It was the custom of the Diwani on succeeding to chief power, to give an ox and twenty pishis of rice to each of the districts, and it was a prerogative of his that all virgin girls should be brought to him before being married—the widespread custom of *jus primæ noctis*. Whenever the Diwani walked out, any ox that he found on the road was slain and eaten, and whenever he sat down a mango tree was planted, a custom that is said to have originated with Mkame Mdume.

Having persuaded the Mazrui to expel the Portuguese, it was not long before their oppression led the people of Pemba to wish to rid themselves of their late deliverers, and they determined to send a mission to Seyyid Said at Muscat to aid them in that behalf. Who composed the mission is a matter of some controversy. The written history says that the Diwani Ngwachani, accompanied by his brother, Diwani Athmani, who apparently assisted him in administering the government, went in person. Tradition has various versions.

One story says that the Sheha Mshoka, Kiago baba Mdogo and Yusuf bin Idarusi went, having been hidden before embarking by one of the Ismaili Arabs, Nasor bin Suleiman. As this Arab's mother was a Mazrui, he undertook this service at some considerable personal risk, apparently with the hope of fulfilling an ambition of becoming Liwali.

Another version says that Nasor bin Suleiman went in person, accompanied by a deputation of three Wapemba, three Masherifu and two Swahilis. Yet another says that the Diwani Ngwachani went accompanied by Mwishoka (who was probably the same person as Sheha Mshoka). The truth seems probably to be that Ngwachani and Athmani went with a representative deputation.

When they got to Muscat they laid their petition before the Seyyid, and he agreed to help them. The generally accepted story is that in return for these services they agreed to pay an excise duty of 5 per cent. on their products and a poll tax of two dollars a head. In addition to that they promised they would do work for the Government free. The written history, however, says that they agreed to bring samli (ghi) and mats to Seyyid Said, and that he might build where he wished. Seyyid Said then sent orders to his Governor at Zanzibar, Mohammed bin Nasor, to expel the Mazrui, and in the year 1822 the Seyyid's army, commanded by Salim bin Suleiman, brother of Nasor bin Suleiman, and Salim bin Nasor, landed in Pemba. Before this, however, the deputation had returned from Muscat, and the Diwani Ngwachani was arrested and imprisoned for twelve months by the Mazrui, with a threat that if Seyyid Said came he would be killed. He was apparently released (as the Mazrui thought that the danger was past) two months before the Seyyid Said's army landed, and made for the Mazrui stronghold of Chwaka, in the north of Pemba. In this place the Mazrui had built a fort, a house for their Governor and a mosque, the ruins of all of which still remain. Their paramount chief, Mbarak, whose name is still referred to by the inhabitants, is buried there, and there are other graves as well, a tomb where two are buried and the grave of a child.

On the grave of Mbarak is an inscription: "The date that Sheikh Mbarak bin Rashid bin Kathib bin Athman Mazrui died was the night of Monday, Rabia el Akhir, 1221" (A.D. 1806). At the time of this invasion, however, the chief of the Mazrui was his son, Rizike bin Mbarak bin Rashid, who prepared for resistance. The Mazrui were defeated and fled to Mombasa, though some of them surrendered and are the ancestors of the present Mazrui in Pemba.

A short time afterwards the Mazrui returned to Pemba under Rizike bin Salim to try conclusions again, bringing many Wanyika in their army. They built a *boma* at Biri Kau, on the northern side of the Mkumbuu peninsula, and Nasor bin Suleiman, who had attained his ambition of being appointed Liwali, prepared to give them battle. He sent his brother Salim with a vanguard and followed up in the rear. When they were a short way from the scene of the action, Nasor's courage failed him and he collapsed on the ground saying he was thirsty. He sent a man up a coco-nut tree to pick him *madafu*, but the nut was split by a bullet and he did not get it. The strain of this was too much for his nerves, and he apparently became unconscious. His followers took the door from a house and prepared to carry him into Chake; the door, however, broke, as the Liwali was a portly man, and another had to be obtained.

One of the six improvised stretcher-bearers was a man named Kombo Baraka, the slave of Abdul Rahim bin Salim el Busaidy. (He is said to have been a man of great strength, and it is related that even if a coco-nut tree fell on him it did him no harm. As a slave all his masters were afraid of him, and he frequently changed hands on this account. If he gave permission to his wife she was allowed to carry water for their master, but if the Arab in question sent her without his permission, it is said Kombo would take the water and douse his master thoroughly with it.)

Meanwhile the rumour had got back to the fort at Chake, which was held by the Seyyid's men, that the Liwali had been killed, and the garrison set out to meet him. They did not get far along the road when they met Kombo and his party carrying him on the door, and they went on to Biri Kau, where the Mazrui were defeated and fled to Mombasa. In the next year they came back to Pemba and succeeded in building a *boma* at Wesha. The victorious Salim bin Suleiman in command of the Seyyid's men came, but not before the Mazrui had succeeded in well establishing themselves at Wesha, and setting up a battery with a large gun at Tiberizi.

One of the Arabs in the Seyyid's army, Salim bin Mohammed el Mendhir, in the course of the battle, told his men to point Rizike out to him. This the soldiers did, and Salim, taking aim, shot and killed him. The credit of firing the shot has also been given to Abdulla bin Fihim Hadim Rumhi, whose grandson of the same name was the Sheha of the district of Ngambwa.

As for the battery at Tiberizi, it is said that the gunner at the fort of Chake Chake took good aim from the top of one of the towers, and succeeded in placing a cannon ball right into its mouth, a piece of good fortune which was attributed to magic worked by the Arabs of the Rashad tribe. The name of the gunner is said to have been Said Msellem el Harusi, who afterwards became Liwali.

This finally broke the power of the Mazrui, who fled again to Mombasa; some say that they took with them the body of Rizike who is buried there, but a baobab tree at Wesha is also pointed out as marking his burial-place.

The Government was now stabilized with the Liwali, appointed by the Seyyid. The Washirazi were left in a semi-independent tributary state under the Diwani Ngwachani, and the taxes paid formed the revenue of the island, which was used by the Liwali in paying for the administration services.

Salim bin Nasor, who had been one of the victorious generals of the Seyyid, was accidentally killed after the war by a spear thrust in a competition of *Razha*, a sword contest accompanied by drums, by another competitor who was returning the spear to him. This started a blood feud, for the Ismaili clan wished to fight that of the slayer Wasuri, of the tribe of Jenebi, but Salim's father, Nasor bin Suleiman, the Liwali, wrote and forgave them, the document being said to be now in Muscat.

Shortly after these events the Diwani Ngwachani died, an old man of about seventy-two. He was buried at the back of Chake Chake town, where he had lived latterly, and a borassus palm marks his solitary grave to this day. He was succeeded by his brother Athmani, who lived only for a short time, and during the reign of Seyyid Majid a man named Ibrahim became Diwani, to be succeeded in the same reign by Kihanuni, another brother of Ngwachani and Athmani.

This man was the last of the Diwanis who carried on with the cruel practice of his predecessors. He lived mainly at Chambani, and had the state drums, called *Kutanga*, with which to summon his people. The natives relate that at the end of the year he was in the habit of sewing up the eyes of any children he could get hold of.

Many other small chieftains during the period of the Diwanis may be mentioned; Sheha Kikamburi who lived and died at Mtambwe during the reign of Seyyid Said bin Sultan, and another also noted for cruelty was Seyyid Mtu bin Kiambani. One of his pleasures was to order people to climb up a perpendicular wall and beat them when, as a natural corollary, they failed. Another thing he did was to endeavour to force people to cultivate by night. "He said he used to do these things because he was a young god, but this only brought him into ridicule, and when he died everyone said that the young god had died."

THE SHEHA OF TUMBATU

The chief of Tumbatu was known as Sheha; beneath him was his prime minister, or Waziri, and below the Waziri, an officer called the Makata. Tumbatu was nominally subject to the Mwenyi Mkuu, but the Sheha was allowed by him a good deal of freedom in his administration.

We have seen that Mwana wa Mwana, Queen of Tumbatu, married Hassan the Mwenyi Mkuu, and legend has it that for her sake the Watumbatu were excused payment of the taxes.

Mwana wa Mwana was succeeded by Ali bin Hassan, brother to the Mwenyi Mkuu, Ali was succeeded by his daughter Fatima, who was, in her turn, succeeded by her nephew, Vuai bin Mkadam. Vuai was succeeded by his second cousin, Mwana Kazija bint Ngwale bin Kombo bin Ali, and she, by her brother Ali. This was the end of the royal house of Tumbatu. Little is known of these people, but the names are interesting, as showing that a woman could freely succeed to supreme power: such a thing would be unlikely to happen nowadays.

C. HISTORY OF MODERN ZANZIBAR

CHAPTER XIII

The Zanzibari-Omani Empire

THE REIGN OF SEYYID SAID

Considerations of space make it impossible for me to devote more than a little room to the history of Seyyid Said, whose name towers out above those of all men who have been associated with the island kingdom. His life, however, is fairly well known, and as it is my object here to avoid giving information which may be easily obtained elsewhere in convenient form, it will be impossible to mention more than the outstanding features of his reign.

Said bin Sultan, grandson of the Imam Ahmed, was born in 1791, and ruled jointly over Oman with his brother Salim until the death of the latter in 1821. Continual troubles in that most turbulent of Arabian states, Oman, ushered in the reign of the prince: these troubles were to continue with very little interruption until his death. His first connection with Zanzibar was in the year 1822, but he did not make his first visit in person to the coast until 1828, when, with a large fleet in his flagship, the *Liverpool*, he fought with the Mazrui and defeated them at Mombasa, after which a treaty was entered into by which the Mazrui acknowledged his supremacy. Leaving a garrison there of 300 Baluchis, he proceeded to Zanzibar, and at once started on improvements, but was later called back to Muscat by rebellion there. In 1837 troubles again occurred in Mombasa, and proceeding to the coast, he captured Rashid bin Salim, the chief of the Mazruis, and sent him and twenty-four others to starve in Bunder Abbas. It may be noted that in 1824 they had concluded a covenant with Captain Owen of H.M.S. *Leven*, whereby they were placed under British protection, but this had been disallowed on the remonstrances of Seyyid Said. In 1832 he made Zanzibar his capital, though he had to pay frequent visits to Muscat, where he returned on the 10th of September of that year. After settling the trouble there he re-embarked for Zanzibar, leaving his third son, Thwain, as Wali of Muscat. Seyyid Said had not been long in Zanzibar before he was again recalled by the rebellion of Seyyid Hamoud bin Azzan, who caused him continual trouble until the time of his death in 1849.

In 1833 Seyyid Said entered into a treaty of Amity and Commerce with the United States of America, and an American consulate was opened at Zanzibar in 1837. The British Consulate was established in 1841, and the first consul was Colonel Hamerton, who became a great friend of the Seyyid's. He maintained excellent relations with Britain, and entered into the first treaty directed against the abolition of slavery (1822), which cost him a loss of 100,000 crowns annually, and for which he declined compensation. He gave his ship, the *Liverpool*, to Great Britain, and it was renamed the *Imaum*.

In 1844 he signed a Commercial Treaty with France, and generally encouraged commerce and recognized free trade. In April, 1856, he was compelled to enter into a humiliating treaty with the Persians, in respect of the territories of Bunder Abbas and other dependencies, which he leased from them. In the same year Seyyid Said sailed from Muscat for the last time on board the *Victoria*. Deeply humiliated by the affronts of Persia and worn out in health, he was destined never to see Zanzibar again —the Decree of Fate overtook him in the sea of Seychelles on the 19th October, and though he directed that in the event of the death he expected he should be thrown overboard, his body was taken to Zanzibar and buried. His last words were a call for his friend, Colonel Hamerton.

At his death his dominions included the whole of Oman, with certain islands in the Persian Gulf, and the coast of Africa from Guardafui to Cape Delgado, with the exception of Lamu, a distance of 960 miles. In addition his sway was acknowledged in the interior, from the coast to beyond the great lakes. He conceived the idea of a series of trading-stations, starting on the coast opposite Zanzibar to end in the Congo.

This one man, by his own strength of character, built up an empire which any power might have envied: had he been better served this empire might have survived till to-day: as it was, it fell to pieces on account of internal dissension and the great rush for Africa which the powers of Europe were soon to start. It may be said that it is owing to Seyyid Said and Seyyid Barghash that Zanzibar to-day still has its own Sultan and its own flag.

Personally Seyyid Said was a "tall, stout, honourable-looking man, with a benevolent countenance, clever, intelligent, sharp eyes, and a remarkably pleasing and agreeable manner: he combined, in a high degree, majesty of figure, nobleness of countenance, and perfect grace of gesture." He was a distinguished diplomatist, a great sailor, a brave soldier, and withal, highly religious. He laid the foundations of Zanzibar's prosperity by insisting on the cultivation of the clove, which was introduced at the end of the eighteenth century. When he died, Zanzibar and Pemba had many clove plantations.

"First in war, first in peace, first in the hearts of his fellow countrymen," he was a ruler any country might be proud of.

THE REIGN OF SEYYID MAJID

On the death of Seyyid Said, his son Majid, who was in Zanzibar, immediately took up the reins of Government; but it was not long before his brother

Thwain, the Wali of Muscat, laid claim to the whole empire. Majid was perfectly content that Oman should fall to Thwain, but was not prepared to give up Zanzibar, and Thwain, in 1860, prepared to send an expedition against him. In addition to this, another brother, Turki, claimed Sohar. The British Government now deemed it expedient to interfere, and the Governor-General of India appointed a Commission to inquire into the claims of the rivals. It appeared that it was Seyyid Said's wish that Muscat should go to Thwain, Sohar to Turki and Zanzibar to Majid. The Governor-General's decision, now known as "Lord Canning's award," was made on 2nd April, 1861, and by it Majid was to retain Zanzibar on paying 40,000 crowns annually to Thwain, who was to retain Muscat. The money was not to be considered as making Zanzibar dependent on Muscat, but to compensate the ruler of the latter place for abandonment of all claims on the richer country of Zanzibar. Majid paid the money until Thwain's death, and in 1871 the arrears were paid by the Indian Government: since the death of Thwain the money has not been a charge on the Zanzibar treasury. From 1861 the fortunes of Oman were no longer mingled with those of Zanzibar, and from that date we can devote ourselves to the history of Zanzibar alone.

The independence of Zanzibar was recognized by England and other powers in 1862: the rest of Seyyid Majid's reign was uneventful, but he paid a state visit to Bombay in 1866, and in the same year Pate and Siu submitted to his arms. Seyyid Majid died in 1870.

THE REIGN OF SEYYID BARGHASH

Seyyid Barghash, who had twice endeavoured to supplant his brother Majid, succeeded to the throne on the latter's death. The clove industry of the island received a serious set-back in 1872, when a cyclone occurred which destroyed practically all the cloves in Zanzibar, though Pemba luckily escaped.

It was Seyyid Barghash who instituted the export duty on cloves, which he fixed at 30 per cent., a figure reduced by his brother Seyyid Khalifa to 25 per cent. In the year of the cyclone, owing to the encouragement of Seyyid Barghash, who was anxious to help trade, the British India Company started a service between India and Zanzibar. The next year the Sultan entered into a treaty with Sir Bartle Frere to abolish the slave trade, and the treaty was finally signed on the 5th of June. The same year Zanzibar Treasury ceased to pay the subsidy of 40,000 crowns to the Sultan of Muscat, who received it from the Political Agent there, with the sanction of the Viceroy of India. It is interesting to note that the Sultan offered France the Protectorate of his dominions, but the proposal fell through, as Great Britain and France had agreed to respect his independence indefinitely. The following year he made overtures to Germany, which were again refused by Bismarck.

In 1875 Seyyid Barghash paid a state visit to England at the invitation of the British Government. He was attended by a numerous suite, and accompanied by Sir John Kirk.

In the same year Egyptian warships, under McKillop Pasha, sailed down the coast of Africa and attempted seizure of the mainland ports, dropping anchor at Kismayu. They finally left under the orders of the Khedive, to whom representations had been made by the British.

Another step was taken by the Sultan towards the abolition of slavery, by a decree ordering the confiscation of slaves brought to Zanzibar, and prohibiting slave traffic by land.

In 1877 he offered a lease of the customs administration of the Zanzibar east coast to Sir William Mackinnon, which was refused, as Mackinnon could not obtain Foreign Office support.

Two years later another link (of Zanzibar) with the

outside world was forged by the laying of the cable, and Seyyid Barghash ceded the small island of Bawe, outside the territorial waters of Zanzibar, to the Eastern Telegraph Company to land the cable. In the same year German attempts at a protectorate over Zanzibar, which had been mooted by Vice-Admiral Livinous in 1875, were renewed, and for the next five years the Germans were very active in East Africa. The notorious Dr. Carl Peters concluded treaties with the chiefs of Mbuzini and Usagara in 1884, which caused some uneasiness to the British Government. The next year Peters obtained an Imperial Charter of protection, and some of the territories of the Sultan were put under German protection in spite of Barghash's protest. He (Barghash) prepared to send an expedition to subdue Witu, but the German Government protested and declared a protectorate. The result of this was a Commission appointed by Britain, France and Germany to delineate the Sultan's boundaries, which resulted in the *procès-verbal* of the 9th June, 1886, which defined his possessions as the Islands of Zanzibar and Pemba and the islets within twelve miles thereof; the Lamu Archipelago, a ten-mile belt along the coast from Tungi to Kipini, at the mouth of the Ozi River, and the ports of Kismayu, Barawa, Marka, Mogadisho and Warsheik.

In 1886 the Sultan accepted the Berlin Act, but excepted his territory from the free trade articles, continuing to levy a 5 per cent. duty on imports as well as certain export duties. On 25th January, 1887, Portugal demanded a rectification of the frontier between Zanzibar and Portuguese territory, stating that Germany recognized Rovuma as the northern limit of Mozambique colony: Germany, however, stated she would not interfere if Portugal came to an agreement with the Sultan concerning Rovuma.

In February the Portuguese demanded the cession of this territory, and as the Sultan declined to yield, broke off diplomatic relations with Zanzibar: Portugal stated her intention was only to occupy Tungi, but rumours of hostile Portuguese action at Zanzibar and the capture of H.H. ship *Kilwa* by the Portuguese, led the English Government to make inquiries and demand explanations.

Portugal, however, now continued to commit acts of war, and in addition to capturing a ship of the Sultan's, occupied Minengani and Tungi, which latter town they bombarded on 18th February. Some retaliation was made in April by the Governor of Tungi contrary to the orders of Seyyid Barghash.

A Commission was then appointed to investigate the matter, which sat, on the arrival of the Portuguese Commissioner, on 10th July. But before this had happened, Seyyid Barghash was taken seriously ill, and died on 26th March, 1888, at the age of fifty-five. Sir Euan Smith, who was acting Consul-General at the time, stated that his "death seems to have called forth but very limited expressions of sorrow and regret from any section of the community," and while it must be admitted that Seyyid Barghash had acted often in an arbitrary manner towards his subjects, frequently seizing their property, it must be remembered that he suffered severely from consumption and elephantiasis, and that the gradual and inevitable stripping of his territories caused him considerable disappointment and humiliation. At this distance of time the verdict of history is more merciful, and Seyyid Barghash can be seen as a great ruler.

He was a remarkable man, and possessed many of the qualities of his father: he was exceedingly ambitious and energetic, but withal, honourable, and had a knowledge of the world exceeding that of his father and his brother.

Before closing this chapter, reference must be made to Sir John Kirk, whose name is even now a household word in Zanzibar, and who retired from the position of Consul-General in 1887. Sir John Kirk was a man of marvellous energy, and his uniform successes were undoubtedly the result of a long practical acquaintance with native manners and methods: "the pre-eminence of his work entitles him to be remembered as one of the greatest pioneers of the Africa of to-day, and when other names are buried in oblivion, not always undeserved, his will stand out pre-eminent as that of a wise and powerful ruler and successful administrator."

TIPPU TIB

One can hardly write of the Zanzibari Empire in the times of its prosperity without mentioning the great traveller, trader and ruler, Hemed bin Mohammed, surnamed Tippu Tib.

The son of adventurous parents, he commenced his career at the age of eighteen with a journey to Ugangi, north-east of Lake Nyasa. After this he undertook to journey on his own, declining to have any supervision or protection, and set out into the interior at the head of a numerous band of followers. After some years of trading and adventures in the interior during which, in 1867, he encountered Livingstone, to whom he rendered considerable assistance, Tippu Tib made for the coast, and after a few incidents reached Dar-es-Salaam, where he found Seyyid Majid and his Court assembled. The Sultan, realizing that the mainland furnished him with most of his wealth, had determined to build a palace and transfer his Government there. The coming of Tippu Tib's caravan excited the greatest interest, and the Sultan loaded him with high honours and entertained him as his guest: Tippu Tib returned with him to Zanzibar, but soon wished to set out again. The Sultan encouraged him and supported him in every way, knowing that it would increase his political influence if his subjects should achieve importance in the interior, and would bring as well rich produce to his country.

Tippu Tib met with a reverse at the hands of the Wangoni, but followed it with a success over Sultan

Taka at Ugalla, and a considerable victory over the Kasembe kingdom of Lunda in 1867. The fame of Tippu Tib as a conqueror now spread, and no resistance was offered to his progress. He passed on to Irande, and subsequently to Utetera, where he was made Sultan, and spent several years as ruler in his territory with expeditions to the country around. In 1874 he met Cameron and rendered him assistance. Two years later, when engaged on peaceful work at Nyangwe and Kwakosongo, Stanley appeared. Stanley and Tippu Tib did not agree, and there can be no doubt that the Englishman had treated the Arab unfairly, as he seems to have ignored the terms of any agreement made: however, they set out together, and had it not been for Tippu Tib, Stanley would have been deserted by his people. In December of 1876 they agreed to part.

In 1879 Seyyid Barghash summoned him to return at once to Zanzibar to settle his affairs with his banker, and a year after Tippu Tib set out for the coast. He reached Tabora, but not without incurring hostilities on the way in which, as usual, he came out successful.

On 7th September, 1882, he was joined by Wissmann, who accompanied him to the coast, and they reached Zanzibar on 13th November of that year.

There he saw Seyyid Barghash, who told him that he had intended to make him Liwali of Tabora, but considered it more advisable that he should return at once to his dominions. However, Tippu Tib remained some time in Zanzibar, and held consultations with Sir John Kirk, who was very interested in the state of affairs at Ugogo, and proposed that Tippu Tib should, in concert with the Sultan, bring the whole country under his control.

Had the Sultan taken this hint, as he could easily have done, he would have averted the loss of his great possessions in Africa, but Barghash had less inclination for extending his political influence than for commercial undertakings, and desired first and foremost to secure the monopoly of trade for his subjects in the new regions. He promulgated a decree that no one should enlist carriers until Tippu Tib was sufficiently supplied. More favours were heaped by Barghash on the famous traveller, and with an unlimited credit he started off for the interior again. At Tabora he heard that the people in Manyema had become refractory, so he pressed on to Kwakosongo, which he reached in June, 1883, and soon restored order.

Shortly afterwards Seyyid Barghash wrote to him to use every means in his power to keep the country under his influence: Tippu Tib thereupon replied that the Sultan must first supply him with arms, and Barghash called him back to talk it over in person.

On his arrival in what is now Tanganyika Territory, he found that the Belgians and the Germans were threatening more and more to force back the Arab sphere of influence, and as Tippu Tib had to force or purchase his ways through the coast, there were clear indications that the Sultan's power was not in the least feared by the natives.

At Zanzibar, Barghash realized from Tippu Tib's accounts that he had indeed lost his hold in the interior, and could only hope to keep the Island of Zanzibar, which even then the Europeans wished to wrest from him.

Tippu Tib's next undertaking was in 1886, when he rendered assistance in the rescue of Emin Pasha.

King Leopold, desiring peace with the Arabs, offered Tippu Tib the post of Governor in the provinces wrested from the Congo state by the Arabs. Tippu Tib therefore set sail with Stanley and journeyed inland, after having passed through Cape Town in 1887. He eventually took up his duties as Governor of Stanley Falls, where he lived on the best of terms with the Europeans, especially the Belgians. At this time he heard of the death of his old patron, who had died on 26th March, 1888, and he at once sent an embassy to convey greetings to Khalifa and assure him of his allegiance: however, he had shortly to return to Zanzibar, as the King of the Belgians informed him that Stanley had brought a case against him for breach of contract, and he started in March, 1890, despite all the protests of his fellow-tribesmen, who wished him to evade justice. In the Arab text of the summons the plaintiffs were given as "Emin Pasha and his people," meaning the relief committee.

Emin Pasha was most indignant at the misuse of his name, as it might give rise to the idea that he was on unfriendly terms with the "uncrowned ruler of Central Africa," and publicly denied his association with the suit. The case never came into court; Stanley apparently failed in his accusations, and as it was shown that he had made false accusations against another European, opinion now turned against him. After that time Tippu Tib did not journey again into the interior. After his departure there was trouble in Congo, the Arabs rising against the Belgians, but it could hardly be said that Tippu Tib was to blame for this, for as soon as his personal influence was removed there was bound to be trouble.

He himself suffered considerable loss, as all his goods were lost. He spent his last years in Zanzibar, an important person in the Council of the island, and always on good terms with the ruler for the time being. He never lost his attraction for the Europeans. He died in June, 1905.

CHAPTER XIV

The Reign of Seyyid Khalifa bin Said to the Present Day

THE REIGN OF SEYYID KHALIFA BIN SAID

Seyyid Khalifa bin Said succeeded his brother on 26th March, 1888. In October he offered a concession of his mainland territories to the British East Africa Company. It will be remembered that this was offered by the last Sultan to Sir William Mackinnon, but refused, as the British Foreign Office would not support the company: on this occasion, however, the concession was signed in 1889, and the Sultan surrendered all control over the company's territory in return for an annual payment. This concession was probably expedited by the action of the Germans. In June, 1887, the German Consul-General demanded the concession of all the port and Island of Lamu: this was refused by the Sultan, and the Belgian Foreign Minister, to whom the case was submitted for arbitration, decided that the Sultan could cede the island where he chose. The Sultan took another step towards the abolition of slavery, by decreeing that all slaves born after the 1st January, 1890, should be free; he later, fearing for his safety at the hands of the Arabs, never published this decree, and it remained a dead letter. Seyyid Khalifa died after a brief reign on the 13th February, 1890.

THE REIGN OF SEYYID ALI BIN SAID

Seyyid Ali bin Said was recognized as Sultan on the 17th February, and June of the same year agreed to the assumption by Great Britain of a protectorate over Zanzibar. This was recognized by Germany in exchange for the Island of Heligoland, and by France on recognition by Great Britain of her protectorate over Madagascar. Thus the last remnants of independence passed from the proud empire built up by Seyyid Said, though legally certain islets, unimportant and few in number, which lie outside the territorial waters of Zanzibar and Pemba, are not within the British Protectorate.

It must be remembered that if this had not been declared, other powers, for instance Germany, would have been but too ready to absorb the weak and powerless state.[1] At the same time the actual territory between the Rivers Umba and Rovuma, including the Island of Mafia, was ceded to Germany on payment of four million marks.

The disposal of slaves was declared illegal in August of the same year by a decree of the Sultan, and in the following year constitutional government was established, Sir Lloyd Matthews becoming First Minister.

In 1892 the import duties were abolished and Zanzibar was declared a free port, and in the same year the Benadir coast was leased to Italy. Seyyid Ali, who had been sickening for some time, died on the 5th March, 1893.

THE REIGN OF SEYYID HAMED BIN THWAIN

On the death of Seyyid Ali bin Said, Seyyid Khaled, a young and ambitious youth, the son of Seyyid Barghash, attempted to seize the palace, but was expelled at once owing to the prompt action of Sir Rennell Rodd, the Consul-General, and Sir Lloyd Matthews. There were two other claimants to the throne; Mahmud, a cousin of Seyyid Ali's, and Seyyid

[1] Germany's attitude towards Zanzibar may be judged from the activities of Carl Peters. See also Chapter XVII, Vol. I, of Sir George Arthur's *Life of Lord Kitchener,* which describes the way the Germans were instrumental in cutting down the Sultan's territories at the Boundary Commission of 1886.

Hamed bin Thwain: of these the latter, a man of forty odd years, was selected and proclaimed Sultan within a few hours of Seyyid Ali's death.

In July, 1893, the Benadir ports and territory were leased to Italy for a further period of three years.

In 1895 the Imperial British East Africa Company surrendered their charter, for which they received a compensation of £250,000, a sum, save £50,000, paid out of Zanzibar funds. Zanzibar and Great Britain entered into an agreement for the administration by the latter of the Sultan's mainland possessions. The Kenya Government pay annually a sum of £11,000 as rent for these possessions, and £6,000 as interest at 3 per cent. on the £200,000 paid to the company.

Seyyid Hamed bin Thwain died, after a short reign of three years, on the 25th August, 1896: he was a man of high culture and literary taste, and a profound student of Arabic literature. Sir Rennell Rodd credits him with a remark which shows him to have been of a liberal turn of mind, "The wise men who made the Law, Christ and Mohammed, lived a very long time ago and made the Law according to their lights, but they did not know many things that we know now, and the world has moved on further since their Law was made."

SEYYID KHALED BIN BARGHASH

On the death of the Sultan, Seyyid Khaled again at once seized the palace and proclaimed himself Sultan: however, a British fleet arrived soon after, in the harbour under Rear-Admiral Rawson: a two-hour ultimatum was sent to him at seven a.m. on the morning of the 27th August, to which he vouchsafed no reply; it is said that the soothsayers had foretold that the British guns would spout only water. At nine a.m. a bombardment commenced, and when it finished, forty minutes later, the palace had been reduced to a shambles, over 500 natives had been killed, and the Sultan's ship of war, *The Glasgow*, sunk; Khaled himself fled to the German Consulate and was given sanctuary in Dar-es-Salaam. On the capture of the latter place in the late war, he was exiled to St. Helena; thence in 1921 he was removed to the Seychelles, and was then allowed to live in Mombasa, where he died early in 1927.

THE REIGN OF SEYYID HAMOUD BIN MOHAMMED

On the deposition and flight of Seyyid Khaled, Seyyid Hamoud bin Mohammed bin Said was proclaimed Sultan (August 27th, 1896). In September of the same year more direct British control was assumed over the Official, Military, and Executive departments of the Government. The final abolition of slavery by a decree of the Sultan took place on the 6th April, 1897.

The 5 per cent. *ad valorem* duty, which had been abolished in 1892, was reimposed in December, 1899, as it was recognized that Zanzibar could not control the East African trade, of which the German share kept increasing despite Zanzibar's being a free port.

In 1901 the Government issued £100,000 3 per cent. debentures in London at par, the principal repayable not later than 1st October, 1931.

To the great regret of all, the Sultan's Prime Minister, General Sir Lloyd William Matthews, K.C.M.G., died on the 14th October, 1901. Sir Rennell Rodd has said of him, "few men could possess so clean a record as was his; soldier and sailor and vizier, he was of the fibre of those simple, God-fearing mariners of the great days who laid the foundations of empire. If few of his own countrymen had had the opportunity of appraising him, no one was ever more sincerely mourned by those of an alien race and dusky skin."

Sir Lloyd Matthews was succeeded as Prime Minister by Mr. A. S. Rogers in November, 1901, and Seyyid Hamoud died at the age of fifty-one on the 18th July, 1902.

He was an intelligent and generous man, of a fine physique, with a courtly and charming presence.

THE REIGN OF SEYYID ALI BIN HAMOUD

Seyyid Ali bin Hamoud succeeded his father on the 20th July, 1902; but as he was under age, the First Minister, Mr. Rogers, was appointed Regent. He attained his majority in June, 1905, and assumed his powers; in the same year the Benadir coast was ceded to Italy for £144,000.

In 1906 the Government was again reorganized and the First Minister given two colleagues, a financial member of council and a legal member of council.

The Zanzibar army was disbanded in 1907, and the defence of the country was entrusted to two companies of the King's African Rifles. In January, 1908, the import duties were increased from 5 to 7½ per cent. *ad valorem*. In June, 1909, the emancipation of slaves was completed by a decree directing compensation to be given to slaves unable to support themselves, for the deprivation of their masters' protection. No claims were to be considered later than the end of 1911. In 1911 the Sultan left Zanzibar to attend the coronation of King George V, and whilst in Europe decided to abdicate: he died in Paris in 1918.

THE REIGN OF SEYYID KHALIFA BIN HARUB

Seyyid Khalifa bin Harub acceded to the throne in succession to his brother-in-law on the 9th December, 1911, and was formally installed on the 16th of that month.

On the 13th February, 1913, Mr. Edward Clark, the last of the long succession of distinguished Consuls-General, died in Zanzibar. In the same year the control of the Sultanate passed from the Foreign Office to the Colonial Office, legal effect being given to the change in 1914 by a new Zanzibar Order in Council which constituted the offices of High Commissioner, British Resident and Chief Secretary. In the same year the Zanzibar Protectorate Council was formed: it consisted of His Highness as President, the British Resident as Vice-President, three official and four unofficial members who represent various communities. The High Commissioner was the Governor of Kenya Colony and Protectorate. The British Resident combines the offices of Consul-General and First Minister. Major F. B. Pearce, C.M.G., was appointed first Resident. Mr. J. H. Sinclair, C.M.G., who had served for many years in the Protectorate, was the Chief Secretary.

On the outbreak of war Zanzibar found herself in one of the theatres of war, and His Highness associated himself with the protecting power by a series of decrees, the first being a declaration of war with Germany dated 5th August, 1914. In connection with Germany and Zanzibar it is interesting to note that the German Chancellor, Von Bethmann Hollweg, states that in February, 1912, it was proposed that Zanzibar and Pemba should be handed over to Germany, in addition to other considerations, in exchange for German concessions in the Baghdad Railway question, and, whatever other result the war may have had, it is satisfactory to think that such a contingency as this is unlikely to occur again.

The first act of war committed within His Highness's dominions by the Germans was the sinking of H.M.S. *Pegasus*, which had been in these waters some time, by the German cruiser *Königsberg* on 20th September, 1914.

Zanzibar's contributions to the war were, for her size, by no means negligible. Besides the formation of a European Defence Force, and the enlistment of many natives in the King's African Rifles, some thousands of carriers, under the Native Carrier's Recruitment Decree of 1916, were recruited, and a sum of £70,000 was contributed to the Imperial

Government as an aid to the carrying on of the war. In addition £245,000 was invested in war loan and £19,500 raised by public subscriptions for the British Red Cross Society. Major Pearce has stated of His Highness that his steadying influence, not only over his own subjects within his dominions, but over the Moslem populations of East and Central Africa, largely contributed to the maintenance of peace among the Mohammedans of mid-Africa during the critical periods of war in these regions.

The principal event of economic importance following the war was the rise in value of the rupee, which was fixed by the Government of India in 1920 at two shillings gold. The British sovereign, which had been made legal tender at the rate of fifteen rupees to the pound in 1908, was demonetized. The import duty was raised from 7½ per cent. to 10 per cent. on the 10th August, 1921.

Since the war much has been done to make up for the years of unavoidable inactivity. In 1920 the Government, wishing to improve the state of education in the country, which had long been sadly neglected, appointed a Commission to inquire into its needs, and as a result of its findings, an ambitious programme was adopted. This was followed in 1923 by a similar Commission to investigate the agricultural industry, which has for long been declining as a result of the apathy of plantation owners, induced probably by the serious debt in which many are involved. Disease has also affected the clove trees, causing loss, though it may be remarked that the production of the actual commodity has been fairly steady at a high figure for many years. Important undertakings put in hand during this period were the construction of a harbour works in Zanzibar, and a system of roads in Pemba.

Other events of importance have been the removal of the King's African Rifles from Zanzibar, and the filling of their place by an augmentation of the Zanzibar Police, who were, in 1922, constituted to act either in a civil or military capacity as occasion demands.

The Laws were codified in 1922 and the Courts reconstituted in 1923, when the jurisdiction of His Highness's courts was made similar to that of His Britannic Majesty's.

The administration of the Island of Mafia, ceded to Germany in 1890, was placed in the hands of the Zanzibar Government in 1916, but was transferred to the Government of Tanganyika Territory in 1922.

Major Pearce retired in 1922 and Mr. Sinclair succeeded him as British Resident, Mr. E. Costley White, O.B.E., becoming Chief Secretary. Mr. Sinclair was succeeded by Mr. (now Sir) A. C. Hollis, K.C.M.G., C.B.E., in January, 1924.

In 1925 the High Commissionership was abolished. In the same year minor jurisdiction was given to Arab Akidas and natives sitting in district courts. Executive and legislative councils were established in 1926. The former is presided over by His Highness the Sultan. The British President presides over the latter, and there are three other *ex officio* official members and five nominated. There are six nominated unofficial members representing the various communities.

The period of Sir Claud Hollis's administration was one of unprecedented development. All departments of Government received encouragement to proceed with measures for the improvement of the conditions of the people, but in no direction was progress more marked than in the construction of roads. In 1924 there were roads from Zanzibar city to Mkokotoni in the north, to Chwaka on the east coast, to Tunguu a few miles towards the south, and to Chukwani on the west coast, and there were no roads in Pemba worth the name. In 1929, when Sir Claud Hollis left, the Protectorate roads ran to nearly every corner of both islands. The effect of these roads not only in commerce, but on the mentality of the people, can hardly be exaggerated.

In 1929, Prince Abdulla, the Sultan's only surviving son, was proclaimed heir to the throne. Shortly after, His Highness proceeded on a state visit to England. This visit was a great success from all points of view, and gave those who came in contact with His Highness there a chance of realizing that which those in Zanzibar have long known, namely, that in Seyyid Khalifa, Zanzibar has a wise and enlightened ruler, who has the interests of his subjects keenly at heart. I have often met people who think that the Sultan of Zanzibar is only a figurehead, and it may be well for me to assert from intimate knowledge that this is far from being the truth. His Highness is a constitutional monarch, but as President of the Executive Council he deals with all the most important matters of his dominions, and with his wide knowledge of all that concerns his people and a judgment that seems almost instinctively right, he plays a very valuable part in the direction of local affairs.

He is a man of great charm and fine presence, and has that rare but royal faculty of always saying the right thing at the right time.

During the Sultan's absence in Europe, Sheikh Suleiman bin Nasur el-Lemki was appointed to act as regent. For this and previous marked services to Zanzibar, he was awarded the C.B.E., and I had the honour of accompanying him as interpreter when, in August, 1930, he received the insignia at a private audience granted by His Majesty the King.

Sir Claud Hollis was succeeded in 1930 by Mr. R. S. D. Rankine, C.M.G. Mr. Costley White was succeeded as Chief Secretary in 1927 by Mr. R. H. Crofton, who has served for many years in Zanzibar.

PART II

ETHNOLOGICAL

A. FOREIGN INFLUENCES

CHAPTER XV

INTRODUCTION

As has elsewhere been said, the present population of the Sultanate may be roughly divided into four principal classes, Africans, Arabs, Indians and Europeans, and when studying the sociology and ethnology of the native, not only is it necessary to describe how the customs of the latter three classes have affected the first, but also what they have inherited from previous colonizers. These peoples have been the ancient races inhabiting the Persian Gulf, the ancient Egyptians, the Greeks, the Malays and Chinese, and, coming to more recent times, the Persians and Portuguese.

In addition to these, many of the customs of a variety of African tribes have been, and are being, introduced into the country. With the exception of the Persians, traces of these early colonizers have been referred to in the historical chapters. In the following chapters I propose to describe the life and customs of the Zanzibar Arabs of Omani origin. It might have been supposed that, exerting such a paramount influence as they have done during the last century and a half, they would have had more effect on the customs of the natives. I think, however, it will be seen that far from doing this they have absorbed many native customs themselves.

The effects of English occupation will be sufficiently remarked in the chapter on Swahilis and freed slaves, while in the chapters on the aboriginal natives themselves many and various customs imported from other peoples will be noted. As the people of Makunduchi have so many customs peculiar to themselves, I have devoted a special chapter to them. The only class remaining is the Indian, and it seems little short of amazing, in view of the prolonged residence of the Indians on the east coast of Africa, that they have made so little impression on the sociology of the native. What is the reason of this? Here are these Indians practising all their rites and customs, bringing up their families in the country, many of them among the natives, and yet, with the exception of a few insignificant superstitions, the native has borrowed nothing, except money, from them.

The reasons are probably to be found in the customs of the Indians themselves. Firstly religion. The Indians are either Hindus or Shiites; if the former they are regarded as heathens, and their religious customs, well known to the natives, are anathema to Mohammedans. Their dress is peculiar: they have their heads almost shaved except for one long top-knot, and they wear round their nether limbs a loose cloth of which the bottom is folded up between their legs. Any native will tell you that the top-knot is intended for the Banyans to be raised to heaven with, and that the loose fold of cloth is intended to catch Issa, whom the Banyans believe is to be born next time of a man! Their methods of burial and customs of marriage are also totally different to either anything African or Islamic, while as regards animals the Banyans will take no life at all, and as natives have often told me, consider that even the chickens that run across the road may contain the souls of their grandmothers. No native would touch a Banyan's food. These, roughly, are the ideas the natives have of the Hindu religion.

To anyone who does not understand Islam it will appear remarkable that Sunnis and Ibathis should consider the Shiites so far removed from themselves, but such is the case, and one must live in an Islamic country to understand the bitter diversity of opinions between these two great divisions of Islam. Ibn Saud, the enlightened ruler of the fanatical Wahabi sect of the Nejd, is stated to have said that he far preferred Christians to Shiites.

This is not the place to describe the customs and beliefs of the various sects of the Shiites, some of which present great divergencies, and it must be understood that in Zanzibar members of all sects and creeds live on friendly and easy terms with each other, although the beliefs of one may be anathema to another.

Secondly, as regards the mode of living. Indians live very much to themselves, and although they live their lives in full view of the natives, they have their own communities in each village or group of small villages. It is rather remarkable that different districts have in the main communities of Indians belonging to one sect, thus Jambangome in Pemba is mainly Bohora, around Mkokotoni in Zanzibar there are chiefly Khoja Ismailis, and at Makunduchi the Indians are all Makumbaro.

Thirdly, as regards occupation. The Indian is chiefly a small shopkeeper, and for the most part business is an occupation at which the natives do not shine, though in some degree, principally among the Wapemba, they have copied him in the keeping of small shops. It is probable that it is but recently the Indians have taken to agriculture, an occupation of which they do not make a success in Zanzibar. The fact of their having taken to it arises out of their money-lending propensities, and this occupation has in some degree been taken up by a certain class of Arab and native.

It is possible that a few of the customs may be traced to ancient visitors from India, but these are sufficiently indicated throughout the book.

As regards the Persians—the Shirazis as they are called locally—I have indicated fully the customs which the natives say are derived from them. The most marked Persian institution is the *Naorozi*, or Siku ya mwaka, the Persian New Year's Day. This is of old Persian or Parsee origin. Those who wish to compare the customs of the Shirazis of Zanzibar and Pemba with those of the modern Shirazis of Persia should consult *The Glory of the Shia World*.

CHAPTER XVI

THE KHAWARIJ

THE fundamental principle of the Shiites is that the Caliphate could only be hereditary from Mohammed, and they quarrelled with Ali because he did not insist on his divine right to succeed, but wished to submit his claim and that of Muawiyah to arbitration. Now the Khawarij came into being on the same occasion, but they quarrelled with him not because he did not insist on his divine right, but because he did not insist on his right as elected Caliph. On the way from the field of Siffin, 12,000 of his followers broke away on these grounds and elected a Caliph of their own. Some of them were won back and others deserted, but about 4,000 gathered at Nahrawan to die for their ideas of what was right.

The battle took place in 658, and the Khawarij were utterly defeated by Ali's superior force. Their spirit, however, could not thus be crushed. Nine of them are said to have escaped, of whom two fled to Kerman, two to Sejistan, two into Mesopotamia, one to Tell Mauran and two to Oman, and in these places they propagated their creed. Later three Kharijites assassinated Ali at the door of a mosque in Kufa.

The Kharijite principles are those of the old Islam of equality and fraternity, which, however, except where these principles have taken root, have never worked. Their two doctrines are that, (1) any free Arab (or later any Moslem) is eligible for election as Caliph if just and pious and with other requisite qualifications, and that failing such a one no Caliph is absolutely necessary, and (2) that an evil Caliph may be deposed and put to death.

The Khawarij are the origin from which the

Ibathis have sprung. They are therefore of interest in the history of Zanzibar, and have a more local interest, as their commentaries are said to have been printed here, though they are difficult to procure. Burton, describing the Khawarij, who are now mostly confined to Morocco, Muscat and Zanzibar (the two latter being the strongholds of the Ibathis), says that the principal Khawarij sects have been reduced to five, of which the first four are, at the present time, common only in books.

The *Encyclopædia Britannica* says that representatives of the sect of the Assassins, founded by a Persian fanatic in the early part of the eleventh century, are found in Zanzibar, but if so I have never heard of them.

They were called Hashishin, a name derived from the drug *Hashish* to which they were addicted. In their early days they were noted for their treacherous use of the dagger, but since the thirteenth century they have become inoffensive.

THE IBATHIS AND THEIR IMAMATE

The word Ibathi, or Ibadhiyah, is derived from the name of Abdulla bin Ibadh (or Abdulla bin Yahya bin Ibadh) et-Temimy and Palgrave's derivation (he calls them Biadeeyah), El-Mubayyidhun, or white boys, is erroneous. It is possible that the name of Abdulla's father is derived from bâdha ("to surpass in whiteness"), though more probably it is from abadha ("to tie or strengthen the legs of a camel") but the meaning of the word has no significance, for the name of the sect is certainly derived from the name of its founder.

Abdulla bin Ibadh lived during the reign of the Caliph Marwan, 744-749, but unfortunately little more is known of him, except that he belonged to the Sarih subdivision of the Benu-Mukais, who were derived from Temim bin Murr, of the race of Adnan and Maadd, descendants of Ishmael, from whom

Mohammed was descended, and therefore of another branch to the royal house of Zanzibar who are descended from Joktan. Barak bin Abdulla, one of the Kharijite murderers of Ali, was also of the Temimy tribe.

We have seen that two of the Khawarij fled to Oman after Nahrawan, and it is just possible that Adbulla knew them or derived his ideas from them indirectly. He is said, shortly after the reign of Marwan, to have been conquered and put to death.

Badger thus sums up their doctrines: (1) The elective principle of the Imamate. (2) They are said to hold predestination in such a sense as to make God the author of good and evil. (3) The commission of a great sin places a man beyond the pale of salvation.

An Arab gentleman, learned in the Sheria, has thus summed up for me the principal differences between the Sunnis and the Ibathis.

The Sunnis say they will see God face to face at the end of the world, but this the Ibathis deny.

The Sunnis say that if God sends a man to hell he will get out later on. The Ibathis deny and say it will be either hell or heaven for ever.

The Sunnis say that a man's deeds will be weighed like silver and gold in scales, but the Ibathis say they will be shown what deeds they have done, and on this they will be judged.

Sunnis say that there is a narrow road laid straight through hell which a good man will pass over, but a bad man will fall off into the fire. The Ibathis deny the existence of a road, and that God will choose out Himself those who have done good or evil.

Sunnis say that you should marry a woman with whom you have committed adultery or fornication, but the Ibathis say this is wrong, as such a course would be a reward of evil.

The Sunnis say that you may marry your illegitimate child, but the Ibathis say this is very wrong, as whether married or not to its parent, it is just as much your blood child.

He ends by saying: "If we look hard we see that the Ibathis follow the truth because most of them are Arabs and know the word of El Quran, they like truth and do not treat religion frivolously, and they do not change the words of their religion from the days of the Prophet till now. The Sunnis are people who have mixed much with savages. They mix religion with noisy play and make great show of it. It is not necessary; God can hear prayer even if whispered."

Palgrave and Burton confuse the Ibathi with the Karamitah, who were a very ungodly crowd, from any point of view, and while the latter is not at all flattering to them and has no opinion of them, the former is simply libellous. Burton says "the faith of the Bayazi is narrow and exclusive, a monopoly of righteousness, a moral study of the infinitely little." That is not a fair statement, but Palgrave says "they very rarely assemble for any stated form of worship; their prayers are muttered in a low and inaudible voice, accompanied by inflexion and prostration different from those employed in Mohammedan devotion. Many on this occasion turn to the north, others in other directions perfectly regardless of Kiblah or Caabah." "I should add that wine is freely and avowedly drunk, especially towards the interior." "A semblance of Mohammedan ways and speaking is often assumed, and the Biadeeyah, a compound of Sabæans, Batineeyah and Carmathians, inheritors of Mokannaa and Aboo Tahir, will at times pass themselves off on strangers as tolerably orthodox Mohammedans. But closer acquaintance has marked them out for infidels. . . ." "As regards tobacco, no people perhaps in the world make a more frantic consumption of that article than do the good people of Oman." "It would be very hard to find a single Biadee in . . . any . . . mosque." "In simplicity of dress and aversion to ornamental display, I fear that Omanees have no better claim to Niebuhr's commendation than the inhabitants of Vienna or in Paris." "Severity on what regards maiden virtue or marriage vows is not a distinctive feature of Oman." Burton and Palgrave's observations on the Ibathis are singularly incorrect. Burton describes them as fiercely intolerant, than which I cannot conceive a more incorrect description.

If one looks for a parallel sect in Christianity, I should consider the Baptists or other Puritans to be nearest them, though my experience of both, having lived for a year in a country of Baptists and Methodists, and for eight in a country of Ibathis, would lead me to choose the Ibathis as being the most tolerant people in the matter of religion I have known. In almost any town in Zanzibar there are Sunnis, Ibathis, Ithnasheries, Bohoras, Memons, Khojas, Ismaili Khojas, Banyans, Quakers, Church of England, Roman Catholics and Parsees. This may not be remarkable in these days when religious tolerance is insisted on, but it has been the case for years before such a state was reached. Ibathis consider others mistaken, as who does not, but they mix freely with all, and eat with even an infidel like myself. They acknowledge that the one God other people worship is the same as theirs, though the method of worship is irregular. Such a thing as intolerance I cannot conceive in connection with them.

As Palgrave says (the only piece of truth in the quotations I have made), they do not make prostrations like other sects, for they believe that the postures adopted are unnecessary; all that is necessary is a proper reverence and attention at prayer. They do not decorate their mosques, as they think it detracts attention from worship. They are thoroughly democratic, and the highest may mix with the lowest. In many ways they are much more liberal in their interpretation of Scripture than other Mohammedans, though in some points rather narrow-minded. For instance, they consider that the Bohoras' Ramathan is of no avail, as they start two days earlier and finish two days earlier.

To show that general tolerance is part of their religious creed, it may be stated that the *Talkein Sibian*, or book of how an Ibathi should comport himself, directs that even if your neighbour is of another religion, you must rejoice with him on his occasion for rejoicing and sorrow when he sorrows, and let nothing cause him annoyance.

In their charities Ibathis are often promiscuous, and will bestow alms or show kindness to those of any creed. I know a very high caste Arab, who has taken a sick Parsee to his house to give him a change of air and set him up. They believe greatly in the efficacy of sincere prayer, be it Christian or Moslem.

These instances of the tolerance and goodness of the Ibathis might be continued indefinitely.

Let us consider for a moment the Imamate.

The Omanis disallowed the claims of the Baghdad Caliphate, and on the principles set out above at the beginning, set up an Imam of their own endowed with civil and religious duties.

From the time of Julanda Masud, the first Imam, to that of Seif bin Sultan, these elective principles were firmly adhered to, but in the case of the latter, the first suggestion of hereditary right appeared. And later, when Ahmed bin Said, the founder of the Albusaid dynasty, was elected to the high office, it ceased to be a truly elective office, and his children succeeded, but were confirmed by election in their appointments. The great Seyyid Said never laid claim to the title, which has dropped out of usage among the rulers of what is now termed the Sultanate of Muscat, though a spiritual Imam of the tribes in the interior of Oman has lately been elected.

Ordinarily the word Imam, which means an example, is applied in five different senses. Firstly, to Mohammed and the Caliphate; secondly, to the heads of the four orthodox Sunni sects; thirdly, to the leader of prayer in a mosque; fourthly, to indicate the book or scripture or record of people; and fifthly, to designate a teacher of religion.

The Ibathis are confined to Oman and Zanzibar, and the Kitab el Milal wa'r Nihal (quoted by Badger) divides them into four sub-sects:

(1) The Hafsiyyah, derived from Abu Hafs bin el Mukdam, who say that between faith and polytheism is a middle course, which is the knowledge of God.

(2) The Yezidiyyah derived from Yezid bin Anisah, who say that God will send a prophet from a foreign country with a book, written in heaven, which will descend upon him at a single time, and he will discard the law of Mohammed and incline to that of the Sabæans.

(3) The Harithiyyah, derived from El Hareth, El Ibadhy, who are at variance with the original Ibadhiyah on predestination, and

(4) Those who affirm that should a man do what is commanded of him and not intend it to the honour of God, yet that is true obedience.

Ibathiism seems to have been slightly tinged with Wahabiism, especially in Muscat, probably because being contagious to the country where Wahabiism is practised, and also probably because to some extent the aims of their founders were similar, namely, to restore Islam to its pristine purity.

CHAPTER XVII

THE ARABS OF ZANZIBAR

THE principal Arabs in Zanzibar are those who have emigrated from, or descended from parents who emigrated from, Muscat. In faith these are nearly all of the Ibathi persuasion, though there are a few Omanis who are Sunnis. The following are the principal tribes represented in the Sultanate: el-Amawi, el-Alawi, el-Afifi, el-Adwani, el-Abdisalam, el-Amri, el-Busaidi, el-Buhri, el-Bauli, el-Bahri, el-Bimani, el-Barwani, el-Bakri, el-Darmki, el-Dorii, el-Emeri, el-Felani, el-Farsi, el-Farii, el-Furkani, el-Falahi, el-Ghassani, el-Ghazali, el-Ghattami, el-Gethi, el-Hinawi, el-Hatmi, el-Hadidi, el-Harthi, el-Hathmani, el-Habsi, el-Hasmi, el-Hbeshi, el-Hamandi, el-Ismaili, el-Jabri, el-Jahhaji, el-Jasri, el-Jahadhmi, el-Jafri, el-Jadidi, el-Jebri, el-Kindi, el-Kassabi, el-Karni, el-Kweti, el-Kharusi, el-Khalasi, el-Khanjri, el-Karrasi, el-Khaifi, el-Kasbi, el-Kumri, el-Khzeri, el-Khalili, el-Kitani, el-Kamshi, el-Khasibi, el-Kanani, el-Keshi, el-Kyumi, el-Ksemi, el-Kasmi, el-Lamki, el-Lahsani, el-Marijebi, el-Mandhiri, el-Mugheri, el-Maskiri, el-Mauli, el-Mahruki, el-Mamiri, el-Msharifi, el-Malki, el-Mharmi, el-Mashuri, el-Mayyahi, el-Marhubi, el-Mazruhi, el-Nahbi, el-Nakhli, el-Nabhani, el-Nofli, el-Nomani, el-Nabhi, el-Nazawi, el-Ofi, el-Rwehi, el-Riyama, el-Rajhi, el-Rashdi, el-Risi, el-Rahbi, el-Rumhi, el-Rkeshi, el-Rastaki, el-Rassadi, el-Ramdhani, el-Sumri, el-Sibuti, el-Sinawi, el-Sarhani, el-Shkeli, el-Shuhhi, el-Siyabi, el-Salami, el-Shwedi, el-Shkeri, el-Sudi, el-Siidi, el-Shhebi, el-Sreri, el-Snesri, el-Sukri, el-Sleimi, el-Subhi, el-Shebani, el-Suleimani, el-Talii, el-Tiwani, el-Wardi, el-Wihibi, el-Yorobi, el-Yahyai, el-Yahamdi.

In Zanzibar Island no tribe appears to have collectively exercised paramount authority except the el-Busaidi, though the el-Harth Arabs, who are said to have migrated to Zanzibar in A.D. 924, were, prior to the coming of the Yorobis and, subsequently, the Albusides, of principal influence. Even at the present they are not on good terms with the Azdite section of the Arab community.

In Pemba the Ismaili tribe in the north and the Mauli in the south seem to have been the ruling classes, though, prior to their rise to power, the Mazrui dominated Pemba as they did Mombasa. These Omani Arabs are the principal descendants of the el-Azd, and are therefore of Kahtanic origin. Kahtan, or Joktan (as he is called in the Bible), had a son called Yorobi, whose great-grandson was Himyar, and these Arabs can therefore trace their descent through Abir, the father of Kahtan, and great-grandson of Shem, to Adam.

They are, of course, true Zanzibaris, and all subjects of His Highness the Sultan, who is their hereditary and titular ruler.

The other most numerous Arabs of Zanzibar are those of the Hadhramaut, commonly known as Shihiris, from the town of Sheher, a southern seaport in the Hadhramaut. Hadhramaut (Hezarmarveth) was the eldest of the sons of Kahtan, Yorobi being the second. Apart from these Arabs of Kahtanic origin, there are also a number entitled to be designated Sherif, who are descended from the prophet Mohammed, through his daughter Fatima, who married Ali bin Abi Talib.

BIRTH AND INFANCY

In Zanzibar the Arabs have adopted, to a very large extent, the customs of the natives at the time of the birth of a child, and the customs described later in the case of the native babies are almost all observed.

There are, however, some customs that are the product of Arabia, and these have been brought and maintained by the Arabs; indeed, those that have a religious significance are often adopted by the natives.

At the time of birth the Arab mother is placed in a prone position on the bed, and the other women of the household are present to assist in the delivery of the child. In practice, in Zanzibar the native Mkunga, or midwife, is often called in. Shihiri women, however, very often have no assistance, and bear their children alone. When the child is born and after the cord has ceased to pulsate, it is tied (originally with camels' hair, but now with anything that is to hand, and can be used for the purpose), and cut in a peculiar way. The cord and placenta are afterwards buried, not burnt, and in East Africa usually treated as the natives treat them. After delivery the mother's stomach is massaged, and a red ointment called Warsi rubbed all over the body. This ointment is often used also to protect the body from the hot wind during the monsoon, which causes the skin to crack and get sore. A medicine is also given internally. The mother is ceremonially unclean during the puerperium for as long as the lochia continues.

As regards the child there are three important days —the day of its birth, the seventh day and the fortieth day—and to each of these days customs appertain.

On the day of birth the parent, or an Arab renowned for piety, repeats the Azan in the child's ear. The right ear is held with the hand and the Azan, the call to prayer, whispered into it. The left ear is then held and the Ikama, or introduction to prayers, whispered into it. Something sweet, e.g., dates, is then rubbed on to the gums with a finger. Both of these ceremonies are symbolical. The first is intended to ensure that matters of religion shall always have first call to the child, and the second that its food may always be sweet and toothsome.

On the seventh day the child is taken from its

mother's room, which it must not leave until that time, and shown to the inmates of the house, each of whom deposits a small money present with it. After the seventh day a feast called Akike must be made, even if it is postponed for some years. Two goats are slaughtered if the child is a boy, and one if it is a girl. This feast must be made in every case of a child born alive, even if it dies before puberty. It is not made for a still-born child. Circumcision should take place on the seventh day, but the period is often very much lengthened. However, the nearer the seventh day it takes place the better. *Sadaka*, or alms, are given on this occasion.

In the case of girls, clitoridectomy is sometimes performed on the seventh day, or afterwards, and *sadaka* may be given, but privately.

After the seventh day the child's eyelashes are blackened with Wanja wa manga (antimony). This is supposed to have the effect of protecting the eyes from ophthalmia neonatorum, and of making them bright and lustrous. The common Wanja, or soot, is smeared on the face to keep the evil eye off. A cowrie shell is fastened round the neck on a string to keep evil away, and *hirizi*, or charms, are used for the same purpose. These *hirizi* consist of a piece of palm inscribed with the *Ayat el Kursee*, and either sewn up in a piece of cloth or encased in a silver box.

On the fortieth day the head of the child is shaved, and the hair put in a pair of scales and weighed against gold or silver. The weight of the hair in gold or silver is given to the poor.

No particular customs appear to appertain to the age of puberty; girls are instructed as to how to fasten the Khirika, or Idaba (diaper), by their parents.

Boys and girls should *hitima*, or know how to read the whole Koran by the age of ten, but the rule is not strictly observed in the case of girls.

COURTSHIP AND MARRIAGE

The first stage in the acquisition of a wife by the young Arab is to send his relations to the parents of the girl he wishes to marry. Only in rare instances will it have been possible for him to have seen his prospective bride in the flesh, but he will have to make up his mind, or will have it made up for him by his father, on the reports of the lady members of the household, as to her beauty and accomplishments. In all probability he will not be the only suitor, but the girl's parents will select the one they deem most suitable from those who present themselves. In any case an answer to this proposal (Khutbeh) is not received at once, and further inquiries have to be made.

When a man makes a proposal to the parents of a girl for her hand in marriage, the parents inquire whether he is a suitable Kufu for the bride. Kufu means the social position of the man. Thus a girl of the Koreish may not marry with any other tribe, and in Zanzibar a woman of the Albusaid may not either. An Arab woman may not marry with a man of alien race.

In the event of his being the successful candidate, the next question is the amount of *Mahr* (dowry) to be paid. This is fixed according to the customs of that family, and half of the sum agreed on has to be paid at once. A day must then be chosen for the religious ceremony. This will be chosen by a *Mwalim* after consulting the stars. After the selection of a day, verbal invitations are issued to the friends and relations, and on the day in question, the young man, with his supporters and friends, and the father or guardian of the bride with him, repair to the mosque, or the house, chosen for the ceremony. The Mwalim, who has got permission from the bride and her guardian, to the marriage, sits down facing the bridegroom and his followers, and asks him: "Will you marry so-and-so as your wife and for what you have agreed between you, and for the dowry of so many rupees of which you have paid so much and of which there is so much due by you?" On the receipt of an affirmative reply, the Mwalim reads the *El-Fathak*, and then all read the *Surat el Hamdu*, and the Mwalim then says: "Praise be to God and to His prophet Mohammed and his people. All ye people witness that I marry so-and-so, son of so-and-so of such and such a tribe, and so-and-so, daughter of so-and-so, according to the word of God in His Book, and the precepts of the prophet Mohammed, that they live together for their good and great blessing, and may everything be well between them, and may they enjoy every good thing that God has prepared for them, and we pray that evil may be removed from them, and that the husband may give his wife everything that is fit, and her dowry, so much on the first occasion and so much on the second, and that everything may be made lawful, according to her assent and that of her guardian so-and-so, son of so-and-so."

This sentence is called Akadin ni kiar, the knot of marriage, the Mwalim then says, "*Kada kabilta,*" and the bridegroom replies, "*Kada kabilth.*" "You agree to so-and-so as your wife?" "For such and such a Mahr?" "For all I have said in the Khutbeh?" *El-Fathak* may again be read. After this, everyone shakes hands, and the bridegroom's people must provide *halwa*; halwa, in the ordinary way, means the sweetmeat of that name, but it is used here in a generic way to indicate not only those sweetmeats, but also coffee and even cooked rice and meat.

The next stage is to find a suitable day for the ceremony of "entering the house"; this again must be discovered from the soothsayers. No marriage can, however, take place in the month of Safar. At the hour and on the date named, the bridegroom goes to the bride's house or she may be brought to his. If, however, the girl's family are strangers, the bridegroom must go to her house, though he can take her away after one day. He will go, accompanied by his friends, dressed in his best clothes and perfumed, with crowds of people following behind, but only a few of his companions will enter the house with him. The companions then have their feet washed and oiled by the women; the bridegroom gives them presents of money and they go out.

Within the house are women singing; the bridegroom removes his heavy clothing and proceeds to the room of the bride, when both he and his wife have their feet washed by the women, for which he pays them. The man then stands up and takes the bride's head in his hands, and either he or someone else reads the *Ayat al Kursee*; at the end of which the bridegroom says: " I acknowledge this woman as my wife. God keep me and her together in happiness." The bridegroom may then go outside and bid farewell to his friends, for whom food is then prepared, and there is much merriment. He then returns to his wife and does not go out for at least three days, though seven is usual.

In Zanzibar the washing and rubbing of the body of both parties takes place before they get into the bride's room, and after a visit there the bridegroom has his body rubbed again.

When left alone with his bride he gives her money to speak to him, and then she says, " *Sabalkheri, Bwana* " (Good day, Master), and then he proceeds to remove her clothes.

Among the lower class of Arabs the women listen outside the door for the girl's cries, and raise shouts of rejoicing if they hear them; and should she prove recalcitrant they will enter and hold her down. A piece of white cloth is put under the pillow with which to remove the blood, and this is afterwards shown to everyone.

During the seven days of the honeymoon, the relations of the wife provide food for the bridegroom. In Muscat the washing described does not take place, nor do the friends enter into the house, and the women are not allowed to make the demonstration referred to outside the door. The custom of seeking for traces of virginity is also purely African.

DEATH AND BURIAL

When a man is about to die, he is laid north and south and the *Yasin* is read over him. After death the body is laid out, with arms to sides, and washed with a cloth covering the hand of the washer, and is then covered from head to foot with a clean cloth; it is forbidden to look deliberately on the nakedness of a dead man. Any clothes that will do for a man to pray in, will do for him to be buried in. White is generally used.

Three, five or seven cloths may be used. The usual number is three, but two, four or six may not be used. If three are used, two wide ones are wound round the body and a small narrow one round the head. Cotton-wool mixed with various spices, kiafor and saffron, is placed in all the apertures of the body in the following order: mouth, right nostril, left nostril, right eye, left eye, right ear, left ear, and then all over the whole face, rectum, beneath the testicles, right armpit, left armpit, between the fingers of the right hand, between the fingers of the left hand. To perform the operation as much of the cloth as is necessary may be removed at a time. The corpse is then put on the bier and covered all over, sandalwood is burnt below and elsewhere in the room, and the shroud also must be scented with the smoke of sandalwood before it is used. Incense is then passed three times below and above the bier. If it is desired, the shroud may be made into clothes, a *kanzu* (khamis) and trousers which must come up to the breast, but the clothes must cover the corpse from head to foot. If cloths are used, the first is wrapped from the head working to the feet, and the second from the feet upwards. The ends must then be fastened top and bottom and waist, but in the latter case the knot must be on the left side.

The bier is then carried head first to the mosque, or other place of prayer, and thence to the grave. At the graveside the body is taken out of the bier head first and placed in the inner cavity of the grave (for description of which see Death and Burial Customs of natives), and laid on its right side, head to the east, face to north and feet to west. The knots are then unfastened and the shroud loosened, the board or flat stones are then laid over the cavity so as to cover the corpse completely. During this operation the grave is covered with the bier-cloths, so that no one can see save the three or five men who bury the dead. When these men have laid the board over the cavity they cover it up and clay up the sides, the cloths are taken off the grave and it is then filled up with earth. Those who have filled in the grave have to wash afterwards.

It is ordered as a religious command to follow the bier of the dead and commended as a good deed. Afterwards everyone says, "*La illahi ila allahum: al hayu allathi laiya mutu.*" "There is no God but God, He is eternal and does not die."

It is said that when covered in the grave, the dead temporarily recover their strength and sit up and hear the Mwalim; if he has been bad through life the dead man sees hell near by, but if he has been good he sees both heaven and hell from afar off and will want to go to heaven, but will realize the time is not yet, and will lie down and go to sleep.

The Arabs believe that the body of a good and pious man never rots in his grave.

The *Talkein Sibian*, an Ibathi book of religious observances, gives the following directions for the washing of the dead. He who performs this operation must wash his own hands first and then those of the dead; the right hand first and then the left. If a person has died of an infectious disease, the body need only be washed from the navel to the foot; the washer must not hold the hands of the dead nor catch hold of the genitals except with a cloth.

Ablutions may then be performed for the dead as for prayer (this is voluntary, but commendable). The body should be then washed with the leaves of the sidr if obtainable, but this is not compulsory. The third washing now takes place in the following order: the right side of the head, left side of the head; from the right shoulder to the foot, and from the left shoulder to the foot; the front of the body, then the back. (In Zanzibar the corpse is wetted at each washing until burial, in Muscat once only.)

If no water is obtainable, sand should be used; lay the body in the sand and do as in the Tayammum, or sand ablution. Take the right hand and rub it in the sand, then the left also, then both hands and rub together.

CHAPTER XVIII

SOCIAL ORGANIZATION

EACH clan of Arabs in Zanzibar and Pemba has its head, or tribal sheikh, who is a senior member of the clan and is generally designated the Sheikh el Kharusi, the Sheikh el Mauli, etc. The word sheikh, in the ordinary way, indicates someone of importance corresponding roughly to something between the English esquire and knight, but it is very loosely applied in these days. To these tribal sheikhs are referred all matters that affect the social life and standing of the clan, as well as disputes between the various members of the family. The clan is *the* important thing among the Arabs of Zanzibar.

OCCUPATION AND RELAXATION

The Arab of Zanzibar is *par excellence* a landed proprietor, and usually has his money in clove and coco-nut plantations. These days Arabs go in for many different kinds of life, and are to be found in Government offices and commerce. The Arab, however, is a bad business man, and has shown himself unable to adapt himself to the new conditions of life engendered by the abolition of slavery; as a consequence he is very largely in debt.

The Arab is looked to by the native as his natural master, and the native accepts his control very readily, each understanding the other perfectly. It must be remembered that slavery was as much a religious as a civil institution, and the life of the Arab is so much bound up in religion that he finds it difficult to dissociate himself from slavery. There are two traces of slavery still existing in Zanzibar in a quasi-legal sense. One is as regards guardianship of females. The Arab is the legal guardian of his female slaves, and the freed slave woman still accepts the guardianship of her late master. It is possible also that the legal guardian of the daughter is also the late master of the mother. The other trace of slavery is as regards concubinage. The Arab could only legally take his concubine from his female slaves; he now takes her, with her own consent of course, from among those women who would have been his female slaves, and the children are considered by the Arabs legitimate, though I am not aware what view a court of law would take if the question were ever raised. Apart from these two traces there are many natives living actually in the state of slavery on their master's plantations, working for their masters without pay, and regarding themselves as slaves and having no desire for freedom.

In his leisure hours the Arab walks abroad, or visits his friends, where he drinks coffee, eats halwa, and discusses current politics or enjoys a quiet game of cards (*Wahedusitin*).

The Arab is as fond as the native of story-telling. Classical favourites are, of course, the stories in the *Arabian Nights*, and the moral teaching of Æsop is also much quoted. There are hosts of modern stories told as well. The only performance or dance of Arabs is the sword dance, *Razha*. In this there is an orchestra of drums, while the performers, armed with swords and jambiyas and small shields of rhinoceros hide, indulge in mimic contests, leaping about and wielding their swords in a truly marvellous way. In a dagger contest, when a man is thrown, his foe makes as though to gorge out his eyes with the point of his jambiya. It is unusual, however, to see this dance performed except by those Arabs known as *Manga*. In Swahili the word *manga* is used to denote the Arab born in Muscat, who has migrated to Zanzibar. *Mwarabu* means the Arab who has been born in Zanzibar. After a short time one can easily distinguish one from the other; the Arab of Zanzibar has a benign, kindly look in his eyes and moves with deliberation, whereas his brother, born and bred in the mountain fastnesses of Oman, has bright, black, piercing eyes, sharp features and a rapid gait, born of the necessity of ever being wakeful for a foe. Many of them are kind and friendly, and enjoy a childish prank. It is always said that it is unsafe to wake up a Manga Arab suddenly, as he will start up, dagger in hand, and strike out at the supposed foe.

The Arab of Zanzibar much appreciates the comforts of modern Western civilization, sits on chairs and eats off tables, very often with knife and fork. In addition to this, he is fond of the music that has been introduced from Egypt; players on the wood and other instruments are eagerly listened to, while they sing their haunting songs of love and fair women.

In conversation the Arabs in Zanzibar speak Swahili, but in writing always use Arabic.

POLITENESS AND HOSPITALITY

It is almost superfluous to refer to the politeness and hospitality of the Arabs, for both are proverbial; courteous, dignified, benign and friendly, the Arab is Nature's true gentleman, and his notions of chivalry and friendly bearing have been inherited from ancestors whom he can trace back to Adam.

Nothing, perhaps, is more important to the Arab than good manners and *heshima*, and he is as particular of his own as he is not to upset the susceptibilities of others. *Heshima* is a very comprehensive and expressive word which means not only respect, but the maintenance of that position to which respect is due. To the Arab it is the most important thing in life, a thing to be jealously guarded and augmented, and it is a term also that includes, besides respect, something of the meaning of honour.

I shall have further to say on the politeness and hospitality of the Arab when I speak of the same thing among the natives, for it is impossible entirely to dissociate the two. However, I give below a translation of the injunctions contained in the *Talkein Sibian* as regards duty towards one's neighbours and towards one's guests, precepts which might well be adopted by other civilizations.

To a European it is difficult to comprehend the open-handed hospitality shown by the Arabs; here in Europe one calls only on one's friends and partakes of their food only when invited, and the doors are always shut. In the East, the door stands hospitably open; one may walk into any house and, if one receives a reply to the call of *Hodi*, will be certain to be invited in to partake, at any rate, of coffee or other refreshment, and to join in a meal if the hour is near. To an Arab feast given on the occasion of a funeral or marriage, hundreds of guests are invited. Coming through one's host's plantations towards his house, one meets crowds of fellow-guests coming and going, and nearer to the house are hundreds of natives waiting to be invited to finish up the remnants. Near the *wanja*, or open space in front of the house, are the cooks still serving up rice in huge piles on big dishes, and meat and curried gravy into large bowls.

One dish of rice and one bowl of meat is then put on a big tray and hurried away by waiting servants, on their heads. The cooking-pots are almost Brobdingnagian, copper lined with tin; each is about three feet across the top, widening out to almost four at the bottom, and they are perhaps two feet six inches or three feet in depth. There will be perhaps about four or five of these standing on iron tripods under which a large fire burns. Each is covered by a large tinned copper tray on which fire is also heaped.

The perspiring cooks have their clothes turned up and in their hands wield enormous spoons quite six feet long, with which they continually push off the lids and inspect the contents, or pile further food on to empty dishes. Nearby, on the roots of a spreading mango tree, lie the pathetic remains of the ox that forms the central feature of the feast—a head with sightless eyes and protruding tongue, and a pile of loose and empty skin.

It is a picturesque sight that confronts us as we turn round, and one which could not be met with elsewhere. The four o'clock sun shines through the green foliage of the mango, and on to the cloves and sweet-smelling, bloom-laden orange trees that surround the space of hard red earth in front of the house. It shines, too, on the yellow mud walls and low, brown, thatched roof of the house, and gives a pleasant, mellow air to the whole scene. On the long and broad verandah of the house, and almost everywhere where there is shade, groups of Arabs sit in circles, round trays, some beginning, some completing, and others in the middle of their repast. Variety and colour are lent to the scene by the continual movement, by the white of the *Kanzus* and headdress of the Arabs, with their bronzed, black-bearded faces, while among them pass to and fro servants bearing the food and wearing torn and tattered clothes.

But we must go and pay our respects to our host. Here he comes, from round a corner where he has been attending to the wants of others, and hospitably welcomes us with outstretched hands. Then he finds a vacant place for us on his verandah, or under a tree, and we squat down with crossed legs in a circle on a mat, while, as if by magic, a servant appears with one of those trays we saw being prepared just now. This he sets down in the midst of us, while another comes with a brass ewer, from which he pours clean water over the right hand of each of us in turn. Our host now bustles off to welcome other guests, and we, with a *Bismillah!*, take up in turn the bowl of meat and gravy, and extracting with our fingers the bits that take our fancy most, place them on the rice before us and pour some gravy over it; thereupon we plunge our hands into the hot rice. If it is too hot, a servant will obligingly fan it, and mixing the gravy and rice into balls, we transfer it as neatly as possible from the dish to our mouths. And very good it is too. That it is good is eloquently testified to by the absence of conversation at our own tray, and at that of the others round us, though there is a continual clatter of trays and dishes. When eating it is good manners not to watch others too closely, not to make an exhibition of the food as one transfers it from dish to mouth, and not to eat noisily. One eats, moreover, in the method of those who eat to live, for one does not linger over food, which at the end of the meal is washed down with copious draughts of clean, cold water.

As each diner finishes he gets up and turns about, while the ever waiting servant pours water over his outstretched hands and gives him a piece of soap. He washes his hands thoroughly, and then in a cup formed by them, sucks the water into his mouth and washes that out too. "*Al Hamdu 'l illah*," each exclaims with feeling, and makes a sound in the throat which is not much admired in Western Society. A servant then brings black sugarless coffee, and waits to pour out the three half-cups which politeness allows. The little handleless cup is then returned, with a shake of the hand to indicate no more is required. Among Oman Arabs the coffee-cup may be only half filled. The Shihiris fill it right up. It is an insult to offer an Omani a full cup.

Invitations for a party like this may be issued for noon. Guests start coming about the seventh hour (1 p.m.), and are going and coming till late at night. A couple of oxen and 300 pishis of rice (about 1,800 lb.) are a usual provision of food for such a feast.

It is an interesting experience to spend a week-end with an Arab landed proprietor on his country estate, and no experience can be more pleasant. Some of the happiest week-ends I have known were spent in this way. I used to mount my donkey and ride through the shambas of cloves and coco-nuts to Kinyasini, about seventeen miles north-east of Zanzibar. Nowadays a good motor road takes one the whole way there, but it was not so when I first stayed there. Turning off the main path, a well-kept clove avenue led to the house, and at the sound of the donkey's hoofs my host used to come out to meet me on the *sikafu* (cement floor used for drying cloves) in front of the house. The house was low and long, and in front there was a cool, wide *baraza* (verandah). I was seldom the only guest staying, and neighbouring Arabs used to drop in for coffee, for my friend kept very open house, and continually asked men of all creeds and colours to enjoy his hospitality. I had to be prepared for enormous meals, half Arab, half European, to which I was expected to do full justice. I give the menu of the lunch I partook of one Saturday when staying for a week-end. It consisted of seventeen courses, of each of which courtesy demanded that I should partake. It was as follows—I give it as my host's son wrote (in English characters learnt at school):

1. Supu	1. Soup
2. Samaki	2. Fish
3. Kababu	3. Chicken hash
4. Kuku wa Kukaanga	4. Braised chicken
5. Kababu ya nyama	5. Meat hash
6. Sambusa	6. Small meat cakes
7. Nyama ya Kukaanga	7. Braised meat
8. Nyama ya kuchoma	8. Roast meat (on spits)
9. Mkati ya kusukuma	9. }
10. Mkati wa lkhokho	10. } Different kinds of cakes
11. Ellkemati	11. } and breads
12. Villosa	12. }
13. Wali	13. Curry and rice
14. Rosi	14. Cooked fruit
15. Pudin [*sic*]	15. Caramel pudding
16. Farne	16. A kind of porridge made of ground rice
and friut [*sic*]	Fruit

Dinner was twenty-six courses, and breakfast was —porridge, four eggs, a whole chicken, meat pies, sweet cakes, tea and coffee. (I may say that it was

(*Upper*) NYANGE DANCE AT MAKUNDUCHI
(*Lower*) WAHADIMU

(*Upper*) MIHRAB OF MOSQUE AT CHAMBANI (SHIRAZIAN).

(*Lower*) INTERIOR OF OLD MOSQUE AT KICHOBOCHWE.

(*Upper*) AN MPEMBA GIRL

(*Lower*) MIHRAB OF MOSQUE AT MKUMBUU (EARLY SHIRAZIAN)

ZANZIBAR DOOR DESIGNS

(*Upper*) FISH WITHOUT SCALES–DOUBLE TAILED–GRENADE SHAPED OBJECT–BECOMES FLOWER VASE. (*Lower*) FISH WITH TAIL–NEXT STAGE, DOUBLE TAILED–THIRD STAGE, FISH–SHAPE LOST–FISH BECOMES PINEAPPLE

(*Upper*) THE WA-PEMBA MAKING THEIR CURIOUS CRY (KIUPILO).

(*Lower*) AN ANIMAL CALLED KURURU, MADE OF

(*Upper*) GOGODUA, OR THE STILT WALKER

(*Lower*) A PEMBA BULL FIGHT

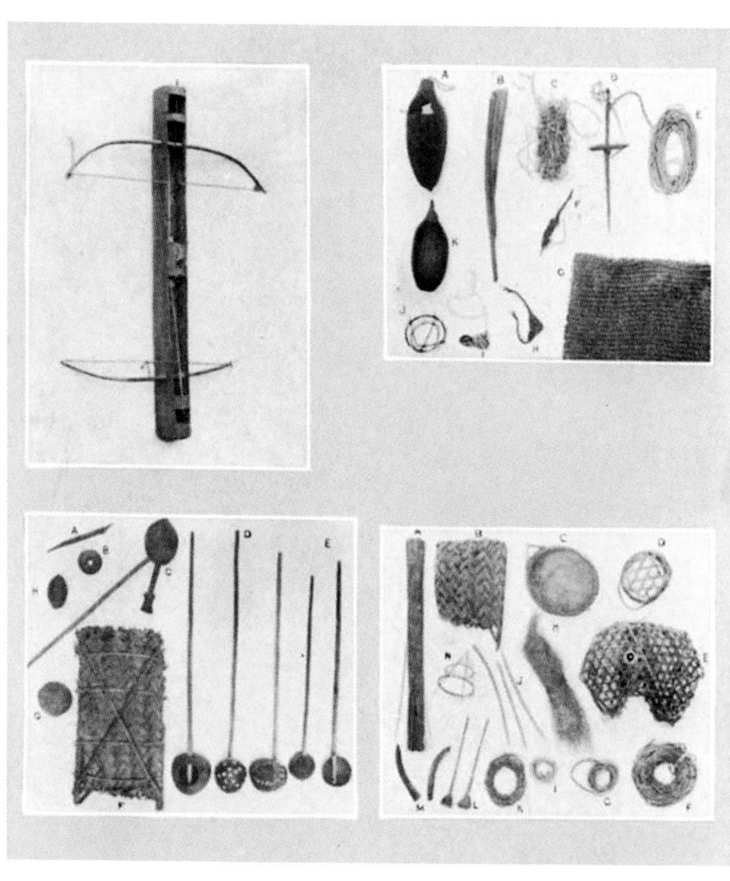

(*Upper left*) RAT TRAP MADE BY SHINEN BIN SAID. (*Upper Right*) a.– CALABASH, USED FOR DRAWING WATER FROM WELL (NDO). b.– NATIVE UMBRELLA. c, d and e.– RAPHIA BEFORE, DURING AND AFTER MANUFACTURE INTO CORD. f.– FISHING LINE AND HOOKS. g.– COIR MATTING. h.–SLING. i.– BIRD TRAP. j.– BIRD TRAP, TOP VIEW. k.– BALER, MADE FROM CALABASH (UPO)

(*Lower Left*) a.–WOOD. b.–ZOMARI MOUTHPIECE. c.–BHANG PIPE d.–UKATA (NOTE INLAID WORK) e.–UPAWA. f.–MODEL OF DOOR. G.– HALF COCOANUT SHELL. h.–MBATA (*Lower Right*) a.– BROOM. b.–FAN. c.–KUMOTO (SIEVE) d.–BASKET FOR SCENTING CLOTHES, MODEL. e.–DEMA (FISH TRAP). f.–KATA (ROUND PAD WORN ON HEAD FOR CARRYING LOADS) g, i, k.– THREE KINDS OF CORD. h.–CHOIR. j.–TOOTHBRUSHES. l AND m.–PAINTBRUSHES. n.–BIRD TRAP, SIDE VIEW.

(*Upper*) DEMA FISH TRAPS
(*Lower*) A SEWN BOAT

(*Upper*) OLD FISHERMAN WITH MGONO TRAP
(*Lower*) CAT FISH FISHERMEN WITH TRAPS

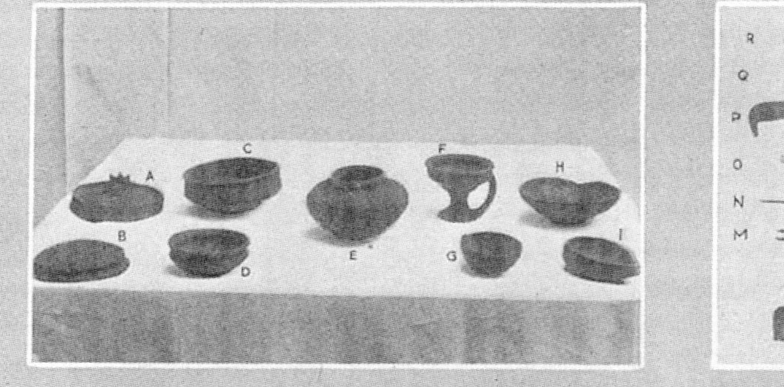

(*Upper Left*) a.–COVER (MKUNGWATANO). b.–DISH FOR COOKING CAKES (KIKANGO CHA KUPIKA MANDAZI). c.–POT FOR COOKING RICE (CHUNGU). d.–POT FOR COOKING CURRY (KIKANGO). e.–WATER JAR (MTUNGI). f.–INCENSE DISH (CHETEZO). g.–LAMP (TAA). h.–FOR SHREDDING COCONUTS IN (MKUNGU WA NAZI). i.–LAMP (TAA). (*Upper Right*) a.–RAZOR (WEMBE). b.–KNIFE FOR MAKING FISH TRAPS (KOTAMA). c.–SMALL KNIFE (KISU). d.–SMALL KNIFE (KOMBA). e.–SHOEMAKER'S AWL (MAHARAZI). f.–MODEL AXE (KISHO-KAA). g.–HOE (JEMBE). h.–DOOR FASTENER AND STAPLE (TUMBUO) i.–CURVED KNIFE (SHEM-BEA). j.–KNIFE (KISU). k.–UNMOUNTED KNIFE (UKENGELE). l.–MODEL ANVIL (FUAWE). m.–TONGS (KOLEO). n.–POKER (CHOCHEO). o.–HAMMER (NYUNDO). p.–SICKLE (MUNDU). q and r.–MORTAR TROWELS (MWIKO LA KUPAPIA CHOKAA). (*Lower left*) BLACKSMITHS AT WORK (*Lower Right*) A POTTERY MAKER, PEMBA.

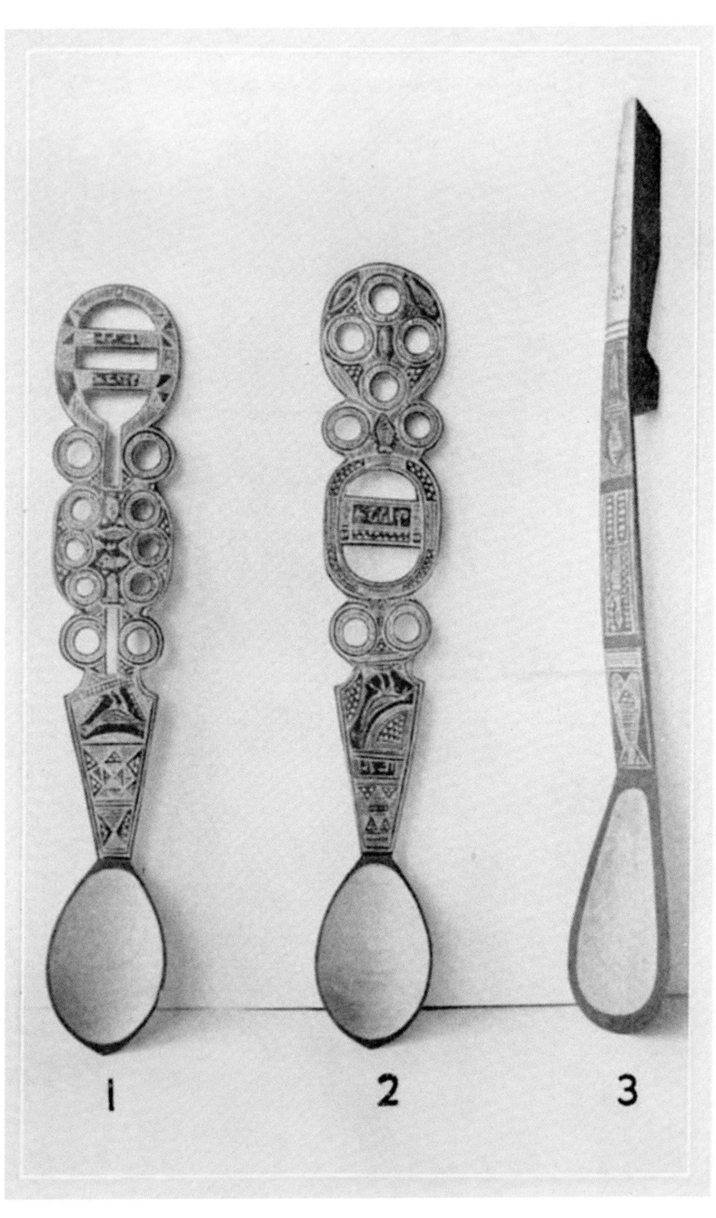

THREE HADIMU SPOONS DECORATED WITH POKER WORK

(*Upper*) ORCHESTRA FOR THE DANCE KUMBA
(*Left*) ORCHESTRA FOR VINGAGO. (*Right*) a and j.–CHAPUO. b.–MSHINDO. c.–TARI NA KENGELE. d.–TARI. e.–KINGANGA CHA MSONDO. f.–KINDIMBA. g.–MSONDO. h.–KINGANGA CHA MAULIDI. i.–TUTU. k.–VUME. l.–KIMININGO.

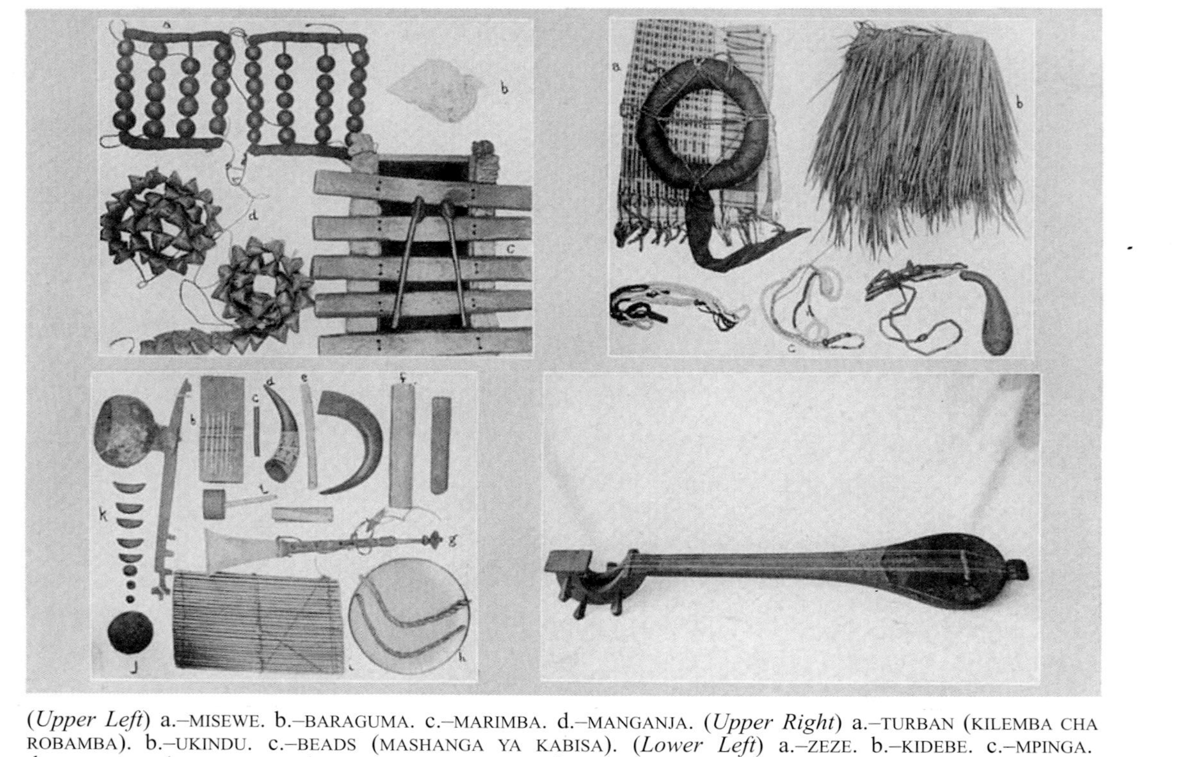

(*Upper Left*) a.–MISEWE. b.–BARAGUMA. c.–MARIMBA. d.–MANGANJA. (*Upper Right*) a.–TURBAN (KILEMBA CHA ROBAMBA). b.–UKINDU. c.–BEADS (MASHANGA YA KABISA). (*Lower Left*) a.–ZEZE. b.–KIDEBE. c.–MPINGA. d.–LELIMAMA (NOTE CARVING). e.–MBIU AND BEATER. f.–MIWALE. g.–ZOMARI. h.–UPATU. i.–KAYAMBA. j.–HALF COCOANUT SHELL. USED FOR BEATING. WOODEN MORTAR IN DANCES. k.–NJUGA. l.–SANJI YA CHEREWA. (*Lower Right*) NATIVE MANDOLIN (ARAB OOD).

(*Upper*) THE QUEEN OF THE MANGUNA DANCE, KIMBA.
(*Lower*) THE PANGA MWAKJUGA, BEMBA.

(*Upper*) PERFORMERS OF THE NYAMWEZI DANCE CALLED "UGIGE" (*Lower*) THE DEVIL HUNT, SHOMOOCH, MAKUNDUCHI.

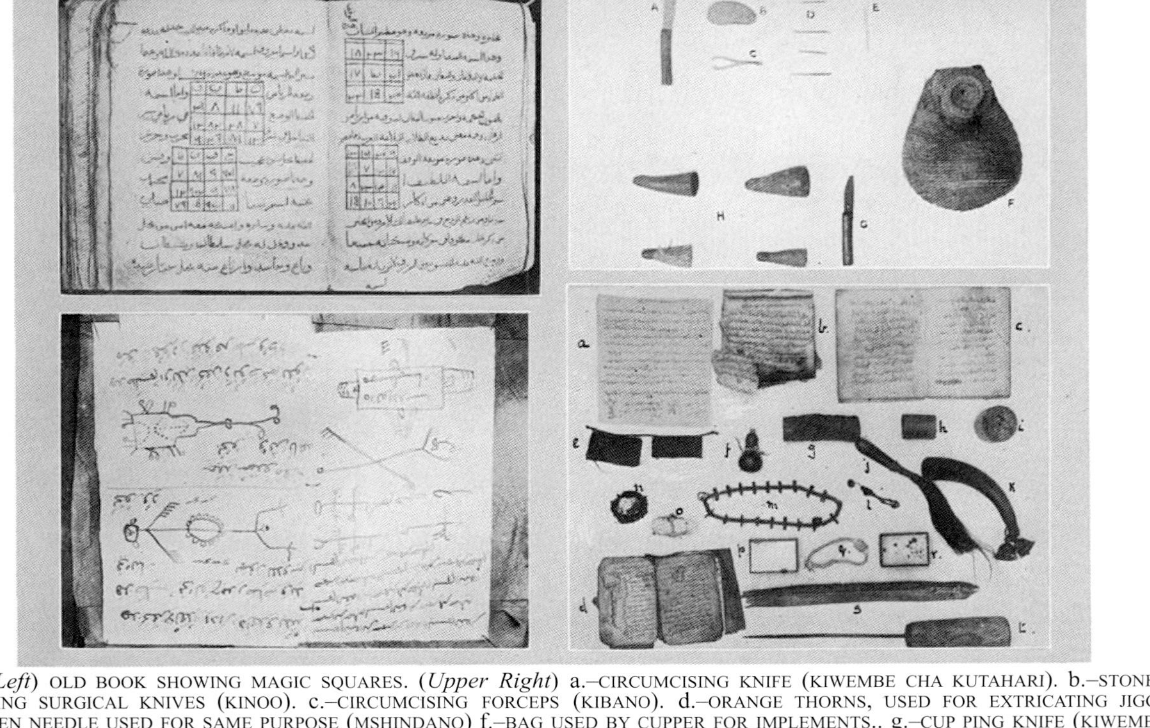

(*Upper Left*) OLD BOOK SHOWING MAGIC SQUARES. (*Upper Right*) a.–CIRCUMCISING KNIFE (KIWEMBE CHA KUTAHARI). b.–STONE FOR SHARPENING SURGICAL KNIVES (KINOO). c.–CIRCUMCISING FORCEPS (KIBANO). d.–ORANGE THORNS, USED FOR EXTRICATING JIGGERS. e.–WOODEN NEEDLE USED FOR SAME PURPOSE (MSHINDANO) f.–BAG USED BY CUPPER FOR IMPLEMENTS.. g.–CUP PING KNIFE (KIWEMBE CHA KUMUMIZA). h.–CUPPING HORNS (CHUKU). (*Lower Left*) RECIPES TO KILL, OR AGAINST DJINNS. (*Lower Right*) a and e.–HIRIZI CHARM WORN BY CHILDREN. b.–BOOK OF MAGIC. c.–RECITATION, "DAWA YA PEPO". d.–BOOK OF MAGIC. f.–CALABASH FOR MEDICINE (TUNGURE). g.–CHARM BURIED IN ROAD TO HARM ME. h.–KILEZI. i.–KOMA. j.–USINJA. k.–PINI. l.–CHARM TO CURE CONJUNCTIVITIS. m.–KOJA. n.–CASSYTHAFALIFORMIS, ROOT AND CREEPER. o.–CHARM FOR BIG DRUM. p.–CHARM TO RENDER WEARER INVISIBLE TO WITCH DOCTORS.

with great difficulty I mounted my donkey to return on Monday morning, and I ate very little for some time after.)

My host was quite upset at my poor appetite, as I never took a large helping, at any rate at the end, and when he met me afterwards, told me his wife was very disappointed that I had not cleared the dish. The food was excellent, but that cannot be said of all Arab food.

Arabs are very hospitable, and feed not only you and your retinue of boys and carriers and grooms, but also your donkey and dogs. I might add that very often, after a meal, the uneaten remnants are sent with you. One's boys come in for this. They have apparently unlimited capacity.

In the intervals of eating these meals, we used to sit and talk on a variety of subjects and gossip with the constant stream of visitors that came and went. At night after dinner deck-chairs were taken out on to the moonlit *sikafu*, and we talked peacefully until a late hour, smoking with our coffee, and drinking in the perfumed air, heavily laden with the scent of ylang ylang and jasmine. Late at night I was shown to a comfortable bed with spotless, scented sheets.

Early in the morning a boy used to bring me tea, and after drinking it, guests used to go in turn to the wash-house across the *sikafu*. Here there was plentiful hot water, Pears' soap, and a large soft towel, for my host knew European ideas of comfort. All Arabs are hospitable, but at other houses I have often had to content myself with a wash from a trough of cold water, ladled over me with a large spoon made from a coco-nut shell at the end of a wooden handle. In the ordinary Arab house one eats one's meals cross-legged on a mat, from an enormous pile of rice and bowls of curried meat, but here, after a comfortable bath and when we were dressed, we went into a dining-room, where a sumptuous breakfast was laid out on a snowy table-cloth. The floor was covered with Persian rugs, and a servant pulled a punkah.

I think these mornings in the shambas (plantations) were the most attractive part of the day. It was yet cool, and one felt fresh. No one seemed affected with liver, and kind inquiries were made as to the kind of night we had had, and everyone used to remark on the paucity of mosquitoes.

The life there was of a patriarchal kind. My host had a large family of boys of all ages, ranging from twenty to seven. The family was always in a hurry for breakfast, but before getting down to it, all of them, from Suleimani, the baby, to Abdulla, the eldest, used to come to their father and kiss his hand when wishing him good morning. They always called him " Sir," and did his bidding at once, though they were very much boys as well. Catapults were the favourite toys of some of them, and they were good hands at knocking a crow off a coco-nut tree. The elder ones would go off to shoot duck on a neighbouring marsh before breakfast.

After breakfast, when it was hotter, our chairs were taken and set under a double avenue of mango trees below the house, where there was usually a pleasant breeze blowing, and a view over waving rice fields. My host always used to remind his guests when it was time for prayer, and produce the necessary mats and water.

Belching is a sign of good rather than bad manners, but the best people put their hands in front of their mouths in an apologetic sort of way, as if they were sorry, but really they could not help it, as the food was so rich.

On parting from one's host many wishes are expressed for your future health, and greetings given you to give your family—" Salaam so-and-so," " Salaam so-and-so." Then many *Kwaheri's* (good-bye), and *Kwaheri sanas*, and one passes on.

I have mentioned under death customs that relations and friends are informed of deaths, and I append a rather amusing letter I received, presumably as an act of politeness, from a young Arab friend who knew a little English.

"*Tuesday*, 2/3/1920,
"WETI.

"To Mr. W. D. INGRAMS,

"We are very glad to notify you that the father of my wife is dead on date 26/2/20 thusday [*sic*] last. Our sympathy in that case was great.

"Yours for ever,
"AHMED BIN SULTAN RIYAMI."

Duty to Neighbours
(From the *Talkein Sibian*)

If feasible you must go and see your relations. You must remove all annoyance of your neighbours, and even if your neighbours are of another religion, you must rejoice with them on the occasions when they have rejoicings. When on safari you must be on good terms with your companions, and give them everything of which they may stand in need. You must not cause doubt in their minds by whispering with others, and you must produce your food and provisions at once on reaching a halting-place, so that they may eat your food and not have to prepare their own. If, though, anyone does evil on safari, you must rebuke him, but still continue to look after him.

Guests

Guests must be fed for three days, and this is compulsory, but after three days it is as alms. When visiting do not outstay your welcome. Wait on your guest and tell him when to pray. Look after his animals and give them food and water, and do not leave your guest long alone.

Do not wait until he asks you for what he wants, but bring everything you have; bring water together with the food, so that he may not thirst. Treat all your guests in the same way, even if there are many, and do not be silent in their company, neither use your guests to perform any errand for yourself.

When entertaining your guests in your house bear in mind their likes and dislikes, and do not put enemies near each other. Do not scold your servants in the presence of your guests.

Letter-writing

The Arab's politeness extends not only to his encounters with his fellow-men, but also to his letter-writing.

It would be impossible to imagine good wishes more poetically or more fully expressed than they are in letters. In official quarters this would be no doubt referred to as "unnecessary verbiage," and in the cold, unfeeling print of official publications is reduced to two letters, "A.C." (after compliments). But is not this "verbiage" more pleasant to read than the obvious fiction written to one by one's superiors that they have the honour to be one's most obedient humble servant? I would therefore recommend this more flowing style to those whose life is spent drafting dispatches among the purlieus of Whitehall.

RELIGIOUS DUTIES IN EVERYDAY LIFE

Among the Arabs, as Captain Colomb says in his chapter "Inshallah," one feels a far greater sense of the abiding presence of God than one does in a Christian country, for religion enters so much into the daily life of the people. In Zanzibar nearly everyone fasts the whole of Ramathan, most people say their prayers five times a day and are thinking of the will of God at all times, and it must be remembered that there is no priesthood in Islam to keep them up to the mark. As an example of the way in which they are continually in thought of their religion, let me give the precepts of *Talkein Sibian*, which regulate the ordinary actions of everyday life.

Before Food, etc.

Before eating food say, " In the name of God, the merciful and compassionate, who has intended this as food of my body to give strength to live. Praise be to God who has given me this food. I eat for His glory and that of Mohammed His apostle."

When putting on clothes say, " In the name, etc. It is my intention to put on clothes to hide my nakedness, and to protect me from illness, and to show that God has given me clothes for His glory and that of Mohammed His apostle."

When going to your wife say, " In the name, etc. I go to my wife, and I pray to God that I will get a child, and to prevent myself from wanting other women, for the glory, etc.," or " I go to my wife to put out the fire of my desire."

Before business transactions say, " In the name, etc. I pray to God for prosperity, and to help me in all my affairs, for the glory, etc."

When going out of the house to go to the mosque, " I go not out ostentatiously to show people that I am good, or to let people know that I go to pray. I go for help and to get the approval of God, and to escape hell fire."

Before going to urinate, " It is my intention to clean myself of urine (or excretion) and everything bad. I abase myself before God and His prophet Mohammed." You then wash the parts. But if the act is not done say, " I put off all dirt for the glory, etc."

Before brushing teeth, " I brush my teeth as a meritorious act before God and His apostle Mohammed."

After killing an animal the blood must be washed away. If water is not obtainable, sand may be used.

Prayers

Prayers must not be performed without ablutions being performed first of all. After urination and defecation, it suffices to wash the parts, but after sexual connection the whole body must be bathed.

Women cannot pray during menstruation, and must bathe after it before praying.

The best water obtainable must be used for ablutions.

First of all water must be put in the mouth, and the first finger of the right hand must be used to clean the mouth three times, and then you must gargle, but not in Ramathan, lest some of the water should escape down the throat.

After this the nose must be washed out three times, then the whole face three times, then the right arm, left arm, head, ears, inside and out, right leg and left leg, each three times, and you must say, "In the name, etc."

It is *sunnaa* (meritorious) to use a tooth-brush first, though it is not compulsory.

Before ablutions and after sleep, the hand must first be washed, and as each part of the body is washed you should pray God, who gave you water to drink, as you wash your mouth, to give you the perfume of Paradise that you may smell clean, then with your nose, that your face may shine, and that on the last day you may be among those whose faces shine.

SUPERSTITIONS

There are a few superstitions peculiar to Arabs, and I therefore give them here.

The cawing of a crow near a house signifies the coming of guests, and the braying of an ass as it approaches a house signifies good luck for the owner of that house. On the other hand, if a pregnant woman hears the cawing of a crow, it means bad luck for herself and child.

Bad luck is also indicated by the lowing of an ox near a house, and the sight of a cat crossing the road also indicates bad luck. In Muscat, although there are many slaves, a black man cannot remove the body of a dead animal.

The month of Safar is unlucky, and Arabs, in order to avoid further bad luck, burn or cut themselves, however slightly, at the beginning, and as a thanksgiving read the Koran at the end. No marriage takes place in this month.

NOTES ON ARAB ARCHITECTURE IN ZANZIBAR

Apart from modern works of a particularly meretricious kind, the evil heritage of Indian workmen from the British-India of the Victorian era, Zanzibar possesses many buildings of charm, and of a style associated with its traditions. The unfortunate circumstance of the scarcity of suitable building material in the island has to a certain extent crabbed the hand of the artist, and fought against the preservation of many interesting works.

While most of the architecture of Zanzibar and of the island is fashioned on the original Arab model, there is in the later work a tendency to assimilate into the detail imported Indian forms, and works of purely Arab origin are comparatively scarce.

The general design and planning are here very much the same as in any other Moslem Eastern town, where conditions of climate, life and habits are the same. They appear to be varied here only by the scarcity of flooring timber, or the length of mangrove poles available with which to carry the lime and stone forming the roofs.

The detail, on the other hand, consists of many of those ancient forms known of antiquity in the valley of the Euphrates and absorbed into the art of the nomad Arabs, and in addition there are many lovely natural shapes adapted from trees and plants in the vicinity. The "traveller's palm," in particular, frequently appears as a *motif* for band ornament in wood.

Carved stone-work is very scarce, but moulded plaster-work overlying coral abounds, chiefly in the interiors of mosques and in the decoration of the mihrab, or praying niche.

The Arab tradition in Zanzibar was debarred by circumstance from giving the world such work as is found in Cairo and Spain, but has left there many humble monuments of grace, good proportions and great charm, despite the rude material of which they are made.

ZANZIBAR DOORS

Zanzibar doors, like Zanzibar chests, are well known, and it seems that this is an appropriate place in which to give a few notes about the meaning of the carving with which they are decorated.

The *motifs* used are of considerable antiquity, and as they portray natural objects, are pre-Islamic in origin.

The rosettes and leaves represent the lotus, associated by the ancient Egyptians, from whom or from the Assyrians the design was probably borrowed direct, with reproductive power. At the bottom of the two uprights are two grenade-shaped objects, and below them three wavy lines. The former are degenerate designs of fish, and the latter represent the sea. The fish design can be traced on all Zanzibar doors, from a well-designed fish to a shapeless grenade, a pine-apple, and latterly a flower-vase with flowers extending out of it up the length of the post. It is possible that the fish represents Atargatis, the Syrian fish goddess who was a protecting deity and associated with generation and fertility. The design probably travelled from Syria by the Arabian seaboard to Muscat and thence to Zanzibar. The water symbol is also of Egyptian origin and signified the production of life.

There remain the chains, one or two of which almost invariably go all round the door: this design, I take it, is intended to represent security, and by a species of homœopathic magic to guard the home against intruders. In the first place, natural chains were no doubt used. In the same way the ornamental brass bosses were originally spikes designed to give an uncompromising reception to unwanted guests. It is sometimes said that the bosses are as a protection against elephants. If this is so, it should be shown that they are Indian in origin, and that they do not appear on the genuine old Arab doors. Many Zanzibar doors have also frankincense-tree patterns and date-tree patterns, the former symbolizing wealth, derived from the Egyptians, and the latter plenty, derived from the Arabs. The symbolism of these designs on a door is too obvious to need explanation; it may be noted that the door was the first part of a house to be erected, the idea doubtless being that its beneficent influences might affect even the ground the house was to be built on.

In some of the conclusions above I have followed Captain F. R. Barton, C.M.G., formerly First Minister, in his article, "Zanzibar Doors" (*Man*, 1924, 63).

CHAPTER XIX

SOME NOTES ON THE LIFE OF THE SWAHILIS AND FREED SLAVES

THE derivation of the word "Swahili" has been elsewhere discussed in this book, and, whatever interpretation is put on the word, it is difficult to define what peoples can be included under that designation. In this chapter I apply it to those detribalized natives and natives of mixed descent living in and around the town, and, although they would not admit it, there is a certain class of so-called Arabs that may be justifiably included under this description. They are of mixed descent but live in the style of Africans. The freed slaves are also classified as Swahilis, but in the main they originated from up-country tribes, the principal tribes being Gindo, Songo Songo, Dengereko, Sagara, Sukuma, Nyassa, Bisa, Zigua, Digo, Manyema, Zaramu and Yao. These people, coming from widely different areas, have many of them brought into Zanzibar their own pantheon of devils and a variety of ngomas. In the main, however, their customs follow those of the rest of the natives, but being quite detribalized and without family influence exerted over them in any way, they have lost much of the results of the herd instinct.

MARRIAGE

They regard their marriage ties very loosely indeed; often no more than five or ten rupees is mahr, and in other cases a sum is named as mahr but none paid at all.

Divorce is frequent, and the women rarely observe their Iddet. Marriage is common when money is plentiful, and before the month of Ramathan. The divorce figures rise and money is scarce after

Ramathan. They are extraordinarily loose and immoral in their manner of life, far more so than the aboriginal tribes.

VILLAGES

As regards their villages, the construction of their houses is better than that of the ordinary native, and the houses are generally fitted with windows and often whitewashed inside and out. A good deal of decoration occurs on houses, consisting of birds such as the peacock, and patterns of leaves painted in black and green. The artists are often Wanyamwezi, some of whom make a profession of this work; for the rest their houses are made to imitate to some extent European and Arab styles, and they frequently have cement floors.

These houses are often arranged in rows on either side of the street in European style, and they decorate them inside with cheap pictures, and have beds of Indian manufacture, often using mattresses and sheets. These remarks, of course, apply particularly to those who live in the town and are moderately well off or extravagantly inclined. Among the poorer classes the furniture is, of course, African.

DRESS, MODE OF LIVING, ETC.

To the town-dwelling Swahili *Malidadi* (finery) would appear to be the ruling word in his life; he must be well dressed and have everything smart. His idea of being well dressed is to wear a fez, a pink-coloured vest, a pair of white trousers, a thin, filmy kanzu and a coat of tussore, or drill, cut with a waist. On his feet he wears socks and a pair of brown and white rubber-soled shoes, while in his hand he carries a cane. It will be seen that this costume is a mixture of Arab and European, but the Arab is being rapidly discarded in favour of the European dress. Recently one has seen objects clad in fezes with coloured shirts and bow ties, blue serge suits, wearing shoes and socks, wearing a monocle, and smoking cigarettes in long, gold-tipped cigarette-holders. Such caricatures are not pleasing sights to see, and even worse perhaps are the gentlemen who have taken to soft hats and heavy boots. Wrist-watches are also in favour.

ORGANIZATION

These people are utterly detribalized and, apart from the Central Government consisting of Europeans, have no one to look after them. Until recently the freed slaves in Pemba had their own Sheha, Fundi Yakuti, a fine, intelligent type of native. Some 4,500 natives up and down the length of Pemba recognized his sway, and he had a number of assistants; since his resignation, however, and subsequent death, these freed slaves have been left in the charge of the local Masheha of the Wapemba, though some few districts are still largely comprised of this class, for instance, Chanoni and Chake Chake town.

OCCUPATION

These people are not much engaged in native industries except for the building of native huts. Many of them are tailors, however, and it should be noted that in Zanzibar no sewing is done by women, except mission girls. The greater number of town-dwellers are occupied as labourers or in domestic service with Arabs, Indians or Europeans, thus picking up a variety of ideas on different ways of living. Those who live in the country do very little work, and scarcely plant enough crops for their own personal use. If one rides through Chanoni, for example, one cannot but be struck at the paucity of native crops, and the untidy methods of planting. The variety of crops is also very small and confined chiefly to cassava. On the other hand, some of them have small coco-nut or clove plantations, and many pick cloves on an Arab's plantation during the clove season.

I should mention also that a lot are employed on transport work as bullock and donkey-cart drivers. Other occupations largely practised by this class are those of charcoal-burners, carpenters, shoe-makers, masons, porters, boat-boys, motor-car drivers, messengers, petty dealers in foodstuff, teashop keepers, etc., and it also comprises a certain number of lower class clerks. The total number of people employed in each of these occupations is not large.

CRIME

The bulk of the jail population is drawn from this class, and here we have the habitual thieves, gamblers and drunkards. Many new types of offence have been appearing lately in Zanzibar; in addition to modern methods of house-breaking, such heretofore unknown methods of crime as pick-pocketing, hold-ups on roads, and robbery by gangs are becoming known, and it is likely that the cinema has had a great deal to do with this.

One of the forms of *Kinyume* is the thieves' slang used by this class.

RELIGION

While retaining a general belief in devils, the Swahilis pay more outward observance to the forms of Islam than do the native tribes, probably because it is considered fashionable. Of the converts to the Christian missions in the island, most come from this class (and Wanyamwezi). Being bad citizens in any case, they make bad Christians, and as they are the type of native Christian most generally met with by the traveller, it is they who give the missions a bad name. (As far as missions are concerned in Zanzibar, there are three classes from which their converts can be drawn. These are, (*a*) the Arabs and native tribes who are all either staunch Mohammedans or animistic with a strong adherence to Islam, (*b*) this class now being described, and (*c*) pagans, such as raw Wanyamwezi; the two latter classes are, of course, much the smaller. Christianity makes little headway in the first class; in the second class it makes some headway, but generally procures bad recruits; the third class makes the best Christians.)

AMUSEMENTS

As this class is of such mixed origin it naturally has a very exotic repertoire of ngomas. In addition it has taken largely to what it euphemistically designs as "bands"; Scotch Band, Marine Band, Tipperary Band—these are but a few of the titles that are bestowed on these crowds of natives who dress themselves in fantastic uniforms, chiefly caricatures of British uniforms, and in which generals and staff officers are almost as common as privates. Swahili women have also taken to dressing themselves in clothing based on the European model for these performances.

In addition to such tunes as "God Save the King," "Tipperary," "If You were the Only Girl in the World," "Auld Lang Syne," "Colonel Bogey's March," and a few others, these bands have evolved a curious kind of music, which is a cross between the ordinary dance music of Europe and the ngoma music of Africa, and while the "band" makes the night hideous with this kind of "music," the "army" forms a circle round it, and either drills in European style, or performs an ngoma in the African style. This type of dancing is often called *Chemka*.

Siku ya mwaka (New Year's Day) has been forgotten by these people, who instead, at the Idel Fitr at the end of Ramathan, which is known as *Siku kuu*, proceed in their best clothes in enormous crowds to watch such entertainments as I have described above, or take turns on swings and roundabouts erected by enterprising Indians. The *Siku kuu* is also notable for the amount and variety of easy methods of losing money on gambling.

One moonlight night at Jembiyani, in the south-east of the island, while watching an ngoma I was asked if I had seen *Kargoss*. Thinking this was another ngoma, I followed my guide to a house where I was conducted on to the baraza behind some large mats called *Jamvis*, which closed the baraza from public view, and effectually excluded the air, thus forming a theatre about thirty feet long and seven or eight feet wide. At one end of this sat a native with a concertina, while behind there was a space of perhaps three feet between the mats and the wall.

Totally unaware of what was going to occur, I was little short of amazed when a marionette dressed in native style made his appearance above the screen. What followed was, in fact, a Punch and Judy show.

Punch, Mwalim Kargoss, had quarrelled with his wife, and a well-meaning friend endeavoured to reconcile the parties, and the end of it was that Mwalim Kargoss successfully slaughtered the wife and the well-meaning friend, and having also slaughtered a couple of policemen capped in red fezes, he decided he would go to his shamba, and sent for his donkey. The donkey threw him once or twice, but he got to the shamba in the end, where he set about milking a cow, an act which he performed with much realism, but with such violence that the cow shook every time he drew milk. Not unnaturally annoyed at this treatment, the cow let out with its hind leg and kicked Mwalim Kargoss, a distance of some yards. He recovered, however, and determining to have his revenge, decided to slaughter the cow and called for a knife. A long table-knife as big as himself was then brought, with which he sawed through the cow's jugular vein, and she expired, uttering protesting "moo-oo's" in a most realistic fashion. After further adventures with a lady whom he desired to seduce, but who, judging from the way she banged him and flung him about, was too muscular for him to overcome, Mwalim Kargoss retired, and the audience was, to say the least of it, startled when a huge, white-bearded face looking rather like Father

Christmas appeared over the screen and sang a comic song in a very gruff voice.

The dialogue of this play was very clear, and the actor behind the curtain changed his voice for each character in excellent style, and pitched it proportionately to the size of the marionette. I was informed by one of the two players that they had been taught the show by a Shihiri Arab. These two natives travelled on foot, with their properties in baskets, every day from village to village, and set up their show on the baraza of a house in the evening, charging two pice for admission. Such a sight may be seen in the town of Zanzibar on *Siku kuu*, but in a village as isolated and as truly native as Jembiyani it seemed extraordinary.

Before leaving this section I would draw attention to the number of English words which are rapidly being absorbed into the vocabulary of this class of natives. Such words are:

Bafu	Bath	Lenketi	Raincoat
Band	Band	Mishin	Christian
Bed shiti	Bed sheet	Motoboti	Motor-boat
Biskuti	Biscuit	Mtwana	A lorry or motor-'bus—originally a slave
Bilanketi	Blanket		
Buku	Book	Motokari	Any motor-car (not a Ford)
Burashi	Brush	Musiki	Music
Buti	Boots	Numbawan	The best
Charki	Chalk or blanco	Pudin	Pudding
Fidla	Violin	(Ku)rouni (-louni)	To walk round (derived from the "rounds" of the Police)
Fodi	Ford car		
(Ku)frai	To fry	(Ku)rosi	To roast
Fruiti	Fruit	Saluti	A salute (the National Anthem)
Fursklasi	Excellent		
Gilassi	Glass	Sharti	Shirt
Juggi	Jug	Soksi	Socks
Keki	Cake	Speshul	Special
Koffi	White coffee	Spiriti	Petrol
Koti	Coat	Tarumbeta	Trumpet
Krismass	A present		
Kurutu	Remnant (derived from recruit; someone without a number; then the last man of a column; something left over, hence, for example, a scab after a sore, etc.)		

The derivation of most of these words is too obvious to need remark. Almost anyone could understand some of the semi-educated town natives who use this form of speech.

B. NATIVE TRIBES OF ZANZIBAR

CHAPTER XX

Life of the Individual

THE MAN

(*a*) *Infancy*

1. When the time comes for the delivery of a child, the father fetches the midwife (*mkunga*), who then attends to the expectant mother. The woman is seated on a low stool, and the midwife sits in front of her and receives the child. When the child is born the midwife ligatures the umbilical cord and cuts it, and she then takes the child, washes it in cold water, and lays it on a cloth in a flour sieve (*unga*) while she attends to the mother.

The mother is washed in very hot water, and then a fire is prepared of coco-nut shells, and she stands over it with her legs apart, after which she will go and sit on the bedstead, which for the moment has no mat on, and a fire underneath it.

At the head of the child in the flour sieve are laid a lemon, a razor, a silver chain and its mother's waist beads. This, I am informed, is to keep the devils off. It is interesting to note that Sir J. G. Frazer in *Spirits of the Corn and Wild*, Chapter I, describes similar customs in ancient Greece, Java, Foo-Chow, China, Bilaspore district of India, Upper Egypt, Punjaub, Gaolis of Deccan, Siam, Travancore and among the Tanalas of Madagascar.

The placenta is buried behind the house and the place marked.

The period of confinement lasts until the umbilical cord falls off, which is usually seven days; during this time neither mother nor child go out, and the lemon and razor, etc., remain at the child's head.

After seven days the father obtains, in the case of a boy, seven coco-nuts, or for a girl three, and two kibabas or a pishi of rice.

The coco-nuts are broken, and some of the rice thrown in each direction with the words, " This is your share, big people." This is, of course, to the devils hovering round, and is intended to appease them and keep them away from the young child, who is so susceptible to their baneful influences.

A fowl is then killed, a cock if the child is a boy, a hen if it is a girl. The rice and coco-nuts are cooked in the usual way, and a curry is made of the fowl in which ginger must be included. This is called *Fuka.*

The food is then divided on to four plates, of which one is the share of the big man of the village, not necessarily the Sheha, one is given to the Mwalimu, the third is the portion of the father and mother, and the last goes to the *Maskini wa mungu* (God's poor).

After this the father gives Re. 1 to the midwife, and she returns the silver chain and the beads, which, like the child, have been in her custody during the period of confinement.

When these ceremonies are over the Mwalimu comes every morning for forty days and pours water on the mother's head. At the same time he reads the *Yasini* from the Koran.

After this period (seven days) the child's head is shaved, and then if it is desired a feast may be made.

The umbilical cord and hair is buried with the placenta behind the house, and sometimes a coco-nut is planted on it. It is considered very bad luck if this subsequently dies. It is referred to as the navel of the child. Seven different kinds of grain are sown, and the child shown the manner of sowing.

An *Mchi* (the pole used for pounding grain in

a mortar) is placed against its throat and it is told not to tell tales. Children are usually not given proper names until they are old enough to choose them for themselves. In Pemba, especially, infant girls are usually called *Kijakazi* and boys *Mtwana*.

2. When the mother is again able to follow her occupation and cultivate, she generally carries her child with her, tied by a cloth either to her back or sometimes to her front. If she has several children the child is often entrusted to the care of an elder sister.

Natives seem, curiously enough, to have but hazy ideas on infantile feeding, and one frequently sees babies, as yet unweaned, having their mouths stuffed with boiled rice and curry. This improper method of feeding is doubtless responsible for much of the infantile mortality, and certainly causes the abnormally distended abdomen so commonly seen in native children. It is also considered essential that they should eat a certain amount of earth, though the habit is not entirely confined to young children. There is a particular kind of reddish earth eaten called *Udongo Mwekundu*, which is popular, and the habit is largely responsible for many intestinal parasites, which are a real scourge to the native.

(*b*) *Childhood*

When the child is of an age to walk about, it is generally left to amuse itself for the day with all the children of the village while its parents are away at work. This happy existence goes on till the child is seven or eight, when the only education it receives commences.

In every little village there is a mosque with its *Kuttab*, or Koran school, and the *Mwalimu* (teacher) attached. Here both morning and afternoon every day for two or three years sit the children of the village, a " slate " with a verse or two inscribed for the smaller ones, or a Koran for the elders. All of them repeat their portion over and over again at the same time, till both intonation and pronunciation are correct, and the noise of their reading can be heard quite a way away. The teacher quickly pulls up anyone who is wrong, and picks out each pupil in a wonderful way, and woe betide the boy who is really thick or wantonly stupid. The use of the stick is by no means unknown to the teachers of Zanzibar.

The tragedy of it all is that with all its fine sounding phrases the meaning of the words and the import of the Scriptures are as unknown to the teacher as to his pupils.

The correct repetition of the Koran is said to be meritorious, and presumably this is the only benefit derived by the scholars. The uselessness of this repetition seems well recognized by the intelligent Arabs and by the Kadis, one of whom referred to it to me as *Maneno ya Kasuku* (a parrot's words), but said, who was to expound it to them?

I have often asked the teachers if they ever expounded the Scriptures to their charges, and all said "No," some even confessing that they could not. When asked what was the use of it, several said that the method was first to teach the correct enunciation, and then those who were specially fitted could go to the city and learn of their religion from the Mwalimus there.

After their education is over, or in their spare time, the children are employed by their parents on running errands to the local grocer, on herding the goats and kindred small tasks.

In play hours they occupy themselves much as do their Western cousins—flying kites, whipping tops or drawing round small wagons, etc. A counterpart of the coloured paper windmills sold by street hawkers is also made from a coco-nut frond, and is called *kititia*. Several round games are also played, many almost exactly as in Europe—touch, under the name of *Tasa*, follow-my-leader, called *Tinga*, and a species of rounders called *Tiabu*. Another game quite popular but rather violent is called *Mali ya ndimu*, in which one boy puts his head down and another knocks it, and the knocked one guesses who did it. If he guesses correctly, the knocker becomes the knocked.

They often amuse themselves by catching rice birds, which they imprison in small cages and sell.

Sailing boats is probably a favourite amusement of children of all countries wherever water is available, and Zanzibar is no exception. *Kuolesha vidau* means to sail small boats, and it is related that an uncle of Seyyid Said, the founder of Zanzibar, taunted him by saying to him when, as a boy at Muscat, he was amusing himself in this way, that he would end up by doing no more than playing with them. The boy, however, " got his own back," for he one day killed his uncle by stabbing him in the neck with his own dagger.

Children's Games

Nyanjuriya. They hold hands in a circle and move as in " Ring a ring o' roses."

(1) Kibuzi, Kibuzi, chamemee, chamemee, Kibuzi, Kibuzi cha mbwana shandi. Mlelezi chooko na kunde mwamu, Ho waitwa shamba ukale matikite na matango kumi na mawele uji upinde uji utie kata kwenu watie kwetu mkambiti; mkambiti ukadoto ya mwana mize funika panya ho!

(2) Kibuzi, Kibuzi, chamemee, chamemee, mwanambuzi Kajamba kajambili mchunga dekedeke malenga mkonotinde manga hawende maka ukachakue funo na upanga kuku simba kalega kalega kongwe kongwe la mwana mzee tumbwi tumbwi la mbwani, wala Haligongele lagona kwamke mbuya la wesha wesha na mashinge na mashegesha ule mtu watenda nduda haokote vitabwa tabwa du sinika pata lako mama usimambe nakuturana nakufonza maungwana mama, ya usiku na mchana mama, kesho kutwa ntakuja mama na kisahani cha mijama.

Oranges and Lemons. Played in the usual way, but the words *Mizinga* and *risasi* (" cannon and shot ") are used instead of oranges and lemons.

I have also seen a counterpart of " Nuts in May," but it is played in a different way, each side sitting down until they have a final tug-of-war.

String Games

There are two games played with string for children, the first of which is in the nature of a " cat's cradle."

(1) Take a loop of string. Put little finger and thumb of both hands through it, so that it passes in front of the palm of either hand. Take with the the middle finger of both hands. Tell the child to put its hands in centre. Release little and middle fingers, take afresh into little fingers and then with middle. Tell the child to lift his hand into the centre of the new cradle. Release little and middle fingers again. This releases the child's hand.

(2) Take a loop of string. Put it over your head. Put right side of string in mouth and then left also. Cross the string in front and put over the head again. Pull it. This releases the head.

(*c*) *Puberty*

Circumcision takes place between the ages of six and fourteen or fifteen, and this rite is as much a Bantu custom as a Mohammedan one.

It is usual to wait until a number of boys are ready for circumcision before the date is fixed, and when a number have been collected, a house is set apart for their use and a fence built round it, both to prevent the boys being seen and to stop them from running away.

When the boys are all collected inside, the *Ngariba*, or circumciser, who is often the Sheha of the village or the Mwalimu of the mosque, comes with his assistants.

A low seat is placed ready, and the assistants catch hold of each child in turn from behind and sits him there holding the child's hands in his hands, and at the same time his legs which he holds apart. The circumciser then catches hold of the penis, gently pushes the prepuce back and cleanses it. He then brings the prepuce right forward, holds it with an *mbano* (forceps) and then cuts it off. Sometimes it is necessary to cut a second time to remove the inner skin.

He then applies a mixture of *wanja manga* (antimony) and simsim oil, and the boy is carried and placed on a seat called *chege la mgomba*, which consists of a section of banana palm. After the ceremony the foreskins are buried.

Further treatment is accorded to the initiates after this until they are healed. In the first place a triangle is made of three pieces of the hollow stem of the leaf of the *mbono* (castor-oil) tree threaded together, which, when tied round the waist, acts as a support to the penis. Every three days cotton soaked in oil is put on the sore to make it soft, for a washing with water stained with mangrove which follows the next morning, after which some other medicine is put on.

The boys stay in the yard twenty-one days after circumcision, and a curious magic medicine is given to some cocks to make them stay with the boys during this time. It is as follows: Chew up roots of Mwaka and Mnyamata with ginger and charcoal. Mix this with rice and give to the cocks, who will then stay with the boys for the twenty-one days.

It is said that the presence of the cocks is required to wake the boys up every morning. Cocks employed in this way are, in Pemba, called *Mayombe* during this period.

Certain songs are sung during the circumcision period and dances played. The usual dance is called *Manyaga*, in Pemba *Unjugu*.

(*d*) *Courtship*

When a boy reaches the age of about sixteen it is considered that he should be married, and he or his parents set about making a match, for bachelors are very rare in Zanzibar, and only idiots and such afflicted persons do not marry, though it is apparently realized that wives may be an expensive hobby, for *mke ni Nguo* (a wife means clothes) is a well-known proverb.

When he sees a lady whom he considers fit for the honour, if he is a young man his father will probably interview the father of the prospective bride; if, on the other hand, he is of mature age and it is not his first venture in matrimony, he will either write or send a representative to the lady's parent.

Bantu ideas of beauty hardly correspond with European. Large breasts and buttocks are considered the chief features, and much is thought of carriage and walk.

If the girl's parent agrees to the proposed marriage, he will ask what *mahari* the bridegroom or his parents are prepared to pay.

Mahari is generally interpreted as dowry, but, strictly speaking, it is not so, as it is given to the bride not by her parents, but by the prospective bridegroom.

These days it ranges from five rupees up to anything in the way of two or three hundred among the natives, according to the youth, beauty and occupation of the bride, a lady who has been many times married or divorced being often content with a few rupees, while such a woman as a catcher of whitebait, or skilled at some other craft, may demand 300, as the demand for such skill is great, and she would be a good investment. Usually though, a virgin bride may be obtained for about thirty to fifty rupees. Part of the mahari is paid at once and part after marriage, though in practice the balance is often not paid at all. If a girl has not been married before, she must do as her parents tell her, and she has no choice in the matter, but if she is a divorcee, a widow, or of age, her consent must first be obtained. The payment of mahari is not the only pecuniary obligation attaching to courtship or pre-marriage ceremonies, as a present must also be given to the bride's parents, which is called *kilemba. Kilemba* literally means turban, but it is also used in a figurative sense to denote a present given on almost any special occasion. The bridegroom also gives a present to the girl's mother, called *mkaja*.

There is no fixed period of engagement, and on a favourable reply being received, the bridegroom goes to the Mwalimu, or Kadi, to arrange for the service to be held.

(*e*) *Marriage*

When the wedding-day comes the bridegroom proceeds with his men friends to the mosque, where the Mwalimu reads the service. After that is finished the bridegroom produces halwa (sweetmeats) and coffee, which is partaken of by his friends, and he pays the Mwalimu a fee of two rupees for his services.

That night the bridegroom or his parents provide a feast at their house, after which he proceeds to his bride's house, or sometimes she is brought to his. But before he enters the house she is in, a sacrifice of a fowl or goat must be made outside and he must step across the blood.

On getting into the house, he finds in the ante-chamber women who are guarding the wedding chamber. To these he must pay money, called *Kifungua mlango*, before they will allow him to pass the door.

On entering the bride's room he finds her swathed from head to foot in the cloths, called *kangas*, and an old woman there, who tells him to remove his clothes, and this done, gives him a new kanga, and then after receiving a small present departs. The man then proceeds to his bride whom he must uncover, but she will resist this until paid a present of up to Rs. 300.

If the girl is a virgin, there is an old woman kept under the bed, and when the husband has had intercourse she will emerge and take the bride and wash her, returning her afterwards to her husband, who remains with her all night.

Outside the house music and dancing is kept up all night, and in the morning food is brought to the man, who comes out and shares it with his friends in the ante-chamber, while outside the house there is, all day, much feasting and dancing.

If the man is wealthy he stays in the bride's house seven days (*mfungate*), giving feasts to his friends every day. If, however, he is not sufficiently blessed with this world's goods, he will make a feast for one day and remain in the house but three. At the end of this period the man goes to his house and if he likes may take his wife with him, though generally she is left with her parents for about a month.

A new custom that has sprung up in the last year or two is that the bridegroom should, before the marriage, send a trousseau to his bride consisting of a number of kangas, each of which is carried by a woman, and each of which contains either a looking-glass, ear-papers, waist-beads or a comb. The bearers dance to the bride's home.

Wednesday, if the last of the month, is the only unlucky day for marriage, though the whole month called Safar or Mfunguo tano is unlucky.

The chief months for marrying are those immediately preceding Ramathan, as it is considered important to have a wife to cook during the nights of that month. After Ramathan many of these unions are dissolved.

(*f*) *Divorce*

Divorce is, of course, controlled by the Sharia, and among the Wahadimu, Wapemba, and Watumbatu it is comparatively rare, and children are numerous and well-disciplined. The most usual ground of divorce is merely a desire for change, though a woman is often divorced for barrenness, or on bearing abnormal children, and sometimes, though by no means always, for adultery.

Adultery is punishable in the man under the Indian Penal Code, but there are very few prosecutions, while the offence is extraordinarily common. It is not unusual for a native woman to commit adultery while her husband is away for a night, in which case he is pretty certain to be doing the same. The only sin about it is, apparently, being found out by the injured party. This generally results in the woman being well beaten, and her lover is lucky if he gets off without a knife wound, or being "murdered."

The methods of divorce are those usual amongst Mohammedans, but the quick method is the one most employed. *Talaka* (I renounce you) said once or twice can be revoked; if said three times it is final, and a man cannot remarry his wife until she has been married and divorced by someone else.

A woman can get a divorce from a Kadi if her husband does not provide her clothes at least twice a year, or does not maintain her.

If the husband desires the divorce he must pay the whole of the dowry over to the wife, for on marriage it is not the custom to pay the whole dowry, but usually about half, though often none is paid at all. Should the husband die, the widow may obtain her dowry or the balance of it from her husband's estate. If, as often happens, the woman desires divorce, she must pay the dowry back, and is often required to pay far more. The practice leads often to abuses, as the husband so ill-treats his wife that she is but too glad to pay any price to get away.

The desire for divorce is, however, as often as not, mutual, and in this case the wife usually forgives the payment of the balance of the dowry.

In the Sunni law impotency or malformation of the husband, such as to make carnal connection impossible, is a good ground for the wife's suit for divorce. This law states that a husband is in the same position as if he were impotent, if his penis is of such a size that it cannot be introduced into the wife's vagina.

The Ibathi law says if the length of the husband's penis is equal to the breadth of twelve fingers the marriage should be annulled.

(g) *Mature Life*

After marriage the young man settles down with his wife in a hut, probably built for him or provided by his parents, and accumulates his bits of furniture and his cooking-pots.

Then the serious business of life begins. For the man it is cultivating his land, and eating or selling the produce. If his father was a blacksmith, or has taught him a hereditary trade, he will follow that, helping his father until death, when he takes over the business; or perhaps lime-burning, which is the principal industry of some villages; or fishing, when he daily brings his catch to the market and it is sold by auction for him, a small fee in cash or kind being paid to the auctioneer.

For the woman it means child-bearing and working in the fields, and in the morning and evening fetching the water on her head from the well, and also the cooking of the evening meal for her lord and master. Perhaps if he is well off he may accumulate more wives, and may marry four, though few exceed one or two, at any rate in the more distant parts. Each must have her own household if she desires it, though the wives generally converse quite amicably during the day, and help each other if they are in the same village. Temporary alliances are often entered into.

The stouter and more prosperous our friend becomes the more respect he is held in, and it is not long perhaps before he is addressed by his equals and admiring juniors as *Bwana*, or master, as opposed to *Mtoto*, or child, which he has been previously called.

(*h*) *Old Age*

"*Jam veniet tacito curva senecta pede*," and he will lose his stoutness, lose his sprightly bearing, and his surrounding of wives and children, and walk bent, with grey hair.

This, however, does not decrease the respect with which he is regarded, for the native aristocracy is one of age, and he is called *Bwana mkubwa*, or "great master," or more affectionately by the older men *Baba*, or "father," and becomes one of the *wazee*, or elders of the village, whose advice the Government will ask before appointing a new chief, if one is required. If one wants information on unusual subjects, or on bygone times, one is told, in a tone indicating the respect felt for them, to ask the *Wazee*.

Presently though, forerunner of death (and at no late age according to European ideas), his faculties fade, and he can do no more than sit outside his hut and eat the food his old wife prepares for him.

(*i*) *Death*

(1) *Before*. "Bwana so-and-so is very ill, he is near to die." The news quickly spreads round the village, and soon the near relations come to the hut of the dying man, who tells them his wishes, maybe, and has his last words with them. The doctor (*mganga*) comes and does his best, but it is of no avail. All the women sit round silent, and presently

comes the Mwalimu, or teacher, from the mosque and reads the *Yasini* from the Koran, until he is dead.

(2) *Death.* When he is dead, all the women must go outside and commence the wailing. Then the bed is laid from east to west, and underneath it a hole is dug (*ufuo*). The corpse, being undressed, is laid on it on the bare cords, no mat being beneath it, and washed, and the water runs down into the hole. After this operation a new mat is placed under the corpse on the bedstead, and it is again covered. This being done, news is sent to everyone concerned, friends and relations, and each replies, "Masha Allah" (Let God's will be done). The grave is dug, and some pice paid both to the washers and the Mwalimu.

When all this has been finished, and the people are gathered together and served with refreshments, the corpse is again washed, and during the operation the Mwalimu reads the "*Kul huwa llahu. . . .*"

The body is then dried and, every aperture having been stopped up with cotton waste (*pamba*), it is wrapped in a shroud (*sanda*), which is fastened by a cord round the neck, waist, including arms, and feet.

(3) *The Grave.* While these operations are carried out the grave has been dug. It is about six feet long, three wide and four deep, and runs from east to west.

On the north side of the bottom of the grave is dug a cavity running the length of the grave, about eighteen inches deeper than it and a foot wide. It is called *Mwana wa ndani*, and in this the corpse is to lie. It is provided with a board, which will cover it up when the body is laid there.

(4) *Burial.* When the body is ready for burial a bier (*geneza*) is brought, in which is placed a mat and the body in its shroud on it. Over it are laid kangas.

It is then carried to the graveside, and followed by the mourners. Arrived at the grave it is taken from the bier and handed to three men, who descend to the first level of the grave. These lay it head to east, facing north, on its right side and with arms to side, in the cavity above referred to. The shroud is then loosened and the cords undone. The right ear must touch the ground and the left is uncovered. Then the board is laid over the cavity and plastered up with clay. The three men now get out of the grave, and then everyone pushes back the earth. When the grave is full, the Mwalimu pours water in where the head lies, and this is supposed to reach the ear, though I cannot say why or for what purpose. This being done everyone reads the *Yasin*. Wailing takes place from death to burial, but mostly as the body is being borne to the grave.

Burton, who makes several remarks on marriage and death customs, says that on Tumbatu Island the late friends, women and debtors indulge in reproaching and abusing the dead, and compares this to Irish wakes. I am told, though, that this custom, which was but rarely indulged in even formerly, has now died out. He also mentions, as a belief of the natives, that most deaths occur "when the tide ebbs, at the full and change of the moon."

(5) *Post-Burial Ceremonies.* When it is all over the relations gather together and subscribe money, which is given to the nearest relation to buy food—rice and fish, fowls or goat, according to the money available—and for three days the men and women of the family sleep at the home of the deceased, the men outside and the women in the hut.

On the fourth day the whole countryside comes to a large feast and service called *hitima*. The whole Koran is first read through, thirty people each reading at the same time a separate Jeza. After this there is much feasting.

When this is over all intone the following prayer: "*Elhamd ul illah, rabi-el-alamina, mungu amrehemu maiti*," of which a free translation is "Praise be to God, the Lord in whom we trust; May God have mercy on the dead."

An Arab woman remains in mourning for five months (*Kalia eda*), and does not appear at all during that period, but at the end gives a feast. The natives do not do this.

Graves are generally kept in good repair and rarely built over. Stones are set round them, and often broken plates, etc. These latter perhaps not so much for decoration, but, I have been told, for the use of the devils. Relations generally visit the graves and see that they are in order.

THE WOMAN

(*a*) *Childhood*

The differences observed in birth ceremonies between boys and girls have already been referred to. The life of a girl of early age differs but little from a boy's. Her games are not so rough, and her spare-time occupations are more domestic. I do not think dolls are of general use among children, though I have once seen a little girl playing with a rag doll, referred to as *mwanangu* (my child).

A girl is generally, when old enough, employed by her mother on such tasks as minding the baby, and later on the small daughter will pound the flour in the *kinu* and sift it in the *unga*, and generally assist in the preparation of food. When the millet or rice is ripening, they will also sit in little shelters in the fields and scare away the birds.

As a general rule girls receive no education and are not taught the Koran, though there are exceptions to this rule, and I have a charm which I saw being copied from the Koran by a little girl about thirteen years of age.

(*b*) *Puberty*

When a girl perceives her menses beginning for the first time she gives warning of her condition by crying out. On hearing this, her mother or grandmother will examine her, and if it is in fact so, will shut her up inside, away from all people, as she is then taboo.

The mother will then go and buy her two new printed calico cloths (*kisutu*), and search for a *somo* (teacher or confidential adviser) for her, who will come, and taking the girl on her back will carry her to a washing place. Here she will take off her clothes and wash her all over. All the women of the village follow and pour a spoonful (*kata*) of water over her. The *somo* will then take her back and will sit her on a white mat.

The women will bring a wooden platter (*chano*) and on it a cup of simsim oil. They then mix *pakanga* (rue-Steere), *pacholi* (?) *maua maulidi* and *liwa* (a sweet-scented wood, like sandalwood from Madagascar—Madan), and grind it. The girl will first be rubbed with the oil and then with the flour, and all of the women present will smear a little on. She will then be taught how to wear a diaper (*piga winda* or *sodo*).

After seven days the girl may emerge from the house, but may not speak to any old women unless each of them gives her money; this prohibition continues in the case of each old woman until the girl gets money from her or bears a child.

Hartland (*Ritual and Belief*, p. 277) has apparently got hold of something of this custom when he says of Swahili girls at puberty, " among them a girl returns from her seclusion in silence, and gives her hand to every man she meets, receiving from him in return a few small coins."

Before they are married girls receive some instructions as to the relations of man and wife. In Zanzibar Island, among the Wahadimu, a special *ngoma* is played called *msondo*, and women imitate, for the benefit of the novices, the sexual relations of men and women. In Pemba, among the Wapemba, in addition to this dance (*msondo* or *unyago*) girls who are to be married are sent for a short course of instruction with an old married couple.

Captain Craster is presumably referring to this custom in his book, *Pemba, the Spice Island of Zanzibar*, when he says: "In each village there is an old woman whose business it is to instruct the girls of a marriageable age in their duties as wives and mothers. She also teaches the girls to dance, and to walk with a peculiar swagger that is supposed to be seductive in the eyes of the men. During their course of instruction the girls usually live in the old woman's hut. If, after marriage, the husband considers that his wife has failed in her duties, he sends her again to the old woman, who gives her further instruction, and sometimes emphasizes it with a stick. And if a wife has any cause of complaint against her husband, she often consults the old woman, and generally receives good advice, for these old women are very successful in composing conjugal disputes. She sometimes also acts as match-maker, but the employment of a match-maker is not considered essential."

It is not by any means considered essential that a young girl should be chaste before marriage, and I should be extremely dubious as to whether there are many girls who are virgins at marriage, at any rate in the town.

Bishop Steere says in a note under the word *bariki ku* (to bless) in his handbook: "Young people are said in Zanzibar to *bariki*, when they first have connection with the opposite sex. Girls are thought old enough between nine and ten."

Craster also mentions that he was told by a sheha who was holding a wedding-feast for his son, that the drumheads would be cut when it was time for the guests to go. I have not heard this.

(*c*) *After Marriage*

The ceremony of marriage has been described under the life of a man, but there is a note of a curious custom in Captain Craster's book (referred to above) which he says takes place in Pemba, though during my stay there I could not find any confirmation of it save in one case, when the Arabic clerk told me it was so.

I quote it verbatim as follows: "When a native marries, he is allowed to choose three married women from his village, who are installed in his house as concubines during the honeymoon. On his arrival at his house he finds the women each wrapped from head to foot in a sheet; and he is required to guess which is his wife. If he guesses wrong he must pay a rupee to the woman he has mistaken for his wife."

As for the life of a woman after marriage there is but little I need mention here, but it should be stated that there are the usual taboos as regards a woman in her courses. She is unclean in every way, neither may her husband have intercourse with her, nor may she prepare his food. If she comes to court as a witness, she may not touch the Koran, but must hold her hand above it to swear.

CHAPTER XXI

FAMILY ORGANIZATION

A LIST of the native names for the various relationships gives a clue to the way in which the native regards his family.

English	*Swahili*	*Kipemba*
Son or daughter (father speaking)	Mwanangu	
Father (son speaking)	Baba	
Mother	Mama	
Father's elder brother	Baba mkuu	
Father's younger brother	Baba mdogo	
Father's brother's wife	Mama	
Father's sister	Shangazi	
Father's sister's husband	Baba	
Mother's brother	Mjomba	
Mother's brother's wife	Mkwe	Hau
Mother's elder sister	Mama mkuu	
Mother's younger sister	Mama	
Mother's sister's husband	Baba	
Father's father	Babu	
Father's mother	Bibi	
Father's father's brother . . .	Babu	
Father's father's wife	Bibi	
Father's father's sister's husband .	Babu	
Mother's mother	Bibi	
Mother's mother's husband . . .	Babu	
Mother's father	Babu	
Mother's mother's brother's wife .	Bibi	
Mother's mother's sister's husband .	Babu	
Elder brother	Kaka or Kake	
Elder brother's wife	Shimeji	
Elder sister	Dada	Mbu
Elder sister's husband	Shimeji	
Younger brother	Ndugu	
Younger brother's wife	Shimeji	
Younger sister	Ndugu	
Younger sister's husband	Shimeji	
Father's brother's son	Ndugu	
Father's sister's son	Ndugu	
Mother's brother's son	Ndugu	
Mother's sister's son	Ndugu	
Father's brother's son's wife . .	Shimeji	Muwamu
Father's sister's son's wife . .	Shimeji	

English	*Swahili*	*Kipemba*
Father's sister's daughter	Ndugu	Kikoi
Mother's sister's daughter	Ndugu	
Mother's sister's husband	Shimeji	
Son or daughter	Mwanangu or Mwangu	
Son's wife or daughter's husband	Mkwe	
Brother's son or daughter	Mwanangu	
Brother's son's wife or daughter's husband	Mkwe	
Sister's son or daughter	Mjomba	
Sister's son's wife or daughter's husband	Mkwe	
Grandson or daughter	Mjukuu	Mkewangu
Great-grandson or daughter	Kitukuu	
Great-great-grandson or daughter	Kirembwe	
Great-great-great-grandson or daughter	Kinyingingya	
Great-grandfather or great-great-uncle	Ba Mkuu	
Great-grandmother or great-great-aunt	Bi Mkuu or Ma Kkuu	
Husband	Mume	
Wife	Mke	

A study of these words shows to whom the native renders obedience, and from whom he exacts it. If he says he must consult his *wazee* (elders), he means all those people whom he calls *baba*, *mama*, *kaka* and *dada*, and more particularly the *babas*, *kakas* when they are living. He will also render respect to his *bibis* and *babus*. *Bibi* in particular is a term of the highest respect, and is applied, not only to the array of "grandmothers" shown above, but to a wife, particularly of another person, to the mistress of a household, and in general essentially means a "lady." In the case of marriage it is generally the father who chooses the young man his wife, and arranges with her parents the dowry to be paid. The father also often builds a house for the young couple. In the case of girls, guardianship follows the rule of the Shafite school of Mohammedan law, which also governs the relationships of a man with his wife or wives. If he has more than one, he is bound, should they wish it, to furnish each with a separate house, and to treat them all in an identical manner.

Custody of the children again follows the law of Islam. The supervision and care of a child which has not reached the age of discernment (in the case of boys, seven, and puberty in that of girls) is primarily a woman's duty and is a right of the mother, even if divorced, which cannot be alienated. In the absence of a mother it devolves on her female relations. When the child is of the age of discernment, it may follow its own preference and stay with the parent it chooses.

In a man's actual family or *fungu* he includes all those relations named in the table given, except *shimeji* and *mkwe*. His own wife is one of his *fungu*. As regards marriage in the *fungu*, the rule is *nyumba mkubwa huingia mdogo*, i.e., the small house may enter the larger. Thus, a grandfather may marry his granddaughter (in Zanzibar as well as Pemba), and a grandmother her grandson. In practice this does not occur, for obvious reasons of age, but a grandfather sells his right over his granddaughter for a rupee or so. This right is not taken very seriously, but it is established custom. Prior claim like this does not exist in the case of a grandmother and grandson.

A man may marry the daughters of his *shangazi* (father's brothers and sisters), whether they are older or younger than his father, and he has a first claim on them. He may also marry his deceased younger brother's wife. He may not marry the daughter of his mother's brothers and sisters or the wife of his deceased elder brother or any other members of his *fungu*. A woman may marry the sons of her *shangazi* and her deceased elder sister's husband. She may not marry her deceased younger sister's husband.

A grandfather has no rights at all over his grandson's wife, but calls her *mkewangu* (my wife) affectionately. In the same manner a grandmother calls her grandson *mume wangu* (my husband).

A man may not marry two sisters while both are living. Incest of father with daughter or of brother and sister are heinous, but liaisons between relations who can marry are of no account.

CHAPTER XXII

VILLAGE LIFE

(*a*) *The Village*

NATIVE villages vary very much indeed. Those of the more " civilized " people, the Swahilis, ape the Arabs and even the Europeans, generally having streets more or less wide, and the houses almost in rows facing each other.

The Watumbatu, whose chief towns are Kichangani (with its principal quarters, Chwaka, Uvivini and Gomani), and Jongoe on Tumbatu Island, build their houses very close together, with no idea of streets or anything else, and it is a very complicated business to find one's way through a perfect maze of houses to the Sheha's house.

There are no outlying huts in a Tumbatu village, which may, of course, be accounted for by the fact that the space suitable for building is rather limited. The Pemba villages are airier and more picturesque, and generally consist of a collection of small or family clumps of houses, but all in a certain radius.

Those of the Wahadimu, or so-called aborigines of Zanzibar, consist usually of large, roomy huts well scattered about, with no suggestion of crowding. They are extraordinarily pleasant places, especially on the north and east of Zanzibar Island, where the houses are generally built of stone and often have two storeys.

Very often the Wahadimu live in solitary huts in the bush, or with not more than two or three neighbours.

These four types of villages have certain public

buildings, etc., common to all of them. These are a mosque, invariably, though of a very simple design, a market, often merely an open banda, a well or two, and sometimes a police station, or a chief's hut.

The simplest form of mosque is a rectangular hut with a kibla, and outside a water-pot and stepping-stones, so that worshippers can avoid soiling their feet after ablutions.

In many villages there is an *mkahawa*, or coffee-shop, where all the gossip of the day is discussed. This corresponds to the "Public House" of English villages.

In a few villages in both Zanzibar and Pemba I have come across ngoma bandas, or theatres, where dances are held, and there is also one at Kichangani, on Tumbatu Island.

A rare building to find is an *Mzimu*, or dwelling-place of a spirit. The only built one I have seen was a small secluded hut, and in it many broken potsherds and rags, placed there as offerings to the devil. Sometimes the Sheha has near his house a small hut where no one lives, but which he uses as an office, or to entertain distinguished guests.

Chicken huts, built on four legs to keep mongooses and civets off, are common objects, and also goat, cattle and donkey bandas, the former often a lean-to.

Outside the villages or behind a cluster of huts is the midden, the chickens' paradise, on which such refuse as empty shells, food scraps, etc., is thrown.

The native paths are proverbially crooked, and they seem incapable of making them straight, even when there are no obstacles. If a tree falls across a path, a new one is made round it, the obstacle is never removed, and even when it is decayed the path still goes round. Perhaps this is why there are so many bends. Near many streams are built platforms of wood with a *kata* near, which are used for prayers. To build over a narrow stream a convenient tree is usually thrown across it (if the bed is deep and the descent difficult). Ferries often ply between adjacent islands and over wide creeks, for which a fare of two pice is usually charged, though, of course, the fare varies with distance.

(*b*) *Moving a Village and Founding a New One*

The old map of Zanzibar is now quite inaccurate and cannot be relied on, at any rate as far as small villages are concerned, as the owners have moved to fresh woods and pastures new.

If a Sheha, or the head of a large family, dies, his hut is not occupied again, and gradually his family round breaks away and builds new houses and founds new villages, each of which gets a different name. If the owner dies before the house is completed, it is left unfinished, but it is possible that this custom is derived from the Arabs. (Princess Salme says it is not from sentiment, but from innate indolence.)

Another reason for frequent shifting is that the land gets exhausted and no longer bears *muhogo* (cassava) in profusion, and fresh land is therefore broken up.

There is one rite that is always observed in the building of a new hut. Before entering the new house to live in it, a sacrifice of a goat or fowl must be made outside the door, and the blood allowed to fall there. The owner does not eat the flesh, but gives it to the poor. The intention of this is to appease any lurking devil, or to stop any spell that has been put on the house.

The same sacrifice must be made before digging a well, and the blood allowed to fall over the place it is to be made, so that the devil living there may drink it and not be annoyed at his dwelling being disturbed.

Native huts are often rented at from two to five rupees per mensem, but a higher rental is, of course, payable for more superior dwellings in important areas.

(*c*) *Shehas and Organization*

Formerly almost every little village had its chief, or Sheha, but when a more direct system of government was introduced and the Shehas, were paid, the number was cut down, and now Shehas control quite large areas.

The Sheha's official function is to act as a kind of glorified policeman, and he has statutory police powers of arrest. If the Administration want to see a particular man, it is to the Sheha that the summons for him is sent; if information or labourers are wanted the Shehas supply them.

A Sheha also unofficially endeavours to settle small disputes, and if a native has a complaint against a neighbour, it is first taken to the Sheha, who endeavours to settle it. If he is unsuccessful, he hails both parties before the Kadi or the European in charge of the district.

Above the Shehas (correct plural *Masheha*) are sometimes placed *Maakida*, and above them again a *Liwali*, but this is an Arab arrangement. The Arab title Mudir has now (1928) been substituted for Akida, and there are no Liwalis left.

The Sheha is also responsible for keeping the paths and village in his district clear and clean, and must provide porters and guides if required.

When a Sheha dies or resigns, and a successor is needed, the elders of the village, or district, are required to select a new man.

Shehas generally have an assistant called a *Naibu*, very often their son. As on a Sheha's retirement or death the *Naibu* is very often appointed to replace him, the office tends to become hereditary.

Each Sheha is provided with a silver or bronze badge, an official waistcoat (*Kisibau*) and a red flag, which he flies outside his house from sunrise to sunset.

Since the above words were written, the Sheha's position has been greatly improved. He is now a member of a district court which tries small criminal cases.

(*d*) *Daily Life in the Village*

If one pays a visit unexpectedly to the village in the morning, one sees very few men, but on each baraza there are several women seated, working, perhaps, at mat-making, which takes the place of the knitting of Western countries, or making coir or preparing flour and other kindred occupations.

There is a general air of peace and quiet, and it is very pleasant sitting on a shady baraza listening to feminine politics.

Their men are generally away at work, save those that are old, and in large villages the local tailor pedalling briskly away at his "Singer."

THE MAN'S DAY

Very often I have been travelling at night, or camping, and up early in a native village about four a.m. when the cocks crow for miles around, and have seen the day start for its inhabitants, and "before the phantom of false morning dies" one hears the muezzin, who is surely the earliest riser of all, call out to the drowsy worshippers to pray, and those that are most pious come hurrying out of their huts to begin their orisons before sunrise.

Otherwise in early morning there are few men who rise before the sun, except in those villages not too far from town, where the milkman is up early to milk the cows before the long ride to town to sell it.

There is soon a ghostly greyish light over the village, and as the sun rises, which it does quickly near the Equator, one sees the foliage begin to assume its colour. Smoke rising from the eaves shows that the women are astir preparing breakfast for their lords and masters. With a clang of wooden bars being thrust back, doors open, men and women stagger sleepily abroad, some to sit yawning heavily on their barazas, others to perform a perfunctory toilet. Goats get up, stretch themselves, and bleat, and cows low. Soon after the village bustles with activity, the men have fed, and after a visit to the mosque, each goes out to his occupation. Even the African realizes that early morning is the best part of the day for work, and wants to get it done before the midday heat.

If asked what their occupation is, most answer "*Kulima*" (cultivating), and very early they go off to hoe up their patch and make the ridges for the muhogo to grow in, and build walls to keep the pigs away, or clear bush in order to break up fresh ground.

Carpenters, blacksmiths and other craftsmen go off to their jobs, the former perhaps to the dhow he is repairing or the canoe he is hollowing out for a fisherman customer, and the blacksmith to the forge to repair his neighbour's hoe, or if it is too far gone, to make him another. Builders go off to the hut they have contracted to build, and so on.

In the northern village of Nungwe, or on the Pemba Island of Mtambwe Kuu and other places, the lime-burners repair to the shore to break the coral rag, and build it up with wood into a bonfire to make the lime they will afterwards export to the city.

About ten or eleven o'clock the market begins to fill and sellers come with their wares—fruits and vegetables and dried fish, chiefly, which are laid out in little lots. Shortly afterwards the fishermen, who have been at sea all night, come with their catch for sale, which they hand over to the auctioneer to sell. After this the purchaser again sells the fish by retail either in that market, or carries them off to one of the smaller markets and sells them there. Women never sell, and but rarely appear in the country markets. In clove time, of course, nearly everyone is employed on picking the crop, and the ordinary routine of life is very much disturbed.

Another skilled occupation is that of plucking coco-nuts, at which one may earn a pice for each tree climbed, and an allowance in cash or kind for the number of coco-nuts felled. Certain songs are sung during this work, as in clove-picking, when the singer tells of passing events, and conversation is often carried on in chant.

At four o'clock all leave their work, and after going home to change their workaday clothes for their spotless white kanzus, go and call on their friends. About dusk the evening meal is ready and served on trays on the baraza, and with the help of friends this is soon dispatched, though first the piously inclined perform their sunset prayers and afterwards the night ones.

After this more visiting or an adjournment to the Sheha's house to discuss the affairs of the nation or tell stories, or perhaps there will be a dance (*ngoma*). Then to bed and so ends the day, which is not always by any means as strenuous as I have pictured it.

THE WOMAN'S DAY

The woman is the housewife and the cook. Her day starts before dawn with preparing the breakfast, which consists of the remnants of last night's meal "hotted up."

Then when the master has gone to his work, his wife cleans up the hut and afterwards goes and exchanges a few remarks with her next-door neighbour, thereafter to the well, where as much time is spent in talking as in drawing the water.

After that, if it is the time for breaking the soil, sowing or thinning out the rice, or keeping the birds and monkeys from the crops, she will go to the fields and work till eleven to twelve, taking with her a hoe and a basket of odd things on her head, including perhaps water to drink and sometimes the latest arrival to the family slung on her back. Both sexes appear to work indiscriminately in the fields, except in the Ndagoni Peninsula of Pemba, where women only do the work. If her work is that of catching whitebait, or shell-fish, she will go with her basket and fellow-fishers to the shore, where two will hold the cloth and the other drive the fry into it, or perhaps if the tide is low they will pick up crabs, or shell-fish.

At noon back to the hut to grind the maize or millet or to pound the flour, and prepare the food for the evening meal. Later, perhaps, she will go out a little way to pick up dead coco-nut leaves or wood with which to make the fire. At four or five again to the well, and whereas perhaps not many have been there in the morning, all seem to be there in the afternoon.

Then presently day draws to a close, the tropical sun has quickly set and the short twilight is over. Cooking starts about five or six, and when the meal is ready, it is soon dispatched by the men who have returned from work.

Talking fills in the gap between "our after supper and bedtime," or perhaps a dance in the slack part of the year (for they are forbidden during the clove harvest), in which case there is no bedtime, for it goes on till dawn has lightened the sky.

GAMES

There are two kinds of games which find especial favour—*bao* and cards.

Bao is a game played on a board, having four rows of eight holes in it, with the grey seeds of a shrub that grows on the seashore. There are three forms, Kiswahili and two kinds of Kiarabu. Kiswahili is very complicated, but Kiarabu is more simple.

The debased form is as follows:

In each hole are three seeds, and two rows of holes for each player. The starting player picks up the seeds from one hole, and passing either to right or to left, drops one into each hole. If the last of the seeds in his hand drops into a hole with more seeds in, all are picked up and distributed till at last one falls into an unoccupied hole. He then picks up all the seeds of his opponent in the two holes immediately opposite. The second player goes on, and the game continues till one or the other captures all his enemy's seeds.

The true form from Arabia is played, using only seven holes in each of the four rows and only two seeds in each hole. Otherwise it is the same as the form described above, except that all movement is anti-clockwise, and if there are no seeds in the opponent's front line, those in his back line cannot be taken.

Kiswahili has a multitude of rules, and requires a lot of careful thought before each move, and a lot of practice before proficiency is obtained.

To explain it a diagram is necessary.

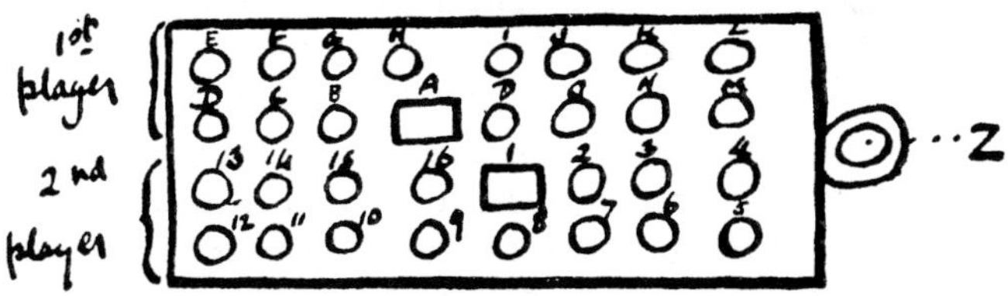

The lettered spaces represent one player's holes, and the numbered his opponent's. The round holes are called *kishimo*, pl. *vishimo*, the square ones *kuu*, and the one marked " Z " *kichwa* (head). This last has no other purpose than a store and does not enter into the game. Each player's front rank is called *mbele*, and rear rank *nyuma*; the seeds are called *komwe*, or *soo*, or *namu* (see later). To set the board for play is *kupanga*. To take seeds is *kula*.

Each player has thirty-two seeds, and the first player puts six in A and two each in B and C, while the second player puts six in 1 and two each in 2 and 3. The balance of the seeds is called *namu*. The object of each player is to capture his opponent's seeds and use them till his opponent can no longer move.

The first stage of the game is called *kunamua*, which lasts until all the *namu* have been played, and the second, which continues to the end, *mtaji*.

In the first move the first player puts a *namu* in either B or C, and taking up the three goes either to right or left placing one in each. The second player does the same, but may put his *namu* also in any hole where there is one opposite. If he does this, he takes his opponent's seeds and places it either in 4 or 13. The game now continues in this way, but if you take more than one of your opponent's seeds, you play from either of your own end front row of holes towards the centre, and if the last one falls into a hole already occupied, you pick up all and continue the way the board is lettered or numbered, and on each occasion your last seed falls into an empty hole with seeds opposite you, you take these and go to either of your end holes and start afresh. Thus any one turn may be a very long one.

There is a slight exception to the choice of ends to start from, in that if the seeds you take are in the end hole, or the hole next to the end, you must start at that end and may not go to the other. This is called *Kimbi*.

If at any stage there is no occupied space in your front rank with an occupied space opposite, you may *takata*, or put a seed in any of your own occupied front rank spaces, and go not to the end, but right or left from the hole in which you *takata*-ed. If there is a choice of holes to *takata* in, you may not *takata* in a hole with only one seed. Of course if your *safari*, or move, stops in a hole with seeds opposite, you take these and go to the end in the usual way. You cannot *takata* from *kuu*, but if there are only seeds in *kuu* you play one to either side, you then place your *namu* with it and go on. This continues until there are only six seeds in *kuu*, after which you may use the *kuu* to *takata*.

When all *namu* in a player's hand are finished, the second part of the game called *mtaji* begins. This consists in taking up the seeds in any hole in which there are more than one, and playing towards the end in which there are most seeds. If this results in taking your opponent's seeds, it is called *mtaji*. If a player cannot make an *mtaji* move, he must *takata* in the same method employed in the first half of the game, except that if no front rank space has more than one seed he must *takata* with the rear rank, and if possible he must *takata* with the seeds in a space, which, on being played, will leave the seed to fall into an already occupied space. He cannot *takata* with only one seed.

The game is ended when a player has either no seeds in the front row and none placeable there, or no hole with more than one seed in it.

Many other forms of this game are played over Africa, and the *bao* is generally referred to as *Mankala*.

Card Games. There are four of these played by the natives, and I shall give the rules of each one in turn.

(1) *Chanis.* Shuffle and cut the pack, deal each player four, and turn up four on the table. The player on the left of the dealer begins. If he has a card of nine pips and there is a 5 and 4 on the table, he takes them and lays them aside, if say, he has a queen and there is a queen on the table, he takes it, and so on. If he cannot take, he discards one to the table. If he has two queens and there is another on the table, he may lay one down saying "*Chanis*," if another player also has a queen, he captures both saying "*batis*," if not the original player takes the card with his remaining queen saying "*batis*." When the four cards in hand are exhausted another four are dealt. The player who gets the most cards wins.

(2) *Wahedusitin*, or sixty-one. 2's, 8's, 9's and 10's are discarded. Three cards are dealt to each player and the next one turned up, and its suit is then trumps. Each player then plays a card; the highest of the suit led, or trumps, wins. Then an extra card is dealt round so that there are always three in hand. To beat a card is *kupika*; trumps are *terufu*. The Jack is always higher than the queen.

When finished the cards are counted as follows: A = 11; Queen = 2; 7 = 10; King = 4; Jack = 3. 3, 4, 5, 6, do not count. The player nearest 61 wins. King, Jack and queen are generally known as *Mzungu Mosi*, *wa pili* and *wa tatu* (first, second and third European.) The low status of the queen is probably attributable to the native attitude towards women.

(3) *Nakshi*, or thirty-one. This is like vingt-et-un. Each player is dealt one card, dealing from below. Then the banker deals more to each player as he wishes. If he stops under 31, he remains as he is; if 31, the dealer pays, and if over, the player loses.

(4) *Komari*. This is even more of a gamble than *Nakshi*. Each player calls a card, and in turn the banker deals for each, two packs, one his, one the player's. If the card called falls in the player's pack, he wins, if not, vice versa.

Gambling is forbidden not only by the law, but by the Holy Sheria (though it is more or less countenanced during Ramathan after sunset). Needless to say, this does not prevent its being indulged in.

Tossing for a pice is a new pastime. This is called *Kamali*, and consists in throwing two pice into a hole. If only one goes in, the others say *maliza* (finish), and the player throws a stone on the one that is out.

The following game is slightly more intelligent. There are 15 bad men (long) and 15 good (short). Arrange them in a row so that knocking out every ninth you leave only the good.

This is the correct arrangement.

ıııı I I I I I ıı I ııı I ı I I ıı I I I ı I I ıı 1

A favourite but concealed sport in Zanzibar and Pemba is cock-fighting. It is concealed (*a*) because gambling is illegal, and cock-fighting would not be cock-fighting without it, and (*b*) because it might be cruelty to animals, which is also illegal. It will be easily perceived that, shorn of these two attractions, cock-fighting would not be much of a sport, not only to natives, but also probably to many who are supposed to be more civilized than they. Good cocks fetch as much as Rs. 10 (I have heard of one for Rs. 15) each; they are let loose and fly at each other, while the lookers on form a circle round and bet.

CHAPTER XXIII

TRIBAL ORGANIZATION

THE aboriginal tribes of the Sultanate are of no great antiquity. Such tribal organization as there was, was gradually built up by those conglomerate peoples, but under Arab and British rule it has gradually declined, and there is now little trace of it, though a good deal of the tribal, or clannish spirit, is still to be observed.

The Wahadimu were apparently welded into a tribe by the Persian colonists, who pursued a policy of assimilation reflected to-day in the numbers of Hadimu who call themselves Shirazis, and claim descent from the old Persian princes.

At their head was a chieftain called probably at first Mfaume (chief), and latterly Mwenyi Mkuu (the great owner). He was assisted in his administrative duties by a number of Waziri (viziers), or Ministers. The Wahadimu (many of whom, by the way, claim only African descent) all owed allegiance to him, and paid him taxes regularly.

There was a good deal of sanctity about the person of the Mwenyi Mkuu, and he was treated with the greatest respect by his subjects. His regalia consisting of horns and drums were also sacred, and used only on special occasions.

The last Mwenyi Mkuu, who was tributary to the Omani Seyyid (Sultan), died in 1865, and no other has been appointed, though his heir is still recognized as such in title by the Wahadimu. The villages of the Wahadimu are far more in the nature of separate settlements than those of the other two tribes, except perhaps to some degree the Watumbatu. In each Hadimu village is a person known as the Mwana Zale, or Mwana Vyale. This man is the senior descendant of the original founder, or father of the village, and on him devolves the care of the sacred places, the homes of the spirits on whose goodwill the welfare of the community depends. The word zale is derived from zaa "bear" (children), and Mwana Zale may be translated "Patriarch." Vyale is the Kihadimu form. The administrative head of the village is the Sheha, who is in the nature of a sub-chief.

Among the Wapemba the organization was very similar, and the chief was also of Persian origin (and nearly all the Wapemba claim Persian origin), though he was called Diwani. The Wapemba became tributary about 1822, when Seyyid Said put the natives on the same basis as the Wahadimu. The Masheha of Pemba were, until a short time ago, the heads of large families, and many of them can give off by heart the names of all their families and relations amounting sometimes to five hundred or so.

Recent reorganization of the shehaships on more or less geographical lines has been responsible for some trouble among the natives, and has been also the means of lessening the authority of the Masheha, as the strange families put under their orders do not easily accept their control.

The organization of the Watumbatu is different again; at the head of the tribe was the Sheha, a minor chieftain, to some degree subordinate to the Mwenyi Mkuu of Zanzibar to whom he was distantly related, but possessing considerable powers in matters of internal administration. Under him was the Wazir, and below the Wazir a subordinate official known as the Makata.

It may be noted that among the Wahadimu and Watumbatu, women acceded to the chief power if in the direct line, but there is no record of a woman attaining this position among the Wapemba. *Jus primæ noctis* appears to have been exercised by chiefs in Pemba, and possibly in Zanzibar.

TAXATION

There is no direct taxation on the natives nowadays.

The Wahadimu have apparently paid taxes consistently to every successive conqueror, Persian, Portuguese and Arab. The Watumbatu are said to have been originally exused from tax-paying by the Mwenyi Mkuu, as their chieftain was related to him.

When Seyyid Said, at the invitation of the natives, expelled the Mazrui, he imposed a tax of $2 per head on all the natives.

Pemba tradition says that there was also an excise duty of 5 per cent. on all produce, and that free labour had to be given on Government works, though a native document gives the price of his aid as the provision of regular quantities of mats and ghi.

In Zanzibar $1 went to the Sultan and the other was retained by the Mwenyi Mkuu.

Apart from this taxation the natives were left to their own devices.

There was a hut tax later (with remissions for clove owners) of Rs. 2/2 per hut, which was finally abolished in 1911.

POLITENESS AND HOSPITALITY

The commonest form of greeting in Zanzibar and Pemba is *Jambo*, to which the reply is also *Jambo*, but this is short for *Hu jambo* and the answer *Si jambo*. It means "How are you?" and "I am well," though more literally "There is nothing the matter," and "I have nothing the matter." Instead of *hu jambo*, *Hali gani* is often asked (what is your health?).

Children, or one of the slave class, often say to their superiors, as do young men to old men and women, *Shikamuu*, and this is an abbreviation for

Nashika miguu (I hold your feet). To this the great one replies *Marahaba* (It is welcome).

Sabalkheri means " Good morning," though it is used all day long in Zanzibar, *Mesalkheri* (Good afternoon) being but rarely heard even among Arabs. They are abbreviations for *Sabbakum* (and *Messakum*) *Allah bil kheri*—" May God make the morning (afternoon) good for you."

An Arabic form of greeting much in use in Zanzibar is *Slamalik* (for Salaam Alekum) meaning " Peace on you," to which the reply is *Wa Alekum es-Salaam*—" And on you peace." *Salaam* alone is generally used only by Mohammedan Indians (to Hindus and Parsees *Sahibje*—" God ").

Another greeting copied from the Arabs is *Kef Halek*—" How are you? ", with reply *Hamdulillah* (El hamed ul Illah)—" I am well (understood), Praise be to God."

" Good-bye " is commonly *Kwaheri*, in plural *Kwaherini* (*-heri* meaning " good luck ") or, copied from the Arabic, *Fiaman Illah*.

When approaching a house or entering the baraza, it is customary to say *Hodi*, the exact meaning of which is doubtful, though it may be an idea of " safety," but which has come to mean " May I approach? " The answer is *Karibu*—" Draw near," or " Welcome "—or even the same word, and without such reply good manners forbid entry.

When passing a house after greetings the owner will often say *Karibu*—" Draw near," to which one replies *Starehe*—" Stay where you are," or *Kaa kitako*—" Remain seated," whether one approaches or not.

Hand-shaking is now indulged in, and often kissing the hands of a superior. In any case it is good manners to bow over the hand being shaken, and when saying " I am well," place a hand on the head and heart. Sometimes one's hand is held for a very long time.

After greetings it is usual to inquire the news,

Khabari gani, or *Khabari za siku nyingi*—" What news? " or " The news of many days? ", to which the reply is invariably *Njema* (good) as is *Si jambo* to *Hu jambo*, though a moment after, your visitor often begins to recite a long tale of woe, or of his bad health. After that one may ask after mutual friends, or the family of our friend—the latter is generally inclusively referred to in the word *Jamaa* or *Nyumba*. I have not noticed that either Arabs or natives in Zanzibar are particular about not asking after womenfolk, and often volunteer information as to their wives' health.

For those desirous of making conversation, "trade," "the weather," "crops," "the Government," etc., are just as useful in Zanzibar as they are in England, and one may every now and then intersperse a " How are you? " in a sort of afterthought tone of concern, or reply emphatically, " I am very well " (*Jambo sana*).

A visitor will always be offered some kind of refreshment—coco-nut milk from the tree, an orange, sherbet, or coffee, or more, according to the wealth of the owner.

Any visitors to your office, although they have no business with you, will send in word they want to *Amkia* (greet) you.

It is a great insult to say to anyone *Hunu abadu* (You have no manners); in fact this often leads to blows and litigation.

When there are two or three together and one sneezes, it is usual for the others to say *Hamdulillah*, which corresponds in this instance to the English " Bless you."

CHAPTER XXIV

LAW

THERE is no regular system of native law in Zanzibar, and traces of it have to be searched for in the customs of the people, and in case reports.

Administration of Law

The chief appears to have been, as in other places in Africa, a law-giver and judge, as well as administrator. Cases are generally settled by compounding, when the local chief, or Sheha, *patanishas* (makes to agree) the parties. Thefts, assaults and trespasses are frequently treated in this way, and settled on the payment of damages.

Criminal Law

Theft. If this is not settled it frequently happens that the injured party takes the value from the thief. That they regard this as a perfectly legitimate action is shown by the surprise with which they receive one's dictum that it is wrong.

Adultery. The rule seems to be, judging from assault, murder and wounding cases, that the wife may be beaten and the adulterer killed, or beaten.

Witchcraft. The only penalty for witchcraft in Zanzibar appears to be ostracism.

Civil Law

Disputed Possession. The claimant enters into possession and picks the crops. If the action is disputed, the case is decided in the usual way by the chief, and the claimant may, or may not, have to pay damages according to the result of the case.

Pre-emption. Apart from Mohammedan law, there seems to be a well-established custom that the neighbour has the right to the first refusal of land bordering on his plantation.

Land Tenure. Roughly speaking, the Swahili rule seems to be that waste land is common property which becomes the property of its cultivator, who in some cases thereafter always holds it, and in some loses it if he fails to keep it in cultivation, though in both cases the wild trees and fruits on it remain common property. In the usual way sale of this land is prohibited, though among some more advanced tribes, sale is allowed to members of the family, and in other cases to outsiders when relations have had the first refusal.

Custody of Animals. Unless a sum is agreed on for the herding and custody of animals, it appears that half the value of the offspring is retainable by the herdsman.

International Law

It may seem curious to consider that there are any traces of International Law among the natives of Zanzibar (though, of course, Zanzibar had a well-defined position as an independent state and treaties with it—many of which are still in force—were entered into by many foreign powers), but the study of the history of the native shows that they have a well-defined idea of the nature of an international obligation. The principle of International Law from the earliest times to the establishment of the Roman Empire has been laid down that states, as such, had no mutual rights or obligations, but that the tribes which were cemented by blood relationship owed each other certain duties. It will be seen, however, that in Zanzibar the natives went somewhat further than this in their relations.

At the time of the Zinj Empire, when it had broken up into separate states, there are many indications that there were international understandings between the different states. It is true, however, that the heads of these states were of the same family, and war often occurred between states that were not of one confederation, as witness Pate, Mogadisho and the Zinj Empire states; but further alliances were entered into at a later date between the Portuguese and Malindi, and in the case of states other than Malindi, the Portuguese seemed to have made agreements which were in some cases respected and in other cases broken by one or other of the parties.[1] Mombasa was always in a state of war with Portugal, Kilwa sometimes broke away from the condition of limited and tributary independence which Portugal allowed her, and Zanzibar appears usually to have respected her engagements with the Portuguese.

It will be remembered that the Wahadimu called themselves people who made promises (ahadi), and they claim that whether with the Persians, Portuguese or Omanis, they respected them. In the case of Pemba, a local manuscript not only describes what were apparently verbal agreements between the Portuguese and the Wapemba, and the Mazrui and the Wapemba, but also gives us an example of a genuine treaty which may be divided into clauses thus:

"Diwani Ngwachani and Diwani Athman journeyed to Muscat and agreed with the Seyyid these conditions:

(1) You shall assist us in every way you can and you shall remove the Mazrui.
(2) We shall be in friendly relations reciprocally.
(3) We shall pay all our taxes.
(4) We shall bring you ghi and shall bring you mats.
(5) You shall build wherever you please.

The Seyyid agreed to these conditions, and we exchanged blood for the treaty which we had made."

This treaty seems to me of peculiar interest. It would be quite easy to translate it into the phraseology of treaties, and it would comply with all the requirements necessary to make it a valid treaty.

[1] A treaty between Portugal and Bwana Tamu Abubakar bin Muhammed, King of Pate, was concluded on August 24th, 1728.

(*a*) The parties to it must be capable of contracting.

In this case the two Diwanis were the rulers of Pemba, and went at the request of their people. Whether Diwanis are to be considered as absolute monarchs, or constitutional monarchs whose tenure of office was to be regarded as to some extent dependant on the will of the people, it will be seen that in this case they had full power to contract on behalf of the Wapemba.

Seyyid Said was an absolute monarch; his position needs no inquiring into; he frequently entered into treaties with foreign powers which he negotiated himself.

(*b*) Ratification is necessary except when an international contract is personally concluded by a sovereign.

In this case the treaty was concluded by sovereigns, but nevertheless a ceremony was entered into which approaches more nearly to an Act of Ratification than a mere signature to a treaty.

We have seen that in the more primitive societies duties were owed to each other by tribes which were connected by blood relationship. The ceremony which took place on this occasion was one which is well known among semi-savage tribes, and was the medium intended to bring tribes, which were not related by blood to each other, within that category. As there was no true blood relationship, the parties gashed themselves and rubbed their blood together, thus being able to consider themselves in the position of people of the same blood.

(*c*) Interpretation of treaties.

(*a*) They must be read according to their plain sense, or where that is wanting, according to their spirit.

There is no difficulty in reading this treaty in this way,

(*b*) So as to give due effect to the fundamental rights of the State.

No treaty can be taken to restrict by implication

the rights of sovereignty. Any restriction of such rights must be affected in a clear and distinct manner.

Nothing could be more clear or distinct than the manner in which the sovereignty and independence of Pemba was restricted by this treaty. The reader may be reminded that the taxes mentioned were subsequently fixed as the poll tax of two dollars a head, and the excise duty of 5 per cent. This treaty was loyally adhered to by the Wapemba until it became extinct.

Treaties of which the object is to seat a dynasty or prince upon a throne, or guarantee its possession, are not subjects of International Law, because such contracts are in the interests of individuals and their personal capacity. Thus documents written by the Sultan and appointing the new Mwenyi Mkuu scarcely came within the scope of the section; however, they are interesting as showing how these appointments were made.

The first of these documents is of that precise nature, the second is in the nature of a new commission issued by the Sultan's representative, the Liwali, to the Sheha of Tumbatu on the occasion of the accession of the new Mwenyi Mkuu.

(*Translation*)

IN THE NAME OF THE MOST MERCIFUL GOD.

The Sultan's Signet.

From MAJID BIN SAID

To All whom it may concern amongst our friends, God Save You.

WE have appointed and installed our beloved friend, SULTAN AHMED BIN SULTAN MOHAMMED, in place of his father in all matters that concern him. Therefore no person shall interfere with him. And Peace is the Best end. Written on 15th Rabial Awwal, 1282.

Written by His Command by his slave, Mohammed, with his own hand.

(*Translation*)

In the Name of the Most Merciful God.

From Suleiman bin Hamed

To All whom it may concern.

We have appointed Msellem of Tumbatu to hold the same position as he used to do in time of Sultan Mohammed, and so he, Msellem, is now (working) on behalf of Sultan Ahmed bin Sultan Mohammed.

No one from amongst Wahadimu of Tumbatu shall disobey his orders, for he is their overseer as much as, and perhaps more than, he was before.

With Compliments. Dated the 28th day of Safar, 1282.

This is written by me, the humble Suleiman bin Hamed, with my own hand.

Signet.

Local Laws

Two examples of what might be termed municipal by-laws, framed for the benefit of the community by the Sheha and strictly observed by the community, occur to me.

(1) At Vitongoje, in Pemba, there are a number of freshwater ponds on which the community depends for their supply of water. These ponds are also the home of tortoises and catfish, which form an item of the native food supply. The method of catching them, however, involves the stirring up of the mud, and the consequent fouling of the water. It is, therefore, in the power of the Sheha to prohibit fishing in several ponds at a time, in order that clean water may be obtained.

(2) At Makunduchi, in Zanzibar, fresh water is scarce and has to be obtained from wells dug with great labour to a depth of eighty feet. Sometimes

the water gets so low that continual drawing of water causes what is there to become muddy. Each well is, therefore, provided with a flagstaff with a black flag. When the flag is up, water may not be drawn from the well.

CHAPTER XXV

THE SOIL

THERE are four chief kinds of soil which are cultivated in Zanzibar.

(1) The black, loamy soil, which is quite the best. It is found generally in the valleys, and planted chiefly with rice.

(2) The red, clayey soil, which is the commonest, and on which nearly everything (and particularly cloves) is planted.

(3) The grey, sandy soil round the coasts—particularly the east coast—which is planted mainly with coco-nuts.

(4) The coral rag in the north, and running along the east coast from north to south, which can hardly be dignified by the title of soil, but nevertheless supports vegetation in pockets of earth. This is in places assiduously cultivated with muhogo and millet by the Wahadimu, who burn and cut the bush off it, and surround it with stone walls two or three feet high to keep off the pigs.

Pemba is also of coral formation, much hillier, and about two hundred feet in height. The commonest soil is the red referred to above, but there is also black and sandy.

Pemba is not so bothered with coral rag as Zanzibar, except in the north.

LAND TENURE

Strictly speaking, no value is attached to the land itself, its price being determined not by the soil, but by its accessibility, and by the economic trees or plants on it. Of course the quality of the soil does count in an indirect sort of way, as a coco-nut on poor soil will be worth only about three to six rupees, while on good soil it may fetch twelve, as it will bear more.

Any native, i.e., Mpemba, Mhadimu or Mtumbatu, may occupy and plant bush land, or *wanda*, as it is called, but he has no right to anything but the crops on it, all land being the property of the Sultan, and prospective right cannot be acquired unless sixty years continuous and undisputed ownership can be proved.

A lot of trouble has recently been caused by natives selling land to Indians and thus alienating it, but I think I am right in saying the above is the policy now (1920) insisted on by the Government, and based on native custom.

PRODUCTS

(1) *Cereals*

The most important of the grain crops is rice (*mpunga*), and in the old days a lot was exported. Zanzibar and Pemba could probably be very good rice-growing countries now, Pemba especially. There are nearly one hundred hill and valley varieties of rice there, some very good indeed. For many years the huge importation of rice from India has made it unnecessary for the natives to plant, but during the war the difficulties of transport and the high prices of rice made it imperative for them to grow it. A lot of land that had been fallow and bush-covered for years was dug up and planted. The great time for preparing the ground is during the hot season. Before the ground is broken up the bush is burnt, and just before the rains begin, in February or March, the seed is sown. This work is largely done by women, and later on they transplant and thin out the crop—a long, back-aching task. When harvest time comes, and as the crop is ripening, the job is to keep the monkeys and birds off, even watching night and day. This difficulty is increased, as the harvesting is not at first done at one time but as the grain is required, the women going out with baskets and breaking the heads off. In some parts the straw is used for thatching, but I think more often it is burnt, thus forming a natural manure for the ground.

The cereal next in importance is *muhindi*, or maize, which as the name, *muhindi*, suggests, was introduced by Indians. It is probable that the natives do not know how to cultivate it properly, as good cobs are quite unusual.

The other two important crops are *mtama* (sorghum) and *mawele* (millet); the latter by no means as common as the former. *Mawele* is much smaller than *mtama*. Père Saccleux gives its scientific name as *Penicillaria spicata*. *Mtama* stalks in poorer Wahadimu districts are often used for building huts.

Another smaller grain is called *wimbi* (*Eleusine coræcana*—Sac.). Mr. Last tells me he has seen the children cut *wimbi* stalks into lengths, heat them in the fire and strike them on the ground, when they explode with a loud bang.

(2) *Vegetables*

The chief is the ubiquitous manioc, called *muhogo*. In Zanzibar it is planted in heaped-up ridges, but in Pemba little patches, about two feet in diameter, are hoed up, and a cutting is stuck in the centre of each. The ridges of Zanzibar are called *matuta*, and the patches of Pemba *makongo*. The plant is propagated from cuttings of the stems, one end of each being stuck in the ground. In *matuta* they all lean in one direction, but in *makongo* they are stuck in any way. Some of us have tried to persuade the natives to plant them with both ends covered, and so get a double amount, but the general reply is that "our fathers and grandfathers have always planted them by one end, so it would be wrong for us to do otherwise." It takes about a year to reach maturity. There are several varieties, bitter and sweet.

Sweet potatoes (*viazi*) are grown in the same way as manioc, and are propagated from cuttings of the creeper. They are plentiful and very good. There are three varieties: the ordinary *viazi*, *vikuu*, which are very big, and *meu*, which, as far as I know, grows only on Tumbatu Island.

Mbazi on first sight one instinctively distrusts as it looks, both in leaf and flower and pod, so like laburnum, but it is a shrub and not a tree. The pods contain peas which are very good. Père Sacclеux identifies it as the Angola pea (*Cajanus indicus*). It is very plentiful in Zanzibar, and is grown in conjunction with *muhogo*, but planted round the patch.

Kunde are beans produced on the *mkunde* shrub, and very popular. They are imported as well as grown.

Mchicha is a weed that makes a good substitute for spinach.

Mboga is the ubiquitous pumpkin; *bamia*—"lady fingers," or *Hibiscus esculentus*; *nyanya* are tomatoes, but very small; its relation the egg fruit, *bilinganya*, is a dark purple colour, and best fried.

The natives also eat the lufah in its early stages. It is called *dodoki*.

Sugar-cane (*miwa*) is popular, though not cultivated as much as formerly; it is usually chewed, and there is but little sugar (*sukari guru*) made now.

There are several more besides these, and so there is no lack of variety among vegetables in Zanzibar.

(3) *Fruits*

There is a wonderful variety of fruit in Zanzibar, but as most of them are well known and but few indigenous, I do not propose to say much about them. Citrous trees are the shaddock, two varieties, one with pink flesh and one with yellow, oranges, several kinds, lemons, limes, mandarins, or tangerines. Of mangoes there are many kinds, but few of them are good, as the natives do not understand grafting. Pomegranates, custard-apples, guavas, pine-apples, dorian, bread-fruit and rose-apples are but a few of the introduced fruits of which there is a great variety.

The varieties of bananas (*ndizi*) are called *pukusa*, *sukari*, *mjenga*, *mladi*, *maua*, *mzuzu*, *sabatele* and *mkono wa tembo*. The two most important economic trees are the clove and coco-nut, the latter of which deserves a chapter to itself, as it is of such importance in the lives of the natives, while the former, though the speciality of Zanzibar, is outside the scope of this book.

The pine-apple grows wild in two varieties and is called *nanasi* (which shows it was introduced by the Portuguese), the *mzambarau*, a kind of eugenia, whose fruit looks like a damson, the *mbibo*, or cashew tree, whose fruit is pear-shaped with a nut of boxing-glove shape below, called *korosho*, and which Europeans reckon superior to monkey-nuts as a relish at dinner.

Choki choki (litchi) is a curious fruit which looks like a large red beech-nut, but has sweet white flesh inside and a stone. The *mkwaju*, or tamarind tree, produces not only fruit but is a good wood for walking-sticks, which are made from its roots. The *mkunazi* tree, brought by the Arabs, who call it sidr, has a small, round fruit like a bitter cherry, sometimes identified with the lotus. It is under this tree that the Mohammedans say the Resurrection will take place. Arab ladies use the leaves as a cosmetic. Its Latin name, *S. Spina Christi*, reminds one that it was of this tree that Christ's crown of thorns is reputed to have been made. The papaw (*papai*) is the commonest of all cultivated trees, so much so that it is not considered *mali* (property), and may be picked by any passer-by.

Almost anything in the way of fruit or berry is considered tunda (fruit), and part of the native's diet unless it is poisonous.

A reference should be made to scented trees which are very popular, though, I believe, chiefly introduced by the Arabs. The chief ones are jasmine, ylang-ylang and frangipani, the first two being the most important. Women often wear bunches of the former fastened on to a black cord ornament round their necks, and men often carry ylang-ylang in their caps (or pockets if they have them).

(4) *Tobacco*

Tobacco is very extensively planted and grown in the north of Zanzibar Island. It is not used for smoking but for chewing, and a native considers nothing so delectable as a *bonne bouche* made of a clove, a piece of tobacco plug, a slice of areca and a smear of lime, all folded up together in a pepper vine leaf and stuck in the cheek. The horrid result is the red juice which they spit all over the place.

The fact that 23,138 coils were exported in 1920 from the Mkokotoni district of Zanzibar to Pemba shows what a large crop is grown. When ready, the tobacco plant is cut whole and hung up to dry round the eaves of the house. It is then plaited and rolled into coils about ten to twelve feet long which sell for Rs. 5 each.

A favourite story says: "When tobacco came into the world, wise men took it and admired it and smelt it. Other wise men came and took it and smoked it. The Wapemba, the fools, thought it was a food, and took it and ate it."

In the more remote parts Indian hemp is cultivated and smoked in a pipe, which consists of a coco-nut shell with one hole at its apex into which a hollow bamboo passes with a clay top to put the bhang into, and another at the side with a longer bamboo. Water is poured into the nut, which keeps the smoke fairly cool as the end of the top tube is in it.

This practice is kept secret as far as possible, as it is forbidden, and the dried leaf fetches a very large price. It is packed in a peculiar roll made of large leaves, or in sacks.

CHAPTER XXVI

THE AGRICULTURAL AND NAUTICAL YEAR

1. There is a calendar, possibly brought by the ancient Persians to Zanzibar, which is in use among the Wahadimu and Watumbatu and is the Solar year of 365 days.

It is divided into thirty-six decades of ten days each and five days over called the Gathas, and the festival of Hamaspath-madin is observed therein. They are supposed to be the days of the creation. The New Year's Day is the vernal equinox, and is called by the Parsees *Jamshidi Naoroz*, after King Jamshid, or Yima, to whom God gave the command, "Enlarge My world, make My world fruitful, obey Me as Protector and Nourisher and Overseer to the world," and he was presented with a plough and a golden spear. It will be seen, therefore, that this is a pastoral festival, symbolizing the creation and resurrection of spring.

The Parsee year, however, was five hours and fifty-four seconds short, and though they made a correction to balance this, the Zanzibar natives do not, and the beginning of the year is therefore now a little out.

Jamshidi Naoroz is called *Naorozi*, or *Siku ya mwaka*, in Zanzibar, and the last Gatha, *Kigunzi*. The year is called after the day it commences on; thus in 1921 it was *Mwaka Alhamisi* (Thursday in early September).

The Siku ya mwaka is still observed, though not in the way it used to be.

The following are, or were, the particular observances: (1) At night or early morning everyone (particularly women) must bathe in the sea, praying for good health during the coming year. (2) At midday a feast is cooked (*karamu*—Kitumbatu, *kiwao*), women cooking the rice and the men the *kitoweo* (relish), which is then dished out to all comers. (3) Immediately afterwards the fires are extinguished with water and lit again by means of *pekecha* (firesticks). The old ashes are carried out and deposited at cross-roads. The floury ash is sprinkled against the back of the house. (4) After this free fights used to take place, very often with fatal endings, but no inquiries were made. It was a great day to settle old scores, and until the practice was stopped Indians used to be thrown into the sea. (5) Ngomas are played all night.

2. The seasons in Zanzibar are well marked. The island is in 6° south latitude, and Pemba about 5°, and the latter island gets more rain than Zanzibar. In fact, in April, 1921, there were 36 inches of rain in Mkoani, South Pemba, and 17 in Mkokotoni, North Zanzibar, about 50 miles apart, though this is exceptional.

The sun is overhead about October 21st and February 21st.

The season of the Kas Kazi (or north-east monsoon) is called *Musimi*, and lasts roughly through December, January and February, when the sun is in the south.

This is followed by the heavy rainy season called *Masika*, during March, April and May. The cool season is called *Kipupwe*, and takes up about the next three months. The final season, which begins in September and includes the *Mvuli*, or light rainy season in November, is called *Mwaka* or *Demani*. This is the spring of Zanzibar, and deciduous trees, such as cotton (*Eriodendron anfractuosum*), take on new foliage then.

There are also light rains in August called *Mvua ya mwaka*.

The south-west monsoon (*kusi*) begins to blow about the beginning of April and drops about

October, when the *Malelezi*, or *Tanga mbili* (two tacks), begins to blow.

The chief hoeing seasons are before the two rainy seasons, i.e., in October and February.

The regular big clove crop is the mwaka crop (August to October). A second one called *mvule* (January and February) is generally small, but there are exceptions, e.g., 1920-21, when the mwaka crop was a failure, and the mvule very large.

The temperature varies from about 70° Fahr. in the cool season, to about 90° in the hot. But by the sea there is generally a breeze, so that it is never really unpleasantly warm.

AGRICULTURAL CUSTOMS

An interesting custom among natives is that of taking the seed rice (*mpunga*) in baskets, before it is sown, to the Mwalimu, or teacher of the mosque, who reads the Koran over it. This, of course, corresponds to the custom of blessing the seed which still obtains in some parts of England.

Further than this I have been unable to discover any ceremonials connected with sowing or harvest, despite extensive inquiries.

One would have thought it natural that some sort of sacrifice or other to the guardians of the crop would have taken place, but many natives assured me that this was not so. The cultivators are far too busy keeping off such material pests as birds and monkeys, to bother about anything spiritual.

I remember on one occasion walking some little distance behind a man carrying a large bundle of muhogo (manioc) cuttings, which he was on his way to plant. I saw him purposely take one of these and drop it at the side of the path, and when I came up, I saw it was dropped on one of the dwelling-places of the Mizimu (which I shall deal with later) at the cross-roads, where there was also a collection of other offerings, including some unripe lemons, grass and dead flowers.

Now it is just possible that this was a definite offering to the spirit dwelling there, given in the hope that it would assist his crop, but it is more probable that it was the almost mechanical act of dropping the offering, however small, which almost every passer-by makes. This offering, however, is usually merely a bunch of grass plucked just before reaching the Mizimu, and as in this case muhugo was offered, it is possible both intentions were in his mind, namely, to make the usual offering, and by giving a part of his crop to enlist the spirit's sympathies.

Standing in every field of ripening crops is a small hut built on piles, which not only enables the occupier to see every part of the field, but also keeps him above the flood water, which, in the rainy season, covers most of the land where rice is planted.

In these huts sit either children or old people, whose duty it is to scare away birds and monkeys, and many of them are armed with a small sling with which they make a sharp crack, and shoot small lumps of clay or stones in the direction of the intruders.

Sometimes these little huts are unoccupied, and inside are small pots of water and dishes of food. I have often asked if this was intended for the *sheitani* (devil), but have always been told it is the food of the usual occupiers, who are away at the moment.

Scare-crows, much the same as their English cousins, are also used, as are old tins and rags on string communication with the huts referred to.

Sir J. G. Frazer, quoting from the *Bulletin de la Société de Géographie*, says, "Among the Mohammedans of Zanzibar it is customary, at sowing a field, to reserve a certain portion of it for the guardian spirits, who at harvest are invited, to the tuck of drum, to come and take their share; tiny huts are also built in which food is deposited for their use."

I have made many inquiries as to the truth of this, but it is always denied. *Ngomas* (dances) are certainly much played at harvest time, perhaps because they are forbidden during clove harvest, and at other times the people are too tired after a day's work to play, and if asked to play they generally say so, but those in which food is given to the devil (i.e., eaten by the possessed one), are all dances for exorcizing. The tiny huts are those I referred to above, and as after a time I had little difficulty with some natives in finding out far bigger secrets, I think it unlikely they would have lied to me in a case where concealment was hardly necessary. In Pemba a charm is buried in each corner of a rice field, to stop people stealing the grain; and the method of cultivation also differs from that of Zanzibar, as the rice is not transplanted. Also free rice meals are given to all comers during the harvest.

The devils connected with certain trees such as baobabs, cotton trees, and solitary mangoes, I shall deal with later on.

You will often observe a double row of mango trees, which makes a beautifully shady avenue to walk under. These were planted by Arabs in the old days to stop bush fires and protect their plantations from wind.

CHAPTER XXVII

FIRE

THERE is no trace of a fireless period. I have never even heard any legend to account for its origin.

Matches are very cheap and almost universal, but sometimes *upekecha* (firesticks) are used in the more primitive places and in special rites. Captain Craster records it in Pemba, and I have seen it in Zanzibar. The method adopted is to spin a pointed stick in a hole in a piece of wood, backwards and forwards between the hands.

Captain Craster asked an old man near Chake Chake, whom he saw, why he did not use a bow-string, and showed him its use, but the man replied that his ancestors had not used it and he ought not to. This is the usual reply when a change of method is proposed, though the non-use of a bow-string is curious, for native carpenters use them both for drills and lathes.

Fires are built with three stones set as corners of a triangle. Inside these the small fire is made of little twigs, etc., and dried coco-nut leaves, and the pot on top. At each side, between the sticks, a long stick is stuck in, and pushed farther in as it is consumed.

SALT

Salt is now generally imported, though when shipping was bad I have known it obtained from sea-water by evaporation. As in Europe so in Zanzibar, salt is associated with bad, or good, luck. Neither salt, nor incense, nor needles and thread, nor ginger, nor eggs, may be sold after dark on peril of every kind of bad luck. I first found this out at an Indian shop, and asked the woman there if it was a custom imported from India. She told me no. I afterwards confirmed from several sources, both native and Indian, that it is purely native superstition, but so strong that the Indians have adhered to it as well. Should one want salt at night the only way to get it is to be given it, but the giver must first either go out and throw some on the roof, or throw some in the fire.

FOOD

(*a*) The native generally feeds twice a day, the chief meal being eaten in the evening, when he puts a good deal away, and only stops when he is *shiba* (full). The remnants of this meal are eaten either cold or warmed up in the morning. (*b*) *Dishes*. Muhogo is the great stand-by. It is eaten either boiled (*kuchemka*—to boil) or burnt in the ashes (*kuchoma*—to burn).

In Zanzibar bitter muhogo is peeled, and then a traverse cut is made in it, and it is hung up on a kind of netting arrangement to dry for some time (I have never seen this done in Pemba), and then it is pounded in a mortar (*kinu*) and flour made of it. This, made with water into pastry, is then baked in a *sufuria* (saucepan) with a lid on, on which fire is also placed (i.e., as well as underneath), and a kind of flabby cake of bread is made.

Grain is also ground into flour and made into cakes in the same way. When muhogo or grain is sufficiently ground with the quern (*jiwe la kusagia*) it is turned into a sieve, or winnowing fan (*ungo*), where it is well shaken up, and the rough bits come to the top and are put back for further pounding.

Rice is much used, and often flavoured with a coco-nut mixture called *tui*, made by mixing ground coco-nut with water and squeezing or straining it. It is then very good indeed.

Curry is popular, and common almost everywhere, but the poor Wahadimu people generally only boil their food, or make the bread above referred to.

Meat is but rarely eaten, and generally only on ceremonial occasions. Chickens are common, but not often eaten. Eggs are not eaten by the natives (they are by the Arabs), but usually left to the hens to hatch. Mongooses and kites generally thin the broods down.

In addition to vegetables, everyone eats either fish or shell-fish, and the poor old people subsist largely on the latter merely boiled. Fish of most species is eaten, and the natives are not at all particular if it is a bit high. Not only fish, but octopus and cuttlefish, and, in fact, almost anything that lives in the deep, forms an article of diet; practically nothing comes amiss. *Majongo* (*bêche de mer*), though, are barred, and the natives think the Chinese fearful *shenzis* (savages) for eating them. There are colonies of Chinese *bêche de mer* catchers in Zanzibar and Pemba.

I should mention *uji*, which is a porridge made of any kind of grain, and boiled in water with a little salt.

Pigs and dogs, of which some African natives freely partake, are, of course, owing to Mohammedan usage, never eaten. One Arab told me that in his sect turtle (and *bêche de mer*) were forbidden, but this is not general (as regards turtle). I think that some natives are not really particular to see that their meat has been killed in the prescribed Islamic way.

Camels are a great delicacy, though rare. Burton says Moslems do not eat pigeons, but I have not noticed that our natives abstain.

Meals among the natives and many of the Arabs are served on large trays. In more elaborate repasts, there is a large plate, or bowl, of rice in the centre, and small ones of curry, etc., all round, and one stretches for anything one wants. Afterwards a servant comes round with a *kata* of water, which is poured over the hands. It is also usual to rinse the mouth out, from the hands, and to spit out the water. This, to European ears, sounds rather disgusting, but is really a cleanly habit. The right hand alone is used for eating, the left being used for other purposes.

DRINK

The natives' natural drink is now chiefly confined to water, and though there is an abundance of clean, good water in wells and springs which is appreciated, and called *maji matamu sana* (very sweet water), yet a very muddy and dirty substitute seems to do as well.

Madafu, or the juice of the unripe coco-nut, is also popular, but the chief drink made from a coco-nut used to be *Tembo* (toddy), either *tamu* (fresh), or *kali* (fermented), but this is now forbidden.

Pombe is made of boiled *mtama* (sorghum), but this is not a drink native to Zanzibar.

The Borassus is not tapped for drink (at least I have never heard of it), but sometimes a decoction is made of boiled nutmegs flavoured with pine-apple, and fermented.

Honey is also drunk when it can be obtained. The method of obtaining it is curious—the gatherer instead of putting more on, as he does in England, takes everything off, and goes for the bees and their honey with a smoking torch of brushwood. Needless to say, he gets a good many stings, but does not seem to mind that very much.

CHAPTER XXVIII

LIVESTOCK

WEALTH in Zanzibar and Pemba generally goes by the number of coco-nut or clove trees owned, but animals have some significance. Oxen are in places fairly plentiful, and are used both for milk and for draught purposes. Comparatively few are turned into beef, at any rate till fairly late in their lives, or for some big feast.

There appear to have been cattle in Pemba from a very early date. Ox bones are plentiful in old wells at Mkumbuu. Teeth are found with beads at all places where the latter are picked up.

From the writing of Lancaster, Marco Polo, Owen and others, it may be surmised that cattle were plentiful in their times, and used for food and riding (Marco Polo).

The species is *Bos indicus*, imported from India, though another type of the same species, the ox of the ancient Egyptians, is imported from Kismayu. It is much larger in build, and has very big horns. Many natives own cattle in both islands; they are herded either *shemeri* (singly, with a rope through the nose) or *kikunde* (in herds).

Goats are everywhere to be found. Most natives keep them tethered, though on Tumbatu Island there seems to be a system of branding, and patterns are clipped out of the ears.

Donkeys are fairly common, and used for riding

and draught purposes, but few of them are of a good size, and many are badly cared for.

There are a few sheep in Pemba on Panza Island, of a reddish colour with long hair and fat tails, but I have never seen any in the country districts of Zanzibar, though black-headed creatures with short hair are imported for eating purposes in large numbers.

Chickens are common, and large cocks fetch good prices. They are used for cock-fighting, but being illegal, it is kept very quiet and one has few cases reported.

The chickens " run to leg " very much, as they have to take so much exercise looking for a livelihood which their owners leave to Providence to furnish. Cock birds are not eaten, as their flesh is believed to cause illness.

Muscovy ducks, funny squat creatures, with red warts on their noses, are not uncommon, and Madagascar, as well as African Guinea-fowl, are often kept.

In many Zanzibar (though not in Pemba) villages one may see old kerosene tins decorating the eaves of the huts in which live tame homer, and white pigeons.

Nearly every hut has a little cage, made from the Borassus palm, outside with a dove or small bird in it.

Geese and turkeys are known, but very rare.

Most villages have their following of pariah dogs which compete with the chickens on the middens and the crows on the shore for refuse. Sometimes good ones are kept for pig-hunting, which is a serious occupation rather than a pastime.

GAME

There is little game in Zanzibar, and so not much chance for the hunting faculties of the natives to develop.

The wild animals trapped and eaten are the Zanzibar Suni (*Nesotragus moschatus*), called *paa*, which abounds on Tumbatu Island and on the coral rag around the east coast in the bush, the rarer Duiker (*Cephalophus adersi*), which, while new to science, has long been known to the natives under the name of *paanunga*, and the Neumann's tree coney (*Dendrohyrax neumanni*), which is found chiefly on Tumbatu Island and Fundo Island, off the west coast of Pemba. Its flesh is much sought after by men who wish to have children.

The *paa* is not at all bad eating if hung for a day, though a little dry. I have not tried the others.

Almost any bird, particularly if it has been killed (*kuchinja*—cut the throat) in the right way, is eaten, but the most important game bird is guinea-fowl, called *kanga*, and the rarer Crested Guinea-fowl, called *kororo*, both found and trapped on Tumbatu Island.

TRAPS

The native traps are varied, and of considerable ingenuity. I shall endeavour to explain them by diagrams. Their chief ingenuity lies in the catches used to release them.

(*a*) Pig Trap (called *fyuka*). Materials required: a pole about 10 feet long, very strong and very springy, so that when it has one end in the ground, if the top is bent down it will not break or remain bent, but when released will spring into its original position. Two pieces of wood about 18 inches long with a hook on, thus:

Two straight and strong pieces of wood about 18 inches long, and about 6 feet of cord with a noose on it, and above the noose an attached piece with a peg tied in the middle, thus:

some small sticks and brushwood. It is built thus:

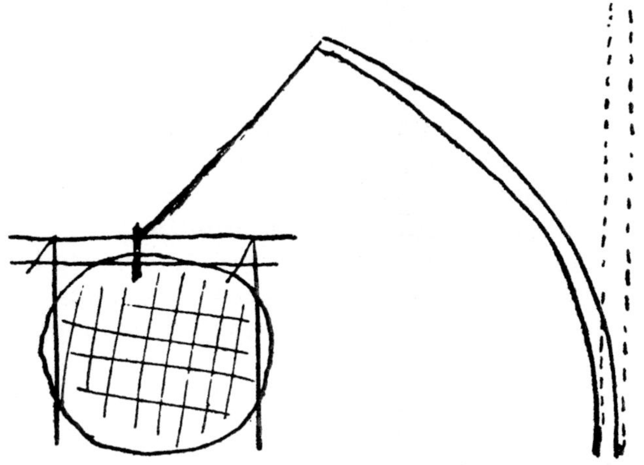

The cord with the noose is fastened to the top end of the spring stick. The two hooked sticks are stuck in the ground about a foot apart, the hooks pointing away from the spring. The first straight stick is put under the two hooks and one end of the peg on the noose cord, fitted under it. To keep it from flying back the other straight stick is placed over the hooks, 2 inches lower than the first straight stick, and the other end of the peg on top of it which also prevents it falling down. Other sticks are now leant against the lower straight stick, and brush, etc., on top of them. The noose is then arranged over the whole.

The pig puts his leg on the brush, and this causes the leaning sticks to press down the lower stick which releases the peg, which in turn releases the spring, which pulls the noose tight and the piggy's leg is securely held in mid-air.

(*b*) Pemba Monkey Traps (called *tenga*). Materials required: a large wicker floorless cage, four long sticks, one hooked stick about 2 feet long, some string and a wooden peg pointed at one end.

Make an arch of three of the long sticks. Under the arch place the cage longways on. This is the cage sideways. It is closed all ways save below.

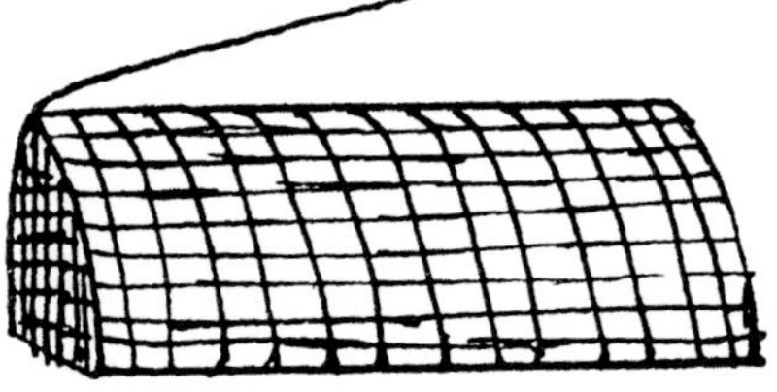

To the front of this hinge the fourth long stick as shown. To the back of the cage tie a large loop of string with the two ends well apart. To the end of the hinged stick tie a string with the pointed peg firmly fastened by its middle to it.

Lift the cage up on its back edge, bring the hinged stick over the top of the arch, put the blunt end of the peg through the string loop and then insert the hooked stick through the bars with the non-hooked end in the cage, the hooked end between the sharp end of the peg and the two sides of the loop which is now taut. On the bottom end of the hooked stick tie a banana or other fruit.

The monkey enters the trap, pulls the banana and this pulls down the hooked stick which releases the

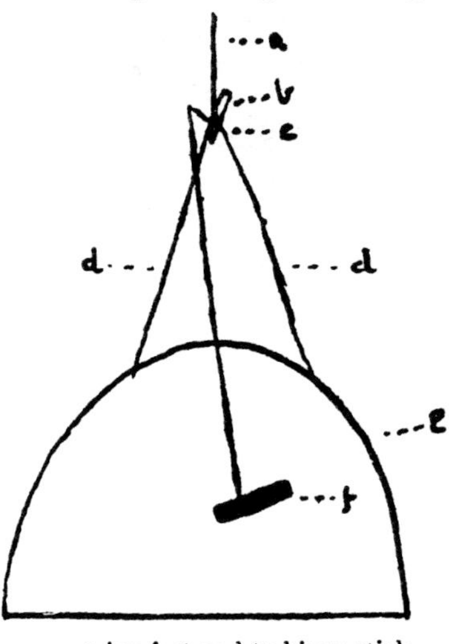

a—string fastened to hinge stick. *b*—pointed peg. *c*—hooked stick. *d*—string loop. *e*—cage. *f*—bait.

peg from the loop, the hinged stick flies back over the arch, the cage falls down, and the monkey is a prisoner.

Back view of the catch on previous page.

(*c*) Tumbatu Monkey Trap. Materials required: spring, a noose as in pig trap, notched peg with cross piece, thus:

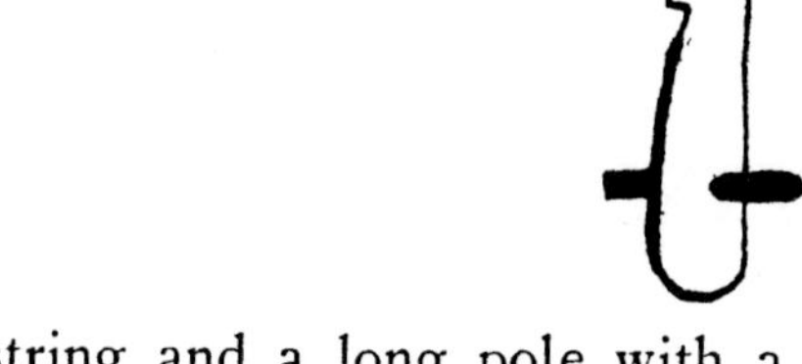

string and a long pole with a kind of wicker horn, which is made by splitting one end into about six ends and then plaiting twigs between them to make a horn, thus:

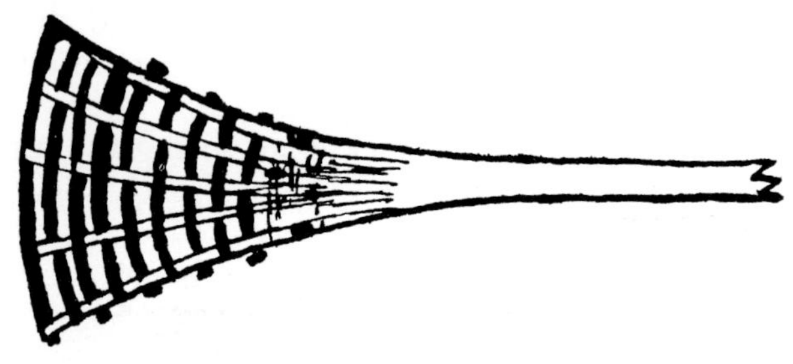

The pole with the horn is fixed to the ground. The notched stick is passed through the wicker-work from inside, so that the notches are above, and so that the cross piece prevents it from passing right through.

A string loop is fastened to the outside of the horn, and made so that when taut its top is level with a notch on the notched peg.

The peg on the noose cord is then drawn down, one end is placed on the loop and one end of a notch on the notched peg. The noose is then passed through the wicker-work of the horn and arranged over its opening.

Bait is placed against or tied to the lower end of the peg. The monkey puts his hand in to get the food; this disturbs the notched peg, which therefore releases its end of the peg on the noose cord, and its other end is thereby freed from the loop. The spring is therefore released and draws the noose tight, which holds the monkey's hand fast against the top of the horn.

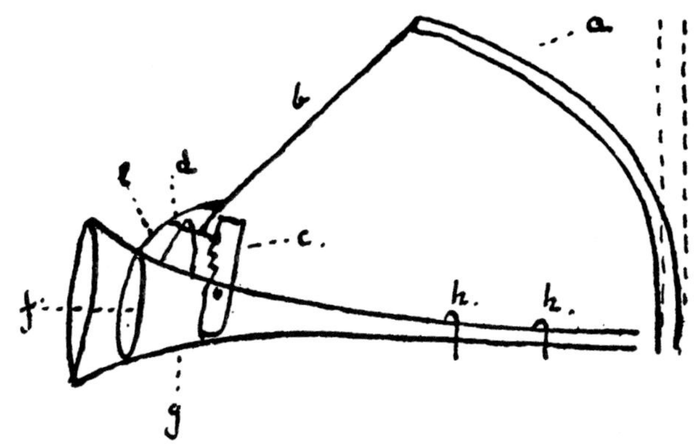

a—spring. *b*—noose cord. *c*—notched peg. *d*—peg on cord. *e*—loop on horn. *f*—noose. *g*—horn. *h*—horn fastened to ground.

(*d*) Genet and Lemur Trap. Materials required: a box cage with barred top and drop door, with bar hinged to top and arch fixed behind door, string, piece of wood with cross peg, pointed peg.

This is somewhat like the Pemba monkey trap, but the catch is different.

The pointed end of the peg on the string attached to the bar (which is hinged to the door and passed over the arch) is passed through the loop of string and made to rest on the top end of the piece of wood with cross peg, which (cross peg) prevents the piece of wood from falling into the cage by resting on the top bars. (See next page.)

(*e*) Bird Traps. Materials: spring and noose with peg, as in pig trap, but very small and much weaker, two small sticks 6 inches long, one very light stick about 12 inches long.

The two 6-inch sticks are set in the ground in

front of the spring, about 7 or 8 inches apart. The peg on the noose cord is brought round one of them, and the top is placed against it; the bottom is placed against the 12-inch stick so that it holds it against the two uprights, forming a perch.

Over this perch the noose is spread, and seed for bait all around. The bird alights on the perch, which then drops and releases the peg, and the bird's feet are caught in the noose.

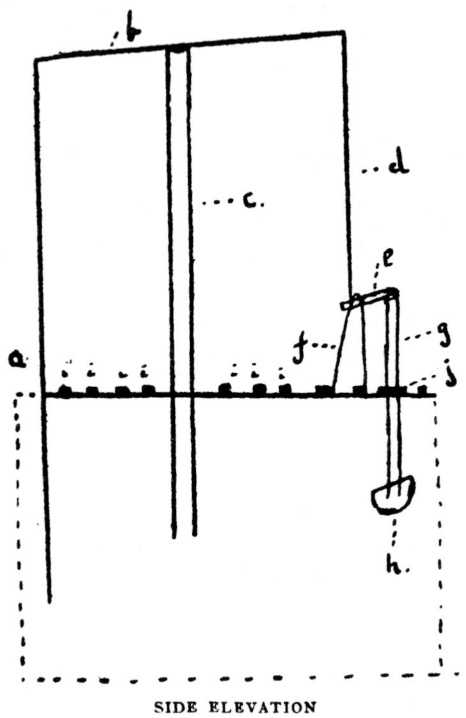

SIDE ELEVATION

a—door. *b*—hinged bar. *c*—arch. *d*—string with peg. *e*—peg. *f*—loop. *g*—wood. *h*—bait. *i*—bars on top of cage. *j*—cross piece.

The plate facing this page shows two more bird traps. The first is placed over an open nest, like a thrush's, and the bird gets its feet caught in one of the nooses which hang from the superstructure. The second is a netting bag placed inside the opening of a nest like a tomtit's, so that the opening of the trap coincides with the opening of the nest. When the bird flies in the string is pulled, and this closes it with the bird inside.

Bird lime, made from Jack fruit, is also used for catching birds.

Gazelles are caught as pigs are, or in pit-falls. Sometimes nets are used, especially by the Wahadimu.

Nowadays many natives know how to shoot, and some have shot-guns.

I should mention a rat trap invented by a clever old man called Shinen bin Said. This is made out of a piece of *mwale* midrib, and has a bow and arrow which is released by the rat disturbing a stick below the bait. This releases the peg holding back the bow and shoots an arrow through the animal's head.

Another simple rat trap consists of an overturned saucepan held up by a very small coco-nut, with a wire or stick stuck into the blunt end and protruding under the saucepan. On this the bait is fastened, and the rat, gnawing this, disturbs the coco-nut, which causes the saucepan to fall down.

HUNTING

The only animal that is hunted both in Zanzibar and Pemba is the pig, and the method of hunting is in both places the same, but the pig varies. In Pemba it is the black European wild pig (*Sus scrofa*), a legacy from the Portuguese, and in Zanzibar the red African bush pig (*Sus potamochærus nyassæ*).

A hunting-party is accompanied by dogs, and is armed with knives, some of them also having spears. The pack goes on in front, and when the trail has been found, the pig is tracked through miles and miles of bush. The passage has practically to be carved out of the bush with knives. The dogs bring the pig to bay in the end, and before he is dispatched he always gets a run for his money, which results in a few ripped-up legs and killed dogs, especially if he is a good tusker, which many of the black pigs are.

The flat, two-edged end of the spear is used for attacking, and the pointed end for giving the *coup de grâce*. It is interesting to note that in Pemba pig-hunting takes place by day and in Zanzibar by night. This is due to the difference in habits of the respective types of pig.

The bow and arrow (*uta* and *mshare*) have only survived in Zanzibar and Pemba as children's toys.

CHAPTER XXIX

FISHING

FISH are caught in many ways, and are very plentiful. With the exception of vegetables, they form the chief food of the natives.

(*a*) Hook and Line. Both hook and line are home-made, and the hook is either baited with fish, dried octopus, shell-fish, or, where obtainable, lug worms. It is weighted with a stone or lead. All the fishermen who go out in canoes use this method, and their catches are considerable.

In Pemba I have seen a row of light sticks stuck in the water with about twenty feet of line on each, with a hook. A bite was at once signalled by the bending of the sticks, and the watchers on the shore removed the fish and rebaited the hooks.

(*b*) Traps. (1) *Dema.* Made of coco-nut palm midrib. They are baited with fish, or other suitable fish food, and weighted with stones tied to the outside. They are also buoyed with the sheathes of the coco-nut flower.[1]

(2) *Uzio*, or *tando.* A long row of sticks is set up in the shape of a V with a bulb at the bottom, in estuaries or on shallow beaches, with the opening facing shorewards, and the uzio, which is also made of coco-nut palm frond midribs, placed up against it. If, however, the net is made of sticks other than coco-nut, it is in Pemba called *tando*.

The rising tide brings the fish in, and the falling tide leaves them in the bulb of the V. The catches of fish made by this method are enormous, but very wasteful, as not even the smallest fry can escape owing to the narrowness of the mesh.

(*c*) By knifing or spearing. This is done at

[1] This trap is of Indian origin, and its wide distribution was due to the Portuguese. See Ingrams, 99 *Man*, 1924. It is also found in Mauritius.

night with a torch, either by canoe in deep water, or wading for small fish in shallow water. The fish are attracted by the light, and then knifed or speared.

(*d*) With seine nets either *jarifi*, which is of large mesh, or *nyavu*, which is smaller. These are both of native manufacture, though nowadays the thread to make the cord for the netting is bought.

(*e*) In creeks by using the thick, white creamy sap of the Euphorbia cactus, which stupefies the fish but does not harm the flesh (Tumbatu chiefly).

(*f*) By women with a piece of calico. Two women hold the calico under the water, and a third drives the shoals of whitebait over it when the other two lift it up.

(*g*) In Pemba freshwater pools catfish are caught with a *kibaba*, which is a wicker trap, looking rather like the conventional parrot cage, with a corded open top and open bottom. The fishermen hold it up by the top, and advance together through the pond, jabbing the trap at each step into the mud. I have seen many tortoises and catfish caught in a short time in this method.

(*h*) The *mgono* fish trap, a conical fish trap made from the coco-nut palm, has a spring entrance in the bottom. It is fastened "in the channel between the breakers," and is peculiar to Pemba. It is probably the fish trap of the *Periplus*.

(*i*) Weights for baits. In deep water over fifteen fathoms, weights are usually fixed to the line, but in water about ten to fifteen fathoms the weight is made detachable, either by tying it to rotten string, when it will break with a jerk, or by fixing it with a bow, in which case a jerk will untie it. Thus the bait, having been taken to the bottom, is then released, and is free to move with the water.

I give a list of the commoner fish, with weights and native names and native remarks on them, and, so far as I could find them, their English equivalents. Anything not poisonous is considered eatable by the natives.

In the column "Remarks" in the following list, the first word refers to native opinion and the second to European, but where the latter is not noted it coincides with the native opinion.

Native Name.	Usual Weight of Fish Caught.	Remarks.
Guruguru	1 lb.	Very good. Sole.
Kambisi	30 lb.	Good. No good.
Mzira	20 lb.	Good. Barracouta.
Sansuri	10 lb.	Good. No good, barracouta.
Chazo	2 lb.	No good. Sucker fish used in medicine.
Changu	3 lb.	Good.
Mpono	3 lb.	No good. Good.
Mkundaje	3 lb.	Good.
Tasi	2 lb.	Good. No good.
Kungu	4 lb.	Good.
Kigombe-Gombe	1 lb.	Good. No good.
Nyaenya	3 lb.	Not very good.
Tawa	4 lb.	Good. No good.
Njana	2 lb.	Good. No good.
Kapungu	6 lb.	No good.
Mzia	6 lb.	Good.
Mwelea	2 lb.	Good. No good.
Mkiki	1 lb.	Good. No good.
Mkule	4 lb.	Good. No good.
Chaa	1 lb.	Good.
Sororo	1 lb.	Good.
Mbawawa	½ lb.	No good.
Kilende	4 lb.	Good. No good.
Mzumeire	1 lb.	Good. No good.
Bange	1 lb.	Good. No good.
Chuchungi	1 lb.	Good. No good.
Chewa	5 lb.	Good. No good.
Mjombo	6 lb.	Good.
Kowana	⅓ lb.	Good.
Bunju	1 lb.	No good. Globefish, poisonous.
Mchumbuluru	¼ lb.	Good. Tough.
Papa Pingushi	40 lb.	No good. Shark.
Papa Amrani	50 lb.	No good.
Papa Upanga	30 lb.	No good.
Nguru	20 lb.	Good. Horse mackerel.
Kole Kole	25 lb.	Good.
Panju	6 lb.	No good.
Nduara	50 lb.	Good. No good.
Taa	7 lb.	Good. No good. Sting-ray.
Kipilipili	1 lb.	Good.
Tuku	3 lb.	Good.
Kangaja	3 lb.	No good. Bad smelling.
Puju	3 lb.	No good. Good Unicorn fish.
Gaio gaio	3 lb.	No good.
Biliwili	4 lb.	No good.
Kitatange	3 lb.	Good. A spiny fish.
Panzi Bahari	3 lb.	No good. A flying fish.

Native Name.	Usual Weight of Fish Caught.	Remarks.
Kuwi	3 lb.	Good.
Komba	3 lb.	No good.
Changu Chole	4 lb.	Very good.
Kaa		Crab.
Kamba		Lobsters. Crayfish.
Kamba		Prawns.
Mgisi	2 lb.	Good. No good. Cuttle-fish.
Pweza	20 lb.	Very good. No good. Octopus.
Kasa		Good. No good unless cleaned. Green turtle.
Chaza		Oyster usually very small.

Customs Connected with Fishing

These are probably many, but I could never get much information, as the fishermen are very reticent about them.

It betokens bad luck for a fisherman early in the morning, on going out to fish, to meet a one-eyed man, and should this occur no fisherman would fish that day.

Nor will a fisherman pick up a fish by its tail, as this is sure to bring bad luck. Possibly this originates from the fact that several fish, notably sting-rays, have stings in their tails.

Fishermen who use uzio fish traps place in the cage a small offering, be it only leaves, so that the spirit concerned may send plenty of fish.

As fishermen approach the shore in their canoes, hordes of small boys rush into the water to help them up, for which service they receive a small "tip" in kind.

It may be noted that in Pemba, at any rate, there is a trace of totemism among the fishermen, some of whom will not catch certain kinds of fish, which they state will come to their rescue if they fall into the sea. Different fishermen have different protecting fish.

SAILING

A great variety of craft may be seen in Zanzibar harbour, especially during the time when the north-east monsoon is blowing, as then come a great variety from the Persian Gulf and from India. The uninitiated generally refer to them indifferently as "dhows," but there are very many different types.

A brief reference must be made to some of these:

(1) *Baggala*. From Muscat and Persian Gulf. Up to 200 tons and nearly 100 feet long. High square stern. Tall poop and long prow. Main and mizzen mast, both raking well forward. Large stern cabin. Muscat make has short, stunted, curved bowsprit. Zanzibar make has no bowsprit.

(2) *Bedeni*. From Persian Gulf. Broad in the beam and very fast. Upright masts. Sharp stern, high rudder-head and perpendicular cutwater.

(3) *Awesia*. Same as *bedeni*, but no prow or head, but only perpendicular cutwater.

(4) *Jehazi*. A smaller type, usually up to about 20 tons, square stern, of Indian origin, but built in Zanzibar and Pemba and on the coast.

(5) *Pattamar*. Indian. Main and mizzen masts, very long yard.

(6) *Batili*. Persian Gulf. Long and low, but with high rudder-head and sharp, high stern. Roomy poop and perpendicular cutwater.

(7) *Ganja*. Cutch. Like a *baggala*, but not so high in the poop or long in the prow.

Various other kinds are the *jalbuti*, with a sharp covered bowsprit, the *kachi* (Cutch) a large *jehazi*, the *grab*, also from Cutch, and the *ukararu* from the Tanganyika coast.

A *tishari* is a lighter, carvel-built like all native craft, broad in the beam, and with a stern like a whaler.

I now come to a class of boat of great interest, namely the *mitepe*, which are not made in Zanzibar, though they may have been formerly. They now hail chiefly from Pate Island, though a small one called *dau ya mtepe* is built at Lamu.

The *mtepe* is a large, open vessel with a long projecting stern, and a long prow made to resemble a camel's head. It is not nailed, but is sewn or pegged together with wooden pegs, and the boards warped close against each other with coco-nut fibre. It is generally caulked in the usual way. Whereas all other vessels are lateen rigged, the *mtepe* is square rigged, and its sails made of coarse matting. It is so fast that the natives often compare it to a man-of-war (*kama manowari*).

It always flies a white pennant when leaving and returning to its home port, and on the bowsprit (usually made of mangrove wood) is a row of charms of alternate leaves of *mkindu* (wild date palm) and *mvinji* (casuarina). Aft is a pole painted with alternate black and white bands, from which it flies its national flag.

It is an object that seems to have been remarked by all the early voyagers to Zanzibar and the coast. Whether historians, geographers, or people who have called there in the course of duty or casual trippers, one and all seem to have noticed these curious objects "sewn like clothes with twine." It will be remembered that the first written account we have of the coast, namely, the *Periplus*, says that in Menuthias there are sewed boats, and also in Rhapta, the very name of which was derived from the word. These boats were known as πλοιάρια ῥαπτά, and the word Rhapta is apparently derived from the Arabic ربط (Rabta = to bind.)

Farther on the *Periplus* says that in Oman there are "boats sewed together after the fashion of the place; these are known as 'madarata,'" which is from the Arabic "muddarra'at," meaning fastened with palm fibre.

Its advantages are that it can sail very close to the wind, and that the elasticity of its make allows it to stand a good deal of hard usage. "Sir John Mandeville" (pseudonym probably of Jehan du Bourgogne, the fourteenth-century Liège physician, who wrote a book of travel full of fabulous stories) says that near Ormuz " there are ships without nails of iron or bonds on account of the rocks of Adamants, for they are all abundant there, that it is marvellous to speak of, and if a ship passed there that had iron bonds or iron nails, it would perish, for the Adamant, by its nature, draws iron to it, and so it would draw a ship so it would never depart from it."

We have seen before that Ibn Said reported that north-east of Mombasa there was a mountain extending a hundred miles into the sea, half iron mines and half magnetic. In the story of the third royal mendicant in the *Thousand Nights and One Night*, there is the following passage: " On the following morning we drew near to the mountain; the current carried us towards it with violence, and when the ships were almost close to it, they fell asunder, and all the nails and everything else that was of iron flew from them towards the loadstone." This mountain of loadstone was no doubt the rocky coast of East Africa, on which many ships, owing to the East African current, before referred to, have been wrecked. The Arabs call it, says Burton, the Bahr el Kharab, or Bad Sea; the mountains el Mulattam (lashed or beaten), el Nidameh (of repentance) and el Ajrad (the noisy); the mountains of Magnet and the " Blind Billows " and " Enchanted Breakers."

Most early voyagers have commented on the danger of these seas.

Here we have, then, the legendary origin of these boats. Knowing nothing of currents, those navigators, seeing themselves impelled by some invisible force on to the rocks ahead, would attribute magnetic powers to these rocks. The Arabs were always ready, like all superstitious people, to attribute the natural to the supernatural. Perceiving that these sewed boats were better able to withstand the rough usage resulting from rocky beaches, it would be supposed that they owed their virtue to the absence of iron nails. The real *raison d'être* of the *mtepe* was probably the lack of these nails at this early period of history; in fact, it seems possible that "canoes hollowed from single logs" were the earliest form of boats, and that sewed boats are second only to them in antiquity.

These boats on the east coast of Africa were probably, in the days of the *Periplus*, as now, sewn with coco-nut palm rope, the word "muddara'at" itself implies it, and that the coco-nut was in East Africa is shown by the fact that palm oil was exported. Marco Polo also mentions these ships, though at Ormuz.

It will be seen from his account also that they were sewn with coir rope. He also makes mention of their being smeared with fish oil, but nowadays they are smeared with a mixture of *shami* and lime mixed with simsim oil.

Duarte Barbosa also says that they are sewn with a cord called "caire" (coir). Ralph Fitch, *flor.* 1583-1591, refers to "sertain shippes made of boards and sewed together with cayro, which is threede made of the husk of cocoes." Friar Odderick also says of Ormuz, "Here also they use a kind of barque or ship called Jase, being compact together only with cords." Jase is, of course, of the Arabic *djehaz* and the Swahili *jehazi*.

The Portuguese called these vessels *pangayo*, and the *dhow ya mtepe* they called *zambuco* (derived from the Arabic *sambuc*) and *luzio*. By the Arabs, the boats are called *muntafiyah*.

Burton refers also to its twin round eyes, painted white like the Ark of Osiris and the Chinese junk which, he says, were possibly, in the beginning, holes for hawsers, though I should imagine that it was rather the other way round, and that they subsequently developed into holes for hawsers.

Chatterton says that "earlier Greek ships had only patches of colour on the bows, blue or purple or vermilion. The painting on the bows was probably to facilitate the recognition of direction taken by the vessel." I myself was told, with reference to a canoe painted in the same way, that it was to enable a vessel to see her way. Chatterton also says, "The eyes painted on the ships of the Greeks and Romans still survive to-day in the hawse holes on either side of the ship's bows. And this belief of the ancients, that by means of these eyes the vessel could see her way, was but one article in the general creed still shared by every sailor, amateur and professional alike, that a ship, of all the creations of man, is indeed a living thing."

It is indeed interesting that the three curiosities of Menuthias as mentioned in the *Periplus*, namely, dug-out canoes, sewed boats, and wicker fish traps, should have survived for two thousand years. We may rest assured that they would not have done so had it not been that they had much to recommend them to a people to whom good results from a small outlay is an important factor in life.

The usual dhow made at Zanzibar is the *betela*, which is of medium size with a curved prow, and the ordinary boat stern of European boats.

Even more typical of Zanzibar are the *dau* and *kidau*, the latter being a small edition of the former. It is a small, open vessel and sharp at the stern. It is used for carrying firewood round the island, or for fishing. Formerly they were rigged with square matting sails, but canvas is now used.

All these craft except the *mtepe* are lateen-rigged, and all except the *bedeni* have masts raked forward.

While sitting in my house at Mkokotoni almost every night, I could hear the music and dancing performed on a *jehazi* to appease spirits of the deep, before it set out on a voyage.

I now come to "canoes hollowed from single logs," which are of two kinds, though a third, the *hori*, is a visitor on Indian dhows. It is wider than the native canoe, and has raised head and stern, and generally has a corner painted.

First of the Zanzibar canoes is the *mtumbwi*. It

is small and feels extraordinarily unsafe, but is not so bad as it looks. *Mitumbwi* do not go out far to sea, though some will carry up to six people and are fitted with sails.

The *ngalawa* is longer and narrower than the *mtumbwi*, and is fitted with outriggers on both sides, which give it great stability. It sails at a great speed, and *ngalawa* travelling is a very exhilarating form of amusement. I have heard of them going from Pemba to Mombasa, a distance of about sixty miles, and I am told that during the war, some captured German dhow crews escaped from Pemba to Tanga in *ngalawas*. They are much used for fishing, and the fishermen are extraordinarily skilful in sailing them, standing on the outriggers and holding on to the sheet. The *ngalawa* is probably of Asiatic origin.

On a recent visit to Mayotte, in the Comoro Islands, I noticed that the canoes had only one outrigger. The Zanzibar *ngalawa* has a rudder affixed to its stern, but the Mayotte *laka* is "pointed at both ends."

The canoes at Ngazija, another of the Comoros, are *ngalawas* proper, but at Nossi Bé, off Madagascar, *lakas* are seen again.

Both *mtumbwi* and *ngalawa* are propelled by a paddle (*kafu*) in deep water, or a punting pole (*pondoo*) in shallow water when not fitted with sails.

There is a proverb typical of the native which says "don't paddle when you can punt."

The knots and hitches used are the clove hitch, half hitch, reef knot and simple knot. "Grannies" are rare, though a succession of simple knots is often used to secure a stone for anchor.

The Song of the Dhow—A Tumbatu Story

When the dhow is going up from the shore the pulley calls "*Watoto, watoto*" as the sail goes up. The rudder says "*ao, ao*" as it scrapes on the sand, and after the dhow goes on the prow shouts "*taa wa saa*" as it strikes the waves, and the dhow goes joyously on.

CHAPTER XXX

CLOTHING

ZANZIBAR and Pemba are now clothed chiefly from Manchester and India, and it is impossible to say what the inhabitants wore formerly. Probably nothing at all, or just something made of vegetable material round the loins, as they are mostly very particular to keep that part covered.

The simplest clothing for a man is a *kikoi* (this has variants) round the waist, with a *kanzu*, a thing like a nightdress or a surplice over for best occasions, and for women a *kanga* fastened round above the breast, and when not working another over the head. I have seen old women on Pemba Island wearing merely a cloth round the waist.

Small children are generally clad only in modesty.

The elaboration of men's costume is the wearing of an embroidered cap (*kofia*), a vest (*fulana*) and a pair of sandals, in addition to the other two articles mentioned.

Those who wish to imitate Arabs and appear fine may wear a turban and a *joho* or *bushti* (kinds of large embroidered overcoats).

The elaboration of women's costume is, in addition to those mentioned, another *kanga* to swathe round the face, and a *buibui*, a black cloak that envelops all, with a veil sewn on to cover the face (sometimes). A pair of elaborate drawers with frilly ends falling over the ankles and a pair of heelless shoes complete the picture.

This is a description of the garments:

Kikoi, a cloth with a coloured border. The cheap ones are made in India, the best are woven in Muscat on hand looms, and the border is of silk.

Shuka. The same but either plain or with a black border. The word is also used to denote sheet.

Doti is much the same.

Kisunga. A checked one.

Kanzu. A long shirt-like garment, which looks simple enough but has a variety of names applied to various parts. (See Steere's *Handbook of Swahili Language.*)

Amazu. A shawl. Not now used; it used to be twisted round the waist.

Kisibau. A waistcoat, generally sleeveless.

Joho. Is generally made of thick blue cloth; the *bushti* is finer, and some are made of camel's hair. It is fuller than the *joho* and in Zanzibar is usually brown.

Kofia, or caps, are often beautifully embroidered, and many town Swahilis make them in their spare time.

There are five varieties of *viatu* (sandals), one of wood with a stud (*msuruake*), two of baobab bark, one plain and one plaited, one of threefold ox-hide loosely tied, and one of the usual imported variety.

Women's *kangas* are printed in Manchester, and have many designs ranging from a flat-iron or an arc-lamp to a sun or a lion or a view on them. They often bear greetings. The women are very particular about the fashions, and Indian traders sometimes tell me they cannot get rid of old patterns. The poorest women only wear a dark blue cloth called *kisutu,* and sometimes over their heads a *ukaya* of the same material with two long ends.

Trousers are called *suruali,* and sometimes the extra *kanga,* used to swathe the face, is of silk and is called *dusamali.*

Kanzus for women, which were coloured and shorter than men's, as well as embroidered waistcoats and *barakoas* (face masks), are not now worn, except by women of rank and position. Another garment no longer used is the *lebwani,* a large square of black silk thrown over all to go out in. The last two are now replaced among the "quality" by a silk *buibui*, with a veil sewn in front of the face.

Arab girls have lately started to wear dresses with high frilled collars, and they look very well in them too. European dress is much in favour, and its use is growing generally. Silk stockings are very popular.

Many natives now own a pair of trousers and a shirt (which is often not tucked in), but the limit of absurdity is reached when they take to soft felt hats. A native somehow looks very ridiculous in European dress.

ORNAMENTS

As with other races so with the Zanzibaris, it is chiefly the women who adorn themselves. Men rarely wear any ornaments. Some have a silver ring, and some wear rosaries (*tasbihi*), but these can hardly be called ornaments. The head is shaved.

Hadimu fishermen plait hats from the dried leaves of the Pandanus. These hats are conical, with a wide brim and a cord to fasten under the chin. The cone of the hat is often used for the carriage of the fishing-line, the coiled line being laid over the cone.

The women plait their hair in ridges, or part it in the middle or plaster it down (this is a new fashion). The comb used for doing this is imported. Their ears are bored and coloured paper rings inserted, three in each ear, and the orifices in the lobe may grow to 2 inches in diameter. Their faces are painted with soot in circles and other figures. Generally the outlines of the cheek pattern is made by putting *wanja* (antimony) round the edge of a coffee-cup and pressing it on. It is then elaborated. Sometimes a nose-ring is worn in the left side of the nose. Fingers and the nails are dyed with henna, and the palm of the hand is treated like the cheek.

Beads are worn on wrists, neck, and round the waist next to the skin. Why, I cannot say, as they cannot be seen there; perhaps it is a survival of the days when no clothes were worn. Formerly bead belts (*kondavi*) used to be worn there, and on the wrists fine wire bracelets called *madodi*, but these are now no longer used.

HABITATIONS

The houses of the Zanzibar natives are all rectangular. The simplest type is made of *mtama* straw or *makuti* (plaited coco-nut), and the better ones of mud and wattle or even with stones built in.

All are roofed either with grass or *makuti*, generally the latter.

This is the method: the materials for the wooden framework are first collected. The requirements are:

Six stout poles 8 feet long for the corners of the house and the door frame, called *nguzo*; more, not so strong, sufficient to fill the spaces between these six at intervals of 1 foot, also called *nguzo*, two stout poles to support the top of the roof about 12 feet long (*nguzo*).

One stout pole to lay across the top of these two, about 16 feet long, called *mwamba*; four stout poles to lie from the corners to the ends of *mwamba*, about 8 feet long, called *kombamoyo*. Others not quite so thick to lie from the walls along the *mwamba*, 7 feet long, also called *kombamoyo*. A quantity of long, thin poles to lie longitudinally on these about a foot apart (*pao*).

A large quantity to tie inside and out about 3 inches apart longitudinally round the walls (*fito*). Two pieces of wood for the top and bottom of the door, *kizingiti* (*Kitum: kisiyangu*). A lot of coir rope (*kamba*). A lot of mud (*udongo*). A lot of *makuti* to make the roof (front and back—*paa*, sides *kisusi* or *kipaa*). A door.

This will make a house with no rooms and no windows, about 26 feet long and 12 feet wide. The rooms can be added afterwards by building partitions, and many people do without windows.

Owing to lack of funds, it is generally a long time before a hut is finished. This probably makes for the better security of the hut, as it allows the mud to settle and harden.

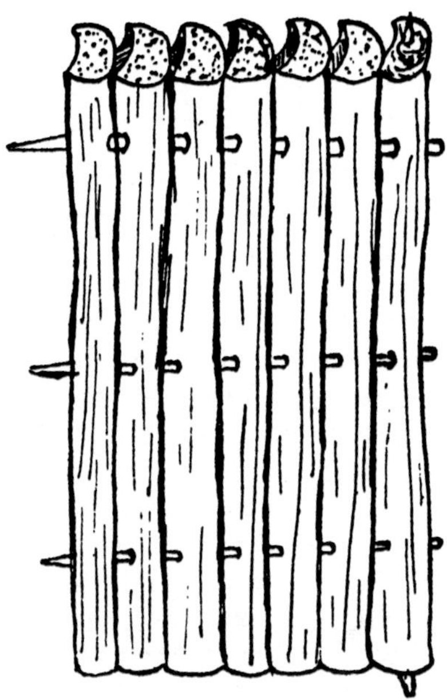

A door of the midribs of *mwale* palm.

First of all the four corner posts are driven in, and a string fastened all round the tops of them, by means of which the tops are levelled. The foundations are about a foot deep. Then the doorway is put in, in the middle of the front. After this the other *nguzo* are placed between these corner poles and door poles at intervals of about a foot, and these too are made level with a string, which should rest on top of them. The tops are then notched and *fitoes* laid over them. Then *fitoes* are tied to the sides, beginning at the bottom and working up about 3 inches apart, one on the outside and one on the inside.

This is the view from the top

and from the sides

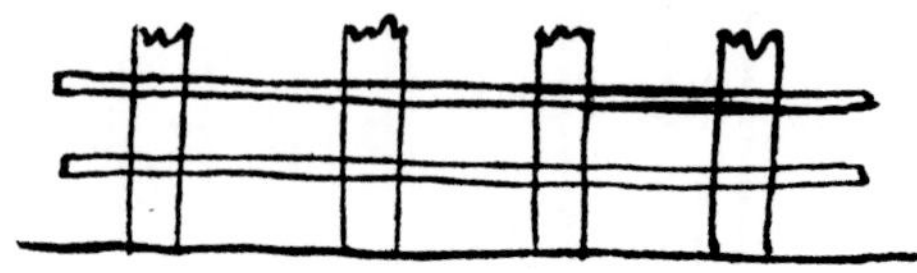

When all the walls are done like this, the two tall *nguzo* to support the roof are placed in the middle, and the *mwamba* across these, for they are notched. The corner *kombamoyo* are then laid to them from the corners of the house. After that the other *kombamoyo* are laid across from the walls to the *mwamba*.

When this is finished the *pao* are tied across these, at intervals of about a foot, and then the house is thatched with *makuti*, or grass, from the bottom upwards. *Makuti* is of two kinds, *kike* and *kidume*.

The roof must be put on first, for if the mud were put in the walls and there was no roof it would be washed out if the rain came.

The Kipemba house has no *visusi*, or ends, to the roof, but the wall goes straight up to meet the roof in the angle caused by the back and front *paas*.

After this, mud well kneaded is built up into the interstices of the walls, and perhaps small stones mixed with it, a style of building called *tomea*. Sometimes the big holes are filled with stones first and mud put round them.

After two or three days the mud sets a little, and then more is put on and it is smoothed off. This process is called *kurudishia*. The door is then fixed in. It is generally bought ready-made, frame and all, and merely requires fastening in position, but simpler people make simpler doors.

The door can be made of *makuti* too, and these are merely tied on to a door-post, but a better door is made by taking the midribs of the *mwale* palm, cutting about a dozen to one length, and fastening them through with a skewer, top and bottom. A spike is then fixed on the top and bottom of one end of the door to revolve in sockets in the frame. If pieces of wood to form the sockets are fixed behind the still and lintel (*kizingiti*) they are called *kimandu*.

DIAGRAMS OF HOUSE IN CONSTRUCTION

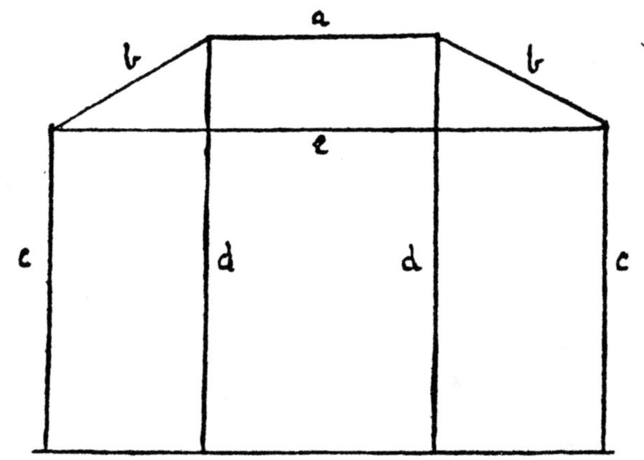

a—*Mwamba*. *b*—Two-corner *kombamoyo*. *c*—Two-corner *nguzo*. *d*—The roof supporters, *nguzo*. *e*—Level of wall, *nguzo*.

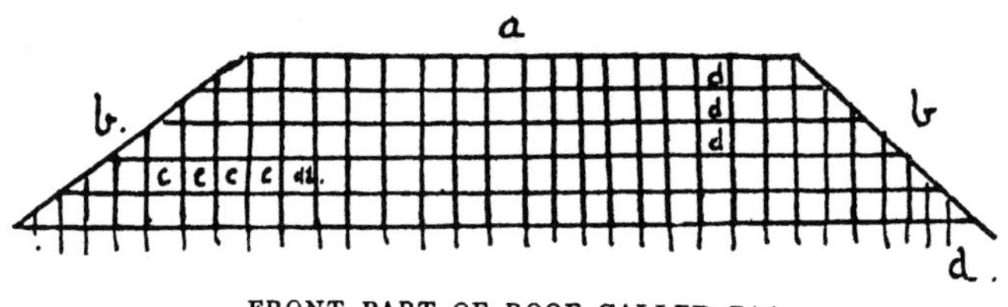

FRONT PART OF ROOF CALLED PAA

a—*Mwamba*. *b*,*c*—*Kombamoyo*. *d*—*Paa*.

After all this, garden walls can be added, and a backyard or anything else required. Often a partial ceiling is made under the roof of *fitoes* on which things can be placed. China and clothes, etc., are generally kept under the bed.

This is a plan of a simple house.

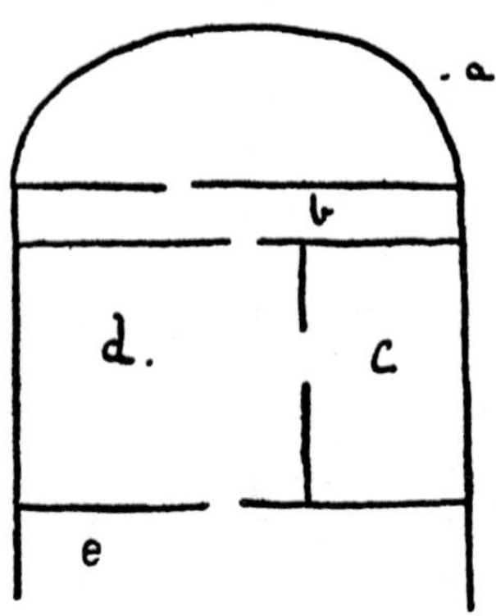

a—*Ua* or *makuti* wall surrounding backyard with *choo* (privy), etc. *b*—*Jiko* (kitchen). *c*—Women's bedroom. *d*—Men's bedroom. *e*—Roofed in *baraza*, to eat meals, welcome guests, etc.

A mud projection is often made round the base of a house to protect it in wet weather.

It is interesting to note that trunks of the wild date palm (*Phœnix reclinata*) are not used by the natives in the construction of their houses, though they last long and are not eaten by white ants. Poles of another species are invariably mixed with them, as it is said that he who lives in a house built only of *mkindu* poles will not live long. There seems to be a general prejudice against timber that lasts long. (See chapter, "Botany.")

CHAPTER XXXI

CRAFTS

POTTERY

THE art of the potter is one of the oldest in Zanzibar, and is practised to-day probably just as it was practised centuries ago. The reasons for this are that there are very few potters (or *wafinangi*), and that for many hundreds of years imported pottery made of a better clay has been known and obtainable cheaply. Thus the demand and competition having been small, there has been no need for improved tools. These two causes, coupled with the fact that the art is hereditary in Zanzibar, contribute to make it a dying art, though none the less interesting for the very primitiveness of the methods which are practised.

The clay necessary is not really common, but in several places there are large pockets, to which the potters go to dig it. Before being baked it is greenish in colour. The potters I have seen generally keep a fair store of it, and when it needs replenishing, repair to the bank from which it is obtained with an old sack. The store is generally kept piled by the side of the hut.

The potters do not keep a stock of articles ready made, but make them to order and at a very cheap rate, though they are usually of a more or less uniform size. I discovered this, as on visiting a potter to give him an order for a set of models of everything he made, it took several attempts and a lot of time to explain that I wanted them far smaller than anything he made for practical purposes.

When they were finished the old man had no idea what to charge me, so the price for all the articles depicted was fixed at about 40 pice by a committee of natives who accompanied me. When I gave him Re. 1 he was overjoyed, though I thought it rather poor remuneration for the trouble he had spent over his work. It is interesting to note that this old man, in common with all the native craftsmen I know, was a real enthusiast at his trade, and would never let anything that he thought poor workmanship pass.

The potter's tools, etc., consist of a flat board or piece of wood, a piece of "coco-nut cloth," that is to say, the cloth-like envelope of the young leaves called *kilifu*, a smooth shell, a piece of wet rag, and one or two half coco-nut shells in which is kept water.

The method is as follows: the potter takes a piece of clay approximately enough to make the vessel (say a bowl) required. This is first roughly kneaded together with water in the same way as one makes pastry, to the required consistency, and made into a rough ball. It is then dumped on to a piece of "coco-nut cloth" on the board to which it adheres, and by pressure with the fingers of both hands it is hollowed out.

When it is roughly of the shape required, though, of course, small and thick and by no means symmetrical, the potter begins to turn it with his left hand while fashioning with the right. It still adheres to the coco-nut cloth, and the board beneath is very polished in the centre from frequent rubbing. By putting his finger inside the bowl the potter makes it larger, and when it is a little too large, with the inside very smooth and the outside rough, he turns his attention to the exterior and smooths that, every now and then pouring water over it to smoothen it. When both inside and out are uniformly smooth, he may make a groove or lines on it with the aid of the wet rag or the shell, and when it is finished, make lines or patterns in much the same way as one decorates a pie-crust.

The pot is now left to stand for a day in the sun, and the next day it is dipped in a fluid bath made of the same grey clay, thinned to the consistency of soup, in a hole outside his hut. If it is wanted to be red it is painted, the red colour being bought and not therefore to be lavished on it.

After this, it is baked in a hole excavated in the ground from which a fire has been raked; when the pots are in the hole, bars are laid across it and the fire remade on top.

Lamps are not now made, though the old potters still know how to make them, as in the last decade or so they have been replaced by small tin lamps imported from India, from whence come also the large water-jars which, being of better clay, have largely supplanted the home-made product. Water-jars altogether are gradually dying out before an invasion of kerosene tins.

Sometimes, particularly in Pemba, women make pottery, but I think it is generally men, and in Pemba there is also a red clay used which I have not seen (though it may exist) in Zanzibar.

BASKET AND MATTING WORK

This industry is entirely in the hands of the women, who make all the articles. Matting and basket-work among the Zanzibaris is of the plaited type, which is one of the things that demonstrate their origin as forest people. The material from which these articles are made is called *ukindu*, and is the dried leaf of the *mkindu*, or wild date palm. The women collect these leaves and clean and scrape them, and then tie them in bundles and put them in the sun till they are bleached white. Some of them are then dyed with imported colours, chiefly red, black, yellow and green, and others are used white.

Mats (*mikeka* and *misala*) and dish covers (*kawa*) are made from long strips which are first plaited about an inch wide. To make an *mkeka* these long strips are sewn together, one of each colour, till they form a broad strip about a foot wide. This is then sewn together edge to edge to form a bag about two feet wide and open at each end, and to the required length. This is then cut down one side and a black border sewn on.

To make an *msala* (prayer mat) the strips are narrow and are sewn edge to edge, but in an ever-widening oval shape so that there is no bag formed. The *kawa* is made by widening the circle gradually, and so building downwards. A tucked border is then added.

Large mats for drying cloves and called *jamvi* are also made, but these are much coarser, as are the circular mats on which the quern is sometimes worked.

Majamvi are often made by old men, especially south of the Zanzibar Island.

Misala (plural of *msala*) are principally made in Mafia Island.

CARPENTRY AND CARVING

Before I embark on a description of the articles made, I must give a short description of the tools used.

All European tools can be obtained in Zanzibar and have their native names, but the ones made, and generally used, by the simpler folk are as follows: saw, chisel, adze, knives, hammer, pincers, drill and lathe. None of these save the last two need a description, as they are of the usual type. The drill is called *kekee* and consists of four parts. The iron (*kekee*), its handle (*msukono*), and the handle this turns in (*jivu*). The bow used to turn it is called *uta*.

The lathe consists merely of a frame of fixed size, which between two nails holds the piece of wood to be turned, on which a bow is fastened to turn it backwards and forwards. It is chiefly used in Pemba to make the stools which are a speciality of the place.

Of carving, chip-carving is most employed, though examples of deep or wood-carving are also shown, as is a kind of fretwork, though this is done by knife and not by saw.

Inlaid work is done with a knife, chiefly on coco-nuts and horns, and inlaid with lime. Mortising is known, and examples are the *buzi*, the chair and the bed. The *buzi* is an instrument used for shredding coco-nuts. The woman sits astride the seat and shreds the coco-nut over the fretted iron head.

The woods chiefly used are mango and jack fruit. *Mvule* and *mvinji* trees are much used for masts, and a good tree will fetch as much as Rs. 100.

The *marufaa*, or Koran desk, deserves notice, as it folds and is made from one piece of wood.

The poker-work used on the *mwiko* (spoons) is always well done. *Ngalawas* and *mitumbwi* are carved from mango trees, which are then burnt over a fire to make them water-tight, and caulked with old rags, bits of coir, etc. Wood is never seasoned. Drums are made from solid trunks hollowed out. Some have inscriptions on them. The ones that belonged to the Mwenyi Mkuu are instances of this, though many have a sentence of Arabic. Good bao boards are made and sometimes have an inscription on the back.

Door frames and window frames are made and carved, some very beautifully.

A dhow repairer cuts out all the damaged bits in an irregular hole, and then cuts a piece of wood to fit it. He then uses a black fluid called his *dawa* (lit. medicine) and paints the hole he has made with it. He then hammers in the patch and makes it fit by shaving off the parts which are blacked by contact with the *dawa* on the hole.

METAL-WORK

Some of the natives are employed by the Indian silversmiths and goldsmiths, and possibly a few work at these trades on their own. However, I do not think that they can have been practised for any length of time.

Lieutenant Ferguson, writing to Colonel Sykes on

3rd May, 1852, says: "The trades carried on by the natives of Zanzibar are building, carpentry, stone-masonry, shipbuilding and manufacturing of inferior cotton goods and trinkets worn by the inhabitants. We also find goldsmiths, silversmiths, coppersmiths and blacksmiths."

The art of the blacksmith, which, like that of the potter, is hereditary, is probably of considerable antiquity, and no native I have asked can remember anything but iron hoes being used or spoken of.

Iron, of course, is not native to the country, but has probably been imported for centuries. The unknown author of the *Periplus*, in the first century, mentions it as being imported into several places on the coast, and though he does not specifically say it was imported to Zanzibar, there is no reason to suppose that it was not.

The geographer Idris also, writing about the twelfth century (A.D. 1154), mentions iron mines at Malindi, and also Manisa (? Mombasa) where the King of Zinjibar lived. ("Les habitants s'occupent de l'exploitation des mines de fer et de la chasse aux tigres. C'est dans cette ville que réside le roi du Zenghebar." Jaubert's translation, Paris, 1836.)

The tools employed by a Zanzibar blacksmith are quite simple, but the class of work turned out is fairly good. The tools consist of an anvil, hammer, tongs and bellows.

The bellows are made of a goatskin sewn up, except at the neck. One side is fastened to the ground, while to the top is affixed a piece of wood with a handle to draw it out and push it down. From the neck proceeds a pipe for the air to pass in and out.

MACHINERY

I propose in this section to deal only with such forms of machinery as I have not dealt with under previous headings. Thus bows, drills and lathes are dealt with under carpentry and carving, and bellows under metal-work.

Such machinery as is employed by the natives is of the very simplest character, and all moved by manual power.

First, and perhaps most important, is the quern, or millstone (*jiwe la kusagia*). This consists of a bottom stone, in the centre of which is a pin, round which a top stone revolves eccentrically, that is to say, the hole in the top one is considerably larger than the pin in the bottom one, and across it, but not diametrically, a small piece of wood is fixed. The top one is fitted on the outside rim with another pin which serves as handle.

The elder natives tell me that *zamani sana* (a very long time ago) the stones used to be made locally, but that whenever new ones are now bought they are imported. There is no great demand for them, however, as, of course, they are handed down from generation to generation. They are used for grinding all sorts of hard grain, e.g., maize, millet, rice, etc.

Another little known but none the less interesting implement is the *pia*, or top, used for string-making by the Wahadimu on the east coast of Zanzibar.

This consists of a sort of glorified crochet hook, over which is fitted a plaque with four notches at equal distances on its circumference. The threads of which it is desired to make the string (generally rafia palm or bark of baobab tree beaten out) are fastened by the ends below the plaque—enough of the thread is then twisted to pass over one of the notches and to take a turn round the crochet top of the centre stick. The threads are then held in the left hand about 2 or 3 feet from the top, and the top is then spun against the right thigh with the right hand. When the length is sufficiently twisted it is wound below the plaque and another length done, and so on. The more primitive fishermen still use this method of making the cord for their lines and nets, but its use is now very limited, as good string can be cheaply bought in most of the shops of the ubiquitous Indian traders.

The use of rollers in moving heavy objects such as boats is well known, and considerable ingenuity is often displayed in lifting heavy weights.

I remember on one occasion wishing to erect as a flagstaff a tree about 50 feet long, and I left the job entirely to the natives to see how they would do it. First of all they tried by lifting only its top end, and by moving along underneath it to get the bottom end into the hole and the tree upright. However, it proved far too heavy. There was then a good deal of palaver, but after a short time they hit on a *shauri* (plan). A long stout rope was fitted about half-way up by a knot so that it gave two free ends, and then two long pieces of wood were crossed near the top and nailed together to form a crutch.

First of all the mast was pushed as high as it could be by hand as before, and then the crutch of the **X** placed under it as far down as practicable, and it was pushed farther up by this means. When it was far enough up for the people on the rope to pull they did so, and by this means the staff was soon erect and planted in the hole.

The native pulley, which is used in some places for pulling buckets up out of the wells, is considerably simpler than the pulley blocks imported from India. It is, of course, possible that the principle of the native one is copied from the Indian, but as the invention of the pulley is of considerable antiquity, there is no reason to suppose that the natives did not develop it on their own.

It looks rather like a series of large cotton reels fastened together, end to end, with a stick passed through them.

Captain Craster, in his book, *Pemba, the Spice Island of Zanzibar*, gives a photo of a native sugar-press, and I have also seen one in the Mwera district of Zanzibar. This, however, is not a local invention.

The one in Zanzibar referred to is maintained and worked by an Indian.

MISCELLANEOUS CRAFTS AND INDUSTRIES

In concluding the occupations of the Zanzibaris, I should just mention a few not worth a section to themselves.

The first of these is lime-burning, which occupies most of the inhabitants of Nungwe village, in Zanzibar, and Mtambwe Kuu Island, in Pemba, though it is by no means confined to these places. A large circular fire, called *tano*, is built up with marvellous care and neatness, of alternate wood and soft coral to form a pile about 10 to 12 feet in diameter and 3 feet high, and on top of this again coral is heaped. The pile is then burnt and the lime sold, mainly to the Government, at Re. 1 a bag. Charcoal-burning is also carried on to a large extent: charcoal is usually made of mango wood, and the tree when cut down is piled into a rectangular heap about 20 feet by 6 feet by 4 feet high. The pile is then covered with earth and fired. The charcoal is packed in sacks with a large wicker end and sold for Rs. 3 a bag.

In nearly every little village one is surprised to see a tailor peddling briskly away at a treadle sewing-machine. The chief articles he makes are *kanzus*, the calico for which he buys from the Indian shop, and women's trousers, generally made from a *kanga* for the top part and calico for the legs and frills.

Rope is made from coir in several parts of Zanzibar and Pemba, and in Zanzibar town there is a place called the "rope walk" where it is made. The coir is first made into two strand cord by women, and several of these are twisted into a rope about an inch in circumference. Four of these are then laid along the ground, and at one end all of them are fastened to an axle on a trestle with a handle at the back end of it. The other four ends are each fixed to a separate axle in another trestle at the opposite end. Each of these axles is also furnished with a handle. The five handles are then turned simultaneously, the four at the one end one way, and the other, which is making the large rope, in the opposite direction.

In former days many other industries must have been carried on, for instance Colonel Sykes (*Climate and Productions of Zanzibar*, 1850) says " one branch of manufacture is carried to a considerable extent, that of round shields 18 inches in diameter made from the hide of a rhinoceros, which, after being soaked and boiled, can be moulded into any form." In these days of peace and prosperity shields are not wanted, and no doubt with increasing civilization more and more of the ancient crafts have disappeared and will continue to do so.

PALM TREES

I think it fairly safe to say if the coco-nut trees of Zanzibar and Pemba could be magically spirited away, the natives would be absolutely lost. The number of uses to which they are put are almost endless. These are a few:

1. The coco-nut (food). 2. The heart of the tree (food). 3. The milk (drink). 4. Toddy—*tembo* (drink). 5. Oil for cooking, light and lubrication. 6. Thatching—*makuti*. 7. Doors. 8. Fans. 9. Baskets—*pakacha*. 10, 11, 12. Three kinds of rope. 13. Pad worn on head to carry heavy weights—*kata*. 14. Fish trap—*dema*. 15. Plaited beaters for gong. 16. Drum-sticks. 17. Bird trap. 18. Chicken cages—*susu*. 19. Basket for scenting clothes. The clothes are put on top and the incense underneath—*Tunda la kufakizia nguo*. 20. Tooth-brush—*msuake*. 21. Brush for sweeping. 22. Fish nets—*uzio*. 23. Toothpick. 24, 25. Two kinds of paint-brushes. 26. Coir for mats, etc. 27. Sieve—*kumutu*. 28. Torches. 29. Floats for fish traps. 30. Bailers for boats. 31. Child's boat. 32, 33. Two

kinds of spoons—*kata* and *upawa*. 34. Bhang pipes. 35. Half nutshell used for beating wooden mortar in a dance. 36. Lip piece of *zomari*. 37. For charms. 38. Medicine. 39. Child's windmill—*kititia*. 40. Timber for props. 41. Firewood. 42. Tops to walking-sticks. 43. Rat traps (Pemba).

1 is prepared from the nut called *nazi* and 2 is called *kilele*. 3 is called *madafu*. 4 is made by tapping the tree and collecting the sap. Fresh, this is called *tamu* (sweet), but fermented *kali* (strong). 5. The nut is dried in the sun and copra made. Oil is expressed from this. 6, 7, 8, 9 are plaited from the leaves; there are two kinds of thatching. 10. Coir rope is made from the husks (*makumbi*), which are taken fresh and buried for five months in the sand below high water. 11, 12, 13, 14, 16, 17, 18, 19 are made from strips of the back of the midrib (*uchukuti*). 20 cut from the flower stem (*upunga*). 21, 22, 23 made from the midribs of the leaflets. 24, 25, 26 made from the coir. 27 made from the cloth-like envelope of the young leaves (*kilifu*). 28. The dried leaves. 29, 30, 31 made from the woody flower sheath (*karara*). 32, 33, 34, 35, 36 made from the shells (*kifuu*). 37 written on leaflets (*ukuti*). 38. Roots. 39 made from leaflets. 42, 43. Immature nuts. The flowers are called *punga*; the small nuts that follow, *kidaka*; a half-grown nut, *kitale*; and when full-grown but before flesh is formed, *dafu*; a half-ripe nut when the flesh is formed is called *koroma*, and a ripe nut is called *nazi*.

A good ripe nut but rattling in the shell is called *mbata*, and a nut that has grown with a white sponge inside is called *joya*.

The juice squeezed from the scraped coco-nut and used in cooking rice is called *tui*.

Copra is the most important product of the coco-nut tree, which, when properly prepared, is the sun-dried nut, and exported in large quantities. Bad copra is made by drying the nuts with a smoky fire.

The coco-nut is celebrated in a proverb, "*Nazi*

mbovu harabu ya mzima"—"A bad coco-nut spoils good ones."

The *mwale*, a kind of raffia palm, is also deserving of mention; its leaf provides an umbrella, and the mouthpiece for the *zomari* (a kind of clarionet), and the midrib, doors and ladders, while pieces of the midrib are made into bird-cages and also used to clap in dances, giving a sharp noise. A rat trap is also made from the midrib.

The Borassus palm (*mvumo*) has many uses, for it also provides umbrellas from its palm, and strips of dried frond are used for making large coarse mats, called *majamvi*, and the rattles, called *manganja*, while bird-cages are made from the midrib. The wood is also useful, being much harder than coco-nut.

CHAPTER XXXII

COMMERCE

THE history of commerce in Zanzibar is the history of Zanzibar itself, and I do not propose to go into it here, as it has been so fully dealt with elsewhere. In this chapter I shall refer only to the small retail trade that affects the natives.

Much of the currency of the Persian traders is to be found on the shores of old settlements in the shape of beads, and there is no doubt that these were used and intended for currency, for many of them have been so misshapen in the furnace and not by the sea, that it would be impossible to wear them, and the occurrence of two joined together sideways is by no means rare. Beads are, of course, still currency in some parts of Africa.

Nowadays the currency is all Indian silver rupees, and Seyyidieh copper pice introduced by Seyyid Barghash, and of which sixty-four equal one rupee. Formerly Maria Theresa silver dollars were currency and worth Rs. 2 pice 8. They exist now chiefly in name at auction sales, but some natives have them hoarded up.

Nafaka means not only coin but corn used as money, and before pice were introduced (1845), *mtama*, or millet, was given as small change; indeed even nowadays change for a pice or two is often given in *mtama* at country stores.

Most of the small trade nowadays is in the hands of the Indians, who live in nearly all the small villages and keep a positively marvellous assortment of goods in their shops.

The following is a list I made of the articles on sale in an Indian's store in the Mkokotoni district: *Kangas* (for women's clothing), calico, khaki drill, cushion-covers, chintz, handkerchiefs, trousers, *kanzus* (men's shirts), sail cloth, *shukas*, *vikoi* (men's underwear), children's clothes, caps and many other cloth things in great variety. Strings of beads of all colours for women. Needles of all sizes, thread, buttons, string. Knives, spoons, tin lamps, wicks, candles, paraffin oil, matches, Muscat fans, sandals, sieves (*kumuto*), *kitanga* from Muscat (woven food plates), pictures, fishing-line, fish-hooks, locks and keys, rosaries, combs, coloured papers for ear-rings, soap, Reckitt's blue, coffee-cups, bowls, glasses, cups and saucers of the "Present from Brighton" type. Dates, raisins, rice (two kinds), *choroko* and *bundi* beans, maize, *mawele*, *mtama*, Huntley and Palmer's biscuits, Cadbury's chocolate, tea, salt, pepper, bread (very stale), *halwa*, coffee beans, dried shark, flour, onions, ghee and potatoes. Sherbet of several kinds, salad oil, *marashi* (scent). Herbs of many kinds, ginger, incense (two kinds), *mangano* (turmeric), curry stuffs of many varieties, dyes for colouring mats, and pots.

It is very interesting to sit in a shop in the country about six o'clock and watch the crowd that comes in and note their tastes.

Lots of children come with little lamps to have a pice worth of kerosene oil, men bring lamps, and buy grain, one buys rice, another buys a few pice worth of *choroko* and a little maize, and so on, and all tie their purchases up in different corners of a cloth and hand over the pice for each article as they buy it. The weights chiefly used for this trade are the *kibaba* and its fractions, and a *pishi*, which equals about 6 lb. and 4 *kibabas*. A *frasla* used for bigger weights is 35 lb.

The Indians also buy up local produce, such as shells (exported and, I believe, used for making cameos), cloves, copra, areca nuts, goatskins, a little tortoise-shell, etc., which he afterwards exports to the city and sells to the merchants at a considerable profit. Some natives take firewood to town and sell it.

The natives themselves engage in trade but little except in Tumbatu villages (where they will not have Indians) and distant villages like Nungwe in Zanzibar and Chwaka in Pemba, but their shops usually contain little but rice, matches, oil, soap and possibly dried shark and a few clothes.

Otherwise the only trading the natives do is in the local markets, where, with much haggling, they sell local produce at as inflated a price as they can, even taking advantage of a scarcity in the market itself to put the price up. There is a kind of wholesale and retail system about this, as some cultivators and fishermen sell large lots by auction in the market, and the purchasers then and there divide their purchases into small lots and sell at fixed prices.

Many of the imports and exports, especially ivory, have been the same for centuries. The antiquity of the import of iron I have elsewhere dealt with, and it is interesting to note that the early Arabian geographer Masudi writes, "on export aussi de ce pays des écailles de tortue" (de Maynard's translation, Paris, 1864). Even to-day in the *Official Gazette* among prices ruling "Tortoise-Shell" is quoted.

CHAPTER XXXIII

LANGUAGES

THE language of Zanzibar *par excellence* is Swahili, and Zanzibar may be said to be the home of this language, not in the sense that its oldest form is spoken there, but because the Zanzibar dialect has come to be known best owing to the writing of such men as Steere, Madan, Sacleux and to some extent Krapf, whose dictionary, however, contains many words in the Mombasa dialect. Also in the days of the opening up of Africa, explorers and traders generally fixed up their caravans in Zanzibar, and these porters and soldiers journeyed into the far interior, some of them remaining there and thus making Swahili a *lingua franca* understood, as Steere says, along the coasts of Madagascar and Arabia, by the Seedees in India and in Central or Inter-Tropical Africa.

The old classical or literary Swahili is known as Kingozi, and there are but few specimens of it surviving, save in poetry. The name is said to be derived from *Ngozi*, the plot of land where the palace of the old king of Pate was. *Ngozi* in Swahili means skin, and the application of the word to the place suggests the story of Carthage and of Kilwa, though there the land was bought from a neighbouring chieftain for the cost of surrounding it with cloth. A similar story is extant at Tumbatu.

The Arabs have made of Swahili a language

full of Arabic words Swahiliized, and this form of speech has been carried by Arab traders as far as the Congo.

It would be difficult to say what is the purest form of Swahili spoken to-day. The word itself is Arabic and means the Sawahil people of the coasts. Kiswahili means the language of these people. Kiswahili may therefore legitimately include words of Arabic origin, as the Swahili people have been intermarrying with the Arabs for many centuries.

In the Zanzibar protectorate there are several dialects. There are also several forms of speech even in the town itself, which vary only as the speech of Whitechapel varies from that of Whitehall. In the Arab quarter of Baghani many words of Arabic are used but slightly disguised. In Malindi the harsh gutturals of Arabs born in Arabia are more apparent, while in Ngambo the speech is far more African.

The speech generally of Zanzibar is known as Kiunguja, Unguja being the native name of the island.

In the outlying portions of the Sultanate there are three dialects, the first of which has several forms.

Kihadimu is the dialect of the Wahadimu. These people live in the south and on the east of the island. The most archaic form of their language is spoken in Makunduchi and Jembiyani, large villages of respectively 1,500 and 400 huts, in the south-east of the island. This dialect is totally incomprehensible when spoken to a person knowing only Kiunguja, owing not only to the number of different words and the peculiar conjugations of the verbs, but to its unusual pronunciation which is very nasal.

Coming northwards up the east coast, the dialect of the next two villages, Bwejuu and Paje, varies again and has forms peculiar to itself. Nearly every village has different forms till one reaches Nungwe, the northernmost village of the island, where, if an inhabitant spoke in his own dialect to a man of Makunduchi speaking his own dialect, they would to some extent not understand each other, and to an outsider would appear to be speaking different languages.

Kizimkazi, the most south-westerly village in the island and the old capital, has a number of forms peculiar to itself, but coming northwards up the west coast, the dialect approaches more and more the Kiunguja proper.

But these dialects are to-day known as Kikale or Kikae, a word meaning archaic, and while they are used in the villages, Kiunguja is known to most of the people.

Separated by a channel about a mile wide from the north-west of the Island of Zanzibar is that of Tumbatu, where the dialect used is called Kitumbatu. This has many forms in common with Kihadimu, but is nevertheless more distinct from the various forms of the former dialect.

The Wapemba, so-called aborigines of Pemba, speak another dialect called Kipemba, which again varies considerably from Kihadimu and Kitumbatu.

In addition to the dialects of every day, there are others used by the witchcraft guilds. In Pemba this is known as Kipepo, and is spoken in different ways by the Robamba, Kumbwaga and Umundi guilds. In Zanzibar there is a similar dialect called Kimundi.

The medicine men have a form of speech, consisting mostly of peculiar names for the trees and herbs they use, which is called Kiganga. There are different forms of this in Zanzibar and Pemba.

Kinyume is not a dialect, but an enigmatic way of speaking. The commonest form, at which many natives are expert, is the transposition of the last syllable of a word to the beginning. This causes a shift of the accent, e.g., *mbengo nguwa faameku naja* for *ng'ombe wangu amekufa jana.*

In most highly developed languages a very large proportion of words are borrowed or adapted from other languages to express ideas for which the original words of the language had no equivalent.

This is largely the case with Swahili which borrows a vast number of words from Arabic, and to a lesser degree from the English, French, Portuguese, and Hindustani languages. When one has eliminated these words there still remains a number which are purely Bantu in origin, and would suffice for the needs of a primitive people untouched by an outer civilization.

Vocabularies of the Kiunguja, Kipemba, Kitumbatu, Kihadimu (Makunduchi, Bwejuu, Kizimkazi and general forms), Kipepo, Kimundi and Shingazija dialects which I collected in Zanzibar and Pemba have been published in the *Bulletin of Oriental Studies* under the title "Dialects of the Zanzibar Sultanate," and space forbids of their reproduction here. I give, however, examples of the grammar, etc. of some of these dialects.

GRAMMAR AND EXAMPLES— ZANZIBAR DIALECTS.

Conjugation of Verbs.

	Know. Kiunguja.	*Know.* Makunduchi.	*Know.* Tumbatu.	*Know.* Angazija.	*speak* (*sema*). Kizimkazi.	*come from* (*toka*). Kizimkazi.
Present	(ni)najua	mvijua	nijua	umjuo	natongoa	naiyawa
	unajua	kuvijua	kuijua	ngojuo	kunatongoa	unaiyawa
	anajua	avijua	kejua	ngujuo	anatongoa	kanaiyawa
	tunajua	tuvijua	twijua	ngarijuwao	etc.	tunaiyawa
	mnajua	mvijua	mwajua	ngamjuwao		mnaiyawa
	wanajua	wavijua	wejua	ngwajuwao	*place* (*weka*)	wanaiyawa
Future	nitajua	chavijua	tejua	ngumjojua	tatua	
	utajua	kuchavijua	tajua	ngojojua	utatua	
	atajua	kachavijua	tajua	ngujojua	etc. regular	
	tutajua	tuchavijua	tutajua	ngarijojua		
	mtajua	mchavijua	mtejua	ngamjojua		
	watajua	wachavijua	watejua	ngwajoujua		
Past	nalijua	nyevunyivijua	nilijua	sundihahatsijua	nilitua	
	ulijua	kuevukuvijua	kulijua	hundihahujua	etc. regular	
	alijua	kevukavijua	kalijua	hundihahajua		
	tulijua	twevutuvijua	tulijua	uondihawajua		
	mlijua	mvumvijua	mlijua	mundihamjua		
	walijua	wevuavijua	walijua	waundihawajua		
Perfect	nimejua	mvijua	nijua (not used as it	tsijua	ntuu	
	umejua	kuvijua	is a term of abuse)	hujua	kutuu	
	amejua	kavijua	amajua, tumajua etc.	hajua	katuu	
	etc.	etc. as present	——	ngarijuwao	tutuu	
			eat (*kula*)	umjua	mtuu	
			nimakulya	ngwajuwao	wametua	
			umakulya			
			kamakulya			
			tumakulya			
			etc.			

	Kiunguja.	Makunduchi.	Kitumbatu.	Shiangazija.
Present negative	Sijue hujue hajue hatujue hamjue hawajue	Sivije huvije havije hatuvije hamviji hawavije	Sije hulije havije hatwije hamlije hawalije	Sije kuje kaje kariji kamje kwawaje
Conditional	ningalijua ningejua	ngevijua ngevijua		engetzejua engehujua engehajua engerijua ngemjua engewajua
Infinitive	kujua	kuvijua	kujua	hujuo

Other Makunduchi forms.

Reciprocal	Najulikana (Kiunguja) Njuikana
	Kiunguja. *Makunduchi.*
I want	Nataka Nachaka Kunachaka Kanachaka Tunachaka Mnachaka Wanachaka
I shall want	Nitakaka Chajakichaka Kuchakichaka Kachakichaka Tuchakichaka Mchakichaka Wachakichaka
I wanted	Nalitaka Nyevunyikichaka Kuevukukichaka etc.
I have wanted	Nimetaka Nkichaka etc.
I don't want	Sitake Sichebu Huchebu Hachebu Hatuchebu Hamchebu Hawachebu
I didn't want	Sikutaka Sidichaka Hulichaka Halichaka etc.
And I wanted	Nikataka Hachaka Ukachaka etc.
I haven't yet wanted	Sijataka Sijachaka

Certain common verbs in Kiunguja do not exist in Makunduchi dialect proper. One of these is the verb to love—*kupenda*—in place of which an impersonal verb is used. *Kinkaza* may best be translated "it gets" or "grips me."

Present.	*Future.*	*Past.*
Kinkaza	Kichankaza	Chevukinkaza
Kikukaza	Kichakukaza	Chevukikukaza
Kimkaza	Kichamkaza	Chevukimkaza
Kitukaza	Kichatukaza	Chevukitukaza
Kikukazani	Kichakukazani	Chevukikukazani
Kiwakaza	Kichawakaza	Chevukiwakaza

Perfect—Kimkaza. *Conditional*—Kingenkaza.

Examples of Kihadimu

The following sentences are an example of the way the dialect varies in different villages. Each sentence means much the same, but the mode of expression is different. "Look out now! don't go upsetting everything! stop it."

Uroa: Babu we! Ah Choo!
Bwejuu: Ee choo ja! Hivyo sivyo vyo sebu vyo!
Makunduchi and Jembiyani: Ee babu we! Njoo ga! Eee Bwana! Sikiliza! maneno una panga vibaya!
Kizimkazi: Sikirize! usizunguruke hivyo.
Unguja Kuu: Ee cho! Utenda usitifu.
Chwaka: Mwanume! sikiliza hivyo, usije uharibu!
Pongwe: Mwinyi wangu! sikiliza haya maneno!
Michamvi: Eee choo jo! usije {uharibu maneno! / utende haya!}
Charawe: Wasikiya sana, mwanume!
Kongoroni: Ajariya kamba! usije uharibu maneno! ajariya kamba!
Fumbi: Mwaname! usije uharibu maneno haya! usije, mwaname!
In *Kipemba* the expression is: Chee! wafanyaje sa!
In *Kitumbatu:* Eee! Kunaliharibu jambo la watu, we!

Can you climb the coco-nut tree? I cannot, it is thick and my arms won't go round it.

Kiunguja: Mnazi utaweza kupanda? Siuwezi, ni mnene mkono yangu haikumbatie.

Kipemba: Mnazi waukidiri kuinjuka? Mnazi siukidiri, mbuni. Mkono yangu haizingilike.

Makunduchi: Mnazi kuchaugoma kukweya? Choo! Siupinge, mnene. Siugoma kupinga.

Kitumbatu: Mnazi kuuvyeza kukweya? Siupinge mnazi mine, kwa ni mnene.

What I want is to go home by that way.

Kihadimu: Neno ja ilyo chakovitaikonde vyangu.

Makunduchi: Neno ja ilyo mchaka nlawe nde vyangu kwa iko.

Greetings, etc., Makunduchi

Kuwamkuu?	How are you?
Niamkuu.	I am well.
Je Kamkuu?	How are you?
Kamkuu.	I am well.
Nyiwekiaga.	Let me place it here.
Kuna lawa viko?	Where do you come from?
Nalawa Makunduchi.	I come from Makunduchi.
Kwendave?	Where are you going?
Kukuko.	There.
Kunaliuzalipi?	What are you asking?
Ngwile.	Catch him.
Ikanya mvua haitukutu.	It rained, but it did not get us.
Haja vano vana maji kumbi.	He knows here there is water certainly.

Kimundi (Z) Songs

There was an invasion of savages and much fighting and raiding, and then they went away: the people sang:

Ni pokuwa boguni ula uzama uzama hatta haja nyumbani
I was in the bush eating in hiding, until there came to the house
Wakubwa wa zama Watu wakenda nyamwezi, mige natazama.

The parents / big ones of the child. The men went to Nyamwezi, I watch them.
A man had a family of daughters, another came and seduced each of them.

Kawadanga, kawashipia, kasaza mpongozi.
He picked them, he finished them; there was left a woman about to bear.

Kizimkazi

Enamba wendo. Nataka kwenda zangu.
I want to go home.

Examples of Kipemba

Mtoto mchesa pao atuzwa.
Mwembale helemewa ni mti tambi zika mwelemea.
Jivule la mvumo liafunika mwekule.
Mkono mtupu haurambwa.
Nataka hajaye nichinje puaye.
Fungato haiumize mkono.
Funika haikulingana na wazi.
Ntiamwana kulia ajalia ye nlezi.
Msafiri hachunguliwe bahari.
Kikunguenda ki kungurudi.
Ajae haulizwa nane.
Mwitu hauchoma taa, mwitu hauchoma mwengi, mkumwilika.
Mchana usiku akutia moto.
Mtutufu kale mbiche.
Ukisema najua, utatanga na njua.
Mwinyi hanyi mwai.
Twemvyetu.
Wauya wapi?

Note.—In Kipemba

sh = s- or -ss-	—e.g., singo for shingo, mossi for moshi (not invariably).
ch- = ki-	e.g., kiakula for chakula.
ch- = sh-	e.g., shupa for chupa.
j- = z-	e.g., zino for jino (pl. mazino).
s- = sh-	e.g., shezo for sezo.

Examples of Kitumbatu

Mkwezi mpe kikweziche pindi ya mnazi ngawa pima; mkwezi mwana wa watu; akigwa huna lazima.

Hanga huingia hangani, je hangani huingia hungoni? (Kingume of Kitumbatu.)
Kata inaingia mtungini, mtungi inaingia katani? (Kiun.)
A ladle goes in a water-pot, will a water-pot go in a ladle?

Utakato nini?	What do you want?
Kuna kwambaje?	How are you?
Kunawa wapi?	Where have you come from?
Nawa Tumbatu.	I come from Tumbatu.
Kunatendaje?	What are you doing?
Sinanavyotenda. Miye na pitakuno.	I am doing nothing. I am passing there.
A! tupite kukohuko.	Oh! you are passing along there.
Kukiwike wape?	Where did you put it?
Niwike pano.	I put it here.
Bono hakipo pano?	Why isn't it here?
Sije! ndo nipo wika pano.	I don't know. Verily here is where I put it.
Kimakugwa.	It has fallen down.
Kunaniuza nini?	What are you asking me?

Kitumbatu Kipepo

Kinyaovu—killa apita anya tu.

Miza kana donda lia kichwa, muyumewe nani?
Miza has a sore on the head, who is her husband?
Ngwajecha kanchinjibu tu kwa kijita.
Ngwajecha has cut her only with a knife.
Q. Mwarabu mkundu humpe mkono. *A. Moto.*
Arab (3) the-red (2) one-doesn't-give (1) a-hand (4) Fire.
Kitandawile changu cha likabu; kina matona, matona ya dhahabu.
Riddle (2) my (1) (is) of (3) difficulty (4); it has spots, spots of gold.
A kitambuaye nane ni ajabu.
May-guess-it (2) he-who (1) is a wonder.

Examples of Kizimkazi

Kizimkazi chajuja usimwone mwidu, ukamba mja; ote wana wa.

(A man) of Kizimkazi is well known don't see him worthless, or think him a slave; they are all children of

Pandu Mkuja weene lindija moja moja.

Pandu Mkuja shows (3) the-brand-of-fire (4) and (1) each (2).

Dunga ya mwana Kiwangwa, ukenda kwa miguu uta rudi kwa kitanda.

Dunga is of mwana Kiwangwa, if you go on foot, you will return on a bed.

Uzi wa hariri tongoo pima, mji shubiri.

Thread of silk, say a pima, wait in the town.

Mwangasiya mbili moja humpona.

He who chases two things, one will miss him.

Kutu piko?	Where did you put it?
Ntuu pano.	I put it here.
Usitue ipo.	Don't put it here.
Unaiyawa piko?	Where have you come from?

EXPLANATORY NOTES ON THE VOCABULARIES

Possessive Pronouns and the Preposition "of."

The vy forms are, except in Kipemba, only used adverbially. *Twende vyetu.* Let us go home.

In the possessive sense pronouns have the ordinary form. *Nguo Zangu.* My clothes.

Robamba is spoken in a drawling way, Umundi and Kumbwaya fast.

The abbreviations Kiun., Kip., Kit. or Kitum., Kih., Kig. are used *passim* for Kiunguja, Kipemba, Kitumbatu, Kihadimu and Kiganga, and these abbreviations have been used throughout the book.

Shingazija is, of course, not properly a Zanzibar dialect. I give it, as not much of it has been published (except by Heepe).

The language of Mayotte, of which I collected a vocabulary of the words given in Sir H. Johnston's *Comparative Study*, when on a visit there in 1927, is called *Shimaore*. It is not unlike Shingazija, but has been largely influenced by Malgash. Examples:

Rongo'ntro ngo za Maore ngema?

Is the news of Mayotte good?

Na wantru navu zao?

And is everybody well?

At Nossi Bé there is a Swahili village, a relic of Seyyid Said's attempt to secure Madagascar, where pure Zanzibar Swahili is spoken. Natives there informed me that they considered themselves *rayia wa Seyyidi* (subjects of the Sultan). One old man asked me how Seyyid Barghash was!

There are about 10,000 Comorians in Zanzibar. It may be said to be a native language in the same sense as Gujerati and Arabic, which are so described in the Code of Regulations, and for a knowledge of which, in addition to Higher Standard Swahili, a bonus of £50 is allowed. There may be said to be a Zanzibar dialect of Arabic, as there are those of Egypt, Syria, Hejjaz, Hadramaut, Iraq and Muscat.

WRITING

Swahili, since Arab influence has made itself felt, has been written in Arabic characters. It has, of course, no alphabet of its own. It is generally considered that Roman letters are more suited to the language, but it will be a long time before they are widely used, or supplant Arabic. But to write Swahili something more than the Arabic characters is required. This is the Persian letters پ (*pe*) and چ (*che*), and a third importation, ڤ (*ve*), is also used. Instead of چ a modified *shin* ڜ is often used. If these characters are not used ب (*be*) is written for پ, ش (*shin*) for چ or ڜ and ف (*fe*) for ڤ. It is generally supposed that the three imported letters are modern introductions, but this is not so. I have seen the character پ in an old document written on Borassus palm leaf. *Fet-ha* (for A), *kesra* (for E or I), *dhumma* (for O or U) are always inserted. The *hamza*, *teshdid*, and *sukun* are also used.

CHAPTER XXXIV

PROVERBS

PROVERBS are as plentiful in Swahili as they are in English. The Rev. W. E. Taylor collected six hundred of them (African Aphorisms). Many of them are connected with the ordinary things of everyday life such as fire, house, etc.

Nyumba ya udongo haihimelie kishindo.
A house of earth won't stand a shock.
Nyumba kuu haina nafasi.
A big house has not room, i.e., there are few chambers in it.
Dawa ya moto ni moto.
The medicine for fire is fire, i.e., like cures like.
Ngoma ikilia sana, haikawii kupasuka.
When the drum sounds very loud, it is near to burst (i.e., a braggart is soon found out).
Mpenzi hana kinyongo.
A lover has no scruples. (All's fair in love and war.)
Hapana maji yasiyo mawimbi.
There is no water without waves.
Kila chombo na wimbili.
Every vessel has its waves to meet.
Kamba killa siku nakata jiwe.
Cord every day cuts stone (on the side of a well). This from the Arabic *habile 'dom yukatah el Kaadah.*
Mfinangi hulia gae.
A potter eats off a potsherd (being proverbially poor).
Haraka haina baraka.
Haste has not blessing. (The natives take this very literally.)

Samaki akioza ni mtungo pia.
If one fish rots so does the whole string. (A sickly sheep infects the flock.)
Kikulacho kinguoni mwako.
What bites is in your own clothes.
Wawili hula ng'ombe.
Two can manage an ox.
Penyi wimbi na mlango papo.
The wave and the channel are close (i.e., the dividing line between safety and danger is fine).
Penyi urembo ndifo penyi urimbo.
Having finery is having bird-lime (i.e., is a snare).
Mtu hajue kuandika, hajue kusoma mwache kuchunga wabuzi.
Leave a man who knows not how to write or read to tend the goats (from Arabic).
Samli ya Pemba haimpati mtu macho.
Butter in Pemba does not get a man's eyes (i.e., is no use to one in Zanzibar).
Amekula ngano.
He has eaten wheat (spoilt his reputation).

Some words are also used in a proverbial sense as metaphors, e.g., *kama maji*—like water, i.e., fluent (of words); *kama chumvi*—like salt, i.e., pungent (of words); *kama pono*—like the *pono* fish, i.e., sleepy. It is said always to be asleep. I have also heard *anaio matako kama mbuyu.*

This is a proverbial saying from Tumbatu:
Mkwezi mpe, kikweziche pindi (ya) mnazi ingawa pima.
Give something to a climber if he climbs the rings of a coco-nut tree, even though it is only a fathom.
Mkwezi mwana wa watu.
A climber is a child of men.
Akigwa huna lazima.
If he falls you have no obligation.

Zanzibar itself became famed in an Arab proverb.

" When you play the flute in Zanzibar, all Africa, as far as the lakes, dances." Nowadays, this proverb is not so true as it used to be, but it still has some of its ancient force.

Proverbs in the dialects of Pemba and Tumbatu will be found in Chapters XXXIII and XXXV.

RIDDLES

The natives, especially children, are very fond of riddles or enigmas, and the variety is endless. They are propounded in this way. The proposer says *kitendawili*—a riddle. The one asked says *tega*—trap. These are some of them:

Q. *Kidani darini fetha mekundu kijamandani.*
A necklace on top, red silver in the box.

A. *Komamamga.*
Pomegranate.

Q. *Nakwenda huko, nashika ng'ombe wangu mkia.*
I go there, I catch my ox by the tail.

A. *Kata.*
A spoon. (Made of a coco-nut.)

Q. *Huko " koo," na huko " koo," katikati simba angaruma.*
Here " koo," and there " koo," inside a lion roars.

A. *Mtungi.*
A water-jar. (" Koo " is a fair imitation of the noise it makes if tapped.)

Q. *Kifaa Kifanana.*
Two useful things very alike.

A. *Tui na maziwa.*
Coco-nut juice and milk.

Q. *Kuku wangu amezalia miibani.*
My chicken has laid in the thorns.

A. *Nanasi.*
A pine-apple. (Because it is a yellow, egg-like fruit growing on a plant surrounded by thorns.)

Q. *Mama nichukue.*
Mother carry me.
A. *Kitanda.*
A bed.
Q. *Bandika, Bandua.*
Put down, take up.
A. *Mguu.*
A foot.
Q. *Shina mshawazi, tambi sokotera, si mbibo, si m'pera. Hun mti gani?* (Kip.)
A. *Mlangamiya.*
Q. *Chini chakula, katikati mbegu, juu mchuzi?* (Kip.)
Below food, midway seed, top gravy.
A. *Muhogo* (cassava; the tuber is eaten, the stem planted, and the leaves provide a flavouring to gravy).
Q. *Tumbili na mbwa, utakato nini?* (Kit.)
A. *Tombwa.*
Q. *Hamadi Bega.* (Kip.)
A. *Kungwa Ndizi.*
Q. *Nyumba yangu kubwa, nzuzo moja.* (Kip.)
A. *Huyoga.*
Q. *Kamba yangu refu haifunge kuni.* (Kip.)
My rope is long, it won't fasten firewood.
A. *Njia.*
A road.
Q. *Nalikwenda Mjini nikasikiya "wifi" nilipotazama sikumwona.* (Kip.)
A. *Mbaazi.* (When the Mbaazi pea bursts it makes a noise like "wifi.")
Q. *Hichohichi.* (Kip.)
A. *Kivule.*
Q. *Nyumba yangu kubwa, ikanya mvua ivuja.* (Kip.)
My house is big, when it rains it leaks.
A. *Mwembe.*
A mango tree.
Q. *Kisima changu cha mawe, ndoo yangu ya mawi, nikateka, nateka changalawe.*
A. *Kungu manga.*

Q. *Nyumba yangu kubwa, haina taa.*
My house is big, it has not a lamp.
A. *Kabure.*
The grave.
Q. *Kuku wangu wote navaa visibau, asikwanacho kisibau si mwanangu.*
My chickens are all wearing waistcoats, if one hasn't a waistcoat it is not mine.
A. *Kunguru.*
Crow. (The African crow is black with a white waistcoat.)
Q. *Nyumba yangu kubwa, haina mlango.*
My house is big, it has no door.
A. *Yayi.*
Egg.
Q. *Kuningwa juu ya dari.* (Kip.)
A. *Nyuki.*

These might be multiplied indefinitely.

When I went to Mauritius I was surprised to find the great similarity between Creole folklore and that of Zanzibar. But it is not really suprising. Many of the Mauritian slaves came from Zanzibar, either direct, as Captain Smee, quoted by Burton, recorded in 1811, or through the slave markets of Madagascar. Many, too, came from other Bantu tribes round Mozambique.

The riddles of Mauritius are propounded in the same way as those of Zanzibar. *Sirandane*, *Sampèque*, corresponds to *Kitendawili*, *Tega*. Examples:

Q. *Dileau pendant.*
A. *Coco.*
Q. *Dileau dibout.*
A. *Canne.*
Q. *Ptit bonhomme, grand çapeau?*
Mbirikimo mdogo, shumbururе kubwa? (Pemba.)
A. *Çampion.* *Uyoga.* (Pemba.)

Q. *Labarbe ene bonhomme, figuire ene zenfant ciel sans taçes, mer sans poisson?*

A. *Coco.* (Husk a coco-nut, it has a beard : take off the beard, you have the mouth and eyes of a child : halve the nut, you have a cloudless sky above, and a sea without fish below.)

The *ngomas* of Zanzibar have their exact counterparts in the *ségas* of Mauritius, and many of the tales are the same. For further comparision see Baissac's *Folklore de l'Ile Maurice.*

The Creole language is derived, as far as its vocabulary goes, almost entirely from French, but its grammar is Bantu, e.g.:

I love	Mo content	*Napenda*
I am loving	Mo après content	*Nina penda*
I shall love	Mo pour content	*Nita penda*
I loved	Mo fec content	*Nili penda*
I have loved	Mo fin content	*Nime penda,* etc.
I do not love	Mo napas content	*Si pende*

A comparison of customs between Mauritius and Zanzibar is interesting. The slaves of Mauritius came, first, from the Bambaras and Yolofs of West Africa; secondly, from the Sakalava and other tribes of Madagascar; and thirdly, a large proportion, two-fifths of the slave population, according to d'Unienville, from East Africa. The tribes represented were, among others, the Makua, Sena, Mashona, Gindo, Maravi, Inhambane, Makonde and Nyamwezi. It will be seen from page 32 that several of these tribes contributed to the slave and African population of Zanzibar.

CHAPTER XXXV

TALES

IN Swahili tales the place of the hare or fox is taken by the *Sungura*. It is difficult to say what animal exactly this is, as the natives call a guinea-pig or a rabbit a *Sungura*, though neither of these animals are indigenous and are only found there in captivity.

The *Sungura* is often confused with *Kibunwasi*, about whom many stories are told. The origin of *Kibunwasi* is Abu Nuwas', the famous poet and wit of Baghdad, who is known to all through the medium of the *Arabian Nights*. Punch and Judy (*Kargoss*) have already been described. *Kargoss* is often confused with the *Sungura* or *Kibunwasi*, and the name is no doubt derived from the Persian *Khargosh*—a hare.

Many of the stories are introduced (e.g., from *Arabian Nights*), and it is difficult to say which originated in Zanzibar.

There is one important one about Liongo, who was apparently a real person and of importance in the history of the natives. Bishop Steere was informed that a sister of his came to Zanzibar, and that her descendants were (1869) living in the city, and he was told by an Arab, Mohammed bin Ali, that he had seen Liongo's spear and other relics preserved by the descendants.

Liongo is comparable to Samson and was, as Sir J. G. Frazer says, an African Balder (there are several others in African legends).

In view of the interest therefore attaching to him I give an abbreviated version of the story of Liongo.

"Liongo, a chief and a mighty man, lived in Shanga, which was once a flourishing town near

Malindi. He oppressed his people, and they therefore determined to get rid of him. One day they bound and imprisoned him, but he escaped. Again they captured him and put him into a small cell, bound with iron fetters, but at last, through the medium of a slave-girl, he got a cake from his mother with files in it. Then, in order to drown the noise that filing would make, he got his guards to play on horn, cymbals and *upatu*, and himself sang. When he had filed his fetters through he escaped and killed many of them. They then plotted to go and kill him by treachery, but he saw through their plan, which was to persuade him to climb a *koma* tree and then to shoot him. Finding in desperation that seemingly nothing would kill him, they told his nephew, promising him the kingdom, if he succeeded, to ask him what it was that was fatal to him, and he replied, 'A stab with a copper needle in the navel.'

"So two nights later, when he was asleep, they stabbed him with a copper needle. He awoke with the pain, and seizing his bow and arrow, he ran to the well, where he died in the attitude of shooting. For three days the corpse deceived the villagers, who dared not approach the well, and they then sent his mother, under threat of death, to speak to him. She found him dead, but they did not give the kingdom to the nephew, but killed him.

"He was buried at Ozi, and his grave may be seen to this day."

Copper or brass needles are used by native women in mat-making.

Several of the *Arabian Nights* tales are current in Zanzibar, and in one, "Abu Mohammed the Lazy," some merchants on a voyage from China to El Basrah call at the "Island of the Zunej, who are a people of the blacks, that eat the flesh of the sons of Adam," and fare badly, as the King has a few of them slaughtered and served up. Zunej is the same word as Zenj.

Swahili tales were very early collected by Bishop

Steere, and there are many of them extant. I give below some of them I have collected at first hand.

Stories always begin with this dialogue: the story-teller says, *Paukwa*; the audience replies, *Pakawa*. Then the moral is expounded or the point explained, e.g., *Mwanangu mwana siti mjino kama chikiche, tamjengea kijumba kibueka kibuazama.* He or she is then pressed to go on; and the story begins as all fairy stories should: *Palikuwa*—" once upon a time there was——"

The first is a slightly improper one of the " Lady Who Had Sense." This is it, toned down a bit from the way it was told me.

Once upon a time a man went to a woman's house and wrote on it, " A woman has no sense." Presently the woman came out and saw this, and was annoyed. So she put on her best clothes and went to see the man who had written it, and started making overtures to him, to which he responded and came to her home. Here they were engaged together for some time, and then the man heard footsteps outside. He said, " Who is that? " The woman said, " My husband, but do not be alarmed, stay quite quiet and I will cover you up."

So she covered him up with clothes, and her husband came in. " What is that? " he said, pointing to the clothes. " I am sure you have a man there." She said, " There are clothes, and if you think I have a man here go and search under the bed in the bedroom." So he went, and while he was away she uncovered the man and he ran away. So her husband came back and said he had found no one, and was glad his wife was faithful. After he had gone she went again to the other man's house and said, " Was I not clever? " and he said, " Yes." And she said, " Why then did you write ' A woman has no sense ' on my door? " And he was confused, but he went and rubbed it off.

Here is a little " Just-so " story:

There was one Mzee Mkono (Old man Hand)

and a Mzee Mbu (Old man Mosquito). Mzee Mbu said to Mzee Mkono, "Let us go and steal the goat of Mzee Shikeo." And they went and stole it. Then Mzee Mbu said to Mzee Mkono, "Let us kill this goat and divide it between us. I shall take the blood and you take the meat." And they did it. For this reason mosquitoes up to now like blood.

A Proverbial Story of the Wapemba in Kipemba

Wapemba wakichinja ng'ombe, wakikaa kitako wakipige mbinda, wakisema. "Mwingi hanyi mwai" wakisema. "Mbwa akiwa mkali akiyuma mkia." "Udandaro wachelewa njiani." "Mtu tufu kali mbichi." Mgema yamtuza moyo, saburi ya vuta kheri. Karibu harabu, nikheri kaufike. Ukisema "sijue" wastarehe na mjiwako, Ukisema "najua" utatanga na jua. "Wakarude, wakaimbana" Bwana Ali si weye, mlauku na mayayiye. Kiambiwa na mwana Baye kuku kimla na mayayi, moyo atia kinaie.

Upo moja anadonda wenziwe wakamfumba, wanambiya "Panyuka kiungu." Akafaham, akawambia "Hapanyuki kiungu." Usiku wa makungu, mtumke gani mteleka kiungu. Lakini mwache wacheka mashama ya mungu. Utapata ya mungu yapite haya yangu. Ukatwende mwamwe, agana kukagawe mwamwe changenya. Usiri wavuta akiwa mkupa kidogo hakuliwaza. Ukiwa mwenezi, simkazi kitako, kadyjanga kiguu mchume kwanenda tusikukaa tu. Kazimbi si mcheso mwema. Kupakwika kuuza kugea. Kilonge lungua. Kibule hama keche (ngaa) Umang'a mang'a (early morning). Mtu mzima kachoma na bocho waopozi wasiende wa toto.

The Virtuous Princess and the Wicked Wazirs

There was once a Sultan whose name was Muhammad; he married a wife and had two children, one a daughter and the other a son named Muhammad. Presently the parents and the son journeyed, and the

Sultan left his Wazir to look after the daughter and his concubines, and the Wazir made a plan and told the concubines that the child was a little mischief-maker, so he created a mistrust of her in their minds. One day the Sultan's daughter was told by the Wazir to massage him, and she said, "How can I do such a thing?" "Am I not to you as your father?" So the child went to massage him, and afterwards the Wazir got sleepy and she went back to sleep in her room, and on the second day she went again and the same thing happened. On the third day the Wazir wanted to make overtures to the girl, and when he saw she was aware of it, he got under the bed and stretched out his hand, and then she took a wooden shoe and hit the hand as hard as she could, and got the Wazir in the face with it, and when the Wazir saw he was bleeding he ran away.

The next morning he told the concubines what she had done, and they asked him why, and he said, "Because I found a man inside and forbade him." And they said, "Master will come to-morrow. Tell him." On the next day the father came and he sent Muhammad down to get news of the girl, and Muhammad went and saw the Wazir and was told that she had hit him because he had found a man inside with her. And Muhammad went back to the ship and told his father, and his father said, "Go and kill your sister." And Muhammad returned to the girl and told her, "Father has told me to cut your throat," and she asked, "Why?" And he told her what the Wazir had told them. Then Muhammad went inside and gave her three purses of silver and a camel and sent her off, and after she had been gone about three hours he returned and got a sheep and a *guruguru* and cut their throats, and putting their blood on his sword, went to his father and said, "I have killed her," and the father was pleased.

When the girl got to the next town, she stopped under a very large mango tree and slept there, and when she awoke she cried from hunger, and about eleven o'clock in the morning she climbed up the mango tree. Now in that city the Sultan had a son who was very fond of shooting birds, and on that day he had gone out for that purpose, and he had arranged to have his lunch at twelve o'clock under that mango tree, and slaves laid mats and he came and ate there, and the child up the tree cried hard, and one of her tears fell on the mat before the Sultan's son. And he asked, "What is this? Is it a bird-dropping or what?" And the slaves said, "No, it's not a bird, but perhaps it is water." And the prince looked up and saw the girl and said, "Go and fetch her down." Then the slaves climbed up and told her, "Lady, we are told you are to come down," and she said, "I can't come down until you have gone away." And they went down and told the prince, and went away. Thus she came down and saw him.

Then he asked her for what reasons she had come there, and she told him that her parents and brother had journeyed and that she had been left with the Wazir, and what the Wazir had done and all he had told her father when he came back, and how her father had told her brother to slay her and what he had done.

"And now," she said, "I don't know what to do or where to get food, and when I saw your food I cried, for it is such food as I would get at home." Then they ate together and he told his slaves, "Go and tell my father I shall be back at two a.m.," and at ten p.m. they started home and he got her inside the house.

The next day the prince said to his father, "Marry me to a room." And the father said, "What child of a Sultan has ever been known to marry a room?" And the son replied, "I have never heard of it, but I want you to marry me to one." So the Sultan beat the *mbiu* to all the people, and when they came he told them the next day he would marry his son to a room. And on that day he made a wedding for seven days, and everybody came and ate at the palace and no one had permission to eat at home, and on the same day the prince had a son, for the room bore one, and he was called *Mbamwezi* (moon-ray), and on another day he got another and he was called *Jua* (sun).

He showed them to his father and said, " I told you to marry me to a room and see what the profit is." In the light Mbamwezi covered his face and in the night the sun shone from the face of Jua. Another day he got another child and he was called *Nyota* (star), and at night his face shone too. After a time his father asked where he had got these children, and he showed him the daughter of Muhammad, so the Sultan made a bigger wedding than before.

And after a month had passed the girl asked her husband to make her a railway, and he told his father to do it, and in seven days the railway was made, and she took a *joho*, a *kilemba*, a *kanzu* and a *kikoi* from her husband, and she asked if the carriage was ready and he said, " Yes." Then she said, " How many people will you give me to go home? " and he gave her thirty-five slaves and a Wazir.

Now the slaves were in the end carriage and the Wazir in the one next to the lady. And one day he saw how beautiful she was, and he went into her carriage at night as she lay there with her three children and he said, " I have come to enjoy you or kill you," and she replied, " I cannot do this," and he said, " Well, I will kill Jua," and he did so and she cried very much.

On the second night he came again and said, " If you won't do as I wish, I will kill Mbamwezi," and she said, " No, kill him," and he did so, and she cried very much. And on the third night he went again and asked, " Won't you do this or shall I finish Nyota? " and she cried, " Finish him. I will not do as you ask." So he killed Nyota. On the fourth night he went and told her, " Now I will do as I want or kill you." But she said, " Give me an hour," and he agreed, and she said, " Pull the cord and stop the train," and it stopped. Then she said to a slave, "Take water in a kettle and put it under that coco-nut tree," and she went to wash there, and the kettle she left on a stone and ran away. The Wazir waited for an hour watching the smoke, and when he looked he found she had gone. So he took the train back to her husband and asked him, "Did you marry a djinn or a woman?" and he said, "Why?" and the Wazir told him how she had gone with the kettle and that later when they went to her they found she had vanished, and her children. And the prince said, "Father, give me a horse and a sharp sword," and he did so, and the prince went to follow her and said, "I will get my wife, or I will die."

Now she had got to a place like a well and lived there, and it was near to her father's place, and he asked who lived there, and he sent her brother Muhammad to see who was there, and he went and made a big feast there and asked her who she was. And she replied, "I am Gharibu." And he asked where she came from, and she said, "I don't know where I come from or where I go." And Muhammad went and told his father, and the next day they went together and made a big feast, and she knew it was her father. After the meal she said to her slave, "Tell the young master when he goes to forget his *kitara* (sword)," and he did so. And when they had gone he told his father, and he said, "Send a slave." But he said, "I would, but it is a beautiful one of gold, and if I lose it how can I get another? I will go myself," and he went. And his sister said, "Do you know me, Muhammad?" and he replied, "I do not remember you," and she said, "Tell father to-morrow to build a big tower and to beat the town *mbiu*," and he went and told him.

On the next day she went there, wearing her male clothes and *jambiya* and sword, and all the men, slaves and everyone, was there, and the women too. And she said, "I am going to speak, and my words have a meaning. You must all sign a paper that if anyone interrupts me or interferes while I am speaking he will have his head cut off." And they agreed.

Now on that day her father, brother and their Wazir were there, and her husband, father-in-law and their Wazir also. Then she began to speak and she told them a story of a long time ago, that there was a Sultan and his wife and they had two children, a boy and a girl, and the father, mother and brother journeyed and left the girl with the Wazir, and at this point her family knew who the speaker was, but could do nothing as they had signed the paper. Then she went on with her story, and when she had got to the part about the kettle, her husband and his father knew who she was, and when all of them had heard her story they believed her and she took off her men's clothes. And her father killed the Wazir and the concubines, and her husband did the same to his Wazir and the slaves.

Then they had a big new wedding and fired guns, and this is the end.

The Story of Zimwi Mroha

There was a man who had three children, two boys and one girl. When the girl came to a marriageable age, she said, "I don't want a husband who excretes in the ordinary way. I want a husband who excretes gold and silver." One day there came a Zimwi and he was told about this, and he said "All right," and he took some finery and bound it round his person, and bound in it some rupees, and he went before her and excreted rupees, and she agreed to him and married him. After three days he wanted his wife to take her to his house, and he was given her and he went with her. After a short time he came back and took his brother-in-law to come and see his sister, and they went on their way, and they took with them bread to eat on the road. And they went on till they came to a sugar-cane plantation, and the Zimwi said, "Let us go and cut some sugar-cane, but cut the young ones because the owners are very fierce towards those who cut the ripe." So the youth cut the young ones, but the Zimwi cut the ripe ones, and he put them at the bottom of his basket and the young ones he put on top. They went on the road, and presently the Zimwi said, "Let us eat our sugar-cane," and the youth said, "It can't be eaten because it is young." But the Zimwi took out his ripe canes and ate them.

Then they found bananas on the road in a shamba in the same way, and he told him in the same way to pick the unripe ones, and the youth picked the unripe ones and he the ripe ones, and put the unripe ones above them. And they came along the road, and he said, "Let us eat our bananas," and the youth said, "They can't be eaten," but he took out his ripe ones and ate. And they went along the road till they came to a forest, and the Zimwi said, "There is a devil lives here. When he says you must throw your bread to him do so, or he will do you harm." When they got there he said, "Wait for me. I am going to relieve myself," but as a matter of fact he went into the forest and sang, and the youth thought it was indeed the devil and he threw him his bread, and the Zimwi ate it and came back. They went on their way till they were near the houses, and he showed him a tree on the road, and said, "This tree is a great medicine for me for stomach-ache. If I have its leaves it is medicine, therefore if I send you, come here." Then when they got to the house food was ready, and he said, "My stomach aches with a pain, go at once and fetch my medicine," and he ate all the food. And the youth returned and went on his way.

After a few days the Zimwi went and brought his younger brother-in-law, and they came to that place where the sugar-canes were, and he told him, "Don't you pick the ripe ones, only the unripe ones, for the owners are fierce." So the Zimwi picked the ripe ones, and the youth also picked the ripe ones and put unripe ones on the top as the Zimwi had done. And when it had got to the time for eating, the Zimwi took out his ripe sugar-canes, and the youth took out his ripe ones too. And the Zimwi was very annoyed and he gave him his, and the youth ate them all. And they went on their way till they got to the banana place, and he told him in the same way, "Don't you pick the ripe ones, pick the unripe ones." But the youth picked the ripe ones and put them under the unripe ones till they got on the road, and the Zimwi said, "Let us eat our bananas," and he took his ripe ones, and the youth took out his ripe ones in the same way, and the Zimwi was annoyed and gave him his, and the youth ate them all. And they went to the place where there was a devil, and he told him, "There is a devil here, when he sings throw your bread to him. Wait for me, I am going to relieve myself," and he went inside and he sang. And the youth, instead of throwing the bread, threw a stone, and knocked out his tooth and hurt him very much, and he said, "Why do you strike me?" And he said, "I thought it was the devil, so I struck him."

And they went on their way till they got near that tree which was the Zimwi's medicine, and the Zimwi told him, "If I am sick come and take for me the leaves of this tree, for it is my medicine." And the youth said, "Very well." The Zimwi went on, and the youth said, "I am going to relieve myself," and he stayed behind, and he plucked the leaves of that tree, dug up its roots and took its bark; everything he took and he concealed it. When they got to the house food was ready, and the Zimwi said, "My stomach aches, go and fetch me the leaves of that tree," and he gave him them on the spot, and he said, "No, I want its roots," and he gave him them. He said, "No, I want its bark," and he gave him it. So the Zimwi was very much annoyed and he didn't eat his food, and the youth ate it all, and on the next day he took his sister and went home.

The Strong Man

There was once a rich man who was very anxious to have a child, and after some time he had a son and called him Pweke. On the day of its birth the child cried, so they prepared some food for him, about one *kibaba* of rice. He ate it all, and on the second day he ate two *kibabas* of rice and two fowls. It kept increasing, till after some years, he ate one *sufuria* of *uji* in the morning, one *sufuria* of rice and one goat for his lunch, and one *sufuria* of rice and one goat for his dinner, and many areca nuts and betel leaves.

One day he asked his father to make him a bow and arrows, and the rich man sent many labourers into his store to fetch iron bars for making arrows, and it took a month to make one arrow, for it was very large. Then he said he wanted a very big bag with three rooms inside, and his father made one for him, and in the first room he put so many goats, and in the second so much rice and water, and in the third some betel leaves and areca nuts. He took his bag and arrows and went away, saying he was going to find a man as strong as himself.

After journeying some time he saw about fifty big cooking-pots and some water-jars full of water; he asked whose they were and whether a feast was being held, and was told, "Do not speak aloud. *Bwana Mswaki-Mbuyu-Mkongo-Mvumo* (Mr. Toothbrush-a-baobab-tree-walking-stick-a-borassus-palm) is asleep. He will kill you when he comes." But the man got excited and ate up all the food, drank all the water and chewed the betel leaves, and when he spat, all the people near him were drowned. He then sent and caught *Mswaki-Mbuyu-Mkongo-Mvumo* and put him in his bag, and went away. After some days he met another man, *Kidevu Mfunge*. His meal was about one hundred cooking-pots, the boy ate all the food and drank the water, chewed the betel leaves, and the people were drowned as before. He then put the man in the bag with the other and continued his journey. After some days he saw a very tall and thin woman sitting opposite a large lake, and he was told she was *Kijiwa Chama Kana Madina*, and she was keeping the birds off her rice-fields. Pweke took up his bag and threw it across to her, telling her to keep it for him, and she picked it up and put it in her pocket, and he was surprised at her strength. He went over to her and was going to sit down on a very large stone about one hundred yards in length, but she took it up to throw at the birds.

Then Pweke, much astonished, went back to his father and told him that in future he would only eat half a *kibaba* of rice and one glass of water and one betel leaf as other people did.

The Sultan and the Wife of the Grand Vizier

Once upon a time there was a Sultan and he had a hundred wives, and his Wazir had one, but she was very beautiful. Now the Sultan went one day to the Wazir's house, and saw his wife and loved her, but saw no way of getting her; so he sent his Wazir on a long journey to inspect an outlying portion of his kingdom, and in his absence went to the lady and told her he wanted her, and she agreed, and he said, "This evening I will come."

When he had gone she cooked thirty plates of different kinds of sweetmeats. In the evening the Sultan came, and the lady bade him eat and he refused, but she pressed him, so he took off his ring, and putting it under a cushion, ate some of the food. When he had finished she asked him which was the sweetest, and he said, "All are equally sweet." So the lady said, "If that is so it is bad for you to want me, for after a few days you will not be able to see me, and all we women, like the sweetmeats, are equally sweet." To this logic the Sultan could not reply and left, forgetting his ring.

The next morning when the Sultan woke he heard

the guns on shore fire a salute to the Wazir, who was returning. At once he remembered the ring, but he had no one to send to fetch it. The Wazir disembarked, and went home and ate; after he had eaten he moved the cushion and saw the ring. He put on his *joho* and went to the *Baraza* (meeting), taking the ring with him. After the *Baraza* was over the Wazir followed the Sultan inside to make his report, and when he had finished he said, "I have come back and I went to see my *Zizi*, which has only one ox in, and I see footsteps of a lion, won't it hurt me?" The king understood and told the Wazir everything, and the Wazir gave the Sultan back the ring and went home to his wife who told him everything.

The Magician and his Pupils

Once upon a time there was a couple who had two children; presently the father died and they were left to their mother, who, when they grew up a little, sent to look for a teacher for them. She eventually found one, and as she had no money it was agreed that when they were taught the teacher should keep one. She sent her children to be taught, and of the two the younger was far the keener to learn. In fact, whenever the teacher was absent the boy would get his big books and read them. When the teacher returned he found out that the boy had been reading the books, for no one else could get such knowledge except in this way.

Now the teacher was really a *Zimwi*. One day when the teacher was out their mother came to give the boys food, and before she went away again the younger said to her, "You must be sure to take me when the time comes, as I am very clever." When the teacher had finished their education the mother came to take one of her sons away. She wished to take the younger, but so did the teacher, and they quarrelled, so that they had to go to the *Kathi* to decide. The *Kathi's* judgment was that as no agreement had been made beforehand as to which child each should have, the mother should have the first choice, and of course she chose the younger.

When they got back home again the boy told her that they could make a great deal of money, as he had the power of turning himself into any animal he liked, and he could do this and his mother take him to the market and sell him, but he said, " You must be sure to take the rope back every time." So each day the boy would turn himself into a sheep, or a goat, or an ox, and his mother would lead him to market and sell him, but she always insisted on the rope being returned, and as soon as he was led away by the purchaser he would seek for an opportunity and escape.

One day the teacher heard that the woman was selling these animals in the market and that she would never part with the rope, so he went there and bought a horse from her for Rs. 200, and when the woman wanted the cord he refused, and she was much disturbed but could not stop him, and the teacher led the horse away by the rope. Now the teacher knew well enough that it was not really a horse but his former pupil, and on the road he told him that he would kill him because he refused to follow him and had gone back to his mother.

When he got him to his place he put him into an iron cage and gave him no food or water. After this he went to a blacksmith's and got arrows made, and during his absence the boy's brother and the other pupils in the teacher's house gave him food and water. When the teacher returned in the evening, he used to ask if they had done this but they denied it. For seven days this happened until the teacher had seven arrows ready, and on that day he was ready to kill him, so he went to the door of the cage and shot the first arrow, but he missed him for while he shot the horse was reading the Koran, so that the arrows missed their mark. Six arrows he shot and the horse knew that the seventh was the one that was bound to kill him, for it was the only thing that could kill him and his charms were finished; so as the teacher drew back his bow to shoot the seventh arrow he broke through the cage and got out, and turning into an *mwewe* (an Egyptian kite), flew away. The teacher did the same and followed him.

When the boy got tired he turned into a *cheche* (a mongoose) and the teacher turned into a dog and hunted him. He got so close to him that the boy thought he was bound to be caught, so he turned into a *kipanga* (a kestrel) and the teacher did likewise. Flying towards the sea, he saw a fisherman bathing and his clothes with some pice on them left on the shore, so he turned into a pice and fell among the others. The teacher then turned into a man and walked up to take the money, but as he approached the fisherman came up and saw him and raised an outcry that he was robbing the poor; but the teacher pacified him and he said he only wanted one pice for which he gave him four rupees and went on his way.

As he was passing over some coral rag on the shore the pice turned into *mtama* (millet) and the teacher turned himself into a chicken, but a grain of this fell into a hole under the coral and the chicken picked up all the rest and ate it; then he saw the lost grain, and as he tried to get it, it turned into a *cheche* and bit the chicken's throat, and it died.

The boy then turned into a man, went to the teacher's house and released his brother, and took the two wives of the teacher and all his property. He and his brother then married the two women.

The Beggar's Son who Married the Daughters of Eight Kings

Once upon a time there was a beggar and a merchant; the merchant had a daughter and the beggar had a son, and the children played together, and one day he seduced the merchant's daughter.

When the merchant found out he hit the buffalo horn to call all people, and asked them if any knew who was the perpetrator. After a search of twelve days his men found that it was the beggar's child, so he was caught, and the merchant had his arms cut off, after which he ran away until one night he came to the town of another Sultan.

He went into the mosque at Alfajar and prayed a petition, and his voice was so beautiful that all the people awoke and came out of their houses to find out who it was or whether it was a spirit, for no one had heard such a beautiful voice. Even the king himself woke up and went to see, and when he saw the boy he took him to his palace and married him to his daughter because of his beautiful voice.

On the night he entered into his bride's house she became pregnant, and the boy ran away at once at night, as he was ashamed to be married to the king's daughter without any arms. He went to the town of another Sultan where the same adventure happened to him, and after that to a third, a fourth, a fifth, a sixth, a seventh and an eighth, and in each case married the king's daughter and she became pregnant on the night of his entering the house.

After leaving the eighth city there were no more states in that country, and so he went into the desert, and about two o'clock in the night a *Pinga* of the night came whose duty it is to fold up the night and spread the day. The *Pinga* asked him where he was going, and the youth said he did not know, and the *Pinga* said, " I know all that has happened to you, and I will give you your arms back if you bring to me the child of your eighth wife." The next day his eighth wife bore a child, and he went in the night and brought the child to the *Pinga*. Now there was a big lake where the *Pinga* lived. When he got there he was told to put the right stump into the water, and when he did so he got a beautiful arm. The *Pinga* told him to do the same with the left, and he got another arm more beautiful than the other;

so he gave the *Pinga* the child in a flour sieve together with razor, grindstone, lemon and beads. Then the *Pinga* said, "Cut its thoat." He did so, and the *Pinga* told him to separate the meat from the bones, and he put the meat on one side and the bones on the other. After he had finished this task the *Pinga* said, "Of all the sons of Adam there is not one more honourable than you, and you have kept your bargain, so good-bye." When he was nearly out of sight the *Pinga* called him back and said, "Take the bones and the meat and mix them together," and he did so. Then he was told to throw them into the lake, and when he had done this the *Pinga* said, "Look away," and when he turned back again there was the child alive with a golden chain around its neck, and the *Pinga* said, "The child is my grandson and my gift is the chain."

Then the youth took the child back and laid it by its mother's side, and when she awoke she saw the chain and wondered who had put it there, and the Sultan beat the buffalo horn to call all men together to see this chain. Now when anyone called to the chain, "Oh, chain of the child, come here to me," it did so of its own accord and fell on the neck of each.

The boy stayed there twenty-four days, after which he said, "I have left home a very long time so I pray permission to take my wife and my child and go there." So they packed everything and took seven camels to carry food for the journey and started off, and in each state that they passed through that he had been through before he stayed twenty-four days and took his wife and child, for all the other wives had borne children, and journeyed on, taking each time seven camels.

When he got back home his father was very pleased to see him, and they made a small town for themselves for there were many of them.

Then the youth accused the merchant before the king, and there was a big case to prove he was not guilty, and the king gave judgment that the merchant and his daughter were to be sewn in sacks and thrown into the sea, but the youth grew more and more prosperous and became Wazir to the king.

The Woodcutter and the Log

Once upon a time there was a poor beggar who earned his living by cutting firewood. One day when he was working he happened to be cutting a big log, and while he was doing this he heard a voice say, "Who are you? Who are you?" He answered, "I am a poor man who cuts firewood to earn my living." So the log begged him to spare it, and when the man did as he was asked, gave him a goat and told him whenever he wanted money he had only to tell the animal, who would drop as much gold and silver as he liked. When the man got home he and his wife immediately tried to prove if this was true, and were overcome with joy on finding that it was so. They became very rich and for some time were very happy, but the husband was not satisfied, and wanted to get a kid by the goat, so he sent the animal to a shepherd in order to get it crossed. He advised the shepherd not to allow the goat to relieve itself and he agreed, but after the owner had gone he was overcome with curiosity and ignored the advice given him. Finding that it produced gold and silver, he kept the goat for himself, and when the owner came to fetch it, gave him another instead. The man did not discover this until he reached home, and then it was too late to do anything.

He went to the log and told him what had happened, so he was given a tray and told that whenever he wanted food he had only to tell the tray and it would produce whatever he wished for. He went home and tried and found that it did so. After a time, again becoming dissatisfied, he sent the tray to a tinsmith's to be cleaned, and advised the man not to tell the tray if he wanted any food. Naturally the man did so out of curiosity, and was so delighted with the result that he kept that tray himself and gave the owner back a nice new one. When the man returned with it to his house he found he had again been cheated.

He went a third time to the log and begged for something else, and this time he was given a stick and was told to go into the house with his wife, close all the doors and windows, and order it to play. This he did, and the stick got up and gave them both a good beating; they tried to stop it and only succeeded after a long struggle. He then took the stick to the men who had stolen his goat and tray, and made the stick beat them until they were forced to give up his property. In this way he got them both back and was happy again.

The Seven Sons of Abdul Karim

Once upon a time there was a Sultan named Abdul Karim; he had seven children, and died three years after the last was born. The seven children quarrelled over the Sultanate, and the youngest, whose name was Muhammad, said that they ought not to quarrel about it, but should go and journey round the country and study it. He told his mother that they wanted a year's food to go on *safari*, and when it was ready they mounted their horses and went.

At the end of the year they were still far away from home and their food was finished, neither could they see any means of getting more. Presently in the forest they came to a tiny house in which an old woman dwelt, who lived on millet husks. She welcomed them and asked where they had come from and where they were going; they told her that they did not know. She made them food of millet husks, which they ate.

One day the eldest said, "I am going to shoot birds." After going through the forest for about twenty miles he came to the end of it, and saw a plain of about another twenty miles in extent which was clear of all bush. In the middle he saw a sheep with a brass horn, which he started up and followed for about twenty miles, until they came to a very high wall which the sheep jumped and where the youth could not follow. So he looked for a door, and having followed the wall for some way round he found one, and in the doorway was a water-jar with a plate over it and glasses on it. He picked up a glass and drank, and immediately he was struck on the head and both he and his horse were lost.

The next day the second brother went off to the chase, and he, too, saw the sheep and got to the door and was lost likewise, and so were the third, the fourth, the fifth and sixth brothers, until there was only the youngest left. He went out and he met the sheep and chased it, and saw it jump the wall, and he looked for a door, but when he saw the jar and the glasses he kicked them to smithereens and went home. On the second day he again chased the sheep and it again escaped and jumped the wall, and when he went to the door there was another glass and jar, and those he also broke and went home. On the third day after he had chased the sheep again and broken the glass and jar, he went and unfastened the door in the wall. He went inside, but he saw no house and nothing but a sandy plain all bare, surrounded by the wall. For two days he went inside, seeing nothing, and then he saw a big stone with a hole inside and within an old woman sitting.

Now the sheep that he had been chasing was not really a sheep but a djinn, and the old woman was one of the ayahs of the djinn, and her work was to keep the entrance. She wanted to destroy the boy, but he read and read and read until he had broken all her strength, and he had 1,000 rupees with him. The ayah of the djinn said, "Men do not come here. Why have you come?" and he replied, "I want the djinn who has taken my brothers." So the ayah said, "I will give you a plan for getting there," and on his giving her 50 rupees she gave him some roots, and she said, "The ayah of the inside will tell you more. Go there at six a.m. and when you get to her bite the roots and puff and her fierceness will go."

When he got there he found the ayah of the inside and did as he was directed, and then told her what he wanted, and she said, "Wait until six a.m. to-morrow." So he waited and came again, then she said, "Go as far as the horizon and there you will see a stone. Move it and enter the hole it covers. If you hear nothing do not go, but if you hear noises go, and at the end of the passage you will see a door. Knock it three times and each time you knock a horse inside will cry; when you knock the fourth time you can enter, and to subdue the horse's mistress you must hold her by her hair." So the boy went on as far as the horizon, and found the stone which he moved. Underneath the stone was a flight of stairs which he descended, and hearing the noise of a horse stamping, he went on to the door at the end of the passage.

This he knocked once, and inside the horse cried out and woke its mistress, and she rose up and gave it food. When it had quieted down he knocked again, and again the horse cried out. Out came its mistress again and gave it water. The third time he knocked, and this time the woman was annoyed and came out and knocked the horse with a *kiboko*, and when she had gone he heard the horse say, "If the door is knocked again I shall not cry out." So he knocked on the door and went in, and passed the horse and entered the sleeping-room of its mistress. When he saw her in bed he took hold of her hair, and by some of it he fastened her on to the bed and the rest he held in his hands; then he woke her. She tried to get up, but she could not as her head was fastened. She said, "Loose me," and he refused, and he said, "I will loose you only if you swear to do me no harm." So she swore and he loosed her, and they agreed together, and then he married her and they lived together for twelve days.

On the twelfth day she said, "I want to wash

my hair." Now there was a river which passed through the middle of the house, and she said she wanted to go to the bathroom to wash her hair, but he said, " I would like you to do it here and I will scrub you." As she washed her hair one hair broke off and floated down the river and outside the house. It floated to the Sultan's palace where the river entered his bathing-place. When the horses went to drink they saw a black thing in the water, and it filled up the whole of the bath, for the hair of a *djinniyah's* are many *pimas* long. Then the Sultan's son asked the groom why the horses did not drink, and he replied, " I do not know." So the Sultan's son went to see, and when he got there he took out the hair and got a horse and put it on it, and it was a big load, and he went to his father and said, " I must marry the owner of this hair." So his father said, " This hair is the hair of a *djinniyah*. How do you think we can get her? " But his son said, " If I do not get her I shall run away." So the Sultan was at a loss, for he loved his son dearly and would do anything to please him, so he called for his Wazir and told him to take the army and look for the owner of the hair, and they followed the river and came to the house of the *djinniyah* and her husband, and she said to him, " There is war. Stay inside and I will go and fight, but when I return you must not speak to me. Hold a glass of water until I say you may speak, then speak."

So she went and fought and slew the Sultan's army save one man, whose ear she cut off, after which she returned. After she had given her husband leave to speak she related everything to him.

On the second day she said, " There are some more coming, about half the number of those yesterday; half of them will follow the stream and half will come the other way. You take on those on the water and I will manage those that come from above." They had a hard day's fight, and the lady killed all her opponents and the youth all but two, and then he killed one of those, but the other killed him. She came back and saw her husband dead, and the survivor of their opponents came inside and tied her up, and called men and carried her off, and when they got to the palace the Sultan's son rejoiced, but the *djinniyah* neither spoke nor ate nor drank day or night.

Now in the house where her husband lay slain, after everyone had gone there came out two rats, which played together, and presently out came two snakes. When the snakes came out the rats hid and watched, and the snakes fought each other until one was killed. Then the surviving snake went to its hole and fetched out a stick which he put on his companion's nose, and he revived, and both went away in different directions. Then the rats came out and played again, jumping over the prostrate body of the youth. One of them picked up the stick, and running towards his companion on the youth's body the stick came near his nose, and he immediately revived and sat up. Then the rats ran away. When he did so he saw his wife was not there and he was greatly distressed, and he went outside and walked a long, long way to find her.

Presently he got to the house of an old woman and asked her the news of the country, and she told him that the Sultan's son was about to marry a woman who neither spoke nor ate nor drank, and at once he said, " She is my wife; make a plan that I may see her." So she said, " We will go to-night," and the old woman dressed him in woman's clothes, and they went to the wedding and to the bridegroom's mother, and the old woman said, " This is my daughter, I married her to your slave and sent to the *shamba*; now I want her to see the bride." So the Sultana said, " Let her go," and when he got to the bridal chamber he and his wife knew each other, and she was overcome with joy. Now he had a ring, so had she, and they exchanged, each putting the ring on the other's finger, after which she said, " To-morrow night before seven p.m. wait for me on the forest path."

The next day she ate and drank and spoke, and the Sultan's son rejoiced. That evening she said, "It is our custom at marriage time to go out in the evening if we wish to," and he agreed, and gave her five Arab women to follow her. At the edge of the forest she said, "Wait here while I retire for a few minutes," and she went into the wood to where her husband was, but while he slept in the undergrowth the djinn held his horse. When his wife came she thought that the djinn was her husband and mounted behind him, but as they went away the smell of her husband grew faint behind her, so she looked and saw that the rider in front of her was not he, so she struck him and killed him and returned to where she had mounted, and found her husband sleeping. She woke him and upbraided him and gave him thirty lashes, and said, "To-morrow come again and wait for me here."

Then she returned to her women and went back to the palace. The next night she did the same thing and found her husband awake, so they got on to the horse and went to their home. The Arab women waited until midnight, and as she did not return they went to the palace and told the Sultan and his son, and they went into mourning.

The *djinniyah* and her husband got home and lived in peace. After a while he said, "I want a plan to find my six brothers." And she said, "Your brothers are ready," and she went to the door of the chamber and unlocked it and opened it, and the six brothers with their horses and their swords came out well and alive.

Now the Sultan's son still wanted the *djinniyah* as his wife, so the Sultan beat the buffalo horn, and all that was left of his army, about a hundred soldiers, came out again, and the Sultan told them to go and make war, but the men refused, saying that they would be killed. So the Sultan's son had to give up, and all the rest lived happily ever afterwards.

The Ingratitude of Man and the Gratitude of Animals

Once upon a time there was a snake, a lion and a man, who lived together at the bottom of a dry well, and when it rained there was only a little water in the well. One day there came a beggar who was thirsty, and he made a rope from the climbing plants of the forest and let down a calabash to draw water. When he got the calabash near the top he found he had caught a lion in it, and being frightened was about to drop him when the lion said, "Don't drop me and I will get you some water." When he got it he said, "There is also a snake down there and a man; help the snake but not the man." So he let the calabash down and pulled the snake up, and when he saw it he was so frightened that he wanted to drop him, but the snake said, "Don't drop me and I will get you water," and he got it, and then he said, "There is a man inside, but don't fish him up."

The beggar went on his way, but reflected to himself, "I have rescued two animals—am I to leave a man, a fellow-human, inside the well?" So he went back and got him and took him home, and they lived together like brothers.

Some time after that the beggar got work under the Government and heard that the king had a very beautiful big sheep, so he went to steal the sheep and hid it, after which he bought another and killed it; then he went to his companion and told him he had stolen the king's sheep and killed it, and he said, "Let us eat the meat and say nothing." Now when the king missed his sheep he searched high and low for it without finding it, and offered a reward of Rs. 500 for its recovery. When he heard this, the man who had been rescued from the well went and caught his companion and said, "You will have to go in front of the king." But he said, "Let me go; it is not right to act like this." But he insisted, "No, you will go," and despite further pleading he struck him and put him in handcuffs, and took him to the king. When he got there the king said, " Where is the sheep? " He said, " The sheep is all right, but I have hidden him." So the king asked why he had done it, to which he replied that he wished to test whether his companion could be trusted, and the sheep which he had killed was another one which he had bought. So the king said, " Bring my sheep," and he brought it, and the sheep was fat and well and had been well cared for, but the king said, " The Government cannot compound such an offence," and he sentenced him to be fastened to a post by his ankles and wrists with his hands above his head, and gave orders that anyone who liked might throw rubbish at him. So he was tied up, and very soon buried to his thighs in rubbish. Then the snake came to him and asked him if he found that the man he had rescued was good, and he said, " I have seen of what kind his goodness is." Then the snake said, " Listen, to-day I shall hide two bottles of medicine here, do you see them? " He said " Yes." And the snake continued, " I am now going to bite the king's daughter." So he went away and bit her as she was going to her bath, and when he bit her she was very cross. The king offered a reward saying, " I will give Rs. 1,000 to the man who cures my child," and many people came and tried, but their medicine only made her worse.

On the second day at about five o'clock in the afternoon, the man who was tied up saw the king sitting in the window of the palace, and the man who was drawn out of the well passed. The king called out to him and said in the hearing of the other, " If you can give my daughter medicine and she recovers you shall marry her." As the man was passing the poor man who was tied up reflected aloud, " If I were unfastened I would go and make medicine for her," but his erstwhile companion said in a tone of scorn, " You indeed," and boxed his ears. The king saw this and called out, " Who are you hitting?

Unfasten him and bring him here." So he took his medicine and went to the king, and the king asked him why he had been struck. He replied, "I only said that if I were unfastened I would make medicine for the lady, and he struck me." So then the king told him to proceed, but first of all he took two bottles of oil and cleaned his legs, then when he had finished he went and spread the medicine on the king's daughter, and afterwards she demanded food, water, and everything else and quickly recovered entirely. After that they were married and had a grand wedding, and feasted for seven days.

At the end of the festival the snake came and said to him, "To-day I am going to bite a rich merchant," and he did so, and they charged the merchant Rs. 1,000 for curing him and his child, and then the snake bit the child of the Wazir, who paid Rs. 1,000, and then the child of a Hindu merchant for which he got Rs. 2,000. After this the snake said, "This I do in gratitude for rescuing me."

One day the lion came and gave him a ring, and whatever he wanted he might ask the ring and it would do for him. So he asked for a big town with beautiful houses in a place away by itself and he got it, then he wanted many retainers and he got them. Then oxen and donkeys until his town was complete and everything inside it. After which the lion gave him medicine and said, "If ever you want me put some of this in an incense dish and I will come. Have I sufficiently shown my gratitude?" and he said "Yes." So the lion went, and afterwards the king gave him the kingdom, and announced to everyone that he was king, and everyone came and rejoiced over his good fortune.

The Lion and the Carpenter

There was once a carpenter going to his work; on the way he met a lion who asked him, "Who are you? Are you a man?" The carpenter replied,

"No, I am not a man, but a carpenter." The lion said, "I am very anxious to see a man." The carpenter said, "I can show you a man if you like," and the lion said "Yes." The carpenter made a very strong but very narrow cage and put the lion in the cage in order to show him a man. He locked the cage at once, and then boiled some water and poured it over the lion, and told him, "I am a man if you have never seen one." The lion was about to die, so he let him go as he could not move.

After some time the lion got better and asked his companions to help him kill the carpenter, so they went to find him. The carpenter had a storied house, so in order to get up they stood one on top of the other, and the injured lion was at the bottom, in this way they managed to reach up to the house. The carpenter came and shouted to his wife to bring hot water, and when the bottom one heard this he ran away and all his companions fell down. Some were injured and some were killed and some ran away, and the carpenter escaped.

The Number of Days in Ramathan

There was an Arab who had an idea for checking the number of the days in Ramathan, so that there need be no quarrelling as to which day of the month it was. He put a stone in a tin for each day every morning. His son noticed this and said to himself, "I will help my father; he is having a lot of trouble with his stone collecting." So he put a lot more in one day. Some friends came to the house and they started disputing as to what day it was, one said the twelfth, another the sixteenth, another the thirteenth, and so on. The Arab said, "Don't dispute, I can settle it. I put a stone aside for each day." So he went to his tin and counted a hundred and fifty stones. He was astonished and saw something was wrong, so he took a lot out and went back and counted again.

"To-day is the fortieth," he announced. All exclaimed at this, but he said, "Forty is a little, there were a hundred and fifty days in my month."

The Young Man and the Dishonest Beggar

Once upon a time there was a very rich Arab and he had a son. After some time he died and the son inherited his property, but he spent it all very soon and was left destitute. One day he was sitting down about twelve noon, very hungry as he had had nothing to eat, and said to himself, "I will do some work and if I earn six rupees I will give two to the poor, with another I will buy food for myself, and with the other three I will trade."

He went out to work and he earned six rupees. On his way home he saw a beggar sitting by the road-side, and reflecting aloud, said, "I made an oath that if I earned six rupees I would give two to the poor, with one I would buy food, and with the remainder I would trade." So he took out two rupees and he gave them to the beggar. But the beggar had overheard him and caught hold of him, and cried out, "Oh, Muslimun, quickly help, he is a thief, he has taken four of my rupees."

People collected quickly, and he was searched and four rupees, being found on him, were given to the beggar, while he was arrested and beaten hard, and they said, "You are a thief to cheat the poor," and he denied it. Then men said, "This is the first time he has done wrong, release him."

After this the crowd dispersed, and the young man, determined to get his money back, followed the beggar who in the evening returned to his companions. Arrived at the meeting-place of the beggars, the beggar recited an account of the affair to his companions, who were six, and like himself, all blind. The beggar was much congratulated on his ruse, and exclaimed, "I have now thirty-six rupees in this pocket that I wear round my waist, so that they are quite safe."

At night the young man followed the beggar to his hut and saw him unfasten the pocket and lay it on the bed, whereupon the youth picked it up and went away while the beggar cooked his food and ate it. After he had eaten he went to the bed and felt for the pocket to tie round his waist again, but without success, after which he hit the cords of the bed with his stick until he broke them, thinking the purse might have caught in them, but all to no purpose, for he could not find the purse and cried hard all night.

In the morning he went to his companions and said, "All my money has been taken," and the first of the other beggars said, "You don't hide them properly. For myself, I hide mine under the hearthstone when I cook." The youth, who was there, heard what he said, and waited until the evening, when he followed the second beggar, who, when he reached his house, turned up the hearthstone, found all his money correct and added two rupees that he had got that day. When he moved away the youth took them all, fifty rupees. The beggar found out when he had finished his meal and cried out, "I am blind and I have been robbed," and the next morning he went and told his companions. The third beggar said, "You yourself are to blame; you do not know how to conceal your money. Look at my *kanzu*. I have a pocket sewn on the inside of it into which I have buttoned up sixty rupees." The youth overheard, and in the evening followed the beggar home, where he took off his *kanzu* and put it on the bed to prepare his food. The youth at once cut out the pocket and took it with sixty rupees inside. The beggar ate his food and then picked up his *kanzu* which was very light; he felt it all over to find the money and cut it up, but it had gone. In the morning he too told his companions, and the fourth said, "I hide mine under the threshold and I always look if they are there. I have seventy rupees there." The youth got the money that evening with little trouble, and the next morning the fifth beggar informed his companions that he hid his in a hole dug under the leg of his bed so that he could always hear if anyone dug them up. The youth took all the money, a hundred rupees, in the same way. The next morning the fifth beggar, when he told his companions of his loss, said, " The thief must be among us and overhears what we say," so that they took their sticks and hit round everywhere, but got no one.

The sixth beggar said, " Well, my money is safe anyway, for I have a hole bored in my stick and in it a hundred and fifty rupees." When they went off to their begging the youth, who had as usual overheard, took a bamboo stick and prepared it nicely and filled it with potsherds, small stones and bits of tin so that it rattled. In the evening he followed the beggar home. When he got to his house, the beggar leant his stick up against the wall to undo the fastener at the top of the door. While he was doing it the youth took it and put the dummy one in its place. When the beggar had finished he took up the stick and at once remarked, " It is heavy." He turned it out and found only potsherds, so he cried out, " Help, I have been robbed," whereupon his companions came up, and after sympathizing with him, the seventh said, " All you people have been robbed but I can hardly lose my money for I have it all, three hundred rupees, sewn into a *kisibau* which I wear under my *fulana* and *kanzu* and never take off." When the youth heard this he was much perplexed, and went home to think over how he could become possessed of it. In the morning he went to a shop and bought a quarter of a pound of ginger and a quarter of a pound of pepper and took them to his wife and said, " Make *uji* and mix them in and prepare also a chicken with *wale* and bring it to the Juma mosque to-night." He then went to find him and said, " I am a blind man and a stranger from Arabia, help me; take my hand and lead me to a place to sleep." The beggar took his hand and led him to the Juma mosque and said, " Sit down here "; after which he conversed with him for some time asking news from Arabia. At ten o'clock the youth's wife came to the door with *uji* and the fowl and bread and said, " *Hodi*," and called out, " I have brought food for my husband who was to have returned from Arabia." The blind beggar got up and fetched the food and endeavoured to wake the youth who had fallen asleep, calling in his ear, " Muhammad, Muhammad." " What is it? " asked the youth sleepily. " Wake up, wake up," said the beggar. " Your wife has brought some food." " You can have it," said the youth, " for I am not hungry."

The beggar drank three cups of *uji*, but it was so hot he burnt his inside and made him perspire so much that he wanted to bathe, which, however, he was afraid to do on account of having to take his waistcoat off. He called, " Muhammad, Muhammad," but the youth feigned sleep, so he quietly took off his clothes and went and turned the tap on; then he returned to the youth who was still feigning sleep, so he went back and started to bathe, whereupon the youth at once jumped up and seized the waistcoat and ran away.

When he returned from his washing the beggar discovered his loss and made such an uproar that many people came, but they did not catch the youth, who got right away.

The Three Sick Wagunya

Once upon a time there were three Wagunya; one of them had itch in his arm, one had a sore on his leg, and the third had a discharge from the eyes. The one that had itch was continually scratching his arm, the one that had a sore on his leg had perpetually to drive flies away, and the third was always having to rub his eyes.

One day when they were sitting together they

agreed that for a whole day the one with itch should not scratch himself, the one with a sore should not drive away the flies, and the third should not take the discharge out of his eyes. They sat together for some time suffering much irritation, but after a while the one with the sore said he had been to see a dance where the performers sang *Panga timba* and clapped their hands over and below their legs, of which he gave a practical demonstration which succeeded, not only in showing his companions the nature of the dance, but in keeping the flies away from his sore.

The one who had itch said he had been to the shore and seen a fish about "this size," with which words he drew his nails up his arm from wrist to shoulder. The one who had the discharge from the eyes said, "Yes, it is so, for I saw it with my own eyes," and here he pulled them down, which allowed the discharge to escape.

The Two Thieves

Once upon a time there were two thieves; one stole a duck and the other stole a gun. They were put in jail, and the one who stole the duck was brought up first to be tried before the *Kathi*.

The *Kathi* asked him if he had stolen the duck and he said, "No, I bought the duck when it was a duckling," and the *Kathi* told the complainant that he had no proof and let the thief go.

When he went back to the jail to get his property the other thief asked him how he managed to get off, and he told him.

So when the second thief came before the *Kathi*, the *Kathi* asked him in the same way, how he had got the gun, and he said, "I bought it when it was a pistol, and I oiled it and looked after it, and now it is a gun." The *Kathi* said, "I am afraid if you are not stopped it will grow into a cannon." So he put that man in jail for some time.

A Cunning Rabbit

Once upon a time during the hot season a collection of animals made a plan to dig a well. All agreed except the rabbit, who said he had got very sweet water for himself. The other animals dug a well, and when the water came they used to keep one animal on duty to see that no animal should get the water other than those who dug the well.

The first time a hyena was put on duty; he was there alone and the rabbit came, singing, "*Ngungu ru Ngunguru* "—" and I fetched a little water at a time from the well." When he arrived the hyena told him not to take any water from the well. The rabbit replied, " Who wants that tasteless water! I have got some very sweet water to drink. If you want any I will give you some." He had honey in his pot, and he gave some to the hyena who found it very sweet and asked for some more. The rabbit said, " I will not give you any unless I tie you very tightly with a rope, because you will fall down after you have drunk this water of mine." The hyena agreed and was tied very tightly so that he could not move. Then the rabbit refused to give him any of his water and went to the well, took as much water as he liked, bathed in the well and went away. When the hyena's companions came and found him tied they asked him, " Who has done this? " He said, " A rabbit." He was found to be useless.

A lion stayed there the next day. The rabbit came as usual and saw the lion who said to him, " Why do you come here? " He replied, " I am going to my work. I do not want your water, I have got very sweet water." The lion asked to taste it and the rabbit gave him some, and he asked for some more, but the rabbit told him he must tie him first because he would fall down. The lion agreed and was tied, then the rabbit did as he liked.

The next day a turtle was put on duty, and he sunk himself under the water in the well. The rabbit came singing as usual, and as there was nobody there, he filled his pot with water, then went in to bathe. The turtle at once caught him by the legs and held him there until all the animals came and found him and they tied him up. They wanted to eat him and he said, "If you want to eat me, you must tie me with a very dry banana tree rope and put me in the sun, then I will become very fat, otherwise you will find me very weak and tasteless." They did as he told them, and the rabbit, on being put in the sun with rotten string, ran away and escaped from the cruel animals.

This story is common in many countries, and is told in Mauritius.

The Chameleon and the Buffalo

All the animals were called to a feast; some went on in front and others lagged behind. The chameleon was a long way behind. Presently he met the buffalo, and the buffalo said, "Why don't you hurry up?" The chameleon said, "I shall get there before you. When are you going?" The buffalo replied, "To-morrow," and the chameleon said, "When you go, pass along here, because I have something to tell you."

The next day the buffalo came and they chatted together for some time until the buffalo said, "Good-bye," and left the chameleon behind saying, "Go, and I will come behind." As he went the chameleon climbed on to his tail.

When he got there the buffalo wanted to sit down. Suddenly he heard the voice of the chameleon: "You big people should look where you are going; you don't consider us small people, and you will hurt us."

The buffalo was astonished, as he had no idea how the chameleon had come, but the chameleon did not tell him and he returned the same way that he had come.

Kibunwasi Recovers the Poor Man's Goats

Once upon a time there was a poor man who had a she-goat, but he had no male goat, so he asked the Sultan to have his she-goat crossed. So the Sultan told him to keep the goat with his herd and when she got kids he might have them. After some time the she-goat had many kids, and the man went and asked for his goats, which were many. The Sultan refused, saying, "They are all mine; if it were not for my goat you wouldn't have got them." The man could not do anything, so he went to Kibunwasi and complained. Kibunwasi was the Sultan's jester, and he said, "When you get the goats, how many will you give me?" He agreed they should be divided equally between them.

Next day Kibunwasi left his house early in the morning with an axe on his shoulder, and passed in front of the palace. The Sultan was standing on his verandah and asked him where he was going to. Kibunwasi replied, "Sultan, I am very busy at present, I will come back later." When he returned he was carrying some very large logs on his shoulder. The Sultan asked him what the logs were for. He replied, "My father has delivered, sir, and I am going to make a fire for him." The Sultan said, "You are telling lies; how can a man deliver a child?" He then said, "Why has your Highness not given this poor man his goats? He had a she-goat and you have a he-goat; how can your he-goat have produced the kids?" Then the Sultan laughed and gave him all the goats belonging to the poor man. Then they divided them.

Kibunwasi Builds a High House in a Day

One day the Sultan said, "Among all my people is there anyone who can build me a very high house in a day?" Kibunwasi said, "I can, but you must get me the stones and labourers." So the Sultan replied, "Very well." So Kibunwasi made a huge kite, and got a lot of string and tied a lot of old tins on it, and sent it up. It flew up to the end of the string and roared in the wind, and the tins clattered.

Then he went to the Sultan and said, "The *fundis* say the stone is finished; send some more and come and have a look at the work." When they got there Kibunwasi said, "Climb up and see how the work is getting on." But the Sultan said, "How can a man climb a string?" And Kibunwasi said, "How can a man build a very high house in a day?" So the Sultan determined to kill Kibunwasi, and he called his *baraza* and gave everyone an egg, and said, "Presently I shall tell everyone to lay an egg, and you must produce your eggs."

After this Kibunwasi came in, and they waited until the end of the *baraza*, and then the Sultan said, "Everyone must lay an egg. If anyone does not lay an egg, I will kill him." So everyone produced an egg except Kibunwasi, but he got up and flapped his arms and crowed loudly. And the Sultan asked why he did so, and Kibunwasi replied, "Is there any animal who can produce without a male? All these people have laid eggs, and I am the cock." So Kibunwasi triumphed, and everyone was ashamed that Kibunwasi could be the only male among them.

Kibunwasi and the Three Thieves

One day Kibunwasi was going along the road with his goat and he met three thieves, who, when they saw him coming, agreed that one of them should pretend to have a stomach-ache and lie down on the ground. Kibunwasi came up, and seeing the man on the ground, asked what was the matter, and he said, "I am in great pain." So Kibunwasi said, "Are you able to hold a goat's string?" and he replied "Yes." So he took the man up and carried him, and gave him the goat's rope to hold.

On the way the thief let the goat go, unknown to

Kibunwasi, who, on reaching his house, asked the thief what had happened to it. And the man said, "I was in great pain, and the string slipped out of my hand."

Meanwhile the other two thieves had caught the goat and killed it, and divided it into three parts, and their companion, who had pretended to be ill, managed to escape from Kibunwasi's house while he was away, and soon rejoined them. When Kibunwasi found out he had gone, he told his wife that he must go and find them, but before doing so he got two gazelles, which he fastened in the yard, and a bladder which he filled with blood. He said to his wife, "I will follow the thieves with one gazelle, and you must fasten the bladder of blood to your throat." And she did so.

He then went and found the thieves, and after talking to them for some time, told them he wanted to join them, and they agreed to let him. Whilst they were going back to his house he hit the gazelle with a stick and said, "Go to my wife and tell her to cook food for three." The gazelle ran away into the bush. When they arrived home at Kibunwasi's house, he called out, "Wife, have you cooked the food?" and she said, "No. Why?" And he said, "Didn't the gazelle tell you to?" She replied, "The gazelle came back and went into the hut and told me nothing." Then Kibunwasi fetched the second gazelle and asked why it hadn't told her, and the gazelle cried, "I told her a long time ago to do it." Kibunwasi then went and knocked his wife down, cutting the bladder at her throat, and she pretended to be dead. The thieves were very frightened, and said, "He has killed his wife." But Kibunwasi said, "She has no sense, so I punished her," and he took a bottle of medicine and let her smell it, then touched her with a stick. When she got up he told her to wash herself and then cook some food, then they all sat down and ate.

After they had finished, the thieves, who had been

greatly struck with what they had seen, asked if he would let them have the gazelle, the stick and the medicine, and after some discussion he sold them to them for a thousand rupees, and they took the things and went away. After they had gone Kibunwasi ran away from that place and went and lived in another country.

One day when the thieves were out with the gazelle, one of them hit it with the stick and told it to go home and tell his wife to cook some food, and it ran away into the bush. When they got home they found nothing ready, and the man asked his wife why she had not done as the gazelle had told her. She said, "No gazelle has come here." And he, thinking she was lying, knocked her down and cut her throat, and she kicked out in her death struggles and expired. He then gave her the medicine to smell and hit her with the stick, but they saw she did not revive and was really dead.

Meanwhile Kibunwasi, having run away into a strange country, had none of his own things with him, so he had to go to a neighbour's house to borrow a saucepan, and when he returned it he returned also another small one. The man wondered at this, and Kibunwasi said, "Oh, your saucepan has borne another." The next day he went to borrow one again, and got such a nice one that he kept it a very long time, and when the owner asked for it he said, "Oh, your saucepan died." The man asked why, and Kibunwasi said, "Oh, everything that has breath and loses it dies."

Further Adventures of Kibunwasi

Once upon a time there was a tom-cat, and he went out for a walk and he met a very beautiful she-cat. So he went home, but in the evening he went to the tabby-cat's house, knocked at the door and said "*Hodi.*" The she-cat called out, "Who are you?" "It is I," he answered. "Who are you?" she said. "I am the child of *Panduna Kame*," he replied. "My brother," she exclaimed. She unfastened the door and came out, and he said, "Now I am going to scratch you." She ran away and he followed her, but he did not catch her, so he returned home to his house, and she also went home.

The next day he did the same, and got hold of her, but she shrieked and the owner came out, whereupon the tom-cat scratched him and ran away.

The owner of the she-cat felt very bitter, but he could not catch him, and wondered what cat it was. He returned inside and shut up the she-cat. The next day he did not come, but on the fourth day he came and got into the fowl-house, where he ate two small chickens. The fowls made such a noise that the owner came out and saw the cat, which ran away.

He went among his friends and said, "There is a cat round here that is a great trouble to me," and he told them all it had done. One of his friends, called Kibunwasi, said, "I have a rat-trap which I will lend you; it is a big rat-trap." And he explained to him how he should put his hand in to prepare the bait. The owner of the cat took the trap home and followed out Kibunwasi's instructions, so that the trap caught him by the hand and he could not get it out again. There were no other houses near his, and no one heard his cries and he died, and Kibunwasi got his property.

Kibunwasi took everything of his and sold them, after which he went to another town on the mainland. After some time the dead man's relations came and found out what had happened, and were told that the trap was Kibunwasi's idea. Kibunwasi, who was on the mainland, heard of this, so he journeyed farther away. When he was a distance of two days away he wanted meat, so he caught a gazelle, and taking it with him went on his way. Presently he met a lion, who said, "Kibunwasi, your time is finished. Give the gazelle to the dogs to eat (for Kibunwasi had two dogs with him), you eat the dogs and I will eat you."

Kibunwasi was very afraid, but he gave the gazelle to the dogs, and then a big frog came out, and puffing his cheeks up to an enormous size, asked what all the trouble was about. Kibunwasi told him, and the frog said, " Yes, do it quickly, and I will then eat him." And he blew himself out to such an extent that the lion said, " Yes, it is true, I think he will eat me." So he went away, and the frog told Kibunwasi, " You are safe now, I can't eat you; take your property and go."

CHAPTER XXXVI

A SPECIMEN OF PEMBA POETRY

THE history of its composition is as follows: Salim bin Masud wanted a wife from the village called Vitongoje. He did not succeed in getting her. So a friend, Nassor bin Khalfan, addressed the first verse to him in a friendly derision. The second is Salim's reply, and the third Khalfan's, and so on.

The first three lines of each verse rhyme at the end and in the middle. The fourth rhymes in the middle with the end syllable of the first three lines, and its own end is unpaired.

The second or reply verse follows the same rhyme as the first in each case.

Nakusikia waposa kwa nguvu na Makelele
Naweye huna mapesa uwape nini wavyele
Domo tupu utakosa kuwowa shoti riale.

Salimu mke sinywele yakhe bure hutapewa.

Hilo kweli niliposa hakika kwa miyezi hile
Mayateni ukhamsa nilizowapa wazile
Nikaona wanitesa na nisai kwetu tele.

Muhibu kurudi kule kufika kwangu niowa.

Yakhe bure hutapewa salimu mke sinywelc
Twaona kuna ghumiwa kakulilia chechele
Kake jenendo lauwa utajifinja vidole.

Salimu mke sinywele yakhe bure hutapewa.

Kufika Kwangu niowa muhibu kurudi kule
Hivi enda chukuliwa kwa shangwe na masokole
Nawe nakwita akhua uje ngoma Kopole.

Muhibu kurudi kule kufika kwangu niowa.

Mshahara wa notisi hudiriki hatta chele
Tena wafanya maposi wenda kwa yule na yule
Huwazi wala hukisi tanabuhi usilale.

Salimu mke sinywele yakhe bure hutapewa.

Mshahara wa notisi hushinda wenye vilele
Kulla siku niarusi kwa fedha yakazi hile
Patole silakiasi dawamu nivile vile.

Muhibu kurudi kule kufika kwangu niowa.

Unyonge unakuweza kijio wala matale
Nabado wautembeza mwezangu wajinga Ole
Huwezi kujituliza nakukhofia na ndwele.

Salimu mke sinywele yakhe bure hutapewa.

Bado haujaniweza shai hunywa kwa magole
Penye rizki huyenza japo tumwa mtambile
Wajifumbiya aziza kula pweza na uwele.

Muhibu kurudi kule kufika kwangu niowa.

Kulla siku twaabiwa msikitu hendi mbele
Kwa kuku hutaozewa ya leo siyo yakale
Watafuta kashifiwa wajijuwa ushongole.

Salimu mke sinywele yakhe bure hutapewa.

Hilo kweli twaambiwa mvivu haba patole
Hodari huchunukiwa japo mpemba wa kwale
Wajaala hujaliwa vyalia vigelegele.

Muhibu kurudi kule kufika kwangu niowa.

Tulizana mposaji hapa ngojea kazole
Baada thiki faraji mwakani machumi tele
Wawatatu ni mmoja usidhani ni wapole.

Salimu mke sinywele yakhe bure hutapewa.

Takithiri maposaji madamu silimi chale
Fulusi ni kama maji maneno yako male
Nipendae tazawiji japo akawa kingwele.

Muhibu kurudi kule kufika kwangu niowa.

Tama ajile na dama ukanambia sumile
Utadhiika daima na kashifa ya milele
Watu wataka ndarama utowe weye wazile.

Salimu mke sinywele yakhe bure hutapewa.

Tammat sitakwandama kwa leo siji keshole
Kwakula mtaka vema huuza japo shambale
Nakwosha vitowa vyuma mimi simtu jefule.

Muhibu kurudi kule kufika kwangu niowa.

I heard that you propose to marry by force and with disturbances, and you have got no money. What will you give to the parents? You won't get a wife with words only, you must have money. Salim, a wife is not hair. You will not be given free.

That is true. I intended to marry for some months past. I have two hundred and five (rupees) to eat. I saw them putting me off, and women are plentiful in our village. My good fellow, when I returned home I got married.

My brother, you will not be given free, a wife is not hair, you seem to be perplexed, the *chechele* bird sang for you. My elder brother, walking will kill you, you will break your toes. Salim, a wife is not hair. You will not be given free.

When I reached home from there I got married. Now she is going to be taken with ceremony and pleasures. And I invite you, my brother, to come to the dance at Kopole. My good fellow, when I returned home I got married.

A summons server's pay won't even pay for rice. Then you propose to marry anyone from anywhere. You don't trouble now, but afterwards you will not get sleep. Salim, a wife is not hair. My brother, you will not be given free.

A summons server's pay is better than that of those who have trees. Every day I can have a wedding for the money of that work. Every day we get more than what you think. My good fellow, when I returned I got married.

In poverty you make a meal of unripe coco-nuts. And besides that you make a show of it. My companion, woe to fools, you cannot get peace, I am afraid of sickness for you. Salim, a wife is not hair. You will not be given free.

I can still bear poverty, I take tea with soft cakes. Having means of life I keep it, even if I am sent to Mtambile. You are making a riddle for yourself, my friend, eating octopus and small grain. My good friend, when I returned home I got married.

Every day people say that anyone who has nothing does not go forward. For a fowl you can't get married; to-day is not like a long time ago. You are looking for disparagement for you know you are a fool. Salim, a wife is not hair. You will not be given free.

This is true, for we are told that a lazy man gets little. A clever man gets things given him even if he is an *Mpemba* of Kwale. Those that are destined to get things get them and make joyful noises. My good fellow, when I returned home I got married.

Stop asking for a wife now, wait until cloves are plentiful. After hardships is ease. In the coming year there will be plenty to pick. He who had three wives now has one; don't think they are mad. Salim, a wife is not hair. You will not be given free.

I will continue to ask for a wife, for I don't cultivate a new shamba. Money is like water; your words are wind. Anyone I like I will marry, even if she is unthinkable. My good fellow, when I returned home I got married.

Finish quickly and I follow you. You told me to get out of the way. You will have trouble every day and disparagement for ever. Men who want money you will pay, and they will take. Salim, a wife is not hair. You will not be given free.

This is the end. I won't follow you to-day. I don't know about to-morrow. For everyone who wants good things must sell even his shamba. I have already paid the money, I am not slow. My good fellow, when I returned home I got married.

This is a very good poem and argument to show a native's way of chaffing and repartee. Salim is, as will be seen, one of the Court summons servers.

ART

The art of the Swahili is not to be found among his drawings, for very few of them can draw any sort of a picture, and when asked to their efforts are most crude, as will be seen from the accompanying sketches.

A duck and a fish

This statement is also true of the Arabs, though there is a notable exception in Zanzibar in the person of Sheriff Mansab, well known to all Zanzibaris, whose paintings in oils and water colours, both portrait

A dhow in full sail and a flying fish by an Mhadimu

and landscape, have a modest fame in the city. He has had several pupils, and there can be said to be

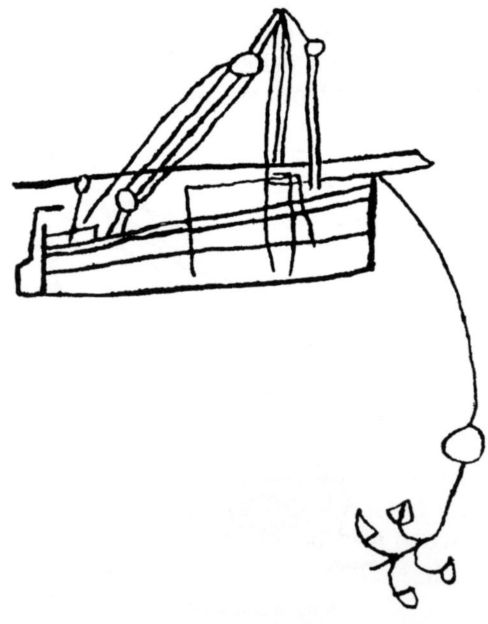

A dhow at anchor by an Mtumbatu

a Mansabia School of artists, for their work is all

characterized by the same style, which shows the same good points and faults, chief of which latter is a lack of proper perspective.

The most interesting form of native art in Zanzibar is probably that to be found in the "poker-work" on the large wooden spoons which are made in most villages: to the uninitiated, the patterns on them have little meaning, but each of them has its name, and they are all derived from natural objects, such as leaves, fishes and lizards.

A picker climbing a coco-nut tree by an Mpemba

Photos of various examples of their work from both Pemba and Zanzibar are to be found in this book, but the best come from the village of Unguja Kuu, in Zanzibar Island. I give a picture of these fine examples. The following is a description of what the various patterns represent.

No. 1. Reading from top. (1) *Ukaia*—the ornamentation on woman's ear paper. (2) Cap decoration. A cock. Grass on top. Two rows of *mtama* (sorghum) for it to eat. Back and front of it a fan. *Mnyamata*—a sea creature found on the foreshore. Three groups of cakes called *sambusa*. Three windows with chains round each. A *sambusa* cake. Borities (building poles). Windows with fish called *kikande* between them. *Sambusa* cakes in corner. Two windows with two fishes, *pono* above and *tasi* below. Two windows with *kikande* fish between. Two round windows with a big one between and borities and fans round. Star at bottom. (There are also stars on the back of the spoon.)

No. 2. Chain. House with windows. Date between borities. *Mnyamata*. Peacock. *Mnyamata*. *Sambusa*. *Sambusa* and *Mnyamata* between two windows. Chain round big window. In the middle above date, chains between two stars. At bottom borities. *Kole Kole* fish. Leaves left and right of window. *Sambusa.* The fish at the bottom are *Mkundaje, Changu* and *tasi.* Borities below (stars on back).

No. 3. Heart (*kopa*=the conventional heart of playing-cards). *Sambusa* above, grass inside. *Sambusa* and two fans. *Bao* or board to put the heart on. Stars. *Kenge* (Nile monitor) chain on each side. Stars. *Kole Kole* fish with borities above, fans in corner and stars around. *Mkundaje* with chain each side. Three stars.

Right Side. Chain. Butterfly, three wings. Fans. *Sambusa.*

Kenge. Borities above and *Sambusa* each side. Grass below. House cap. *Mnyamata.*

Left Side. As right. Date with chains above and between.

The rope and chevron patterns, which are of considerable antiquity and found on ruins in Pemba, are popular. They are above referred to as "chain," as they were so described to me by the carver of the spoons.

Interesting patterns are also embroidered on the beautiful caps worn by all natives, all of which are called by separate names.

The patterns of the wood carvers, as shown in several examples in the book and especially on doors, are also worthy of attention.

Arab art on copper, brass and silver ware is somewhat outside the scope of this book. The work of Ali Muhammad, a Comorian, on jambiyas or curved daggers is very famous, and specimens of his work command high prices and are scarce. One speaks of Ali Muhammad jambiyas as one does of Chippendale chairs.

CHAPTER XXXVII

Music, Songs and Dances

MUSICAL INSTRUMENTS

I SHALL first give a list with short details of the musical instruments, under which heading I include anything that makes a noise.

(*a*) Drums—*Ngoma.*

Vume, big drum; one end oxhide, one goatskin, with a charm fixed inside. *Chapuo*, small variety of *vume*, both ends goatskin.

Msondo and kinganga chake. Used in women's dance *msondo.* The former is covered with oxhide and the latter with goatskin. The skin is usually shaved after being fastened on.

Mshindo. Three-legged, hollow inside, and no bottom. The top is the skin of *Cephalophus adersi.*

Tutu. Drum used to signal news of ngoma to be held. The top is the skin of *Nesotragus moschatus.* The only drum beaten with a drum-stick (of coco-nut midrib).

Rewa is used as a gong, as well as in the dance *rewa.* Top of oxhide. A large edition of *tutu.*

Kindimba. Formerly used in Zanzibar in the dance *marinda*, which is now forgotten. The top is the skin of *Varanus niloticus.*

Kiminingo. The top skin is of goat, used in the dance *kidebe* and others.

Mrungura. A Pemba drum. Top skin of goat. Small drum on three or four legs, which are all on a stand. The drum legs and stand are all carved from the one piece of wood, and often beautifully decorated with carving. Used in dance *msembwi* and others.

Vume, *chapuo*, and *mshindo* are used in most dances.

(*b*) Tambourines—*Tari*.

Tari used in the dance tari. Skin of *Nesotragus moschatus*. *Tari na kengele* with bells used in the dance tari. Skin of *Cephalophus adersi*.

Kinganga. Used in *maulidi*. Skin of *Cephalophus adersi*.

(*c*) Wind Instruments.

Baragumu, a large shell with a hole in the side, used to announce the fact that fish is in the market.

Zomari. Made in Pemba, a kind of clarionet. It sounds like bagpipes. The players get high fees, and are trained from youth to get distended cheeks. The mouthpiece is of *mwale* leaf, and the lip piece of coconut, note-part of metal, key-part and horn of wood.

(*d*) String Instruments.

Zeze, a kind of banjo, played for amusement and not in dances. *Kinanda*, a mandolin.

(*e*) Miscellaneous.

Kayamba. Flat rattle used in most dances.

Miwale. Pieces of midrib of *mwale* palm, used in some dances as cymbals.

Upatu. Brass gong used in most dances. When not obtainable a kerosene tin is used.

Mbiu (not mbui as Steere). A buffalo horn beaten with stick in some dances.

Lelimama and mpinga. Horn and beaters. Used in the dance *lelimama*.

Sanji ya cherewa. A tin rattle used in the dance *cherewa*.

Misewe. Worn on the legs in a dance. Seeds of the *cherewa* tree with beads in.

Njuga. Iron bells each with a different note, tied to legs and worn in *msondo* and other dances.

Kidebe. A new invention played by children, and used in child's dance of same name.

Manganja. Made of shavings with seeds inside, worn on the legs in *kidebe* and *manyema* dances.

Marimba (Xylophone). Played with beaters with rubber ends. The rubber is gathered from wild rubber vines.

The orchestral accompaniment to dances is very monotonous, and this produces after a time a kind of hypnotic sensation. This is precisely the effect aimed at, and natives much prefer their own music to European tunes for this reason.

DANCES

I now come to consideration of the dances themselves. The following is a list of some of the dances native to, or extensively played in, Zanzibar: Robamba, Lelimama, Komero, Kinyawa, Kigala, Rohania, Magani, Kidebe, Miulani banda, Kumbwaya, Manyago, Tahari, Rewa, Kibisa, Sediriki, Jinga muto, Cherewa, Mwamba, Bwende, Msinda, Msondo, Kihiyao, Kidagaa, Tiari, Kibundi, Tari, Kitimiri, Nyunja, Mchanga, Mdebe, Umunde, Chapauringe, Bondogea, Mdema, Ngwale, Kunguwiya, Vinyago, Unyago, Kikwayakwaya, Mabugu, Kidahariro, Sakata and many others.

There are two others, now prohibited, called *bora* and *kiumbizi*, which latter consisted chiefly in knocking your neighbour over the head with a big stick.

Maulidi, or the celebration of the birth of Muhammad, might also be included, and the Pemba bull-fights must also be described.

The following is a brief description of some of the above dances. It will be noted that there are many dialectical words in the songs. I give the interpretations given me. (They were translated into Kiunguja for me).

(*a*) *Kidagaa* (Hadimu).

Instruments used: *mshindo*, *chapuo*, *zomari* and *upatu*.

Some of the words:

Pwane kidagaa we, Pwane kidagaa.
Nataka mcheso kidagaa we, Nataka mcheso kidagoa
Wana Wa membe wendaye Funguni.
Jehazi imetia nanga. Teremkani.

Go to the shore, Kidagaa, thou. To the shore, Kidagaa.
I want the play, Kidagaa, thou, I want the play, Kidagaa.
The children of the sea-gulls go to the shoal,
The dhow has let down its anchor. Go down.

A kind of small fish. Said to refer to a man who is impotent. The players shuffle round in a circle, shrugging shoulders from side to side.

(*b*) *Tiari* (Hadimu).

Instruments used: *mshindo*, *zomari*, *chapuo* and *upatu*.

Words:

Nitendeje chombo, mwana wa miza
Nambiye wongo, tendeje chombo,
Nilipokwenda majini ya chukiwa
Tendeje chombo uziwa.
Kule mjini kuna mambo, mkobelene mtenda hando.

What shall I do, Chombo, child of miza?
I am told lies, what shall I do, Chombo?
When I went to the djinns, they were angry.
What shall I do, Chombo? Has it (the devil) gone to the sea?
There in the town there is business, play till you reach the woman.

This is played in the same way as Kidagaa.

(*c*) *Kibundi.*

Instruments used: *chapuo*, *mshindo* and *upatu*.

Food used: honey, sugar-cane and bananas.

Words:

Kina mama msakose mayowe,
Kwende tendeje mchana kibandani kwa mtwana,
Ukitake nikatia kanga, siutake msugunda
Siafu wandruma, ndruma siafu.

Thou, woman, make song.
What did you do in the day in the slave's hut?

If you want to, cut me a cloth; I don't want a black one.
The ants are biting me, biting me, the ants.

This is played when a man is sick (in head, chest or stomach). He is put on a bed and the drum is beaten, then the afflicted one shakes his head and the devil is then located there. Then he falls in with the women and men. First the women in a line on one side, and the men opposite. The lines approach and join and then go round in circles face to back very fast. The dance starts at twelve noon and ends at sunset, when the food is given which (as in all these exorcizing dances) goes to the devil really, though the patient eats it.

(*d*) *Lelimama*.

Instruments: *mbiu*, *chapuo*, or *vume*, *zomari*, *upatu*, *mpinga*.

Words:

Mwanzo wa lelimama ni lala, lilipoanzwa lelimama.

The start of *lelimama* is lying, when *lelimama* is started.

Swaying movements—no motion. Played at weddings or for amusement only.

(*e*) *Rohania* (Pemba).

Instruments: *chapuo*, *vume*, *upatu* and *zomari*.

Food, etc.: *Yungi Yungi* (blue water lily—*Nymphæa stellata*), sugar-cane, ripe bananas (*mpukusa*) *halwa*, dates, raisins, granulated sugar, lump sugar and bread.

Words:

Sikuapo atokea maziwa, misiwapo miende, akumbiwe. La mnyonge hilo jiwe.

I was not there when the milk came out; the goers were not there, he was told. This stone is not a musical entertainment.

Used for exorcizing or amusement. *Rohan* is a storm devil.

(*f*) *Magani.*

Words:

Tata, tata, tata wambia kijana hakinacha, tumehasiana imependeza wawili kukumbatiana.

Tangle, tangle, tangle, tell the youth not to leave off. We have gone apart. It is pleasant for two to embrace.

All sit down, no instruments, hand-clapping only. For amusement.

(*g*) *Manyago.*

Instruments: *njuga* and *misewe.*

The wearers of *misewe* also wear a short dress of wild date-palm fronds (*ukindu*).

Words:

Hainama dondore
Kitambihiki chako bwana
Mkongwe, anikera kwenda minya
Natufike Kichane mataa ruma umande.

He will not bend down to pick it up. This piece of cloth is yours, master. An old man is worrying me to go to kill. Let us get to Kichani. The dew is on the spokes of the wheels.

Played at circumcision.

(*h*) *Kumbwaya.*

Instruments: *chapuo, vume, tutu, zomari, upatu.*

Words:

Si wewe, mwambia jambo, si wewe.

Not you, bid him greeting, not you.

For amusement and to exorcize the devil *Kumbwaya.*

(*i*) *Rewa.*

Instruments: *rewa* and drum-sticks, two *chapuo, upatu* and *zomari.*

Food: millet, *halwa*, dates, raisins, flour, sugar-cane, ripe bananas, bread.

Words:

Makame juma, Mpunga rewa, kitumbo.

Makame Juma, exorcize *Rewa*, stomachwise.

To exorcize the devil *Rewa.*

(*j*) *Kibisa.*

Instruments: four *misondo.*
Words:

Kumbiye mwaka wendao Bara umhimiza maneno.

To exorcize. The bead dress shown is worn.

(*k*) *Tari.*

Instruments: *tari* and *kinganga.*
Words:

Shungia ngoma, jini akija, Shungia ngoma.

Increase the pace of the dance; when the djinn comes, increase the pace of the dance.

Played moving backwards and forwards. To exorcize or for amusement.

(*l*) *Cherewa.*

Instruments: *Sanji ya cherewa.*
Words:

Nipigie cherewa, kimaulidi bwana.
Beat *cherewa* for me, like Maulidi, master.

For amusement.

(*m*) *Mwamba.*

Instruments: two *vume, chapuo, upatu, zomari, tutu.*

The exorcizing implement *usinga* is also used.

Food, etc.: sugar, sugar-cane, raisins, cardamom, cinnamon, betel, *madafu* (coco-nut milk), eggs, bread, flour, *mnyonoro, dalia* (yellow cosmetic), *wanja* (black cosmetic).

Words:

Tumekuja kiringeni, mambo mtendayo sio
Tulizana we, kaini, tukunyamaza hilio.

We have come to the devil dance; you are not doing it properly. Stay you of a hard heart, that we may silence your cry.

To exorcize.

(*n*) *Bwende.*

Played as *Mwamba*, but different words. A turban is used like that in the dance *Rohamba*, but white instead of blue.

Sikuapo, nalikuwa Potowa, nipokuja mwamba unalia, nilikuta chumbani goa.

Kisu changu cha ngereza mpini wa rezareza, nyoka, kamwambiya mkunga kama leo takumeza, mpikia mchuzi wa pweza leo, Hivi ta bwereza, maliza habari ya nyamwezi. Nagopia takweleza, nimechoka upagazi mzigo mkubwa siwezi.

I was not here, I was at Potowa (a village near Mkokotoni). When I came you were singing *mwamba*. I met the Goan in the room.

My knife is English, the handle of *Reza Reza*. And the snake has told the midwife. If to-day I shall swallow it, cook gravy of cuttle-fish to-day. In this way I will delay, finish the business of the Nyamwezi man. I fear I shall tell it. I am tired of the carrying of a big burden, I can't do it.

(*o*) *Msinda.*

Instruments: *vume*, two *chapuo*, *zomari*, *upatu*.

Food, etc.: sugar-cane, *Yungi Yungi*, dates, raisins, *halwa*, granulated and lump sugar, bananas (*kisukari*), eggs and bread. All to be served on a *chano*, and the following Koran text written on a saucer and dissolved in water.

La llahi ila Allah, lla hua, lli hayu, lli kayumu lli tahutha, Sinatu walla naumu llahi maji. Samawali walla aretha, walla ya uduhu kifithu huinu llialihu llathimu.

Words:

Ya kwanza, ya kwanza wa kurufumzi, mkewako
Ya kwanza mwambwa yeye.
Taireni waganga mwarikuja kirimgeni
Taireni waganga.

The first, the first was one who had been initiated, your first woman spoke well. Give permission, medicine-men, for the initiate to come to the devil dance, give permission, medicine-men.

To exorcize.

(*p*) *Msondo.*

Instruments: *msondo* and *kinganga chake.*

Words:

Tito yayo kukaole, kibonongwa
Uka usifu ya ngombe, unyago Zingwe Zingwe.

Played with the utmost secrecy by women when a girl is ready to be married.

(*q*) *Manyema*, or *Kumba* (Pemba, but imported).

Instruments: *chapuo*, *zomari* and *manganja.*

Words:

Mulume wangu lungu. Tubengele tumkwa mbe kibanda lelele. Awini nyamile witamba leyo nami hali kaleta ndo mitambe miye kibande ah ah, mulume wake ah ah.
(From Craster's *Pemba.*)

In this dance extraordinary head-dresses of feathers, etc., and even cast-off European ladies' hats are worn, and the faces are whitened in some cases with elaborate patterns in chalk. The chief feature of the dance is the extraordinary contortions which the women players are capable of performing with their hindquarters.

The Manyema are Congo people, and during the dance time they speak no language but their own.

(*r*) *Kitimiri.*

Instruments: *vume*, two *chapuo*, *tutu.*

Food: sugar-cane, raisins, *lozi* (almonds), *kungumanga* (nutmegs), granulated and lump sugar, flour and *mnyonoro.*

Words:

Watu waginda kisingere wa mi nauya kisingere.

(*s*) *Kihiyao.*

Instruments: *kiminingo*, *kinganga*, *msondo* and *likuti* (I do not know this instrument; it is not native).

Words:

Che che che che chambara, manda ngala jangu ndima dire natiji ngatole kaje kuazimana ardamilile wati korondo neso.

This was given to me by a mainland policeman who helped me a lot, and that is the real reason I give it. He told me that the meaning is:

"A woman was calling her son, who was taken away by *Zimwi*, a devil, 'Come at once, I left my water-pot at the well.'"

(*t*) The appropriate foods in the important devil dance *Umunde* (which it will be remembered has a dialect of its own) are in Pemba:

Uvumba (incense), ambergris, musk, saffron, sandalwood, nutmeg, *visukio* (kachiri), honey, sugar-cane, cloves, *ngongote*, *mayunge* (either water-lilies or another plant of the same name, much used in magic), *mkadi*, eggs and bananas.

The words of the foregoing dances are not complete, and in some cases I managed to get but a few. I give now the performance called *Robamba*, which is in full, and also gives an example of a good piece of Kipemba dialect.

Robamba.

Instruments used: two *chapuo*, *vume* and one *upatu*, *zomari* and *miwale*.

Words:

Tumwombele muungu, koma na mizimu yache
Kama Nyange tambua kama hapa
uwanjani pana pembe.
Wamli wao waganga kuku wangu wamuhanga
wamli wao waganga.
O Niteremke nipande vilima niteremke.

(Here the devil climbs the head of the sick man, who cries out:)

Mwanangu usilile, ngombe utapewa wako uchinje.
Mke mwenza Mwenambia kwega nikwegege na nguo moja.

(Here the women shuffle backwards and forwards where seated.
Then the *fundi* having seen the devil satisfactorily seated:)

Mshipe wangu wishagwia nyama
Mchukua we mtoto mchanga hana mfupa
Wachawe hao wawiya kwanza.

(Then play in circles, and the possessed ones are crowned with turbans.)

Wachawe wote wakutana Chambani
na Mvumo moja.
Ho arembwera mtoto mchanga.
Wangojewa wewe urendo waja faggia wanja tule nyama,
Mkongwe msimeno karanga ufundi.
Mafundi wenda zao kapu na ifungwe
Baaba ya kunita na utaka msare wa mwanangu unipe
Banja kungu.
Mamie mwana na babu mwana labe.
Tangulia, naja nabanja. vitondoo viangu kwanza.
O Seya Manga namwola ye mpenzi wangu naze
Uvinji welea na maji mvinji.
Kikira cha mbuzi, faggia ulalapo
Mchuchile Kembe mtima wa nitwanga.
Leo ni leo, we kesho twanagana.

(Here the *fundi* dances round with the women, one at a time, much like Sir Roger de Coverley, but in one figure they clasp toes.)

Nipaninile mtima wende na moyo
Wa robamba wendavyo na urendo.
Wimbe elemeya miuja.

(If the devil is now ready to be allowed to depart in peace, before he is allowed to do so he is asked a lot of questions as to whether he will behave in future, and exhorted not to make a nuisance of himself.)

Translation.

We are asking God His blessing, and the *mizimu* below.

If you are a doctor where the horn is kept outside the home. The doctors have eaten my fowl of the sacrifice. O I will come down; I climbed the hills, and I will come down.

My child, don't cry, you will be given an ox to kill.

My fellow wife, you didn't tell me to shuffle back and fore; how can I play with one cloth. My fishing-line has already caught the meat (devil). Take you a young child without bones. The witch-doctors are coming from their play. All the witch-doctors, they have met together at Chambani (a wizard's heath in Pemba), at the one Borassus palm.

Play well, my devil.

People are waiting for you to play, other people are coming; clean the *wanja*; let us eat meat. An old toothless man pounds *karanga* (grain). The *fundies* are going home, the basket must be tied up.

After calling me, I want a piece of cloth of my child, give me. Break an almond.

Mother of the child, father of the child, I am here.

Go ahead, I am coming, I am breaking my *tondoo* first.

O seye Manga, I see him, my lover himself. A *mvinje* tree floating in the water, a *mvinje* tree. The last of the goat; clean this place; you will lie. Soothe the devil, my spirit is beating me. To-day is to-day, to-morrow we shall be gone. Give me to eat, my soul and heart are going. The *robambas* are going with their journey. The waves are retiring with the sickness.

This is not by any means a literal translation, but is in great part the *fundi's* explanation of the meaning of the words.

Mngware.

Played by inter-village "teams," this game or dance is well worth watching. The players stand in a circle. The *fundi*, or leader, sings, and the circle gives the responses. The time is given by hand-claps. No instruments are used. The claps go in series, three with the hands, four or five with the hands, and three on the hollow between the breast and arm, hopping at the same time on one leg. The movement of the circle is backwards and forwards and round the circle. Only loin-clothes are worn.

In the centre, contests between individuals of opposing sides take place. A challenger goes and touches a foe, and they wrestle. When one or other party is down, the ring breaks up and surrounds the contestants, shouting the *kiapilio*, the peculiar barking noise of the Wapemba.

The Ugoe is wrestling, and a clever throw is used, which is made by hooking the legs in a peculiar way.

This dance is peculiar to the Wapemba, and said to be very old. Old men say that in the old slaving days, when warships came to the east coast of Pemba, contests at it took place with the British sailors, who always won.

Fundi: Moyo ukiwendekeya mengi usipolalani hawache kupoteza. Kukutia matatani Hija Naufuatiya ukanitupo njiani.
Najuta la layitani na la mumoyo yangu.
Chorus: Warile Nyanja.

Fundi: Dimbweye mnyamazani dimbwe
Karouni, Karoun kipene kangang'anya kitunga
Haina moto bangi.
Mpenzi nimewasili kitako najikaliya umpe yako shauri
Njema iliotuliya ya jana siku ya kiri sikuweza
Vumiliya, nikipe kinacholiwa, kilacho mto pekeye,
Dunia, dunia.
Karibisha, karibisha, mgeni
Pemba ile umeiona
Kijinu kilitipemba kikinamiya Unguja wa
Pemba na masherifu wakenamiya kumoja name
Ni panga la Sefu, kutongoa sina hoja mlililene
Mwenzenu kufa hakuna moja.

Chorus: Naumia, Naumia.

Fundi: A jabu ya midirara kulla ukimkumbuka mbono
Nane mwanikera na mimi nasumbuka kupenda
Si masehara kunalava na masharka mutasema
Mutachoka, kinda sina budi naye.

Chorus: Lainama, lainama.

Fundi: Hodi, fundi wa mazengo nalitumwa nikijumbe jitiye nguo ya shingo anakuja yule ng'ombe, Kandoro akake kichango kukinendea mazumbe nipane nguo, hamcheze ng'ombe? Kandoro aniliya mwanawe, toto geupe.

Chorus: Sagabeni, Sagabeni.

Fundi: Napata nitafutaye nimepumua masharka napata
Nimpendaye mwelewa, asiye sharka napata takete naye
Si mwezi wala si mwaka napata nashuwarika
Moya unatabasamo.

Chorus: Ilikuwa miye ngiwana.

Fundi: Njoo! Waziri nakwita, Njoo! usitaahari najumla ya mambo, yengine udahadari lubune yangu labuda in Shaabani, ahiri, kimeazimu safari
Hatuwa ikinondoa.

Chorus: Yes, yes.

Fundi: Washirike masalata yatakago Msalite nawewe
Ukafuata maneno ya ugalate bilashi ukanileta kwa thana na tiyate ya sheraffa libinate ni eleza ukosha wangu.

Chorus: Nainyo nyote, Nainyo nyote.

CHAPTER XXXVIII

Music, Songs and Dances (*continued*)

VINYAGO

A DESCRIPTION of the dances played would be incomplete without a reference to Vinyago, which is played by descendants of slaves from Nyasaland, and is quite the nearest thing to acting to which the natives attain.

They will consent to play it on no occasion save on a pitch black night with no moon, and they are quite right in doing this, for with any light the effect is quite spoiled. In the dark one can just see enough to be impressed, and the vagueness of the outlines gives a realistic flavour to the performance.

The properties for the dance are made in strictest secrecy in the middle of the bush, with outposts around, and anyone who attempts to approach gets warned off, and if he persists a rough handling results. The properties used are burnt before sun-up on the night of the performance.

The drums used are *msondo* and *mrungura*, which give a very hollow note, and are just appropriate to the performance. *Sanji* rattles are used and accompany each figure.

The performance consists of a series of figures, which, with the exception of the first, are supposed to represent some animal or well-known object. The animals represented are generally mainland animals, and the names are mostly unknown to me. The animals or other figures are made from branches, palms, etc., tied together with forest vines, with men in them. The figures are brought into the ring by men with rattles, and make their bow rather like circus animals.

The first figure is called *ndoara*, and consists of a chain of white figures, each holding the one in front by the waist, and rushing round in this formation at a great speed and in all directions.

The next figure is always *manyani*, or apes, and consists of about a dozen naked men leaping about like apes, and they are very realistic too on a dark night.

After this figure there generally appear about seven or eight figures from the following repertoire: *karuru* (a rabbit), *jongoo* (a millepede—one I measured was seventy-five feet long and had twenty men inside—it was very good indeed), *stima*—the Pemba steam-launch complete with awning and funnel. I have seen one also with wings. The maker had seen a hydroplane, he informed me (the hybrid between a steam-launch and a hydroplane was weird and wonderful), *bunda*, *kiparamoto* (a man covered with glowing pieces of dried stalks—very good indeed), *chui* (leopard), *jogoo* (a cock, and easily recognizable), *kasa* (a turtle—recognizable), *donga*, *ngombe* (an ox), *mbawara*, *kasenga*, *kuchi*, *nguruwe* (a pig—recognizable only from its grunts and method of progression), *tunga meli* (H.H.S. *Cupid*, with funnel, masts, etc.), *mashua* (a boat, and easily recognizable), *motokari* (a motor-car), *peleleza*.

None of these beasts are recognizable except those I have marked. In addition there is a performance on stilts called *gogodera*, which is played in the day-time, presumably owing to its hazardous nature.

SONGS

Most of the songs that are not accompanied by dances and music are sung by sailors and fishermen, and I give a few here.

(*a*) *Mwakimburo sese, mwache mwana apunge urembo; oo leo sese, mwache mwana apunge urembo.*

(*b*) *Ukenda pwani nambiya usimle mwana kikoa, kibora pumua kutomba mwenyewe kesha tambua.*

(*c*) Part song—1. *Mwana juma twende zetu.*
Child of Juma, let us go home.
2. *Nangojea kitambaa changu kwanza.*
I am waiting for my clothes first.

A variant:
Dada mwajuma kantwalie kitambaa changu kwanza.

(*d*) *Mwache angurume, mwache angurume, Simba hamle mwanawe, urongoo.*
Let him roar, let him roar. The lion is not eating my child, it is false.

(*e*) *Mwalimu we, mama mwalimu we, ukinenda kamwambie nahoza nimeingia mtoni gangawiya.*
Teacher thou, mother teacher thou. When you went did you tell the captain I have gone into the river Gangawiya?

(*f*) *Pararara pontia, pararara pontia, pararara pontia, mamie mwari naumia.*
This is very like "Ta-ra-ra-boom-de-ay," and is sung like it.

(*g*) *Kimeni choma, kimeni choma kijiba cha mchongoma. Si kweli, mpenzi sijakuona.*
It has pricked me, it has pricked me, the thorn of the mchongoma[1] tree. It is not true, I have not yet seen a lover.

(*h*) *Ndo wiro kwenu wapi, shungi mbili na mnyororo.*

(*i*) *Zezee inalia, zezee inalia, mwaka jana hailia zeze, mwaka huu inalia.*
The banjo cries, the banjo cries; last year the banjo did not cry, this year it cries.

Unfortunately I was unable to record the tunes of most of these songs, and of the dance songs, having no knowledge of music, but from constant repetition I learnt the tunes of (*c*), (*e*), (*f*), (*g*) by heart, and give the airs of them on the page opposite.

The *Askaris* (police) are very fond of singing, but chiefly mainland tunes. "Tipperary," however, is very popular.

Children have their songs, and the following is a child's part song called *Duwe*. The first word is sung by the leader, and the second by the chorus and so on:

[1] Thorn bush.

(c)
Mwana Juma Twende ze - tu Nangojea ki - tambaa changu kwanza
(e)
We, mwa li - mu, we - e - e Mama we - li - mu
We - e - e ukinenda kamwambie nakoja ni - meingia
M - fa - ni Gan - ga - wi - ya
(f)
Ki - me - ni - cho - ma Ki - me - ni - cho - ma
Ki - ji ba cha m - chon - go - ma
Si kwe - li m penzi si - ja - ku - a - na
(g)
Pa - ra - ra - ra pon - ti - a pa - ra ra ra
pon - ti - a pa - ra ra ra pon ti a

Mbagale nayale kidusi chanona nazifu koroma
Je tembo lamgema Mjini mwenu taawa kituatua kyawawa
Je hija njoo dase Yupi utakae.

The meanings of some words are unknown, but some of them are as follows:

A parasite—gets fat. A coco-nut—an unripe coco-nut. Is there tembo? A tapper. To your town—I will go. A little bush. I will come out. When I come. Come and touch. Whom? Anyone you like.

We have an expression in English "Whistling for wind," and the natives of Zanzibar also have a corresponding method of calling it up. This consists in calling softly "kuru, kuru, kuru, kuru," on the one note [musical note]

I must now give the incantations used for summoning local devils in the Ngezi rubber forest in North Pemba, and for keeping them off. These are also given in Captain Craster's *Pemba*, but I can confirm them, as I checked them with the natives at Verani.

Hodi Muamu. Nakuja kuamsha na ni ujima.
Wenzi wetu watungoja nawe toka hima hima.
Niwageni wa kingeja leo ndenge itavuma.
Ramka twende ngoma pia mkulala.
Muamu hi kuamsha ndipo wa zidi koma
Walla hu-u siulazio ulalo daima.
Ramka twende ngoma pia mkulala.
Muamu wewe mkubwa jamii sini masnuma.
Yafaa kupita mbele wadogo tukawa nyuma.
Ramka twende ngoma pia mkulala.

The above is to summon devils, the following to drive them away:

Watendaje hapa pwani Kichege
Maandamo hayo mchagoe mume chaya.
Binti Kirimbo upo? mipo.
Ngombe kakata haya haya
Haya bado hajalala haya.
Banja, Banja wewe yai moja
Kuku wane vuapi alizali.

Toka kuzaliwa sijaona
Ngombe wa mavani kuzalia
Tiro Tiro ngombe tuicheze.

The songs sung at circumcision are as follows:

When the circumciser first arrives at the house set apart for circumcision, and is preparing his instruments and sharpening his knife he sings: "*Kwembeya, Shungira wageni,*" which I am told means "I am coming. I am glad to have these children." The purpose of this, a circumciser informs me, is to frighten the initiates.

As I have said, the initiates remain in the *kumbi* twenty-one days, and each day the circumciser comes, and as he approaches sings out "*Wario?*" to which the initiates reply "*Hoo riambo. Yamsimangiti pawani kwa zumbe, kuri miti na misasarimbo, Hili na Hili tupe, kungwi tupe.*" The meaning is "*Hodi,*" and the reply, "Come in. We are all right in the place that has been cut. It is a little better, but still there are sores. Give us some medicines and some songs."

After this he sings as follows:

Wari, Mtiwao nyumbani, Juma 'nne ndio ngema ya kuaviwa vitanda, viti vyombo alama shoka ya mwinyi mngwachani, Iketwa ikagozama, M'takuwa kiranja nani, naje tumle nyama, Msikuwa kiranja nani, nakai nyuma nyuma, 'Makungwi amkuwani tufunze wana yatima. Tunakua usozoni mambo yetu yakusema. Mola, tupe salimini, tuwawe bandari salama.

A free translation of this is:

Ye initiates who are inside. Tuesday is a good day to take out the beds and put the stools, the indication of the knife of the circumciser, inside. These things were asked for and were brought; who will be the first, let him come to be circumcised. Let him who will not come first stay behind. Attendants, make a noise to drown the cries of the children. We have finished our affairs of cutting. God give us safety that we may come out of the house safely.

In addition to this there is a repertoire of enigmatical songs, some of which I cannot get the exact meaning of, but which mainly refer to that part of the initiates' anatomy which has suffered during the rites.

I have probably not got all of them, but the following are examples :

Naona mataajabu, shupa kuingia mkono, Ikangia wajakazi, watu kumi na watano, Ikangia na watwana watu kumi na watano, Ikangia mashemere mchunga lete Kiamo. Hiyo nifumbo kwa fumbo, wafumbuzi fumbuwani.

I see it a wonder, a hand going into a bottle, and there went in female slaves fifteen people, and there went in male slaves fifteen people, and there went in a pregnant cow tied by a rope. Herdsman, bring a milking bottle. This is a riddle, who can discover it, let them.

Baharini kuna nyama, Msirifu, Msipembe. Atafunae tambuu akipa watu uchembe, uchembe wake nidawa, unawatibu viyumbe; huyo simbuzi wala singombe watambuzi tambuweni.

In the sea there is an animal, not long, hornless. It will bite betel. If it gives people a drop, its drop is a medicine, it cures human beings. This is not a goat, neither is it an ox. Who can make it out, let them.

Naliona mataajabu kuku kuvaa viyatu kanyoosha shingo yapata dhiraa tatu, Warabu mwaitwa Masikati kwa Rashidi mla watu.

I have seen a wonder, a fowl wearing sandals. It stretches its neck, about three *dhiraas* (a measurement of length, the elbow to the tip of middle finger). You Arabs are wanted at Muscat at Rashid's the cannibal.

Kasungura kanyama kadogo kanya mavi ya mviringo.

A rabbit is a small animal having round dung.

Kisusuri kisusuri sikitege hakigwiya, Mbawaze huyumba yumba, munakula kisusuri hamwempa nadota.

Kisusuri, kisusuri (probably a bird). Do not trap it to catch it. Its wings hang about. You are eating *kisusuri.* You have not given *nadota.* (I cannot find the meaning of this word in Kipemba. *Kudota* means to tap very lightly.)

Nifunge safari yangu ya wima wima, Mkadamu mbele, mwalim nyuma. Ukenenda kantakire mwanamke mwema.

I prepare my *safari* in haste, the sub-overseer in front, the *mwalim* behind. When you go, arrange for me a good woman.

Mnazi mkinda mtambaa komba, hauna tembo, wagemewani?

A young coco-nut tree, a creeping-place for lemurs. (This is literal, *mtambaa komba* is said to mean of a coco-nut "not yet erect.") It has no *tembo*, why are they tapping it?

The circumciser sings this song while washing the boy's sores:

Pwani kumti shini ya jiwe, Tawi zimile, shina ling'owe Imjakuchimba ndiye mwenyewe.

On the shore there is a tree beneath a stone. The branches (*zimile*), the trunk is uprooted. He who digs it out is indeed the owner.

Students of Kiswahili will note that many words are unusual. Many of the words belong to the Kipemba dialect, but some of these in the first songs are not even found in the Kipemba in ordinary use in Pemba.

MAULIDI

The festival of the *Maulidi* occurs on 12th Rabi-el-Awwal, and it is then that the biggest performances are held, though small ones are often held at other seasons.

I saw an exceptionally large one at Mangapwani, where I was informed that 1,800 performers from all parts of the island took part.

A huge enclosure was built of bamboo and decorated with flowers and much paper. All the women had new clothes (they do for an important affair) and I should say most of the men; certainly the *kanzus* were spotlessly clean. The enclosure was brilliantly lit with arc-lamps, and the moon shining down through the palm trees made a wonderfully impressive scene.

My friends and I were played up by a band hired from the town to a small *banda* where refreshments were served, and we were then escorted to reserved seats. There were four Maulidis going on, and about 100 to 150 men in each, kneeling in two rows facing each other and clad, as I say, in snowy linen. Their movements were all in unison, and woe betide anyone who failed to move with the others, for "the conductor" or "stage-manager" was down on him in an instant. Between the two rows incense was burnt and sprayers of rose-water walked up and down, and mullahs performed the tricks which will be elsewhere described.

I give a description of the Maulidi by Captain Cooper, once a District Officer in Zanzibar.

"A Maulidi is a singing of the Koran, and is extraordinarily tuneful and beautiful, and the music reminded me very forcibly of the priests in the Temple of Vulcan in 'Aida.' The soloists sit on the ground facing the chorus, who kneel together in a row about twenty in number, dressed in white Kanzus, and as they sing they sway in perfect unison. The accompaniment is soft on tambourines and gongs. The whole effect is extremely fine, and they must practise very hard to get it so perfect. The singing is all unison, of course, and of a Gregorian type, all in a minor key. The women sing, but they are placed behind a grille. Incense is burnt, and that and the flickering lamps make a wonderful scene. It is the most striking thing of the kind I have ever seen, and vastly different from a Ngoma."

PEMBA BULL-FIGHTS

Bull-fights as practised in Pemba are a relic of the Portuguese occupation. Curiously enough, they are never performed in Zanzibar, though apparently Pemba is not the only place where the Portuguese introduced them, as Major Tremearne mentions them as being played in Nigeria. The accompanying diagram gives a very good idea of the arena.

It is usually on an open sandy place, set in picturesque surroundings among palm and mango trees. The four o'clock sun, shining through this greenery, on to the white *kanzus* of the men and the coloured *kangas* of the women, makes a very pretty picture.

Before the start young Wapemba usually run about in small companies uttering their curious cry, a series of short, sharp, staccato barks peculiar to them, and then suddenly rush to another spot and repeat the call. Then the matadors usually line up and salute—perhaps a kind of *Morituri te salutamus*.

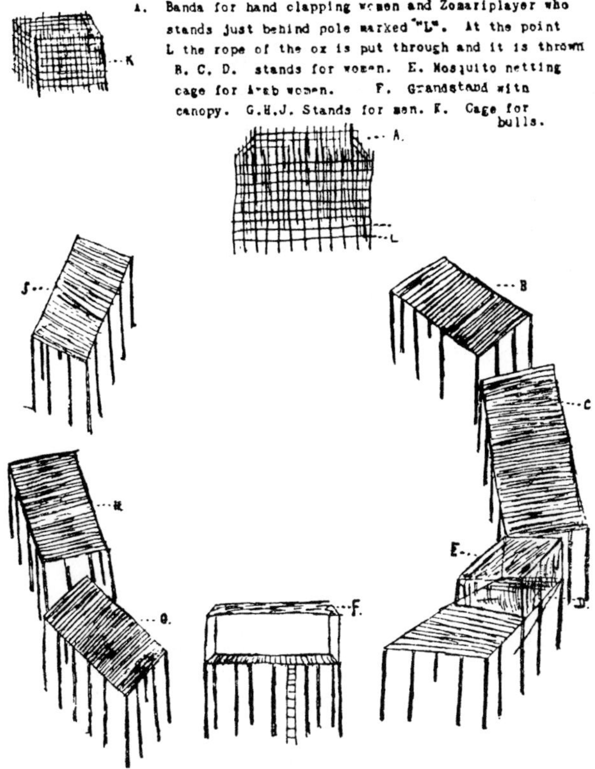

The orchestra then begins. This consists of a man playing on a *zomari* in the corner of the cage of the women, who clap their hands and chant low and monotonously.

The next appearance is that of the bull. If one expects anything fierce one is grievously disappointed. The animal trots in looking perfectly meek at the end of a long rope (called *ngoweo*), and another thin one fastened by a noose to its hind leg.

The long rope is then passed through, behind the

bottom of the right-hand pole of the cage where the women are. It is then pulled short and the bull thrown, after which the leg rope is removed and a perfectly fiendish din made over the poor brute, who becomes thereby thoroughly bewildered and is then loosed. He springs to his feet and charges wildly; sometimes he gets a matador or one of the many adventurous youths who throng the ring. Some of the matadors are very skilful in enticing the bull on, and then twisting to one side to avoid its rush. After a really good turn the matador will come up to salute and receive applause.

If the bull shows any tendency to leave the ring, it is checked by a pull on the rope. Each bull's turn is about twenty minutes, and its feats are warmly cheered by the spectators. In fact, during the whole of the time it is in the ring the place is in a perfect uproar.

At the end of its turn it is again thrown by the women's *banda* and a ring put through its nose, and it is then allowed to wander away. There are generally three or four bulls played in one afternoon.

Interesting features of the ring are the coffee-sellers and betel merchants, who go round selling their wares during the performance, just as girls sell coffee and chocolate in a European theatre.

Those who use the stands are charged two pice each, which goes to pay the hire of the bulls and the fees of the matadors and the clarionet-player. The price of the performance of a good bull may be up to Rs. 10, a matador may receive Rs. 20, and a *zomari*-player Rs. 5.

The Kipemba word for the stands on which spectators sit is *dungu*, for the pen in which the women clap *bigile*, the leg cord used to lead the ox on or away *mbungo*, and the peculiar cry of the Wapemba *kiapilio*.

Bull-fights are played to induce rain in times of drought.

CHAPTER XXXIX

Nature

THE ELEMENTS, ETC.

The winds (*pepo*) are well known in Zanzibar, as indeed they must be to so nautical a people.

The north-east monsoon is known as the *Kas kazi* and the south-west as *Kusi*. The *Kas kazi* blows roughly from December to March, and the *Kusi* from April to November.

During the time of the latter monsoon, from July to November, the wind drops about two p.m. and an easterly wind blows up called the *Matalai*. This is extraordinarily convenient for sailing, as it enables one to go one way in the morning and return in the afternoon.

Rain is *Mvua*. The rain spirit has the same name.

Thunder is *Ngurumo* (onomatopœic). It is said to be the direct voice of God.

The Wapemba believe that the earth is carried on the horns of an ox, and the ox in its turn is borne on a sting ray (*tenga*) which swims in the sea, and the sea is carried by the wind, and the wind by the will of God. Others say that the ox is carried by a mosquito. When the ox tires of its burden it shifts its position by tossing it a little, and thus causes earthquakes.

As regards the daily rising and setting of the sun they say that there are 360 holes in a circle, and that the first morning of the year the sun rises from the first and sets in the second, on the second day it rises from the second and sets in the third and so on, although it always appears to us that the sun rises in the same place each day. The distance the sun has to travel daily would take a man five hundred years to do on foot.

The moon in similar fashion has holes to rise and set in, and some say that eclipses are caused by the sun and moon getting accidentally into each other's holes or each other's paths, but in Pemba it is generally said that if the eclipse is black it is an eel (*mkunga*) that is eating it, but if red then a crab or an octopus. I am told you can tell which by putting water in a flat pan and looking at the reflection when you can see the monster. When an eclipse is on, the Wapemba forgather in large crowds on shore, beat drums and sing, "Eel, eel, give us our moon and go to the shore and eat little fish." In Zanzibar it is said that it is a snake that eats the moon.

I asked several people why the moon waxed and waned, and was informed that it prayed on the 15th of each month and gets fatter at the thought of it. After the 15th it wanes when it reflects on its sins.

Stars (*nyota*) are not much known save the Pleiades, which are called *Kilimia* from *l'ima* (cultivate), as their rising signified the time for starting to cultivate, i.e., October. It is said that if they set in fine weather, they will rise in wet and vice versa.

Shooting stars are called *kimwondo*, and are said to be missiles thrown by the angels at the *Jini*.

Most natives know *el thuhura* (Venus) but few other planets. Of Venus, the Arabs say that there were once two other stars who wished to wed her, but she continued to put them off, as she wished for time. Both these stars could fly, but Venus could not, so she promised that if they taught her she would marry one. But when she had her wings, she managed to fly out of their reach, and so every day she flies up and drops down in the evening when they are away.

The tides are said to be caused by the water being swallowed and disgorged by a whale or oyster, or big fish called *chewa*.

BOTANY

This ought to be a very large section, but as I have dealt with a good many species of plants, etc., in Chapter XXV and shall give a great many more under Medicine and Magic, I give no more here.

Plants are very well known and even varieties have their own names, e.g., each kind of grass or fern is differently called. Their chief uses are as food or in medicine.

Père Saccleux gives the names of a great many flowers and plants, and I believe a flora of Zanzibar is now being prepared.

Almost any tree has a variety of uses, and interesting studies may be made in each case. As an example I append an account of the Cassia. Experiments have recently been conducted with this wood in Zanzibar to see if it would be useful as timber in constructional work. There is a good deal of it in the Ngezi forest in Pemba.

Cassia. Swahili name Mwavi

This is a large tree and has several economic uses. The wood is exceptionally hard and is said never to rot. For this reason it is particularly used in the construction of cesspits and bridges where it is exposed to damp. I am told that a bridge was recently demolished near Chake Chake to be replaced by a concrete structure, and although it had been built many years before, and before the memory of the neighbouring people, the *mwavi* poles used in its construction were as sound as if they had been put in only a short time before.

It makes excellent charcoal and burns long, and for this reason is much used by blacksmiths in furnaces, though I am told it is not used by silversmiths. The reason apparently is that its use is considered unlucky, and there is a saying that he who uses *mwavi* will never become prosperous.

I am informed that its foliage is preyed on by a species of hairy larva which reaches 6 inches in length, and is eaten by mainland natives. I do not know what species it is, nor have I seen a specimen.

The different parts of the tree have medicinal uses, as follows:

Internal use.

Stomach-ache. Boil the roots in water and drink the decoction.

External uses.

Ugonjwa wa chavi. Grind the bark of the trunk, mix with water and apply to sore place.

Swellings. Grind the roots and the potato of *kiviza* together. Mix with lime-juice and apply.

Upele (spots). Boil bark in water and apply.

Caution.—The medicine man who produced the latter recipes tells me that it is dangerous to teeth and eyes. (But in the first recipe one is told to drink it).

Magical uses.

If the roots are buried in a plantation anything near will die (i.e., rice, cassava, etc.).

To remove your enemy. Find the cut stump of a *mwavi* tree, get eight male (i.e., the point) ends of half coco-nut shells, a bunch of *nyassi* grass (the kind used for thatching), small pieces of *mwavi* wood, small pieces of the wood of the tree called *mkame chuma*, a piece of grass found on a patch of ground usually swept clear by the movement in the wind of an over-hanging branch, and wood of the tree called *mvimbi ashi*.

Lay out these ingredients round the stump of the *mwavi* tree and set fire to them. Read *Yasin* from the Koran eight times and eight chapters of Ahali Bederi, and at the end the Hetima of the Koran (i.e., the bit at the end after the text). These operations must be performed on a Tuesday, must begin at seven a.m. and end at two p.m. Your enemy will remove from your neighbourhood and trouble you no more.

ZOOLOGY

(1) The natives are very good zoologists, at any rate as far as mammals and birds are concerned, and nearly every animal has its name; at least, when asking natives the name of a bird I had seen or whose call I have heard, I have always had a name given me.

Zanzibar is rich in birds, but poor in other fauna. Very often species which occur in Zanzibar do not occur in Pemba, and vice versa.

(2) The following is a list of mammals with their names, English, scientific, and native:

English	Scientific	Native	Distribution
Order 1. *Primates.*			
General native name for monkey—*Kima.*			
Kirk's Colobus	Colobus kirkii	*Punju*	Zanzibar local
Syke's monkey	Cercopithecus albigularis	*Ngedele*	Zanzibar and Tumbatu
Grey monkey	Cercopithecus rufoviridis	*Tumbili*	Pemba
Order 2. *Lemuroidea.*			
Galago	Galago crassicaudatus	*Komba*	Everywhere
Order 3. *Chiroptera.*			
Bats, all sorts		*Popo*	Everywhere
Order 4. *Insectivora.*			
Great elephant shrew	Rhyncocyon adersi	(north) *Kirodo* (south) *N'gombo*	Rare
Small elephant shrew	Petrodromus sultani	*N'gombo mweupe*	Rare
Order 5. *Carnivora.*			
Leopard	Felix pardus	*Chui*	E. Zanzibar
Civet	Viverra orientalis	*Ngawa*	Zanzibar
Genett	Viverra megaspila	Pemba *Ngawa*; Zanzibar *Fungo*	Everywhere
Bdeogale	Bdeogale tenuis	*Kitu*	Zanzibar
Mongoose	Mungos gracilis	*Cheche*	Everywhere Z. Rare Pemba
Order 6. *Cetacea.*			
Whales		*Nyamgumi*	Rare
Porpoises and dolphins		*Pomboo*	Everywhere
Order 7. *Sirenia.*			
Dugong	Halicore dugong	*Nguva*	Rare
Order 9. *Hyracoidea.*			
Tree coney	Dendrohyrax neumanni	*Peleele*	Fundo Tumbatu
	Dendrohyrax adersi	*Peleele*	Fundo. Elsewhere rare

Order 10. *Ungulata.*

Duiker	Cephalophus adersi	*Paa nunga*	Zanzibar rare
	Cephalophus pembæ	*Paa*	N. Pemba
Suni	Nesotragus moschatus	*Paa*	Zanzibar Islets, E. Zanzibar
Pigs	Sus scrofa	*Nguruwe*	Pemba
	Sus potamochærus Nyassæ		Zanzibar

Order 11. *Rodentia.*

Rats		*Panya*	Everywhere
Mouse		*Panya nunga*	Not common
Giant rat	Cricetomys gabianus	*Buku*	Zanzibar
Squirrel	Paraxerus palliatus lastii	*Chinde*	Zanzibar

(3) I now come to a list of birds, and this must not be taken as being in any way complete, but only as a selection.

Order 1. *Passeres.*

Java sparrow		*Zawaridi*
Black-billed Bishop Bird	Pyromelana nigriventa	*Chekeche*
Kersten's weaver-finch	Symplectes kersteni	*Kinanda*
Paradise flycatcher	Tersiphone crustata	*Shore Kishushungi*
Layards Bulbul	Pycnonotus layardi	*Shore*
Black African Drongo	Buchana assimilis	*Mramba*
Orange-yellow weaver-bird	Hyphantomis aureoflavus	*Mnana*
Brown's red-faced weaver-finch	Pyletia afra	*Tunguribi*
Southern grey-headed sparrow	Passer diffisus	*Jurawa*
African roller	Eurystomus afir	*Jore*
Senegal bush shrike	Dryoscopus senegalensis	*Kipwe*
African crow	Corvus scapulatus	*Kunguru*
Finches	Fringillidæ	*Chiriko*
Sunbirds	Nectariniidæ	*Chozi*
Flycatchers	Muscicapidæ	*Tiva*
Swallows	Hirundinæ	*Kijumba mshare. Mbayo wayo*
Starlings	Sturnidæ	*Kwenzi*
Canary		*Kurumbizi*
A little black and white finch		*Koma kanga*

Order 2. *Picariæ.*

Black and white hornbill	Laphocerus melanoleucus	*Thembe* (south) *Kwembe* (north)
White-eyebrowed lark-headed cuckoo shrike	Centropus superciliosis	*Tipi Tipi*
Pied kingfisher	Ceryle rudis	*Dete Pwane*

Long-tailed bee-eater	Merops persicus	*Keremkerem*
Nightjar	Caprimulgus fossei	Zanzibar *Kipasua sanda.* Pemba *Baba watoto*
Wood hoopœ	Irrisor erythorhyncus	*Gore Gore*
Cuckoo	Chrysococcyx cupreus	*Mtama wa bibi*
Lesser woodpecker	Campothera caillianti	*Gongnola*
Order 3. *Striges.*		
Barn owl	Strix flammea	*Bunde*
Order 4. *Psittaci.*		
Parrots		*Kasuku*
Order 5. *Columbæ.*		*Njiwa*
Green fruit pigeon	Vinago delalandei	*Ninga*
Tambourine pigeon	Tympanistria tympanistria	*Pugi or Puji*
Half-collared turtle-dove	Stroptopelia semitorquata	*Hua*
Vinaceous turtle-dove	Stroptopelia vinaces	*Hua*
Large dove		*Mwigo*
Order 6. *Gaviæ.*		
Gulls		*Chakwe and Membe*
Order 7. *Limicolæ.*		
Curlew		*Sururu*
Curlew sandpiper	Tringa subarquata	*Kitwitwi*
Dotterel		*Chekehukwa*
Order 8. *Grallæ.*		
Moorhen	Fulicaridæ	*Kuku ziwa*
Order 10. *Gallinæ.*		
Common guinea-fowl	Numida mitrata	*Kanga*
? Crested guinea-fowl	Numida cristata	*Kororo*
Order 12. *Accipitres.*		
Egyptian kite	Milvus ægypticus	*Mwewe*
Kite		*Kipanga*
A speckled kite with bluish back		*Kozi*
A black and white fish eagle (Pemba only)		*Korho*
Order 13. *Anseres.*		*Bata*
Dwarf goose	Nettapus auritus	*Bata mtoni*
Wild duck		*Salili*
Order 14. *Herodiones.*		
White and black egret	Herodias alba	*Korongo*
Grey reef heron	Ardea gularis	*Yange Yange*

(4) Reptiles are not common in Zanzibar, at least there are not a great many varieties.

Order 2. *Chelonia.*		
East African sternother	Sternothærus sinuatus	*Kobe* (Pemba only)
Hawksbill turtle	Chelone imbricata	*N'gamba*
Green turtle	Chelone midas	*Kassa*

Order 3. *Lacertilia.*		*Mjusi*
Geckoes (at least four kinds)		*Mjusi*
Small lizards (at least four kinds)		*Karakaka* (Pemba) or *Mjusi*
Chameleons, 1 kind Zanzibar		*Kinyonga*
1 kind Pemba		*Kigaogao*
Monitor	Varanus niloticus	*Kenge* (Zanzibar only)
Large burrowing skink		*Guruguru* (Zanzibar only)
Order 4. *Ophidia.*		
Python	Python sebæ	*Chatu*
Large snake	General name—	*Joka*
Small snake	General name—	*Nyoka*
Boomslang	Dispholidus typus	*Gangawiya* (Pemba)
Black-throated cobra	Naja nigricollis	*Kipili*
Egyptian cobra	Naja haji	

(5) Of Amphibians there are only frogs and toads. Toads I have seen only in Pemba where they are very common—perhaps two species. Of frogs I have kept about a dozen species, including a variety of Xenopus and tree frogs (one of the latter *Megalixinus fornasinii*). They are all known as *Chura* (Vyura).

(6) Fishes I have dealt with elsewhere, but I must just mention here a peculiar little fish with a box-like coat of armour and two horns in front which looks like some weird submarine, and called by the fishermen *Kibupembe*. It is not eaten, but considered a great curiosity.

There is a legendary sea-monster called *Chinusi* which holds men under water and drowns them, but it has never been seen. Perhaps the origin is a giant octopus.

(7) Of Invertebrates, snails are called *Konokono*, and each variety of shell-fish and crustacean has its name.

Insects are called generally *mdudu* (*wadudu*), and this includes such things as spiders, scorpions, etc. These are some names: Butterflies, *pepeo* and *kipepeo*; grasshoppers, *panzi*; spiders, *buibui*; scorpions, *nge*; millepedes (and *bêche de mer*), *jongo*; ringworms, *choa*; flies, *nzi*; mantides, *vunjajungo*; wasps, *manyigu*; gadflies, *paange*; ants, general name *chungu* and *sizimizi*; soldier ants, *siafu*; red tree ants, *maji ya moto* (" hot water " from bites); bees, *nyuki*; centipedes, *taandu*; cockroaches, *mende*; fleas, *kiroboto*; termites, *mchwa*; jiggers, *tekenya* or *dudu wa kepu*; firefly, *Kimuri muri*.

I think the lists I have given, though by no means complete, will give a good idea of what good naturalists the natives are. Some remarks require to be made.

Owls and chameleons are thought especially unlucky and killed whenever possible, the latter especially in Pemba, where no native would touch one, and those brought to me were always brought at the end of a long pole. It is thought that they can spit a peculiarly potent poison into your eye. Of the nightjar it is said in Pemba, that where they fly wizards follow.

The existence of a crested guinea-fowl on Tumbatu I can vouch for, as I have kept two caught on that island. I have mentioned no animals save those found in the Protectorate.

As in England so in Zanzibar, the calls of the birds are often translated to words, and many of their names are onomatopœic, e.g., *tipi tipi*, *kitwitwi*.

The half-collared turtle-dove's call is variously interpreted as *Mama a kafa, babu akafa nimesalia mimi tu*. " Mother is dead, father is dead. I am left alone by myself." Or *Kuku mfupa tupu, mimi nyama teli*. " A fowl is only bone, I am plenty meat."

The Mwigo holds conversation as follows: "*Coo-oo*." One answers "*Mwigo*." "*Coo-oo*," says the bird. "*Niagulie*" (Prophesy for me), says the traveller. "*Coo-oo*." " Kwema nendako? " (Is the going good?) "*Coo-oo*." But if it answers not "*Coo-oo*," it is a bad omen. My donkey-boy told me once he never asked, as he was afraid of a negative reply.

A little canary-like bird called *Kurumbizi* is

almost as inquisitive as a robin. It is said that if he sees a man talking to a woman, he hops round saying, "*Mtu anasema na Mke*" (A man is talking to a woman).

Owls are said to cry as follows: Male bird, "*Shimegi niazime mkufu*" (Sister-in-law, lend me a chain); female bird, "*Usiku huu*" (to-night).

Monkeys are said to be the descendants of some men, who were transformed into them by God for a wicked misuse of a thin bread called *mkate wa bisi* while in a dhow. *Libero cuidam, post purgationem anum pani deterserunt.*

CHAPTER XL

Religion

RELIGIOUS BELIEFS

While every little village has its mosque, which is kept up by the villagers, and its Koran schools, which every child attends, to learn and become efficient in the parrot-like repetition of the Koran in a foreign tongue, which even the teacher does not understand, for several dreary years, the veneer of Islam is but a flimsy veil for the simpler beliefs of the African. Occasionally revivalist movements take place, and a few years ago a young man who had been taught religion in the city of Zanzibar returned to his people in the south, and in a campaign of earnest preaching told his people that their regard for the devils of their ancestors was wrong, and that they should throw down their altars and return to the worship of the one God. As a result of the inspired words and example of the young man, by name Daudi Musa, now nick-named Daudi Mizimu, the dwelling-places of the Mizimu and the Wamavua devils in a few villages were deserted, and thickets where formerly spirits dwelt were cut down and crops planted. But such an event is rare, and generally all that Islam does, when as in Zanzibar so little of it is understood, is to lend itself to, and to be adapted to, the more efficient (in the native mind) practice of magic, and even receipts for killing one's enemy are headed, " In the name of God the merciful, the compassionate."

Sudden sickness with no knowledge to interpret it aright may easily be attributed to supernatural agencies, and to deal with all these terrors around, soon classified into various groups of devils, unusual methods are required, and thus the beginning of religion, magic, is called in.

Magic in Zanzibar and Pemba is at a high state of development.

ISLAM

If one excepts the numerically few converts of the Christian missions working in the islands, and a few pagans, generally raw Wanyamwezi, who, however, are usually rapidly converted either to Islam or Christianity, according to what surroundings they fall into on their arrival in the country, the whole of the native population profess the Islamic faith.

The predominant sect, which, however, comprises only Arabs, and is therefore in numerical minority, is the Ibathi—A.D. 749. Of this sect His Highness the Sultan is the head. The tenets of this sect came to this coast probably not earlier than 1698, when the Omanis under Seif bin Sultan conquered the Portuguese.

We have noticed previously that the natives of the coast are Sunnis, and as they are of the Shafi school it will be well to make a few remarks on that one of the four great branches of the Sunnis. Its founder was Muhammad bin Idris esh-Shafi, and he was of the prophet's tribe, the Al Quraish, and a descendant of Abdul Muttaleb, the prophet's grandfather. He was born at Askalon in Palestine A.D. 767. His early life was spent at Gaza, and from there he went to Mecca, and thence, in A.D. 813, to Baghdad, where he started his work, gave lectures and wrote. Thereafter he went on the Pilgrimage, and afterwards to Egypt, where he died in 822. His two great works were the al-Usul on the fundamental, and the Sunan and Masnad on the traditional law. At the present day the Shafi sect is chiefly met with in Arabia and Egypt, and Ibn Batuta says that in his time the coast natives were Shafites. These facts, therefore, in conjunction with those previously recited, make it likely that the greatest time of proselytism on the coast was in the latter part of the ninth and early tenth centuries.

ANIMISM

I now proceed to the question of spirits or devils (general term *sheitan*), and before passing from revealed religion to that of the primitives, the first class to be dealt with are the Djinns (*Majini*), in whom all Moslems believe. They are the genie of the *Arabian Nights*, and are mostly harmful. They are Moslem in belief, and certain sheikhs are credited with leading them in prayer.

They are, of course, "imported" into the Zanzibar pantheon, and therefore credited by the natives with being able to travel by sea. Some natives say they are only to be found at sea.

There are also Afriti, allied to Djinns, which may be summoned up by the use of magic formulæ. They were originally seventy, and were subjects of Solomon.

Of purely native spirits there are, firstly, the ghosts who live in the *Kuzimu*, which are the ghosts of the dead; they do not appear to man, and those manifestations which we should ascribe to ghosts are by the native described by no more specific name than *Sheitani*, or devils; powerful men of the past, such as the *Mwenyi Mkuu* of the Wahadimu, or *Mkame Mdume*, the chieftain of Pemba, are credited with keeping in control large numbers of devils, which even now appear in their former haunts. The Wapemba call ghosts *Mkungwe pare*, and say they live in the *jongo mayo*, which corresponds to the Swahili *Kuzimu*.

Then there are the *Pepo*, a group of spirits of many different names, which may be known as personal spirits, as they are the kind which possess people; they are not all really harmful, and may even be called up if the occasion warrants it, to take possession of a person for his or her good; if they become obstreperous they can be exorcized by the use of their particular *ngoma*. In the fasting month of Ramathan these spirits are enclosed by the medicine men in bags. The following are the names of some of the *Pepo*: Masewe, Kigalla, Kinyassa, Magadi (affect women only), Kingindo, Kizaramu, Wabia, Manyema, Watheramu, Watumbatu, Wahadimu, Kiwingo. Nearly all these are the names of tribes, and I learnt from witch-doctors that each tribe has its own devils, and devils of one tribe will not affect men of another.

Thirdly, there is another family of important devils called *Mizimu*, who have their abodes in trees and caves, in each of which there is a seat or altar to which flags are tied and offerings made and incense burnt; they are far more common in Zanzibar than in Pemba, and among the Wahadimu the Mwana Vyali is especially charged with the sweeping of their habitations, and with the responsibility of seeing that the proper offerings are made.

There is then a class of what may be called local and personal spirits, which are known as *Pango*, meaning also a cave or cleft in a rock; these are common in Pemba, and manifest themselves through the witch-doctors, who, on sitting down at the seat of the devil, become immediately possessed by him in a most uncanny way; the voice is changed, the eyes are strange and unseeing, and the witch-doctor usually ends his trance frothing at the mouth, and finally collapses to wake up as out of a deep sleep.

There are also the *Zimwi*, several of whom are met in the tales in this book. They were supernatural beings masquerading as men, and generally mischievous. In the tales one also meets the *Pinga*, whose business it is to fold up the night and spread the day. *Mizuka* are evil spirits under control of witch-doctors, which can be imprisoned in charms and bottles and buried to harm passers-by or a particular passer-by.

Then the words *nafsi*, *moyo*, *roho*, *mtima* must be dealt with when considering the question of soul.

Firstly God. God is considered, besides many Mohammedan attributes, as a being of somewhat limited powers, at any rate as far as foreknowledge goes, and yet is responsible for most things that happen, chiefly misfortunes. If one takes the omens before doing a thing, and it goes wrong, it is *Shauri ya Mungu*—" God's plans "; if it goes all right the fortune-teller and not the Deity gets the kudos. Not only misfortunes and diseases are put down to God, but also the vagaries of the *Serkali*. If the Government does not do what the witch-doctor says it will, or does something considered disagreeable, it is still *Shauri ya Mungu*. The Deity has a lot to answer for.

The *Mizimu* are, as I have said, purely local spirits, who may exercise an influence for good or for evil. Very often it is for good, and they are classed together—God and the *mizimu*, e.g., *Tumwombe muungu koma, na mizimu yache* (Kipemba). " We are interceding with God and His *mizimu*."

They haunt the caves on the seashore or deep holes or ruins or trees, particularly the baobab tree, but also the cotton trees, and when isolated, away from civilization, the mango tree. Offerings are made to them chiefly of potsherds, rags and other valueless trifles.

I have found many *mizimu* in Zanzibar Island, particularly in caves on the coast, but I had not found one on Tumbatu, and the following record by Captain R. S. F. Cooper is therefore interesting: " The western shore (of Tumbatu Island) is very rugged and fine, and there is a great gorge made by the sea, shutting off one part of the coast completely. It is supposed to be the abode of a very fierce devil, and the natives hang up flags and leave offerings to appease him. They besought us not to smoke in the gorge for fear we should offend him, and bring misfortune on the village and ourselves. We complied, of course, as there is no point in trampling on their superstitions."

Many spirits dwell at cross-roads, and here the

offerings are very worthless—a handful of grass will do, though I have seen unripe fruit, a piece of tobacco, a stick of muhogo and other odd things. Anyone who takes away an offering to *mizimu* takes misfortune too. The Ngezi forest and Pembe Island, Pemba, should be mentioned as special haunts of *mizimu*. The devils called *Pango* have specific names. There is quite a celebrated one near the town of Chake Chake, Pemba, which consists of a deep pool in which formerly a large fish lived, but which presumably has died, as it has not been seen for some time. The pool, however, is still considered as haunted and offerings regularly made. The name of the spirit is *Mwana Mashungi*.

I also found another *pango* called *ginyingi*, which is haunted by a devil *Mwakungu*. It is near the village in Pemba called Chambani, the witch-doctors of which place profess to have an invisible stone house where they conduct their ceremonies.

I have not succeeded in finding the site of the house, though I have been shown the neighbourhood in which it is situated.

Although I have seen many women alleged to be possessed with devils, and having them exorcized by witch-doctors with the particular *ngoma* necessary, I think that the most impressive possession I have seen was that of this *pango*. The haunt of this devil is in a cave in a rocky water-course, which is quite dry during the dry season; the witch-doctor whom I saw possessed was usually of a happy disposition, which was reflected in his face, but squatted in this cave, stark naked, as the medium of the devil, his face seemed to reflect only utter and evil savagery, his eyes were bloodshot and staring and yet unseeing, his face was distorted in a horrible grin; he seemed to display a double personality, his own and that of the devil, which was supposed to be possessing him. After speaking a few words in a strange voice, he fell into a fit, his body writhed and twisted on the earth, as if Juma bin Hasan the witch-doctor were wrestling with Mwa Kungu the devil, his hands clutched at his throat and his legs kicked, as if he were attempting to remove an opponent. He was in such a state that an Arab who was with me endeavoured to calm him by saying, " In the name of God, gently, gently." He gave a cry of " I go my way, farewell," in the voice which was supposed to be that of the devil, uttered a fearsome shriek, and after one colossal struggle fell back motionless. He awoke in a moment or two his normal self. My Arab friend claimed that it was the invocation of the name of Power that caused the devil to retire.

The other spirits I will mention again when I come to Possessions and Exorcisms.

Next, the soul. The African distinguishes between soul, heart and mind, and heart, as in English, has a double meaning, both the physical organ and the seat of his emotions.

The soul is considered as being in every part of the body, and if part of you is amputated you lose a corresponding bit of your *roho*. Amputation of the left leg is considered especially bad. It is for this reason that hair and nail parings if left about can be made so dangerous to their former owners.

Soul is *roho*, heart is *moyo*, mind is *akili* (intelligence).

Roho, *nafsi* and *akili* are all importations from the Arabic, but *moyo* is a bantu word, and the word *mtima*, which is seldom heard, save among the old people in distant villages, means rather more than *moyo*, and I think is really *roho*. Both *moyo* and *roho* are often confused. Examples: *Anasema maneno mazuri, lakini moyo yake mbaya.* " He speaks fair words, but his heart is evil." *Moyo yake anakwenda sana.* " His heart is beating fast." *Mtima wende na moyo.* " Soul and heart are going." *Roho amekwenda peponi.* " The soul has gone to paradise."

Nafsi is often used merely to emphasize—self, e.g., *Mimi nafsi yangu*—" I myself."

I once asked an Arab if he considered we should all go to the same heaven. He replied, "No, we shall all have separate towns, but as you and I are friends we can have a house on the outskirts and speak across to each other."

It may be wondered why I have omitted all reference to Mohammedan feasts, but as I am endeavouring to deal as far as possible with the "three tribes" only, I think such reference would be out of place, particularly as the only one that they really take any serious notice of is Ramathan, when many certainly do fast. On the Siku kuu (Id-el-Fitr) they make up for it and will not do any work at all.

SUPERSTITIONS

The European superstitions as to luck from meeting cross-eyed women or touching hunchbacks, and bad luck from other reasons, have their counterpart in Zanzibar.

Superstitions as to salt, etc., and fishing I have related under their appropriate headings, and here there are just a few that cannot be classified elsewhere.

It is bad luck to meet on going out of the house in the morning a one-eyed man or a hunchback, but if on first leaving your house you meet two men on the way together, or a man carrying a load, it is good luck.

The one-eyed man and the hunchback apparently being not sound of body cannot be prosperous, but it betokens prosperity to see two men bent on a *shauri*, or a man carrying a load which means property.

It is bad luck to hand scissors to anyone: they should be put down for the other to take up.

CHAPTER XLI

Medicine

SURGERY

The practice of surgery is in a far more primitive state than that of the sciences we shall afterwards consider. There are only two operations that really deserve the dignity of being called surgical—cupping and circumcision. Cupping (*kumumika*) is performed by a cupper (*muumishi*) with a cupping-horn called by the Wahadimu *chuku*, but in the town *umiko* or *ndukiko*. It is an operation for blood-letting, and corresponds to the use of leeches in Europe; it is generally resorted to in cases of high fever.

The horn is the top end of a cow's horn with a hole bored through the thin end and a lump of bees-wax then stuck on to it. The knife is a small, locally made instrument with a square point. The operation is performed by making small incisions on the back while the patient lies on his stomach, to the number of about four, and then putting a horn over each and sucking vigorously. When all the air is drawn out the operator closes the hole by biting the bees-wax with his teeth. When the cups are removed or fall off in about twenty minutes they are full of congealed blood.

A simpler operation is simply *kuchanja*. This consists merely of cutting gashes with a razor on the back. The cuts are deeper than those for cupping, as the blood has to come out without being drawn out. When sufficient blood has been "let," the bleeding is stopped by an application either of crushed *mbaazi* leaves (a kind of pea that resembles laburnum) and lime, or of the sap of the *mbono* (physic nut tree —*Yatrofa curcas*).

Chanja kwa ndui, to cut for smallpox, is a term that is now applied to vaccination, an operation which is performed also by Swahilis in Government employ.

Circumcision (*tohara*) is carried out by a circumciser (*ngariba*), who is often also an elder, or Sheha, or Mwalimu of the mosque. To circumcise is *kutahiri*, though an euphemism *kuingia kumbini* (to enter the porch, i.e., to be excluded from the house) is also used.

The whole idea of *tohara* is circumcision in the purifying sense of Islam, and *kutahiri* means to circumcise in the Mohammedan way. As I have explained, however, in previous chapters, there is a dance used on these occasions.

Wounds are not sewn up, at least I have not known it done, and many gaping scars can be seen.

The only other "operation" a native is called upon to perform is the removal of those unpleasant parasites, "jiggers" (*Sarcopsilla penetrans*). This is done either with a thorn—orange thorns are often used—or a pointed wooden needle. Some natives are extraordinarily skilful at removing these lady jiggers whole with bag of eggs and all, thus saving the ulcer that results if the bag is broken.

Sometimes the Wakikuyu who, unlike the Zanzibari men, bore their ears like women, wish to get rid of the disfigurement, and this is done for them by cutting out a few inches of the ring of flesh into which the ear lobe is distended, and binding up the two short ends. This heals in a few days.

Among a collection of bones recently excavated in making a road in Zanzibar is a fragment of skull

—left parietal bone—which bears evidence of successful trepanning; successful, because the margins of the opening are healed over. There are no indications as to race and few as to age. It is probably the second oldest of eight skulls or fragmentary skulls from the same place, all buried in tidal sand. The external surface is deeply eroded and it is very friable. From the history of the spot where it was found, and its condition compared with that of the other specimens, one may assume that it is at least a hundred years old. It is the first record of a trepanned skull to be found in Zanzibar, and is now in the Zanzibar Museum.

The Arabs of Zanzibar know of the operation, but I have never heard of them performing it.

Massaging—*kukanda*—is a common practice and many women are skilled at it. They "crack" the joints of the fingers and the backbone, and perform most of the operations known to Western masseuses.

Physics

THE PRACTITIONERS

The word for a doctor or medicine man is *mganga*, and this not only includes a dealer in medicine, but also in white magic. Under this heading, though, I shall not refer to charms as cures for diseases, but only definite medicines as we understand the word in English.

The practice of an *mganga* is hereditary and is passed down from father to son, from generation to generation. Some doctors have recipes for some things, some for another; none will communicate these recipes to each other. I had the greatest difficulty in compiling the Materia Medica I made, and when each medicine man was explaining his herbs, everyone else had to be excluded from hearing, save he and me. I had to pay them pretty well too.

Another curious thing is that they have a sort of language of their own, at any rate as far as concerns the names of the herbs they use; this is called *kiganga*. Especial care had to be taken to check the names, and this I did by resummoning each man after a few days and presenting him with the roots or leaves in turn, asking him what they were and what their uses were. In order to get the scientific names it was necessary to get the flowers, and I had a lot of trouble about this. One old gentleman brought a huge bunch of flowers, and as I called out a name he fitted any flower on to it. I found this out by checking.

Lemon grass is grown outside most huts. Natives make an infusion and drink it in fever. The use of balsam is also known.

The figures in the "Quantity" column indicate the number of pieces of root required. The pieces (*vipande*) are about two inches long.

* denotes leaves and not roots.

Anything else than roots or leaves, e.g., bark, is stated.

D=days. M.E.=morning and evening.

Snake bites are rare; I have only learnt of one, and in that case the patient had in the end to resort to the mission nurse for treatment. The *mganga's* treatment was to tie a charm on and apply a concoction of leaves and dung to the bite.

Burton says that the Arabs make an infusion with papaw seeds, and that it has a similar effect to the compound I have numbered 7 below.

MATERIA MEDICA

No.	Native name of disease or ailment.	English name.	Medicine name of herbs.	Native name.	English or Scientific name.	Quantity.	Method of preparation.	Directions.	Time.
1	Tego	Syphilis from witchcraft	Mbabu Haji 1 Mpinguzi 2 Mikarafu 3	 Mpinga 2	 Cloves 3	3 4 7	Boil together and strain off water	Drink	3 D.M.E.
2	Tumbo la sheitani	Excessive menstruation	Miwali wali 1 Muuyaawali 2	 Muakikale 2 Ubani 4	 Red silk 3 Incense 4	4 3	Tie roots together with red silk, put with a little incense in pot and boil	Drink half and apply rest to affected place	7 D.M.E.
3	Buba	Rupia	Kibubu 1	Kitue 1 Mawele 2	Ord. Solanaceæ solanum (sp) 1	7	Make porridge of *mawele*, boiling the *kibubu* in it. The *kibubu* should be then cleaned and used till end of treatment	Eat porridge	7 D.M.E.
4	Mwana mimba	Pregnancy (Recipe to procure abortion)	Mng'anga 1 Mnanuzi 2			4 3	Boil together, strain off water	Drink. Take another bit of 2 and cook in porridge	3 D.M.E.
5	Mtegofla vidonda	Syphilitic sores	(*a*) Misiliza 1 Mpingozi 2 (*b*) Kiviza (*c*) Mviru 1 Mkatikati 2 Mpukusa 3 (male) Mukongeze 4	 Mvingoze 2 Mviza Mkwamba 3 Kihongeze 4	 Ord. Euphorbiaceæ securinega 3 See No. 9. 4	3 6 9	Boil and strain off water. Boil and strain off. Grind to flour and sieve through a piece of cloth	Drink Wash sores Apply to sores	7 D.M.E. 7 D. 7 D.

MATERIA MEDICA (*continued*)

No.	*Native name of disease or ailment.*	*English name.*	*Medicine name of herbs.*	*Native name.*	*English or Scientific name.*	*Quantity.*	*Method of preparation.*	*Directions.*	*Time.*
6	Kutapika	Vomiting	Msinduzi 1 Mpilipili 2	Pili fili 2		3 4	Boil, pour in *kata*, drop in a piece of burning ash, cover with hand immediately	Drink	Once only
7		Impotency (an aphrodisiac)	Mpaza 1	Mpava 1 Tangawizi 2	Ginger 2			Chew together	
8	Chovia	Swelling all over	Mtikitumbo 1	Ubani 2	Ord. Nyctaginaceæ mirabilis julapa 1 Incense 2	7	(*a*) Boil together, strain (*b*) Make flour of another piece of (1)	(*a*) Drink (*b*) Apply all over	7 D.
9		Delayed child-birth	Muhongeze	Kihongeze	Phyllanthes Euphorbiaceæ and/or Demodium/Leguminosæ Known under this name	*	Crush leaves together, mix with water	Drink some and pour some on head	
10	Uma ya tumbo	Stomach-ache	Taka kuva		Cleatantrus?	*	Boil and strain	Drink	3 D.
11	Vidonda	Sores	Taka kuva		Cleatantrus?	*	Pound .	Apply to sores	

MATERIA MEDICA (*continued*)

No.	*Native name of disease or ailment.*	*English name.*	*Medicine name of herbs.*	*Native name.*	*English or Scientific name.*	*Quantity.*	*Method of preparation.*	*Directions.*	*Time.*
12	Uma ya tumbo	Stomach-ache	Mkaiokaio	Mkaiago		7	Boil and strain	Drink	3 D.
13		Giddiness result of hit in testicles	Mfursala 1	Mfarafaji 1	Ord. Moraceæ norus nigra 1	9	Grind to powder, mix with water	Drink	
				Pili pili 2	Chili seeds 2	7			
14	Mimba tumbo	Constipation	Mnavu		Ord. Solanceæ solanum nigram	*		Chew and swallow	
15		Stomach-ache	Mkakakake				Grind a little and mix with water	Drink	
16	Homa	Fever	Mboga		Ord. Cucurbitaceæ cucurbita pepo	*	Grind	Smear all over	
17		Constipation	Mtundu kanga 1	Mlangamia 1	Cassytha filiformis 1 A fallen coco-nut 2	*	Grind both and then grind together, boil and strain	Drink	
18	Pumu	Shortness of breath	(*a*) Mchakaki 1 Mumbuzi 2		(*a*) Ord. Verbinaceæ lantana	4	Boil and strain	Drink	
				ubani 3	salvifolia 1 incense 3	3			
					(*b*) leaves of both	*	Grind together	Rub over chest and throat	

MATERIA MEDICA (*continued*)

No.	*Native name of disease or ailment.*	*English name.*	*Medicine name of herbs.*	*Native name.*	*English or Scientific name.*	*Quantity.*	*Method of preparation.*	*Directions.*	*Time.*
19		Ear-ache	Kunjuu (stem)		Ord. Aroideæ amorphor-phallus rivieri		Heat stem in fire	Squeeze juice in ear	
20	Kaka	Swollen foot	Mwengele 1 Mbarika 2		Ord. Anpel-ideæ vitis grantii 1	*	Wrap 1 in 2, put on fire, when cooked, take 1 out of 2 and crush	Spread on swelling	
21	Baridi ya ndani	Internal cold	(*a*) Mtukutu leaves 1 (*b*) roots of above	mafuta uta 2	Simsim oil 2	* 7	(*a*) Squeeze out juice, add oil. (*b*) Boil in water, strain	Drink Drink	3 D.M.E.
22	Tumbo la mshipa		Mpinga		Ord. Liliaceæ Gloriosa superba	6	Boil in water, strain	Drink	4 D.M.E.
23		Pain in leg as result of witchcraft on road	(*a*) Muiya amali 1 Mnanua sihui 2 (*b*) roots of both	Mua Kikale 1 Mtapiko chui 2	"That which makes the leopard sick" 2	* * 4 3	(*a*) Pound together, mix with a little water (*b*) Boil and strain	Apply to affected place. Drink	5 D.M.E.
24		Eruption result of bewitched food	(*a*) Mpambuiya 1 (*b*) Roots (*c*) Mwisha viwe 2	(*a*) Mkole 1 (*b*) Roots (*c*) Mchewe 2		* 5 *	(*a*) Pound, mix with water (*b*) Boil and strain (*c*) Boil in water	(*a*) Apply (*b*) Drink (*c*) Pour mixture in bath water and bathe in it	7 D.M.E.

MATERIA MEDICA (*continued*)

No.	*Native name of disease or ailment.*	*English name.*	*Medicine name of herbs.*	*Native name.*	*English or Scientific name.*	*Quantity.*	*Method of preparation.*	*Directions.*	*Time.*
25	Kifua cha pumu	Asthma	Mzimia Marathi 1	Ukindu (top ends 1 in. long) 2	New Needle 3	7 7*	Bind root, ukindu and needle together and boil	Drink	7 D.M.E.
26	Buhuete or Kisonono	Gonorrhœa	Hapingwa 1	Mtunda ngombe 1	Cloves 2	7 7	Boil together and	Drink	7 D.M.E.
27	Homa	Shivering fits	(*a*) anaiwinja jini (*b*) hapitwa nyuma	(*a*) mwamba mji (*b*) mkindu	Phœnix senegalensis	* 5	(*a*) Pound, mix with a little water (*b*) Boil and strain	(*a*) Apply all over (*b*) Drink	7 D.M.E.
28	Kifua cha kukaza	Bad cough	Mpesua marathi 1 (bark)1	Mpesa 1 Popoo 2	Areca nut 2	1	Boil together and strain.	Drink	3 D.M.E.
29	Nyenga	Sting-ray poisoning	Mpepua 1	Mchechepwa 1 Tangawizi 2	Ginger 2		Scrape and mix with a little water	Apply until recovery	
30		Burns	Mwondo adue	Mtambuka choyo		*	Crush	Apply until recovery	
31	Homa, presence of devils on road	"Somebody walking on your grave"	Mparamse bark				Grind to flour and place in small calabash called Tungure	Smell as required	
32		Cause sneezing	Mtule			*	Grind in hand	Snuff up	

NOSOLOGY

The natives suffer from many diseases, which are nearly all ascribed by them to the effect of witchcraft. The diseases most common to the eye of a layman are:

(1) Ankylostomaisis (*Sufura*).
(2) Malaria (*Homa*).
(3) Venereal Diseases (*Tego* and *buhuete* or *kisonono*).
(4) Tropical Ulcers (*Vidonda*).
(5) Tuberculosis.
(6) Elephantiasis (*Matende*).
(7) Eye troubles.
(8) Leprosy (*Ukoma, Jethamu*)
(9) Yaws (*Buba*).
(10) Bilharzia, a helminthic disease common in both islands.

There are also the usual cycles of endemic and epidemic fevers and diseases, such as smallpox, dengue, which derives its English name from the Swahili name *Kidinga popo*, meaning literally a "going round like a bat," and various forms of dysentery, etc., etc.

A few words must be said of ankylostomiasis, which is extremely prevalent, affecting something like 95 per cent. of the native community.

The individual is infected by the larvæ of the ankylostome entering through the soles of his feet, travelling up the blood stream and eventually finding its immediate host in the intestine, where it develops into the hook worm and thrives and multiplies exceedingly. Large quantities of ova pass out with the fæces, hatch out, infect the ground and start the cycle again.

It is a distressing disease, in so far as it lowers the victim's vitality; he suffers in the advanced stage from profound anæmia, naturally robbing him of energy and initiative, and the disease is largely responsible for the *bado kidogo* (not yet awhile) trait in the native's character.

Numerous complications are commonly seen, such as heart disease, œdema, ascites, big sloughing ulcers, etc., resulting from prolonged attacks of ankylostomiasis.

The victim responds readily to treatment, unless too far advanced, but much has yet to be done in teaching and training him in better sanitary conditions, and also in the wearing of some covering on his feet.

Malaria. This does not require any description here; it is enough to say that the native has no protection whatever against the mosquito (*anopheles*), and in childhood has so many repeated attacks that it is recognized generally that a child of eight years has acquired some immunity, and later in life, unless he is out of condition from some other cause, does not have frequent attacks.

Venereal diseases are rampant, as in all coastal towns, and are considerably lowering the birth-rate.

The difficulty here is that the native cannot always be made to see the necessity of a prolonged course of treatment, and will frequently, during this period, return to his native doctor, imagining the disease is due to some magic spell.

Tuberculosis is a great menace, and is increasing rapidly owing to the moist climate, which is an ideal culture media for the tubercle bacilli. This danger is, of course, increased by the native's habit of expectorating on every possible occasion, and their congested and airless scheme of housing.

Nothing but segregation can combat this, and this is always a difficult problem when dealing with the native, as has been proved numerous times when dealing with lepers.

Elephantiasis is due to a prolonged filarial condition carried by the culex mosquito.

Its name exactly describes its appearance. The parts mostly affected in men are the scrotum and the lower limbs, which assume tremendous proportions.

I have myself seen an amputated scrotum weighing 60 lb.

In women the breasts, or vulva, are most commonly affected, although the condition may appear in any part of the body.

These unfortunate conditions are operable, but more to remove discomfort than as a radical cure.

Eye troubles are due to the glare of the sun and dust, and also as a complication of other diseases.

Cataract (*mtoto jichoni*—lit. a child in the eye) is of frequent occurrence.

Yaws. Unknown in Zanzibar, but prevalent in the north of Pemba.

This begins with skin eruption, rapidly involving and disfiguring the whole body. It resembles syphilis, but is not venereal in origin.

CHAPTER XLII

Magic

POSSESSIONS AND EXORCISMS

The spirits which can possess people are of many different kinds, all have names, but grouped under one heading—*Pepo*.

Jini, the imported Arab spirits, do not so much possess as hover round and make a nuisance of themselves.

Illness is often considered to be the possession of a devil, who must then be made to behave himself or leave. Though devils can be exorcized completely, they are generally merely made to be good tenants, but people often like being possessed, and then a devil can be made to come in as a tenant.

(1) Calling a devil for possession (Hadimu).

Take a piece of *mnanuzi* root, and three of *muiza jini* (*mweusa jini* in Kiunguja, order Leguminosæ—Cassia occidentalis), and boil together in a new pot. When it boils, place a pad on the patient's head (to stop burning) and place the pot on top of it. The patient will then shake her head, but the pot will not fall down. The medicine man then gives the patient some of the mixture to drink. The devil will now come, and though he may go away for short periods, will always come back. After this the medicine man will drop the *muiza jini* down a ruined well, so that it is out of the way of mischief-makers, and the other root will be fastened to the leg of the possessed person, where it will stay seven days. The corresponding Pemba recipe is to take the leaves of *nahakai* (Kip.), or *mchakaka* (Kig.), and *kivumbani*, or *kivum-*

basi (Kiun.), or *jembe la waganga* (Kig.), and put them in water. You then stand in front of the patient reading *Yasin* and sprinkling the water over him. He will then become possessed.

(2) The following amongst innumerable others are some of those devils who may make their presence felt: *Robamba*, *Bundi*, *Rohania*, *Kumbwaya*, *Rewa*, *Kibisa*, *Tari*, *Mwamba*, *Bwende*, *Msindu*, *Timiri* and *Dumgumaru*.

Robamba is a very important Pemba spirit, though apparently he has also penetrated to some Zanzibar districts.

Bundi is probably the spirit who manifests himself as an owl.

Rohania is a storm devil (Pemba).

Kumbwaya is another Pemba devil.

Besides these Steere and Madan mention *Milhoi*, *Kinyambala* (a storm devil living at cross-ways), *Kilima*, *makoka*, *koikoi*, *kizuu*, *kisimwe*, *Mwana maua*, but these are not known well now. I asked about them all, but though several of the names were recognized, my informants said they did not now exist.

All these require dances to exorcize them, with special food, and many of them I have described under Music and Dancing. Those that do not require dancing I shall describe here.

It is generally women who are possessed.

(3) Prior to exorcism, the patient must be prepared for it in this manner (Hadimu).

Take seven leaves and seven seeds of *mkuu* (order Urticaceæ—Ficus sycamorus). Boil in water in a *chungu* (clay pot). When boiling place pot between the legs of the patient and cover her from head to foot with clothes, allowing steam a free passage around her private parts.

The devil can then be exorcized.

(4) To exorcize.

(*a*) Sometimes when a woman is ill she is said to be possessed of a *pepo* and the *dawa ya pepo* is read over to her, and at the same time a *upatu* gong is beaten.

The patient sits before the medicine man covered all over with cloths, and he gabbles off his recitation, and someone else beats this gong incessantly till her head begins to nod up and down. She cries out and the devil retires.

The recitation is long and very nonsensical. This is its beginning: "O Sultan Koran, come to us, O Sultan Han. O Sultan Sultan, pat me. Where are you, O Sultan? You are one of the subjects of Solomon, the son of David the prophet, together with your following (of djinns) born from the hottest water," and so on.

(*b*) An instrument for exorcizing *pepo* is called *pini*. It consists of a cow's horn with two bells fastened through a hole at the end, and is filled with the following magical ingredients: three pieces each of *ambari*, *udi uvumba*, which are kinds of incense: three pieces each of the roots of *mkadi*, *mkua usiku*, *rahani*, *mana afu* and *mvumbisi* (Kiunguja—*kivumbua*, order Labiateæ—Ocimum canum.); a dog's nose and the thread made from a tree called *utugwa* are also inserted and the horn sealed up with yellow, black, and white earth, after which before being ready for use it must be smoked with incense. The doctor dances round the patient with this at arm's length, touching the patient and reciting the *dawa ya pepo*.

(*c*) Yet another instrument used in exorcisms is the *usinga*, a piece of hairy ox-hide rolled up to look like a tail stuck in a handle. This is placed on the patient's head while the *mwalimu* or *mganga* reads from a book of magic.

WHITE MAGIC

Let us now consider white magic, that is to say, magic that has no harm for its object but either to cure, to combat evil in black magic, or to make such "medicine" as love charms. Each will be dealt with in turn. All are within the province of *mganga*.

(1) To cure. This corresponds to medicinal recipes and is intended to serve the same purpose, namely, to cure sickness or disease. It goes about its purpose in a different way, however, and instead of being in the form of a drug or an application, is something perhaps to be worn, which will produce the desired effect if the directions are carried out.

The following are examples:

Kilezi—for use in the delirium of high fever. Take a section of bamboo and place inside it, in quantities and order named, the following roots: *mweusha jini*, three pieces; *muweka* (Kiun. *tanda*), two pieces; *muuya amali*, three pieces; *mpindu pindu*, two pieces; *mtambuzi*, three pieces; *mpukusa*, two pieces; *mwamba mji*, three pieces; *mpesi*, two pieces; *mcheka na watu*, three pieces; *mbabuhaji*, two pieces; *mchonjoma*, three pieces; *mkindu*, two pieces; *mpepe*, seven pieces.

When they are all safely tucked in, place your *kilezi* in a *chungu* (pot) with water and put it on the fire. Then take a long piece of *ukindu* (dried strip of the leaf of the wild date palm) and repeat, "*Kul hua llahu ahad llahu samadu, wala mialidi, wala miuladu, wala mia kullahu kufan ahad*," forty times. After each time of saying, tie a knot in the *ukindu*, till at the end there are forty.

Then plunge it into the pot, which by now is boiling furiously, and the boiling will immediately subside and with it the fever of the patient, who, however, must have some of the medicine to drink and to be bathed in.

A charm to be worn to cure conjunctivitis consists of a string made of goat's hair and a blob of some sort of composition at the bottom. It is threaded on to a necklace and worn there. It is of Shihiri manufacture. In Pemba the medicine man professes to cure sick persons at a distance, by putting the ground leaves of *mwopoa habari* on the face of the messenger who brings the news.

Kombe (cup) are a variety of charms which consist of Koranic texts written on saucers with soot, which is afterwards dissolved in water and drunk, both to cure ailments and to combat or ward off evil.

To assist a pregnant woman to deliver, the medicine man in Pemba takes seven pieces of root or seven leaves of *mfukufuku* (Kip.) or *muwaawanje* (Kig.) and holds them in his hands, clasping a man in his arms. The man breaks forth from the embrace, and the herbs are then boiled and the decoction given to the woman, who will then deliver safely.

(2) Into the next class fall such things as love charms, etc. These are examples:

Love Charm. Recipe (a)—(Hadimu).

Take roots of *mlaza laza* (Kiun. *mvumbua*), *mnyamuta* (Kiun. *mnyamata*, order Verbenaceæ), *muweka* (Kiun. *tanda*). Grind the *mlazalaza* on a stone and scrape the *mnyamata* and *muweka* over it with a knife, then grind all together again. Mix this with a little *marashi*. Put some of this on a corner of your lady's clothes, and scatter more in her washing-place and where she sleeps. Then rub some on your own hands and face. After this go to the lady and, under pretence of business, make a pretext of touching her. Thus you will gain her affections.

Love Charm. Recipe (b)—(Hadimu).

Take roots of *mvunja chuma*, *mpamba wake* (male). Grind the *mvunja chuma* and scrape the *mpamba wake* over it, then grind all this together again with the *mvunja chuma*. Put the powder in food and give it to your lady to eat, and at once she will love you.

Love Charm. Recipe (c)—(Hadimu).

Take roots of *mjuja* (Kiun. *mfuru*) four pieces, *mjaza kapu*, three pieces. Grind together, mix the powder with water and put some on the lady's clothes in her washing-place. This will achieve the desired result.

Love Charm. Recipe (*d*)—(*Hadimu*).

Take seeds of *mchunga* (Kiun. *mchungwe*). Grind and mix in food. Give this to the lady, whose affections are then yours.

There are many more but mainly of these types, either contagious or acting through a philtre.

(*e*) Sir J. G. Frazer (*Taboo and the Perils of the Soul*) refers to a charm used to catch runaway slaves. In these days when there are no slaves it is also used as a love charm. The method is as follows: Take a piece of coir cord and recite a passage of Koran seven times, at the end of each recitation tie a knot. Take the cord to the lady's house, call her name seven times and leave the cord on the door. The lady will come.

Some love charms can be made to call a woman from a distance.

(3) *Recipes for Invisibility.* (*a*) *Tumbatu*, (*b*) *Hadimu*, (*c*) *Pemba.*

(*a*) Take the potato of *matunda kanga* (Kiun. *mlangamia*, order Cassytha filiformis) and shred it. Add hairs from the back of the neck of a black cat and feathers from the back of the neck of a black chicken. Put them all into a *chungu* and roast to ashes on a fire. Powder up the result and place it on the back of a mirror. Cut a small vertical cut above the nose in the middle of the forehead and rub the powder with the mirror into the cut. Turn the mirror round and look. If you are still there, rub again, when you will be invisible.

(*b*) While walking along a path where Cassytha filiformis is growing, swallow as you go seven of the white buds (they look like pills) one after another. You will then be invisible.

(*c*) Cut the throat of a black cock, take its blood and rub the roots of a tree called *mwaka mwaka* in it, and then smear them on your face. This should be repeated until looking in the looking-glass you can no longer see yourself.

Another Pemba method of securing invisibility is

to write "*Wa shems watheraka tofadamdama*" on a piece of paper with the blood of a black cock mixed with the *mwaka mwaka*. Put this in your mouth and smear more of the mixture on your face.

Under this heading also might be included such charms as the one which is fixed in the big drum to give it its note.

An interesting form of white magic is that used for catching thieves. It is not native but an importation, and is performed in Zanzibar exactly as described in Lane's *Modern Egyptians*. A magic square of 15 is used and certain incantations, including verse 21 of Sura 50 of the Koran, "But we have taken off the veil from thee, and thy sight is becoming sharp this day" (Rodwell's translation).

The magician procures generally a small boy, not arrived at puberty, though Lane says a virgin, a black female slave or a pregnant woman will do equally well.

The square is drawn on the boy's hand and a pool of ink in it, the magician makes passes and recites incantations, and burns charms in a dish of incense and commands the thief to appear. The boy then sees a reflection of the thief in the ink and describes him.

This is very often correctly performed, as is well known. Possibly the explanation is thought-transference, but I have no doubt that the magicians believe in their charms rather than in their powers of suggestion, hypnotism, etc.

In Pemba should you wish a divorced wife not to be married again, take the roots of *munga nyungu* (Kig. *hang'ongwa*) and wrap in calico. Put this charm under a log, saying, "I fasten so-and-so, I fasten her by a cord." If you want to break the spell you have only to remove the charm.

(4) The feats performed at *Maulidi* (which, as I have elsewhere explained, is a religious recitation accompanied by music to celebrate the birth of the

Prophet) are perhaps more in the nature of conjuring tricks than magic in the sense of the word as I am now using it.

They are three and are not native, being imported from Arabia.

The first and the cleverest is swallowing fire. The Mullah walks up and down between the rows of chanters, holding a dish containing burning incense in his hand and praying with uplifted head, but every now and then blowing on the red-hot ashes of incense. Then he takes some up in his fingers and places it in his mouth, and the glowing incense and the smoke issuing out is there for all to behold.

The next feat is performed with an instrument called *debussi*, which is a long nail as sharp as a needle, fixed in a wooden handle. The Mullah apparently bores this through his cheeks after prayer, and then withdraws it with no mark on his cheek.

The third trick is not so marvellous. The Mullah bares his stomach, and calling on Allah, plunges the sword against it, and it does not cut him.

I have examined the nails (and possess one) and the swords, and they are certainly sharp and not false, and I have asked the performers how it is done. Of course the only reply I ever got was that it was done by prayer, and God would not let the fire or the nail or the sword do harm to a holy man.

(5) In the next class I place charms intended to ward off evil. The following are examples:

Koma. A charm to keep off enemies from a dance-ground, and to stop the players from quarrelling. (Hadimu.)

Take a section of bamboo and stuff in one piece each of the following roots in order (Kiunguja names and scientific names, if known, in brackets): *mlazalaza* (*mvumbua*), *mtandika* (*mbu wa mwaka*), *mpinguzi* (*mpinga*), *mualikia Mbali*, *mbarika*, *mbabu Haji*, *maliwali*, *mtarawanda*, *mpingozi* (*mvingozi*), *muya amali* (*muakikale*), *muiza*, *mviru mshike* (*mshikia hanye*, order Amaranthaceæ, A. chryanthes aspera), *muambe mji*, *kichinja uzia*, *mtakasa*, *mpukusa* (*mkwamba*—securinega), *mpinduzi* (*mwanga kwao*—a fern), *msukuma* (*mlandege*), *haotajwa* (*mlachole*, order Verbenaceæ lippia), *mjuvi*, *muhegaawa* (*mchongoma*), *mtopetope*, *mshinda jemaa* (*kisinde*), *mpekuzi* (*mfaggio*), *mshinda* (*mcheje*, Fimbristilis extilis), *mwangakwao*, *mpite wote*, *mnvamuta* (*mnyamata*), *mpevuatu* (*mpepe*), *michali* (*mjoma*), *mtoga* (*mtarawanda*), *mshika jemaa* (*mkwaju*, order Tamarindus indica, Tamarind), *kongapingu* (*golegole*), *mtawa*.

Seal both ends of the section with *ubani* (incense) and *uvumba* (gum copal). The day before the dance take the *Koma* to the dance-ground, dig a hole and place in it more *ubani* and *uvumba* and burn it. Hold the *Koma* over it and say :

" *Koma we, tunakuweka hapa katika wanja wa ngoma,*
Koma thou, we are placing thee here in the ground of the dance;
adui akitoka kusini mwongushe hapa asiondoke, akitoka
an enemy if he comes from the south make him fall here not to get away; if he comes
matokea jua, mwongushe hapa asiondoke, akitoka kaskazi
from the east, make him fall down here not to get away; if he comes from the north
mwongushe hapa asiondoke, akitoka machwa ya jua,
make him fall here not to get away; if he comes from the west
mwongushe hapa asiondoke, akiwa adui mwana mke, aanguke
make him fall down not to get away. If it be an enemy female let her fall;
akiwa adui mwana mume, aanguke, akiwa mweusi
if it be an enemy male let him fall; if it be black
aanguke, akiwa mwekundu aanguke, na wewe, koma,
let him fall; if it be red let him fall. And thou, Koma,

uzuwiye watu hapa katika wanja wa ngoma wasigombane,
stop men here on the ground of the dance from quarrelling
wala wasipigane, wa rithihe furahaya ngoma basi.
or fighting and content them with the joy of the dance only."

Then bury it in the hole.

After the dance the leader of the dance can take it away, but in a *mkoba* (pocket or sachel), and it can be used again many times.

Under this heading also may be inserted the vast variety of charms falling under the name *hirizi*, which are chiefly Koranic charms, consisting mainly of parts of Suras 113 and 114 of the Koran, which are considered powerful medicines for combating evil.

Sura CXIII—The Daybreak

I betake me for refuge to the Lord of the *Daybreak*
Against the mischiefs of his creation,
And against the mischief of the night when it overtaketh me,
And against the mischief of weird women;[1]
And against the mischief of the envier when he envieth.

Sura CXLV—Men

I betake me for refuge to the Lord of *Men*,
The King of men,
The God of men,
Against the mischief of the stealthily withdrawing whisperer,
Who whispereth in man's breast—
Against djinn and men.

Most children wear a necklace with two or three little wallets bearing some of these sentences, and they are also fixed up in huts to keep evil away in the same way that texts are in Europe.

Some, however, although Koranic, are merely

[1] Literally, who blow on knots. According to some commentators an allusion to a species of charm.

disjointed words and sentences, with astrological or talismanic signs at the end. (Hadimu.)

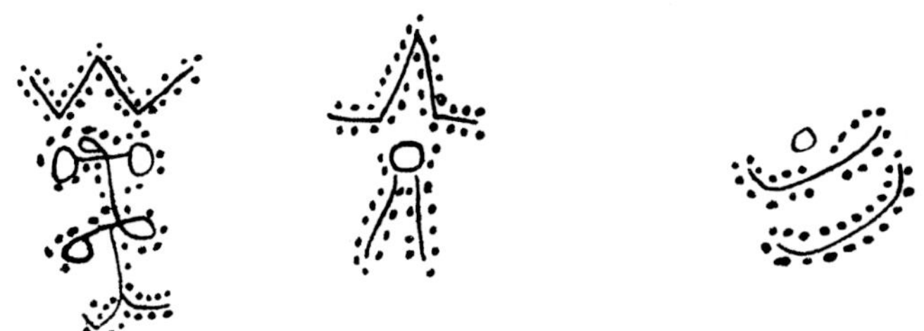

These I was told were *nyota* (stars), and the one on the right the moon.

Another interesting charm under this heading is the *koja*, a chain of wooden beads worn by children. In the long beads are stuck bits of a reed called *ndago*. If anybody of evil intent approaches a child wearing this, the child will vomit, thus disclosing the malignant influence.

To ward off blows in Pemba, the roots of *mvunjashoka* (Kig. *mwambakua*) can be worn in the waist-fold of the loin-cloth. To achieve success in any undertaking, wear the roots of *shinde* (Kip.) or *kishinda wa shindani* (Kig.).

(6) Under this heading come those charms employed to combat black magic, and they are all protective.

(*a*) To enable you to see witch-doctors. (Tumbatu.)

They are usually invisible. Take leaves of *mchu* (Brugeria?) and *mchakati*. Pound these together and smear on your face and over your eyes. You will then see the wizards.

(*b*) To make a witch-doctor stand still until released, or to make them stand without being able further to approach your house, etc. (Tumbatu.)

Take leaves of *msufi* (cotton tree—eriodendron anfractuosum) and write on it three times السّاق با ساق (*asaki bi'saki*). Write it also on small pieces of paper. Wrap and sew these up in cloth, a leaf and a piece of paper, as many as you require to make your circle, and bury it in the ground where you wish the witch-doctors to be stopped. Write *asaki bi'saki* three times on another piece of paper, sew it into a cloth, make an armlet of it and wear it.

(*c*) To prevent djinns being sent by witch-doctors to worry you. (Tumbatu.)

Draw diagrams, shown in illustration, on a piece of paper, and your name, or that of your client, under it, and you or your client, as the case may be, whoever requires the protection, will wear it in an armlet on the arm. Should a witch-doctor send a djinn to you it will return and eat him.

While walking through sleeping villages at night, I have sometimes seen a curious phosphorescent patch on doors. I investigated this, and found that the bones of a certain fish which are charged with phosphorus had been fastened there. My donkey-boy told me it was placed there to keep evil spirits and wizards away.

(*d*) To dispossess witch-doctors of their clothes. (Pemba.)

Take the principal root (called the navel) of *mvuma nyuki* (Kig. and Kip. *mvuma*) and wrap it in calico with ambergris and sandalwood. Say "*Kiafu wal kuran el majid bali yabibbu*" and "*Idha zul zilat el aruzu zid*," seventy times each. Go to the place of the witch-doctors and hold the charm in front of your face. They will think you are a tree and hang their clothes on you. You can then run away with them.

Here are two magical formulæ of Mkame Mdume. The first is as follows:

(1) *Ukitaka kutumia Afriti katika Maafriti wa Suleiman bin Daud Alaihima assalam ukae faragha mahali safi na nguo zako safi na mwili wakosafi ufunge siku sabaa na wewe usome kulla siku marra wahedi waarbainina usiku usome sura kulhuwallahy marra elfu umia uhidaashara atakuja usiku ule watatu na watano na wasita Afriti yule uliomwita yeye na watu wake atakupa miadi yeye na watu wake.*

The first one reads in English: "If there be one who would wish to summon up and have at his bidding an Efreet of the Efreets of Solomon, the son of David, on whom be Peace, let him dwell apart in a clean place, clad in clean apparel and his person clean. Let him fast for seven days, and let him read every day forty-one times and at night one thousand one hundred and ten and one times the chapter of the Koran beginning 'Say He is one God.' There will come to him that night, the 3rd, the 5th and the 6th, the Efreet he has summoned, he and his people. He will do your bidding, he and his people."

(2) *Ukitaka kuondowa mtu wazimu au uchawi twaa kondoo waeili mweusi na mwekundu uwatundike uwafunge miguu uwatundike juu ya mti mkubwa wa zamani ulio na matawi makubwa uwachinje ukusanye damu yao tena uchukuwe maziwa na asali na maji uwandike dua kwa maji yale umuoshe, mgonjwa yule ikiwa niwazimu au uchawi atapona.*

The second, which is protective, means as follows: "If you want to remove madness or the effects of witchcraft from a man, take two sheep, one black and one red. Hang them up and tie their legs. Hang them on a tree, a big one and an old one, one with big branches. Cut their throats and collect their blood. Then take milk and honey and water and write 'Dua' with that water and wash him. That patient will be cured whether he be with madness or the effects of witchcraft."

The reasoning is probably as follows: Black and red are the colours of the men who may have worked the madness or put a charm on the patient. If they are killed and their blood put on the patient, their virtue or wholeness will be transferred to him.

BLACK MAGIC

Medicine, exorcism, white magic, all these are the province of the *waganga*, who are useful members of society and who may practise their calling openly.

We now come to consider that person of evil, the *mchawi*, or wizard, whose province is wholly evil and who is not at all popular, save with those who wish to call in his services to do evil to their enemies. This does not mean that the two are not sometimes combined.

Pemba has got a reputation in East Africa as the home of instruction for budding wizards. On a visit to Nossi Bé in Madagascar, I learnt that there, too, it was well known. The magic of Pemba is characterized by what is known as the guild system. The guilds (*chama*) are organized secret societies which have terrorism as their object. Different degrees have to be passed by the initiate to these guilds. The first is merely a test of nerves: on some suitable night the initiate will awake to hear the barking of dogs and the hooting of owls near his abode. When he ventures forth he may see or hear dark crouching figures passing about in the bush or undergrowth. Read in broad daylight this sounds tame, but it can be an extraordinarily eerie experience, as I know from personal knowledge.

The next step includes the actual entry to the outer circle of the guild, and at a meeting convened on the witches' heath, the initiate is required to promise a bag of rice and a goat. When this is forthcoming he is considered as a member of the guild.

Entrance to the inner circle is purchased by the provision of a child; the initiate or his sponsor is asked if he can "provide a man" (*tupa mtu*); it is said that the offering of an infant has to be made, and that the child is eaten by the guild. It may be said at once that there is a good deal of doubt as to whether this actually takes place, and most people consider it wholly improbable, as Pemba is well organized and administered, but in view of the secrecy observed by all classes in this respect, it is difficult to state definitely that this practice does not take place, as no inspection of dead bodies is required, but only a registration of the death. The registration of births is often more honoured in the breach than the observance, and a new-born child could probably be easily disposed of. All I can vouch for is that the candidate is asked if he can provide a man.

My information as to the procedure necessary to enter these guilds of witch-doctors is gathered from first hand. In 1922, accompanied by an Arab friend and disguised as an Arab, I had an opportunity of going as a prospective initiate to a meeting of a guild of witch-doctors. After a long ride through the night we met our guide at the edge of a plain of silver sand covered with cashew trees, called Gyinyingi, which is the witches' heath of Pemba. The night was inky black, but the silver sand of the plain made it possible for us to follow our guide fairly easily through the trees. As we went along I traced rough arrows on the sand with my stick at frequent intervals in order to be able to find the way in daylight; after we had gone a little way an owl hooted in the distance, which gave us rather a shock; the guide changed his direction and made in that whence the sound had come. After a few minutes he stopped again, an owl hooted so close and so suddenly that we were both badly startled, and did not realize at once that it was our guide who had made the call. An answer came from quite close at hand; the guide softly clapped his hands, making a hollow sound; answering claps came from nearby; the bush we were passing through became thicker. Suddenly somebody dropped from a tree with a rustle as he passed through the leafy branches; he brushed by us touching our clothes and had gone almost before we were aware of it; the whole atmosphere was extraordinarily uncanny. Then the whole place seemed alive with black, almost invisible forms; one could make out vaguely naked figures which plunged by into the undergrowth and were gone.

We came at last to a circular clearing, and at a sign from our guide squatted down. The hooting of owls became frequent; distant calls were answered nearby; with it was mixed the howling of dogs and incessant hollow clapping of hands on bare arms. Not a voice was to be heard, but rustling in the bushes and snapping of twigs indicated that there were a lot of people about. Our eyes were now thoroughly accustomed to our surroundings, and presently we made out the bent figure of an old man who came into the centre of the clearing. Behind him followed a procession of nude forms in single file; we could distinguish both men and women, and as they came they clapped their hands on their arms. They squatted round the clearing in a large circle; the old man addressed our guide and asked whether we were both there. Other sponsors were also asked if the initiates they were introducing were present, and the dialogue was as follows: Old man: "Is . . . there?" Answer: "He is here." "Has he come for good or evil?" "For good." "What does he bring?" "Nothing, but he will bring that which is usual." "A goat and a sack of rice?" "Even so." "Can he give a man?" (*Atavyeza kutupa mtu?*) It was this last question that confirmed for me the stories I had heard of a child being demanded. Our guide said that we could do no such thing, and there followed a muttered conversation between him, the old man, and some of his followers, and we were told to come again on the night of the New Year. Nothing, however, came of this, and I think it is probable that the guild had suspected something of my identity.

As we went back I looked for the arrow marks, but the guide, seeing me peering about, said that they had been erased. The guild had no intention of letting us know their meeting-place.

We asked to be taken to the invisible house, and Juma bin Hassan, our guide, led us off there. However, after a few minutes' walk a cock crew, and he informed us that at cock-crow the home and the wizards vanished!

The magic of the Hadimu of Zanzibar is characterized chiefly by the use of potent poisons, and by the fact that witch-doctors are credited with the powers of being able to keep leopards under control and to send them at will to do harm. Many stories are current concerning these practices, and I shall refer to them again shortly. Not only the natives, but also the Arabs firmly insist that the witch-doctors have these powers.

The magic of the Watumbatu as contracted with that of the Wahadimu shows much less trace of foreign influence. The latter people use Koranic charms to a very large extent, and make greater use of the numbers 3 and 4 and their total.

All sorts of wonderful powers are attributed to witch-doctors; they can become invisible at will, can pass through a ring, or ride upon a millet straw. They can turn themselves into animals or raise the dead. They can control wild animals and send them to do harm. They can provide you with most potent medicines to kill anyone.

For many months I tried to go and see a witch-dance in Zanzibar, but the difficulties seemed insuperable. However, I finally managed to do so by preserving the strictest secrecy and confiding only in two trustworthy people, and by donning the disguise of an Arab.

Hearing in a roundabout way that witch-doctors were going to dance at a certain place in order to cause the death of a sick man near, who would not pay Rs. 100 to save his life, I proceeded about midnight in the direction the dance was to be held. I was wearing the white *kanzu* of an Arab, barefooted, with a cap and a beard and a brown face. I also, to enter into the spirit of the thing, wore a charm to render myself invisible and a charm to enable the user to see the witch-doctors.

As I was proceeding in the direction the performance was to be held, I saw some way ahead a pale blue light go vertically up in the air and with no report seem to burst and fade away. Soon after I heard a weird calling as of dogs, and the hooting of owls, and presently came on some lonely mango and cotton trees, which appeared to be the scene of the dance. There was a species of "follow-my-leader" in progress: a chain of about a dozen young men and women dressed in black were following each other silently but quickly in and out round the trees, uttering no words, but slapping their bare arms in a peculiar way, and every now and then barking or hooting.

Not only did the barking and hooting come from the procession, but every now and then it would be from the trees, and forms would drop with a rustle through the leaves and join in the procession darting about among the trees. Although I was right in the midst of it in a very white *kanzu*, on a moonlight night, not the slightest notice was taken of me, and I stayed watching for over an hour, till the procession moved away in the distance, though I could still hear the clapping, the barking and the hooting.

The native who was with me then accompanied me to my canoe on the shore and went home. When he got home (he told me after) he washed his face and went to bed. Presently he heard the hooting and barking just outside and turned out again. He could see nothing, however, as he had washed the charm off his face!

The end of it all was that the proposed victim got off on payment of Rs. 100.

I once nearly got to a performance where the wizard was to turn into an ox, but the arrangements unfortunately fell through!

It is very easy to make too much out of witchcraft, but it is just as simple to underestimate its power over a people who emphatically believe in it.

Indeed many doctors who live among natives are convinced that these wizards can work evil for this very reason, and once in Nairobi a doctor told me the case of a man who came to him one day and told him that he had had witchcraft put on him and would die on a certain day at two p.m. My friend examined him, found him perfectly fit and told him so. Nevertheless, as the day approached he grew weaker and weaker, though for no apparent reason. On the day in question he was so bad that my friend and another doctor put him to bed and asked the name of the wizard. It was a witch, and having brought her there they told her to remove the curse. She refused, so they tied a rope round her neck and throwing one end over a tree, pulled on it. When the old lady's toes were off the ground, she signified her willingness to remove the curse, and two p.m. being near, she was hurried in and made some passes over the man, who was really at the point of death. However, he got up after this and walked away as well as he had ever been.

Early in 1921, a leopard made its appearance in my district, and in a few nights accounted for eighteen goats. I went out to try and get it, and sat up all night for it in a tree over a kill, but it was of no use, and the natives and even the Arabs, especially two very intelligent men, said I might have saved myself the trouble, as an *Mchawi* had *fuga-ed* (tamed) the leopard and it would go where he told it.

One of my Arab friends (who knew the district and natives well) gave me the names of the responsible people, but inquiries would have been, of course, useless.

This is firmly believed by all people. They say that the Wahadimu witch-doctors alone have the power to do it. They hide these leopards in holes or caves in the bush, tied up, and then send them to kill their enemies' goats. On exploring a cave at Kufile in the south of the island, I was shown a dish with the remnants of food inside one of the inner entrances, and was told that this was placed there by the leopard's master.

The Cadi of Mkokotoni told me a story of a leopard's activities. He said that a few years ago in Chwaka the same thing happened and many goats were killed. So he tried to find the culprit. This apparently came to the ears of the Wachawi concerned, for on opening his door one morning the Cadi was confronted with the leopard. Having no gun, he slammed the door and went to the window—but there was the leopard again. So he had to wait in till it went. Having received information as to who the Wachawi were, he sent for them and took them to the mosque and made them swear "*Wallai, Billai, Tallai, Wallai El Athimu*" (a peculiarly sacred oath) that they did not control the leopards. They must have perjured themselves, for the Cadi informed me that two days afterwards they were both drowned fishing, and after a time a leopard was found dead in the bush.

Black magic is usually either homœopathic or contagious. An example of the former is the common practice of making images of your enemy in bees-wax and damaging them, so that your enemy suffers corresponding hurt, and of the latter, working him harm through something that has been in contact with him or part of him, e.g., hair, nails, teeth, clothes.

Thus the Pemba method of wrapping up a live fowl in a cloth of your enemy's and burying it, is contagious magic, and the death of the fowl acting through the cloth will kill your enemy.

Some time ago, too, the Government wanted porters for the mainland, and letters were sent to say so. In a Pemba village the Wachawi were consulted, and they advised sewing up the lips of a goat with proper invocations, and the fact that the goat could not speak would prevent the Government likewise from doing so. However, the Government apparently was not sufficiently like the goat to be stopped talking, and another demand came. It is alleged that then a baby's lips were sewn up, and this was investigated, and a child was certainly found buried under the eaves of a hut where the informer said it would be found, but there was not enough evidence to convict anyone of murdering it. This was homœopathic magic.

Names, too, can be used by unscrupulous persons

to work you harm. On a visit to a cave in Kizimkazi, the *Mwana vyale* (custodian of the sacred places) directed my attention to a pillar of stone. " Hear the story of Miza Miza," he said. " Many, many years ago, a man of Kizimkazi took to wife a young girl of Jembiyani. There was a great wedding, and people feasted for seven days. Now he had another and elder wife, who soon grew jealous at the attentions paid to her young rival. One day though, she bade her come with her, to draw water at this cave. Miza was warned by two other women, that whatever she did, she must not call anyone by name in the cave, or the devil would destroy them.

" Down the hill they came, the elder woman leading the way. At the bottom here, she stopped, and rapidly filled her jar, and then told Miza to do likewise.

" The girl obediently stooped, and commenced her task, and the other wife climbed quickly up the slope. When she reached the top Miza was kneeling, and about to raise her jar, to put it on her head. ' Miza, Miza,' called the woman, and Miza knew at once that doom was before her. ' All right,' she replied, ' you have done your worst, but go in peace.' They were the last words she spoke; she started weeping, but never moved again. Soon her husband and others found out, and came to see what had befallen her. They found her turned to stone. The tears coursed down her graven cheeks for seven days, but all they could do was of no avail. They slaughtered white goats down here, and called in all the magic they could. Miza, as you see, remains here to this day, as she knelt so many years ago, and still every year the people of Jembiyani, her people, come here and make a feast in honour of that poor girl who was destroyed by the jealousy of a wicked woman."

I examined the stone closely, and with a little imagination, one can make out the features. The nose, the eyes, and the shoulders and arms are there, though to be sure Miza is now no beauty. " No, age has not improved her, as it does not improve any of us," remarked my guide when I mentioned this.

The following are a few recipes for black magic:

(1) To kill your enemy. (Tumbatu.)

Draw the diagram shown on a piece of brass and write the name of your enemy below it. Bury the brass in the fire. Your enemy will die a lingering death.

(2) To kill your enemy—another method. (Tumbatu.)

Draw these symbols and write your enemy's name on a papaw, pick the papaw up and dash it to the ground. Your enemy's demise will be sudden.

5555 55-5

-.555 55--

(3) To send a snake to bite anyone. (Tumbatu.)

Draw the diagram on a piece of *makuti* (coco-nut leaf) and write on it the name of your enemy, hold it over burning incense and say, " I am sending you to so-and-so to bite him." Then put it in the bush, and it will change into a snake and go and do its work.

(4) To make your enemies fall down unconscious. (Hadimu.)

Take leaves of *mpamba*, *mdume* (Kiun. *chomeko*, order Malvaceæ—urena lobata), *kongwa* (order Commelynaceæ, Commelyny benghalencis), *kitumbwi tumbwi* (order Safundaceæ, Cardiospermum halicacabrum), *dumguza* (order Malvaceæ, Thespesia populuea). Grind them together and put in the hollow stem of the papaw leaf. Get as near to your enemy as you can. Blow it in his direction and he will collapse unconscious.

How long he will remain so, I do not know!

The following magic herbal recipes are used in Pemba:

(1) Take the stems of *mpofuo macho* (that which blinds the eyes, Kip. *muam*, Kig. *muamtu*) and squeeze the juice out. Mix it with rice. He who eats it will die. The antidote is *tumbwi*, a coco-nut in the stage between *dafu* and *kokoche*.

(2) Take a *bêche de mer* and the leaves of *mfaggio* (Kip. *mkama kuuna*, Kig. *mzima kiwanda*), *ubondwe* (Kig. *mwagiliza*) and wild date palm. Roast and grind on stones. Take the ashes and put them on a tree in a plantation. All of that kind will die.

(3) Grind the leaves of *mwagiliza* (Kig. *mchinja uzia*) with chillies and mix with water. This sprinkled on the faces of people you dislike is a powerful irritant.

(4) Take leaves of *mtakawa* (Kig. *Muopoa kiale*) and in each leaf wrap three thorns of the wild date palm. Tie them up in calico and throw them where people wash. They will turn to ants and bite them.

(5) This is a very celebrated recipe and said to be much used. Take seven leaf stalks of *mtope tope* (Kig. *mchakwe*, Kig. *mcha kuzi*). Cut a piece off a disused beehive and a piece of *koa*, burn them all and grind the ashes. Smear on seat of the *buzi* (instrument for grinding coco-nut).

If anyone commits adultery with your wife, he will get syphilis. The antidote to this is for the husband to eat cooked *mtama*, covered with *mkungu* (almond) leaves. He must then cover the face of the sick man and urinate over him. Ground leaves of *mtu nguja* should be applied to the sore. Only the husband can do this.

Charms can also be buried on the road to harm only the person for whom intended, and I have one which was buried for me. It was a section of bamboo stuffed with roots.

The powers of wizards are hereditary, but initiation into a "Guild" (*chama*) when one becomes a follower, but not a principal, can be purchased as described above.

There seems little doubt that dead bodies are sought after and perhaps eaten, but it is certain that they are used to prepare the magic poison known as *unga wa ndere*. This is prepared by hanging a corpse up by the heels over a bowl, and a particular juice is said to drop from the neck which is dried and used as a poison.

Children are peculiarly subject to the attention of devils and devil doctors. If they are albino, it is said that before the birth the mother slept without a light and the devil came and changed the unborn child. If they are pale, they are especially subject to the attentions of devils and their faces are blacked.

It is also said that twins and malformed children, being both abnormal occurrences, are the work of the devil and are killed, and for my part I should not like to say that this is not so, as shortly before I left Zanzibar, a Sheha reported to me he had found two baby graves about a month old, and that he had had no notification of birth or death. Investigations were made and the bodies exhumed, but nothing could be proved except the non-registration. But the non-registration of death is so unusual that it seemed to point to the children having been done away with.

Other magic poisons used are *mumyani*[1] or mummified blood, which is imported, and a composition of the dried and pounded stomachs of the chameleon and a large skink-like lizard, called the *guru-guru*, both of which are classed with the owl as affairs of the devil. This is called *punju*. In Pemba, where the

[1] *Mumiani* is obtainable from the shops of the Indians and is used as a medicine, especially in the case of fractures. The broken bones are set and then the ends "ground" together. Cooked *mumiani* is then inserted in cuts made round the fracture and it is set in splints. The patient also takes *mumiani* in his food.

When I was in Nairobi in 1926 with my boy Zayidi bin Bukheti, an Mtumbatu, he informed me that he had been shown, in the heart of the town, the house where *mumiani* was made. It is a general belief of the Swahili that the substance is of European or Parsee manufacture. "How else," I have been asked, "could men's blood be obtained and *mumiani* sold openly in shops?"

guru-guru does not exist, *punju* is made of the stomach of a small burrowing lizard, called ***kiuma*** *mbuzi* or *gonga-gonga*, the tail of the green whip snake, *ukukwi* and the tail of the chameleon. The Pemba antidote is a ground-up concoction of Cassytha filiformis and *mwagiliza* (Kig. *mchinja uzia*) mixed with ghee.

During my investigations into witchcraft I also succeeded in obtaining four books of magic, full of various recipes and written in Arabic and Swahili: one a big one, is well written, but the others show poor penmanship. They are full of diagrams, magic squares, etc., the big one especially, and the magic squares I shall deal with when considering the use of numbers.

This book is said by the Oriental Manuscript Department of the British Museum to have been written between 1800 and 1830, a great age for a native book. It is written entirely by hand, and the compiler apparently died before finishing his work. It is remarkable for the excellence of the handwriting. (It should be noted that books of magic are generally written with each letter separately, and not in the cursive form.) It consists mainly of medicinal white magic, but there is some black. Many of the charms give directions for pronouncing words in a certain way to produce the desired effect. For instance, it directs that if you wish the husband of the woman you are attached to, to kill your rival, you must enunciate, in the way prescribed, certain formulæ against him.

A smaller one is said by the same authorities to have been written at the end of the last century; it consists of a jumble of charms, magic squares and Koranic texts.

A printed book of magic much used in the town is called *Shems el maarifa el kubra*.

CHAPTER XLIII

NUMBERS

In all the magic and medicine given in previous chapters, it will be noticed that numbers are much used, and that certain numbers frequently recur.

Those most used are 3, 4 and 7, and these have always been considered perfect numbers; they are used time and again in all sorts of different books and places, e.g., the Bible. They were the sacred numbers of the Chaldeans, and possibly were brought by the ancient Persians to Zanzibar. They are also connected, for $3+4=7$. Perhaps for the same reason use is also made of 3, 6 and 9 in one recipe. I do not understand the use of 40, though that too is an important number and occurs in several places in the Bible.

Two of the books of magic I have (one particularly) make use of a large variety of magic squares, most of them squares of 3, 4, or 7 figures each way, and the most popular one is the 15 square.

4	9	2
3	5	7
8	1	6

Other squares are 34, 56, 72, 129 (3 and 4 square), 78, 124, 57, 998, 92, 67, 177, 231, and so on, but many of them are not perfect squares.

There is, besides, an endless variety of talismanic signs, etc.

The squares can all be solved by the use of the following table:

A.	ا	1	S	ص	90	H	ه	5
B.	ب	2	Th. hard	ض	800	Y	ي	10
T.	ت	400	T	ط	9		١	1
Th. soft	ث	500	Th. hard	ظ	900		٢	2
J.	ج	3	A	ع	70		٣	3
H	ح	8	Gh.	غ	1000		۴ , ٤	4
KH	خ	800	F	ف	80		۵ , ٥	5
D	د	4	Q	ق	100		٦	6
Dh	ذ	700	K	ك	20		٧	7
R.	ر	200	L	ل	30		٨	8
Z	ز	7	M	م	40		٩	9
S	س	60	N	ن	50		٥ , ٠	0
SH	ش	300	W	و	6			

Figures and letters are used indifferently and in conjunction.

Letters as figures are used in combination, e.g.: ط ج=39.

Very often the dots under letters are left out and letters badly formed.

The two following figures I am unable to decipher:

˥	┘	T
⊢	┌	—
L	┘	⊥

⌒	∠	∠	١٨٧	>
⌒	⌒	>	<	T
<	/	ʎ	١	)

DIVINATION

No one having any important undertaking on hand would fail to consult a fortune-teller first.

There are two methods of fortune-telling on sand, and the stars may also be consulted.

The fortune-teller's apparatus consists of a small board, some fine sand (generally brought from Pemba Island, off the north-east coast, as there the waves are so rough that the sand is exceptionally fine) and a stiffish piece of grass or coco-nut leaf.

The sand is first smoothed all over the board thinly, but to cover it completely, and the one whose fortune is being told traces his finger over it asking what he wishes to know or expressing his desire.

This done the fortune-teller smoothes the sand over again, and to tell "*Kibuzi*," the simplest form, he draws six lines like this:

not counting the arches as he does it. When the six are drawn he starts ticking the arches off in twos from the bottom one and the right-hand side, thus:

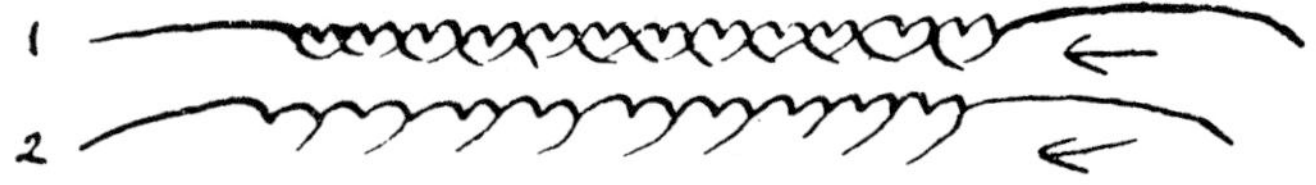

and so on upwards. If there is one over as in the bottom line it is said "*Kusimama*" (to stand); if it goes out evenly as in No. 2, it is said "*Kupita*" (to pass).

Each of the six lines refers to something, thus:

(1) *Nafsi*, self. What state one's inner self is in is told by this.

(2) *Saiili*, question. This line answers the questions asked.

(3) *Mji*, town. This concerns the state of the town you are interested in.

(4) *Haja*, desire. The fulfilment or not of your wish is decided by this line.

(5) *Nakia*, enemy. This tells you if you have an enemy.

(6) *Ghaibu*, distance. Either of time or place. How far off the fulfilment of your wish is or how far away your enemy is, etc.

The key is as follows: If 1, 2, 5, 6 from the top pass out they are good. If 3 and 4 "stand" they are good.

The other method, called *Ramli*, is more complicated. There are sixteen stars alternatively male and female (the female are said to be the wives of the male), each with a symbol. Sixteen lines are drawn with arches, which are ticked off in twos as in *Kibuzi*, four lines go to a star. If a line "stands" it counts =, if it "passes" it counts –. I think the following list of stars with symbols and meanings will make the system clear:

Shemsi Hathihi	– – = =	male	good luck
Mkewe kibla Hela hathihi	= – = –	female	good luck
Zuhura (Venus)	= = – –	male	good for wedding
Mkewe kausa	– – = –	female	good for travelling or marriage
Utharidi Hathihi	= = = =	male	trouble, words, quarrels
Mkewe Jetemai	= – – =	female as male	bad luck
Kamari	= = – =	male	good for thieves and cheats; but bad for others
Mkewe tariki	– – – –	female	same
Zohali Hathihi	= = = –	male	very bad people find this a lucky star
Mkewe sini cafu	– = = –	female	very bad people find this a lucky star
Mshitara Hathihi	– = = =	male	good star for travellers and performing good deeds
Mkewe u tubatu dahela	= – – –	female	good star for travellers and performing good deeds
Mirihi Hathihi	= – = =	male	war star
Mkewe nakiu	– = – –	female	war star
Harifa Hathihi	– – – =	male	discord (*fitina*)
Mkewe kabuthu elharia	– = – =	female	discord (*fitina*)

In addition to these, as I have said, the stars are consulted, and no one will carry out a private undertaking unless the moon is in a good quarter. I say "no one," but this should be qualified to mean no one who has adopted or heard of astrology, for the system was introduced into Zanzibar by the Arabs.

The names of the stars and their significance is given below:

Names of Stars.	*Remarks.*
Sharatini	Neither good nor bad.
El Buteni	Neither good nor bad. Perhaps divorce—not very good.
Thureia	Good. Kilimia—Pleiades.
Dabarani	Neither good nor bad.
Hakaa	Neither good nor bad. Illness.
Hanaa	Neither good nor bad. Illness.
Tharaa	Good.
Nasara	Good.
Tarufa	Good.
Jabuha	Good.
Zabura	Good.
Sarufa	Good.
El awah	Very good.
Smaku	Very bad.
Elerofa	Good.
Zabanane	Good.
Akiliti	Good.
Shola	Good.
Naaimu	Very good.
Bildah	Neither good nor bad.
Saadah Zabihuh	Very bad indeed. Death.
Saadah Baradah	Good.
El Akhbir	Neither good nor bad.
Saadah Sorudi	Superlatively good.
Furadha El Makadamu	Neither good nor bad.
Furadha El Muaheru	Neither good nor bad.
Batini el Huti (chewa)	Very good indeed.

CHAPTER XLIV

THE PEOPLE OF MAKUNDUCHI

In the south-east of Zanzibar Island is a large village called Makunduchi, the population of which is, according to the native census of 1924, 1,190 adult males, 1,531 adult females, 615 boys and 575 girls. Total 3,911. The number of huts in 1,579. The name Makunduchi is derived by the inhabitants from the name of a village on the mainland, opposite the south part of the island and called Konduchi, whence they state they came.

North of Makunduchi is another village called Jembiyani; this village shares with Makunduchi the peculiar dialect of Kihadimu, already illustrated.

Legend has it that many years ago an Arab visited the shore before there were settlers there, and while waiting for his slave, took off his *jambiya*, or curved dagger, which every Arab wears fastened to a belt round the waist, and rested. When he went he forgot the dagger, which was subsequently found by a native coming to the shore to get firewood.

Not knowing what it was, he went back to his village in the interior and told his people. An old man recognized it as an Arab *jambiya*, and it was left where it was on the shore, to avoid any charge of theft being made should the Arab return. He never did return, and for years and years the *jambiya* was left there, the spot being always kept clear of bush and grass. The *jambiya* finally perished entirely, but the spot is still kept clear and the village known as Jembiyani, or the "place of the dagger."

The population of Jembiyani is 465 males, 565

females, 238 boys, 218 girls. Total 1,486. The number of huts is 593.

These villages are of exceptional interest, not only on account of the dialect but because certain other curious customs are observed there which are known to no other part of the Sultanate of Zanzibar. The people are Wahadimu, but different in many ways to the rest of that tribe. They are remarkably law-abiding, and many display unusual intelligence.

Makunduchi is the only place in the Sultanate where transport is carried on with camels. These are mainly the property of the Indians, who are known as Makumbaro. With the exception of some in Zanzibar city, Makunduchi is the only place with a settlement of these Indians, whose home is in Cutch and Kathiawar. The word is derived from the Sanskrit Kumbhakar, a potter, and there are about thirty families of them settled there. They live in great friendliness with the Wahadimu, are very obliging people, and bring up their families in the country. The children speak Kihadimu as fluently as the natives. The women of Makunduchi and Jembiyani make coloured mats with a fringe from the fronds of the wild date palm. This fringe is called *ndevu*, or beard, and is not made on the mats of other villages. Many of them make a good type of pottery.

I now turn to a description of the customs which make Makunduchi so different to any other place in Zanzibar.

The dance *nyange*. This exorcizing dance is played by women, the orchestra only consisting of men. The instruments used are a drum on three legs called *mrungura*, a small barrel-drum (*chapuo*), a brass gong (*upatu*), the native clarionet (*zomari*) and another three-legged but bottomless drum (*mshindo*). Under a *makuti* (palm leaf) shelter, crowds of women dance backwards and forwards. Under the shelter and at one side is a small tent, made of the coloured cloths the women wear, in which sits the woman possessed of the devil the dancers seek to exorcize.

Every now and then the women dance out at one end of the shelter in the sunlight, to fall back again together into the shelter. The movement is extraordinarily reminiscent of the waves on a sandy shore, as they dash up, break into foam and catch the sunlight, to fall back again into the unbroken sea.

About a dozen of the women carry iron tridents affixed to long handles, one or two have swords, others ivory-handled knives, a few carry model *ngalawas* (outrigger canoes), and some model paddles in size too big in proportion for the canoes. Canoes and paddles are painted red with wavy white lines on them.

In Zanzibar dances special food has to be provided for each devil; the appropriate nourishment in this case consists of dates, cardamon, raisins, cinnamon, white bread (called at Makunduchi *pufudo*), pumpkins and pomegranates.

The devil cannot understand the local dialect, and can only make its wants felt in such incomprehensible syllables as: *Zijejera zizejejera Nzujajajajira.* The former is said to denote a desire for food and the latter for water.

The devil *nyange* is said to be contracted only at sea, and the result of inquiries as to its origin was that many years ago three women went down to the shore to catch *kidagaa* (white bait). There they saw a devil riding towards them in a canoe and holding in his hand a trident, and at the sight of him were afflicted with madness. No one knew how the devil, stranger as he was to their pantheon, could be dealt with, but the remedy was revealed in the night in a dream, and the dance *nyange* is the result.

Apart from this dance being an interesting example of homœopathic magic, no one can fail to be struck by the likeness of the sea-devil with a trident (a weapon unknown in Zanzibar and used by the people of Makunduchi only in this dance) to the story of Poseidon, and there can be little doubt that it is a relic of the worship of that deity, brought by the Greeks of old. These jealous gods were of the same nature as the spirits of the Africans, and one can easily imagine that to a simple fisher-folk the worship of Poseidon would make a strong appeal.

The madness caused by the sight of the devil is reminiscent of Pan, but I am unaware if similar madness was caused by the sight of the other nature gods.

Pungwa and *shomoo*. *Pungwa* is the passive form of *punga*, and *kupunga pepo* means to exorcize a devil.

Owing to the activities of witch-doctors, and the evil they may do and plant about the country for the unsuspecting traveller, the people of Makunduchi have evolved a guild of devil-hunters.

Prior to the hunt, *pungwa* is played all night to get the " pack " into the proper psychic state to enable them to trace the evil spirits left about by less scrupulous people. Men only take part in the ceremony, which is performed in much secrecy, to the accompaniment of two drums, *mshindo* and *chapuo*.

In the morning the *shomoo* takes place. Carrying such exorcizing implements as a *pini* (a cow's horn, with two bells attached, and stuffed with roots and a dog's nose, as a dog is a good tracker) and *usinga* (a cow's tail affixed to a stick), the devil-hunters search all over the countryside, now running about, now crawling, now crouching, but always together. When they get a scent they follow it up, and digging with their hands, smelling with their noses, they finally unearth charms buried by the witch-doctors, and in which an *mzuka* (evil spirit) is imprisoned to do harm to the passer-by. A man accompanies them with a bucket full of herbs and water, of which the hunters partake or with which they are sprinkled.

The *Wamavua*. The *Wamavua* of Makunduchi have now practically died out. At their most, they consisted of about twenty-five individuals, members of a few families who were known by that name, and followed the cult of rain spirits of the same name.

Their habits were peculiar: they wore no head-dress, never slept on beds, and had a white flag tied to the outside of their houses. They originally only married among themselves, and only the eldest son or daughter belonged to the guild.

Their place of worship was a cave, called *genge la mavua*, to which they went to intercede with the rain spirits.

They entered the cave on hands and knees clad in a short white *kanzu* only, and kneeling or prostrating themselves round a small circle of stones and fragments, in the middle of which was a stick, to which white cloth was tied from time to time, they burnt incense on a small fire of coco-nut shells, and prayed to the spirits for rain or to avert sickness. Their food consisted chiefly of *chuwali*, a mollusc common on the shore, and which appears to be a species of *murex*.

Their cave was always kept swept and tidy, and though deserted for many years, was still tidy when I visited it, though the white cloth had almost entirely rotted away with age.

The best known of them was an old lady named Mame Hodi, whose grandson, Karibu bin Hodi, and another ex-member of the *wamavua*, informed me they had seen her walk out over the sea, where she remained for three days. She is also remembered as a teller of the future, and said to have foretold many events, including an outbreak of smallpox. She never failed to obtain rain.

The *wamavua* spirits which, unlike many Zanzibar devils, can travel by sea, were for that reason in all probability and like the djinns imported from some other country. They are now said to have left, so their worship has broken up.

Naoruz, or *Siku ya Mwaka*. In addition to the customs observed on New Year's Day by the rest of the Wahadimu, Watumbatu and Wapemba, described in Chapter XXVI, the people of Makunduchi have two other customs. They build a small hut, or *banda*, of dried coco-nut leaves and put two people inside. They then set fire to the hut and throw stones into the flames. The two men are supposed to remain inside, but in reality escape unseen through the back of the hut.

After this the old men dance round the grave of a bygone patriarch whose name is forgotten, but who, like Mame Hodi mentioned above, could walk the waves at will.

Tanga Tanga. As an instance of the way in which new devils become known, may be recited a story of Paje, the next village north of Jembiyani.

Recently (1923) a large buoy marked *Bajang* was washed ashore there; it probably came from Java. Emitting a hollow sound when tapped, it soon gave the natives the impression that it was the dwelling-place of a devil, and as it was quite a new species, a new dance was invented in its honour. The devil and its dance were called *Tanga Tanga*, obviously an onomatopœism from the sound the buoy makes.

CHAPTER XLV

SWAHILI PSYCHOLOGY

A STUDY of the chapters preceding this will give many a clue to the psychology of the native. In this I purpose chiefly to indicate the lessons that may be learnt from them.

In order to learn anything of the character of natives, sympathy with them and unbounded patience is necessary. One must endeavour to " think black." These are the principal desiderata, but a knowledge of their language and of something of the subject under discussion is also important, and, above all, one must never betray disbelief in their beliefs. If one has these attributes, one will generally find that, with a little lead in the desired direction, much information will be forthcoming.

In this way particulars of customs, magic, folk-lore, songs, dances, etc., will readily be obtained. For the rest a close observation of them, a study of the cases in which natives are concerned, and a hundred and one other little incidences of daily life will give the clue to their character and their outlook on life.

Psychology in Folk-lore, etc. Many sidelights on the native's character may be seen in his folk-lore, and it is not necessary for me here to give more than a few indications of the points that may be looked for. In stories will be seen, of course, that there is a great leaning to sexuality, but that, on the other hand, a good moral is appreciated. Cunning is always applauded, sometimes if it is criminal, but the wicked generally come to a bad end. Parables are favourites with the native, and in dealing with him one frequently uses them in order to bring a point home. A form of reasoning favourite with them is the *reductio ad absurdum*.

The lesson indicated in the proverbs is generally caution and deliberation combined with warning to avoid unnecessary trouble. The native's sense of justice, and his somewhat childlike simplicity, is clearly indicated in his folk-lore. From the study of the riddles and art, one sees that he has a strong imagination. His explanation of natural phenomena indicate total lack of scientific reasoning; cause is rarely properly connected with effect, or rather the real cause, but man must have some explanation, so it is invented (anything may be believed provided it is suggested by the herd).

Childhood. It is hardly necessary to say that to get a more or less true idea of the native child one must look for it in a spot not habitually brought into contact with civilization, and the native child in his natural surroundings is truly attractive, as well as being interesting.

As a general rule he will be found to be shy but not frightened, for fear of things material may be almost said to be non-existent; he grows up with a natural fear of the unknown—a something that must be constantly propitiated to be appeased. The devil world is so real and vivid to his adults that it can hardly be less so to the child who is born with these ideas inherent in him, ideas strengthened by outside influence from his earliest days. It is but natural that superstition and fear of the unknown should become part of his nature when it is realized that they are made to govern most of his doings of every-day life, and even his childish aches and pains are "charmed away."

In spite of his natural shyness, which is portrayed in his big wondering eyes, the native child is remarkably precocious, mainly due to the fact that from the time he can crawl his parents leave him to his own resources, and he discovers the dangers and trials of childhood for himself. This early independence tends to sharpen his wits and intelligence. Elsewhere in this book have been described the native games and toys, and when it is remembered that the native child is the sole manufacturer of most of his playthings, it gives one a good idea of his natural capabilities. There is no doubt whatever that he is intelligent and quick to learn, but this, unfortunately, does not increase with his years. When puberty is reached the consciousness of sexual desire, which has lain dormant but been inevitably fostered in the home, is actually active even at that early age, and begins its work of absorbing all other interests, and starting to become the hub of existence. This is hardly to be wondered at when it is realized that the native child, far from being sheltered from knowledge of life, is brought up in an atmosphere teeming with sexuality, and therefore these matters enter into his thoughts and conversation from his earliest days.

Sex. Sex plays such a large part in the life of the natives that, however unpleasant the subject may be, it seems necessary to give it proportionate emphasis. I have elsewhere quoted a remark of Bishop Steere's, that girls are thought old enough for sexual intercourse at the age of nine or ten, and the conversation even of small children often turns on sex. This is scarcely to be wondered at when it is made the central feature of their lives, and no restraint is placed on such talk or actions by their parents.

The puberty rites of both boys and girls are entirely centred on sexual matters, and the songs have as their subject sexual intercourse. The central feature of marriage is sexual gratification, most of the dances are sexual, many of the tales are concerned with sexual subjects, and even magic is used to further sexual wishes; sexual desire is responsible for much of the crime, so that the whole of the native's life may be said to be bound up in this subject.

In *Nyago* and *Msondo* dances young girls are

taught by women how to behave in sexual intercourse; the motions of the women during these dances can only be described as revolting; a fair notion, though by no means an extensive one, of these motions is known to anyone who has seen the *Manyema* dance, which is played in public. Girls are taught also how to be seductive, and instructed in the way to carry themselves; the chief features of beauty to a native are buttocks, breasts and bearing.

Men may be said to be always ready for sexual intercourse, on walks, at wells, and everywhere. It is said that most natives fulfil their desires at least once or even twice in twenty-four hours; it may be also noted that the female desire is as keen as the male.

Under these circumstances, it is not surprising that prostitution is common, and that there is general immorality of both sexes, particularly among the Swahilis and freed slaves.

Polygamy and frequent divorce are no doubt contributory factors to this state of affairs, and infidelity in married life is the rule rather than the exception. Among these town-living women there is great dislike to child-bearing, and figures in a recent census in Zanzibar are very illuminating in this direction, as they show the minute percentage of children among the Swahilis near and in the towns.

The percentage is very much higher among the native tribes. This state of things has been commented on by other writers on Zanzibar, notably Burton.

Before closing this chapter, a note should be made of the fact that old men beyond the physical act still retain their sexual desires, and many of them have women in their household as masseuses (to massage = *kukanda*).

As regards unnatural offences, sodomy is infrequent; there are occasional cases of men living as women and even wearing women's clothes.

I have only become aware of two cases of

bestiality with a donkey and a ewe respectively. Incest is not uncommon.

Emotions

Fear. This is the strongest emotion felt by the natives, and is responsible for many strange customs and beliefs. Fear of the unknown—death, illness, thunder and the elements generally. But there is little fear of that which is understood. Thus it may be that a man will not fear death if he knows how it is coming to him—if he can connect cause and effect. There are frequent instances of cases in which Swahilis have not feared either corporal or capital punishment, because they can, in these cases, connect the effect with the cause. They must not be considered courageous, indeed they are far from it, but they will regard things that they can know and understand, and which would terrify other people, with a greater indifference than say the suspected presence of devils.

Love. Love as understood by us is a rare phenomenon in Zanzibar, though it is by no means non-existent. Love of a father for his children is, however, more common than that of husband for wife and vice versa. As a general rule fathers show more affection towards their children than do mothers, though instances of the latter showing intense devotion are by no means lacking.

As divorce is so easy of accomplishment, it becomes easier to separate the cases of real affection between husband and wife, and I know but few cases where marriages are of very long standing, though in the few I know there is intense understanding and affection between the parties, although in some cases the husband has other and younger wives.

Hate. Hate is rarely violent; as a general rule the native is not capable of a deep enough feeling to enable him to hate thoroughly. He is very easy going and tolerant. Dislike is frequent, but I have never heard a native express hate for anyone.

Joy. Joy is an emotion frequently expressed by natives, but usually at only simple things. The native is at his best when he is holiday-making. *Ngomas*, feasts, marriages, funerals even, all these induce joy.

He feels content, if he has enough money, with a wife and a home. As regards employment, while many work well and I think enjoy it, I do not think that lack of it, provided they are equipped with the aforesaid money, wife and home, causes any depression.

Grief. Grief is only seriously felt by a few. Loss of a wife induces but a very temporary grief, and while a child may cause more it is soon over. The native is happy by nature, and adversity cannot depress him for long. This is probably due to his fatalistic attitude to life.

Jealousy. Jealousy is usually sudden and, while it lasts, excessive, generally causing the native to lose complete control of himself. Such jealousy is usually the result of a husband or wife finding the partner paying more attention than he or she considers right to someone else.

Anger. The native is subject to sudden fits of anger, which subside as quickly as they arise. His temper when it arises is almost uncontrollable.

Disgust. Disgust is rarely exhibited. Bad smell, bad food, disgusting sights produce no expression of repulsion from the native. Anything that is ceremonially unclean may, however, induce disgust.

Curiosity. Curiosity is very strong in natives. Though good at concealment of their emotion, they can rarely abstain from a desire to investigate, to such a degree as their courage will allow them, anything new.

Self-Assertion and Self-Abasement. The native shows plenty of the former to those whom he considers his inferiors, and too much of the latter, which, however, is often assumed, to those he knows to be his superiors.

Gratitude. Gratitude is practically unknown. The native is never really thankful for anything. Anything that they do for each other is done as a matter of course or as a matter of duty almost by instinct. There is no Bantu word to express thanks.

Instincts

Gregariousness. The native of Zanzibar and Pemba is, for the most part, a thoroughly gregarious animal. But a study of the types of villages previously described will show to what degree each tribe varies. Among the Wahadimu it is more of a family instinct, though in its widest sense, among the Wapemba it is also family, but somewhat narrower, while among the Watumbatu it has come to be a tribal instinct. Natives hate being alone. Solitary confinement is the worst punishment that can be inflicted on them, and unless they can help it they do not travel alone, particularly at night.

The only cases one gets of solitariness are among the Wahadimu, when old men will sometimes leave their villages and live alone or with perhaps a wife in solitude in the bush. It seems to be also an instinct with those suffering from infectious diseases, particularly smallpox, to isolate themselves. This applies particularly to the Wahadimu.

Thus as a rule anyone who breaks away from the herd is apt to be considered unusual, perhaps even a menace, and to be credited with supernatural powers, i.e., to be in alliance with devils or to be a wizard.

Reproduction. The reproductive instinct has been debased to a large extent to the simple desire to gratify sexual appetite. It is, however, a general rule that most natives desire children, but they desire far more sexual gratification than is usually considered normal.

This sexual desire is at the bottom of a great many

of their social institutions, and results in a very unmoral method of life.

Feeding. This is a strong instinct, and the native often feeds entirely by instinct; that is to say, he will often not keep regular hours of meals, but eat when he is hungry and when opportunity offers. This means that they frequently overfeed.

Acquisition. This instinct is strong, but if one may call it so it is temporary. Thus the native woman will collect an enormous number of clothes, many of which perhaps she has used but once, but she will part with them for the acquisition of cash. Perhaps she will part with clothes less readily than other articles of domestic use, for it is quite easy to buy most things a native possesses, and he is often quite ready to part with them.

He is anxious to acquire money in the easiest way, and it is generally spent on food or clothes. The native is not a collector, and therefore not acquisitive in the same way that a European is.

Construction. The constructive instinct is not strong—no native wishes to construct more of anything than is absolutely necessary. In the same way his destructive instinct is almost lacking, for he will destroy nothing that is not in his way simply because it is too much trouble to do so.

Self-Preservation. Self-preservation is as strong among the natives as most other people but tempered by a resignation to fate, i.e., as a rule they will give up easily if they believe fighting is hopeless. They are perhaps too easily convinced of its hopelessness.

General Summing up of the Character of the Native of Zanzibar

The character of the Zanzibar native differs considerably from his cousins of other tribes on the mainland. The reader should not fall into the error of supposing that all African natives have the same characteristics. The Nyamwezi, for instance, is a hard worker and the soul of thrift, but the Swahili dislikes work as strenuous as that done by the Nyamwezi, and is one of the most improvident people in the world. There is, too, a difference between the natives of Zanzibar and those of Pemba, and still more those of Zanzibar town. The manners of all are affected by their Islamic profession, but the Mpemba is far more polite than the Hadimu; anywhere in Pemba a stranger is received with all marks of respect, those near stand up and one is continually replying to salutations, but in Zanzibar the stranger rarely gets a *jambo* unless he gives it first. Both the Pemba and the Hadimu natives are hospitable, but the exclusive Tumbatu goes to almost any lengths to drive the invader from his island. The manners of the town tough corrupted by evil communications are often beyond description.

On the whole, though, certain general characteristics apply to most of them indifferently, and the average native may be described as utterly improvident, inordinately vain at heart, lazy, untruthful, much given to procrastination and very sensual. He is always ready to dispossess himself of responsibility, and with no other scapegoat available, loads the blame for things that go wrong on to the Almighty with the words *Shauri ya Mungu* (All is God's affair).

Zanzibar, as the late Miss Thackeray, who lived there more than forty years, once said to me, is the land of *kesho* (to-morrow), and *Haraka, Haraka haina baraka* (more haste less speed) was nowhere else more literally observed. *Dasturi* (custom) rules his life and he will do anything, however shady, to increase or preserve his *heshima* (rank, position, respect). Despite all this, though, he is usually cheerful and rarely sulks; as a general rule polite; generous to the point of extravagance, he hates stinginess in others; tolerant in all ways, he has a sense of humour and dislikes sarcasm levied at himself. He has a strong sense of family affection and loyalty to his friends.

Burton says the Waswahili have inherited the

characteristics of Arabs and Africans. Arab, he says, are their shrewd thinking and practice in concealing thought, their unusual confidence, self-esteem and complacency, fondness for praise and honours, keenness but short-sightedness in business and horror of responsibility and regular occupation. Their tolerance, suspicion, duplicity, dishonesty, untruthfulness, foul language, nonchalance, carelessness, improvidence, procrastination, cowardliness, sensuality, he attributes to their African ancestry, as also their dislike of overt request, combined with inveterate begging habits. Their manners he describes as rough and free, yet dashed with a queer African ceremoniousness. Their conversation turns wholly on women and money, and they hold that old custom, because it is old, must be good for all time.

Their characteristic good points, he says, are careless merriment, an abundance of animal spirits, strong attachments, and devoted family affection.

As regards their untruthfulness he says, "When they assert they probably lie, when they swear they certainly lie. The favourite oath is *mimi wad* (or *M'ana*) *harami*—I am a bastard if, etc., and it is never respected." I once listened to a discussion on lying between a coast Arab and a few natives. The Arab said it was very wrong to tell lies, except to one's wife. One of the natives said it did not matter how many lies you told even in court if you only swore *Wallai* (By Allah), but if you said *Wallai, billai, tallai, Wallai el Adhim* (By God, by God, by God, by God, the Almighty), you must in self-defence speak the truth or you would assuredly die. I think this is the general attitude.

I give two little stories humorous to a non-native, but which illustrate to some degree the difference in the point of view between Westerns and Africans; one I heard myself and the other was repeated to me. A native was telling me about some coast places he had visited; having heard of Shimoni I asked him about it. His reply was, "Allah. Shimoni. You are not going to Shimoni? You had far better go to jail than go there."

The other is of a native servant who had left a very comfortable place. He was met by a lady who knew him well and who asked him why he had left. On being pressed he replied, "Well, bibi, there is so much brass in that house and it is always so polished, you'd think Allah was coming to tea every day."

Some of their humour, while quite witty, is also rather of the doubtful variety, and they are quite clever at repartee. The following example of this is better left in the original Swahili. One said to another, "*Huwezi kula mboga*," taunting him. Like a flash came the question, "*Kwanini, shimeji?*"

Character, no less than religion, seems to be the result of environment.

As regards the Zanzibaris, their character seems to be exactly what one would expect it to be. Zanzibar is a hot, sunny land, where rain and cold are the exception, a land where no one need work, for the fertility of the soil would not allow one to starve. It exudes an atmosphere which conduces to nothing more than lying down, and sleeping and being at peace with all men, taking the easiest path always.

Faults the native has in abundance, but he is a lovable person, and repays sympathy and interest.

Also it must be remembered that their code of honour and their ideals are entirely different to ours, and cannot be judged from the same standpoint.

An Englishman finds at once that they are addicted to bribery and corruption, but he must remember that it is not bribery and corruption to them, and that "payments made for services rendered" are considered perfectly right and reasonable.

CHAPTER XLVI

DREAMS AND GHOSTS

Records of dreams and ghosts are of great value in studying the psychology of a people. However, it is extraordinarily difficult to obtain examples, or to get good descriptions of the first class. The African element places no importance on dreams, and I have never had even a suggestion as to what causes them.

The commonest type of dreams are those connected with money and women; many of each have been related to me but only in two or three lines.

The Arabs make quite a science of dreams and interpret them according to regular rules. This is a common feature of all Semitic people. They also have methods of inducing dreams. For example, to obtain a dream of the prophet Mohammed recite " Ina Artenaki el Keuton," sleep alone and pray to see him.

Ghosts and hauntings are common, but attributed not to ghosts as we call them, but to devils.

Haunted houses are by no means rare. There is a house at Chake Chake where the apparition of an old man with long white beard who mounts the stairs at midnight, so that they creak, and walks round the bedroom, has been seen not only by Arabs, but by Goans. Tundua Bungalow is said to be haunted, and no native will sleep inside it alone. The same remark applies to the ruins of the old towns of Mkumbuu, Chake and Pujini in Pemba, and the Ngezi Forest is haunted. It is said that when huts were being pulled down at Zanzibar to make room for the British Agency, an old woman who was evicted pronounced a curse on the ground, manifestations afterwards occurred and the Bishop was called in to exorcize the ghost.

Doctor Spurrier's story of Dunga Palace is now well known, and is to be found related in Major Pearce's book. The ghosts of Dunga, in Zanzibar, are as famous as those of Pujini, in Pemba. A missionary told me a tale, which I forget in its details now, of two of his colleagues who slept in one of the old palaces of Zanzibar, one on a verandah and one in a room. The latter had to evacuate in the night as the feeling was so unpleasant, and he received a distinct impression that a child was being murdered there. It transpired subsequently that such indeed had been the case years before. In Chake Chake town the apparition of two small children walking hand in hand down the main street at night has been frequently seen. The phenomenon of stones, etc., being thrown by invisible hands (poltergeists), of which instances are given, is well known, and the late Bishop of Zanzibar has also described it.

When editor of the Zanzibar *Gazette* I published a series of ghost stories therein, and the curious will find them in the volume for 1927. The best is the one of a haunted necklace, which was the first in the series.

(*a*) *Dreams*

Omar Hasan dreamt that I gave him five rupees in the office and told him to buy chickens. He woke up and found himself in his home.

Another time he dreamt he was seized by the legs, which were pulled up above his head and shaken. He shouted out and woke up.

. . . .

Sheha of Chambani. "I dreamt I was in my house counting rupees. I woke up and found nothing."

This man has a great deal of property, but has many wives and sixteen children. He is, therefore, always in need of ready money and thinks in rupees.

Omar Hasan. "I dreamt that I had on a *ubinda* and that the *pepo* had entered, and people were playing an *ngoma*."

This man is the leader of an *ngoma*.

. . . .

Juma. "Four days ago I dreamt I went past the market in Chake Chake town to Chachani with Zayidi, and I saw a vast quantity of pice, so many that I could not collect them."

Juma and Zayidi were house-boys of mine. Juma had been in want of money for a long time. His pay was small and his manner of living modest. He therefore thinks in pice.

. . . .

Abdulla Mbaruk. "I dreamt I was in a stone house, and there was a table with glasses and cups on it. A man came in with a beautiful glass, a quarter full of yellow wine. He said, 'Drink,' I said, 'No.' He said, 'Drink.' I said, 'Is it not wine?' He said, 'Whisky.' I said, 'I cannot drink. I don't drink whisky.' He said, 'Drink. You will see no harm come of it,' and then I agreed. I did not find it strong, but like water, and it did not go to my head. I said afterwards, 'I have done wrong,' and then I woke. I had been dreaming.

"I told Mohammed Suleiman about it, and he said, 'If you dream of a thing you don't use you will get honour and profit.' I went to Abdulla and he told me the same thing. After a short time I got the Fourth Class of the Brilliant Star."

Good Mohammedans, of course, do not drink intoxicants. Sheikh Abdulla bin Mbaruk is an "akida" in Government service in Pemba.

. . . .

Abdulla Mbaruk. "I was staying in Zanzibar during the month of Funguo mosi, and one night I dreamt that an *askari* of the police came and told me I was wanted at the police station. I went and found a European there, who said, 'There is a road in Pemba. Go to Weti and do not get off at

Chake.' I said, 'Very well.' On mail day I went on board, and at Chake Chake I said, 'I will get off for the day and return to the ship to-night.' On shore I met Mr. A, and told him, and said, 'I do not know the reason,' and he said, 'I do not know either, but Mr. B says you must go to Weti.' So I returned to the ship. I woke up and found myself at home.

"I told my dream to some friends in the morning, and after having been out to do some business in the town, I returned and found a messenger, who told me that I was wanted at the Government offices, and I was there told that I was to go up to Weti (to which place I was a stranger) to do some work in connection with the road there."

(*b*) *Hallucinations and Ghosts*

Saleh one day left Ngambwa, a native village in the Chake district of Pemba. He was walking along the road and he heard a man following behind, and he looked behind but saw nothing. When he came to the river he crossed and heard as though a hundred men were crossing together, and when he got to the other side he felt dizzy and lost consciousness. Afterwards he sat down and laughed and chewed betel and played a *kinanda*, although he had no idea what he was doing. Nothing further happened, but the next morning a man came and warned him not to go on that road late at night, after what had happened to him on the previous night.

. . . .

When Mohammed bin Mbaruk was "akida" (a post of authority) of the police, he went one night to the market in Chake town to inspect the policemen on duty there. It was midnight, and standing in front of the mosque was a weird figure of a tiny black man, with a very thin face and very thin hands, wearing a white cloth from waist to knees.

He looked at the "akida," who, hypnotized with

terror, stared at him for fifteen minutes, and then managed to turn his head away. When he looked again the apparition had vanished.

. . . .

When the death of a member of the Mauli tribe occurred in Muscat, a mysterious voice would announce the news in Pemba, and when such a death occurred in Pemba the voice would inform the people of Muscat in the same way.

On these occasions a letter would be written to say that the voice had announced the death of so-and-so on such and such a date, and invariably a confirmation of the news was received.

. . . .

About fifty years ago, Abdulla bin Khamis, a sub-" akida " was going from Mkanjuni, a village near Chake town, to Mzambaraoni Samli, another village close by.

It was night, and as he was going down the road leading to the village, he was terrified by a sudden apparition of a crowd of children in front of him, and he turned and ran home in fright.

. . . .

One day when Yahya was asleep in bed he woke up suddenly, and to his great fear saw the wall of his house split open, and through the opening a lamp was shining outside.

When at last he overcame his fear and got out of bed to see, it became pitch dark, and by the time he had lit a candle he found the house was whole again.

. . . .

One day a man called Saleh left Gambani, in the Chake district, to go to Mkanjuni, another village. When he was going over a bridge in a place called Selem, he was startled by a tremendous crash, as of a very large tree falling, and as he stood still for a moment, listening, the apparition of a child of about six years of age, brushed him closely. He hurried on, and a little farther he saw before him an animal eating grass, something like an ox but as big as an elephant.

When he had passed it and was making his way up a hill a man came behind him and beat him with sticks, but he could not feel the blows. He stood still in the road, and then he saw the form go immediately in front of him, still hitting out blindly: frightened, he took out a knife and struck it many times, and suddenly the apparition vanished, then there was silence, and he reached home and nothing further happened.

. . . .

A member of the Friend's Industrial Mission in Chake, Miss Hutchinson, had an interesting experience while visiting a Bohora woman.

This woman, who had consumption, lived in her father's house mothering her widowed brother's children. One day she told Miss Hutchinson of a voice she heard calling to her, and her brother confirmed the story, and as Miss Hutchinson was puzzling over their statements a high-pitched voice from behind her, apparently from the kitchen, called "*Bibi hujambo?*" (Lady, how are you?) The woman whispered, "Did you hear? That's it. Listen." It said again, "*Bibi anywa chai?*" (Lady, will you have some tea?) Then no more, and the people told her how it had thrown bits of mortar, coco-nut shell, charcoal from the fire, etc., into the room, how it had asked for an orange, which had disappeared, and how the voice had asked forgiveness for taking it.

The children treated it as a huge joke; not so the adults, who were convinced it was a djinn and the sole cause of the woman's illness, for had not all the medicine failed to cure her? So they engaged an Arab teacher to come and read the Koran and exorcize it, and the voice would tell which chapter to read.

This went on for many months, and Miss Hutchinson heard it many times when visiting the house. One day she went and found the woman in great distress: on asking what had caused it, she told her how the night before when she was alone the voice had said to her, "On Friday I shall take your fat and drink your blood," or words to that effect, and the woman had taken it as a warning of death. Miss Hutchinson told her she should not believe such things, and that it probably had no such meaning.

However, on Friday afternoon she went down again only to find that the woman had died that morning. From that time the voice was never heard in that house again.

. . . .

Khalef bin Nasor and his wife went to spend the night in a new house at Kaole. He lit a lamp and arranged everything in the room. Then turning down the light, they went to bed. Later in the night he woke up, and to his great fear saw the light was turned up, and the chairs, which he had previously placed against the wall, arranged in a circle round the lamp. Too terrified to get up, he stayed in bed until dawn, when he got up and replaced them, as his wife would have been frightened. In the morning, although he knew it would have been impossible for her to reach the lamp even on a chair, he asked her about it, but she knew nothing. He then went and asked his uncle for advice, and he came and put charms in the rooms. However, although nothing further actually happened, Khalef still heard the noise at night of things being moved about and of someone bathing in the wash-house, which was, of course, securely locked up. Also every time he filled the tank it was emptied, although it had no leak.

. . . .

One of the jail warders, an Indian, Mera Bux by name, had a disturbing experience on one occasion of being beaten with a stick by an invisible hand when lying down.

. . . .

Thwain bin Khalif used to bring strange women into the house when his wife was away, and these used to be beaten by invisible hands.

Mamie Sadi was a mad woman at Kaole, who was constantly having sand and stones thrown at her by invisible hands.

On one occasion Mohammed bin Seif and Salim were going down the road with her and they both saw stones thrown at her, but could not discover whence they came. They sent for a slave called Zaid to take her by the hand, and then this stopped, and they took her down the shore and put her under a huge cooking-pot they found there, and when she was inside stones came raining down on to the spot. Afterwards she was taken to the fort, where the devil that possessed her was exorcized.

. . . .

On the 19th April, 1920, Juma Wadi Mambo entered a house with wide, staring eyes, obviously out of control, and behaving like a madman or as if drunk. Being a man of excellent character, it was surprising, and he was sent for medical examination which, however, proved he had not been drinking.

His own story was that he was passing, on the road to Kizimbani, a village in Weti district, when under a mango tree appeared a very, very tall white figure which startled him so that he went mad with terror.

To the peculiar behaviour of this man and his wild, staring eyes I can bear witness, as I was sitting in the house with the magistrate when he entered, and overcame him with the aid of the police.

. . . .

One night Abdulla Nasur was going home from the market in Chake Chake town to his house, which was on the site of the present hospital, when he met a monstrosity, very tall, with a head like an enormous saucepan. He fled home shouting with terror, and was found in a panic-stricken condition.

. . . .

Khalef bin Nasor was going home from the market in Chake town about ten-thirty to his house, in the native quarter of Kichangani, when he heard the breathing as of a man who had fallen and was in pain, and he went to see what it was. To his great fear he saw sitting on the baraza of a hut, a monstrosity, with a head about two feet broad and a small body with very short arms and legs, which he was waving about—and he was making the noise Khalef had heard. He turned and ran away in terror.

. . . .

Thenian bin Khalef was going from Kaole to Mkanjuni, in the Chake district, with some companions and they saw a "Komanzi" standing by a *mchikiche* (oil palm) taller than the palm, in white clothes, and in the moonlight they could see he had a turban on. They were frightened, and the donkeys could not move with terror.

The "Komanzi" then ran away, and the noise of his footsteps were like trees falling.

A Komanzi is perhaps the commonest form of bogey. Many natives and Arabs say they have seen them, and describe them as enormously tall creatures, very thin, with big heads. The natives are not much afraid of them, as they say they are great cowards.

Knowing the strong imagination of the natives and their terror of night, which they think is peopled with all sorts of bogeys, I should be inclined to suggest that the origin of the Komanzi is the coco-nut tree. In the uncertain light of the moon a solitary coco-nut tree, perhaps with a deformed trunk, and standing among other trees with its branches waving always in the wind, might well be taken for a bogey. Gusts of wind resulting in the moonlight being suddenly thrown on a palm tree and turning it white, and then the palm tree being as suddenly thrown into dark again, might cause a delusion that it was something supernatural appearing and disappearing.

CHAPTER XLVII

PHYSICAL CHARACTERISTICS OF THE ZANZIBARIS

THE negroids of Zanzibar are woolly-haired, though a few are to be found whose hair is of the peppercorn description. Their faces and bodies, with the exception of the pubes and the axillæ areas, are as a general rule almost hairless, and even in the places mentioned the hair does not grow strongly. Moustaches are usually present but very scanty, and the beard, if not entirely absent, is scantier still. Owing to their mixed race, however, there are some notable exceptions to this, and the appearance of strong, bushy beards is not a very uncommon sight among natives claiming to be only of Pemba, Hadimu or Tumbatu parentage. The skin varies from all shades of yellowish brown to black, chocolate brown predominating, but the really black native is the most uncommon. The average stature of those I have measured is nearly 64 inches, 66 inches being an unusual height. The span, always longer than the stature, averaged 70½ inches. The teeth are usually very good and regular, but the cusps are almost always worn away in a man of thirty. They are typically dolichocephalic, but there are a large number of mesocephalic heads, and brachycephalic are not very uncommon. The nose is always platyrhine, but is often well-shaped, and prognathous faces are not common. The ears are small and well-shaped, lying closely to the head; "cabbage" ears are never seen. The cranial capacity of skulls I have measured varied from 1,280-1,340 c.c., but skulls are difficult to acquire.

The natives sleep on their sides, with knees drawn up and an arm under the head.

The head is usually covered in sleep. They are very alert sleepers, and when wakened suddenly lash out with the disengaged arm with a backward movement. This habit is born of the necessity that there used to be in the old times of always being prepared for attack. It is a dangerous thing to wake a Manga Arab suddenly, as they usually sleep with a weapon to hand.

They generally retire between nine and ten and rise at six or six-thirty. During the night a small lamp is usually kept burning.

When resting, natives sit with crossed legs either in the traditional attitude of the tailor or with knees up. It is curious, however, that they are now in a process of developing new ideas of comfort, and nothing is more popular than a hard-seated, straight-backed chair, and this type of seat is rapidly becoming universal.

When resting as opposed to sleeping, the native does not lie down but nearly always sits up. When resting for a very short time only, and to perform necessary acts the native sits on his heels. Kihadimu has a special verb for this.

This attitude is also adopted for drinking.

Loads are always carried on the head. In the ordinary way a native cannot conveniently carry more than 30 lb., but trained porters carry far heavier loads for short distances up to half a mile. These vary from bags of cloves of about 80 lb. to bags of salt weighing 225 lb. Loads of over 100 lb. are usually carried on the head and the back, the porter inclining his head and back into one plane at about 70°.

Physically there are not many very strong, and compared with other natives they are but slightly built.

One sees few deformed (possibly these die early), and the fact that the women are well set up and straight, and that their bodies are not restrained, probably also accounts for the scarcity of congenital malformations. Of such deformities, talipes, infantile paralysis, and dislocated hips can be seen, but compared with civilized countries they are scarce. The occurrence of a sixth but useless finger is not rare, and a few hare-lips are to be observed. Idiots and epileptics also occur. Owing to bad midwifery, umbilical herniæ are a common sight, and I have seen them protruding two or three inches.

They are great walkers and think nothing of twenty miles or so. Even on wide roads single file is usually the rule, though there are frequent exceptions. It is obviously a habit born of long use of narrow paths. As a result of going unshod the skin of the toes often cracks and resists all attempts at healing. For the same reason the toe-nails are very short and worn. They dislike cold, but often remark if the sun is very hot. Not many ride donkeys, but all (including women) ride astride when using them.

They are skilful climbers and shin up a coco-nut tree with remarkable rapidity. The way this is done is to make a loop about a foot or eighteen inches long and twist it into a figure of eight. A foot is then placed in each loop, and reaching up the tree as far as he can, the climber holds on and draws his feet up as far as possible, and then stretches himself out again and repeats the performance. Swimming is done with the overarm stroke, though when under water they swim like frogs with the forearm to the sides. The big toe is not opposable at all, but is often used to hold things with (between big and second toe) especially by carpenters.

The native of Zanzibar does not live long. He matures quickly and is an old man at forty. Sixty is a ripe old age, and though there be some that come to three score years and ten, few reach four score years. Forty to fifty is an average age for those who attain to manhood. I have seen two old women for whom a century of years was claimed. Disease accounts for a large proportion, and there is heavy infantile mortality. Debility, tuberculosis and malaria are given as the principal causes of death.

As a general rule, when meeting with a native in the ordinary way his facial expression is no index to his thoughts.

The impassive look on his face, however, is rapidly transformed by circumstances to one either of pleasure or of fear.

These two expressions are readily ascertainable and most marked. A less frequent one is a sulky set look. Wonderment is to be noticed sometimes, but rarely interest.

As regards the personal appearance of the natives opinions have divided.

Marco Polo's description is amusing but inaccurate, as it was obtained only from hearsay. He says: "In their person they are large, but their height is not proportionate to the bulk of their bodies; were it otherwise they would appear gigantic. They are, however, strongly made, and one of them is capable of carrying what would be a load for four of our people. At the same time he would require as much food as five. They are black and go naked, covering only the private parts of the body with a cloth. Their hair is so crisp that even when dipped in water it can with difficulty be drawn out. They have large mouths, their noses turn up towards the forehead, their ears are long and their eyes so large and frightful that they have the aspect of demons. The women are equally ill-favoured, having wide mouths, thick noses, and large eyes. Their hands and also their heads are out of all proportion large."

Burton says: "The Waswahili of the island appear physically inferior to those of the seaboard: as in the days of Marco Polo, they are an emphatically ugly race. If the girls in early youth show traces of prettiness, it is of the grotesque order of the *Beauté de diable*. Some of the men have fine, large, strong and muscular figures, without being able to use their strength, and as amongst uncivilized people generally, the reality falls short of the promise.

"The national peculiarity is the division of the face

into two distinct types, and the contrast appears not a little singular. The upper or intellectual part, though capped by woolly hair, is distinctly Semitic with the suspicion of a caricature—as far as the nose-bridge, and the more ancient the family the more evident is the mixture. The lower or animal part, especially the nostrils, lips, jaws and chin is unmistakably African. There are a few albinos with silk-cocoon coloured hair, and tender red eyes, their pinkish skins are cobwebbed by darker reticulations and rough from pellagrous disease. Leucosis, however, is rare; we saw only two cases, one on the island, the other a youth near Tanga.

"The Waswahili are by no means a jet-black people, as Pritchard, misled by Dr. Bird, has assumed; nor, indeed, is this the distinction of the Zanzibarian races generally. The skin is a chocolate-brown varying in shades, as amongst ourselves, but usually not darker than the complexion of Southern Arabia. About Lamu and Patta the colour is yellow-brown; at Mombasa and Zanzibar dark brown; and south of Kilwa, I am told, black-brown. Mostly the hair is jetty unless sunburnt; crisp and curling short; it splits after growing a few inches long, and often it is planted like the body pile, in distinct 'pepper-corns.' The barbule is a degeneracy from the Arab goatee, and the mustachios are short and scanty. The oval skull, too dolichocephalous to be purely Caucasian, is much flattened at the walls, and sometimes the upper brow (the reflective region of Gall) is too highly developed for the lower. The eyes, with dark brown pupils and cornea stained dirty bilious-yellow, are straight and well opened, but the nose is flat and patulous, the mouth is coarse and ill-cut; the lips often everted, project unduly; the teeth are obliquely set, and the jaw is prognathous. The figure is loose and pulpy, and even in early manhood the waist is seldom finely formed; in many men I have seen the nipples placed unusually low down, whilst the women have the flaccid pendulous breasts of negresses. Both sexes fail in point of hips, which are lank and angular, whereas those of the inner savages are finely rounded. The shanks are bowed forward, the calf is high raised and bunchy, the heel is long, and the extremities are coarse and large. There is another proof of African blood which can hardly be quoted here; many overland travellers have remarked it amongst the boatmen of Egypt."

It may be that the appearance of the native grows on one, but personally I prefer to side with Lieutenant Ferguson, who wrote in 1852 that "the women are only of moderate stature, well made, rather plump, and in many instances very pretty. The features of both men and women are well proportioned and refined, with fine jet black hair and eyes, good teeth and in general small hands and feet." Of the men he wrote that they were "tall and lean, but very muscular." Their height is not great, and I think it is well agreed that their muscular strength bears no comparison with that of some of the natives of West Africa, for example.

Whatever opinions may be as to the look of the women, everyone must agree that they have a fine carriage, born probably of the custom of carrying burdens on their heads.

Albinoes are not uncommon. I recollect seeing quite a dozen. Their skins are quite white, but easily damaged. Their eyes are blue and they are very shortsighted, almost blind, especially in bright sunlight. Albino men seem to marry quite freely and their children are black. Albino women are never married.

And thiſ iſ the end of the ſtory of the Zanzibariſ
and iſ in anything I have tranſgreſſed the truth
I crave pardon; but God knowſ beſt: from Him
alone comeſ guidance and through Him
only do we attain to the truth.

BIBLIOGRAPHY

Africa, Parliamentary Papers relating to,

Africa Pilot, Part III. London, 1915.

Arabian Nights, The. Translated by E. W. Lane. Edited by S. Lane-Poole. 3 vols. London, 1883.

ARTHUR, G. *Life of Lord Kitchener.* London, 1920.

BALL, N. *Zanzibar Treaties.* 1910.

Barbosa, Duarte, The Book of. Edited by M. Löngworth Dames. 2 vols. 1918.

BEECH, MERVYN W. H. *Aids to the Study of Ki-Swahili.* London.

BRETSCHNEIDER. *On the Knowledge Possessed by the Ancient Chinese of the Arabs, etc.* London, 1871.

British Museum, Handbook to the Ethnographical Collections. Oxford, 1925.

BRODE, DR. H. *Tippoo Tib.* London, 1907.

BUDGE, SIR E. A. WALLIS. *The Queen of Sheba and her only Son Menyelek.* London, 1922.

BUDGE, SIR E. A. WALLIS. *Egyptian Magic.* London, 1899.

BURTON, RICHARD F. *Zanzibar; City Island and Coast.* 2 vols. 1872.

BURTON, RICHARD F. *Camoen's Life.* London, 1881.

BURTON, RICHARD F. *The Book of the Thousand Nights and a Night.* 17 vols. London, 1886.

CANDOLLE, A. DE. *Origin of Cultivated Plants.* London, 1884.

CHATTERTON, E. KEBLE. *Sailing Ships and Their Story.* London, 1909.

CHAU JU-KUA. *Chu-fan-chï.* Translated by F. Hirth and W. W. Rockhill. St. Petersburg, 1911.

COLOMB, CAPTAIN R. N. *Slave-Catching in the Indian Ocean.* London, 1873.

CRABTREE, REV. W. A. *Primitive Speech.* London, 1922.

CRASTER, CAPTAIN J. E. E. *Pemba, The Spice Island of Zanzibar.* London, 1913.

CROFTON, R. H. *Statistics of the Zanzibar Protectorate,* 1893-1927. Zanzibar, 1928.

DALE, THE VEN. GODFREY. *The Peoples of Zanzibar.* London, 1920.

DALTON, SIR C. N. *The Real Captain Kidd.* London, 1911.

DARWIN, CHAS. *Coral Reefs.* London, 1889.

DEVIC, L. MARCEL. *Le Pays des Zendjs ou la Côte Orientale D'Afrique au Moyen Age après les écrivans arabes.* Paris, 1883.

DIXON, AINSWORTH. *The Regalia of the Wa-Vumba.* Man, 1921, 20.

East Africa, Uganda and Zanzibar, Handbook for. (Annual to 1907.) Mombasa. (Contains valuable historical notes.)

ELIOT, SIR CHAS. *The East Africa Protectorate.* London, 1905.

FITZGERALD, W. W. A. *Travels in B.E.A., Zanzibar and Pemba.* London, 1898.

FLURY, S. *The Kufic Inscriptions of Kizimkazi Mosque, Zanzibar.* 500 H. (A.D. 1107). J.R.A.S. 1922.

FRAZER, SIR J. G. *The Golden Bough.* 12 vols. London, 1920.

GARNIER, J. *The Worship of the Dead.* London, 1904.

GASTER, M. *The Sword of Moses.* Hebrew Magic. London, 1896.

GUILLAIN, M. *Documents sur l'Histoire, la Géographie, et le Commerce de l'Afrique Orientale.* Bertrand. Paris, 1856.

HAKLUYT, RICHARD. *The Principal Voyages of the English Nation.* Vol. IV. London.

HOBLEY, C. W. *Bantu Beliefs and Magic.* London, 1922.

HOGARTH, D. G. *Arabia.* 1922.

HOGARTH, D. G. *The Penetration of Arabia.* London, 1904.

HOLLIS, A. C. *Notes on the History of Vumba, East Africa.* J.R.A.I. 1900.

HOLLWEG, BETHMANN VON. *Reflections on the World War.* London, 1920.

HOWORTH, SIR H. H. *Buddhism in the Pacific.* J.R.A.I. Vol. LI. 1921.

HUGHES, T. P. *Dictionary of Islam.* London, 1885.

INGRAMS, W. H. *Sindbad the Sailor in East African Waters.* Zanzibar, 1927.

INGRAMS, W. H. *Khaled bin Barghash: A Memoir.* Zanzibar, 1927.

INGRAMS, W. H. *Said bin Sultan: An Appreciation.* Zanzibar, 1926.

INGRAMS, W. H. *Chronology and Genealogies of Zanzibar Rulers.* Zanzibar, 1926.

INGRAMS, W. H. *Zanzibar, An Account of its People, Industries and History.* Zanzibar, 1924.

INGRAMS, W. H., and HOLLINGSWORTH, L. W. *A School History of Zanzibar.* London, 1925.

JACKSON, CAPTAIN R. N. *Principal Winds and Currents.* London, 1904.

JOHNSTON, SIR HARRY H. *A Comparative Study of the Bantu and Semi-Bantu Languages.* Oxford, 1919.

JOHNSTON, SIR HARRY H. *The Colonisation of Africa.* Cambridge, 1905.

Kenya Colony and Protectorate, Handbook of. London.

KRAPF, J. L. *A Dictionary of the Swahili Language.* London, 1882.

Lancaster's Voyages to the East Indies. London, 1877.

LANE. *Manners and Customs of the Modern Egyptians.* London, 1836.

LENORMANT, F. *Chaldean Magic.* London.

LOCKYER, SIR NORMAN. *Stonehenge.* London, 1906.

LYNE, R. N. *Zanzibar in Contemporary Times.* London, 1905.

MADAN, A. C. *Swahili-English Dictionary. English-Swahili Dictionary.* Oxford, 1903.

MASUDI. *Muruju 'l dhahab.*

MCTHEAL, G. *History of Africa South of the Zambezi.* London, 1916.

MOHAMMED ABDULLA BIN HUMEYYID BIN SALIM EL-SALIMI. *Talkein Sibian.*

MOHAMMED AMIN EL-BUGHDADI. *Sebaike Dheheb Kabaile el-Arab.*

MOREHEAD, A. E. M. ANDERSON. *The History of the U.M.C.A.* London, 1897.

MUIR, WM. *The Life of Mahomet.* 4 vols. London, 1858.

MUIR, WM. *The Caliphate, Its Rise, Decline and Fall.* Edinburgh, 1915.

Native Histories of Zanzibar and Pemba.

Several coast native histories have been published and are referred to in this bibliography (Kilwa, J.R.A.S., Vumba, J.R.A.I., Pate, J.A.S., Mombasa in Owen's *Voyages.* I have heard of another history in manuscript at Dar-es-Salaam). The following manuscripts have been discovered by Mr. J. S. Last, Assistant District Commissioner, or by myself in Zanzibar :—

Zanzibar. Tumbatu MS. History of Shirazi advent and genealogical trees of the Ba Alawi. No date.

Kizimkazi MS. Genealogical tree of the Sherifs of Kizimkazi. Dated 10th Rabi-el-Awwal, 1229 H. (A.D. 1813).

Pemba. Ndagoni I. MS. Probably fictitious. An attempt to derive Shirazi from Shiraz, son of Malik bin Fahm, and thus to make the Shirazis of Mkumbuu, Ndagoni (see page 50), of Arab descent. Gives the story of Malik bin Fahm and his son Sulaimah. The Sebaike Dheheb does not give the names of any of Malik bin Fahm's sons as Shiraz. No date.

Ndagoni II. MS. Account of purchase of land to settle by the Shirazis from the Aborigines. Dated 1st Moharram, 910 H. (A.D. 1503).

Ndagoni III. MS. History of the Shirazis in Pemba from their coming to the time of Seyyid Said. Written on Borassus palm leaf. Dated 27th Shaban, 1267 H. (A.D. 1750).

Ndagoni IV. MS. Genealogy and arrival of the Shirazis who settled at Mkumbuu, Ndagoni. No date.

Kisiwani MS. Modern copy of collection of fragments of old histories, giving a variant of the Kilwa story, and particularly relating the arrival of Shirazis at Pemba, Zanzibar and Tumbatu. Together with genealogies. Includes copy of Ndagoni II. Dated (in part) 22nd Safar, 1255 H. (A.D. 1838).

Jambangome MS. Later dealings of Franks (Portuguese ?) with Pemba. Manuscript undated, but story starts on 4th El Haj, 1014 H. (A.D. 1606) (J.S.L.).

Other minor manuscripts refer to transactions of the Mwenyi Mkuu, etc. (see section IV). There is in Pemba a book of

Khutbehs (sermons) attributed to Mkame Mdume, and in Zanzibar a manuscript Koran of the Mwenyi Mkun dated 1188 H. (A.D. 1773).

All the above papers are treated as communal property of the tribes concerned.

NEWMAN, H. S. *Banani.* London.

NICHOLSON, R. A. *A Literary History of the Arabs.* London, 1907.

OWEN, CAPTAIN W. F. W. *Narrative of Voyages.* 2 vols. London, 1833.

PALGRAVE, W. G. *Travels in Central and Eastern Arabia.* 2 vols. London, 1865.

PEARCE, MAJOR F. B. *Zanzibar, The Island Metropolis of Eastern Africa.* London, 1920.

Persian Gulf Pilot. London, 1915.

Polo, The Travels of Marco. Ed. Yule. London, 1908.

RAVENSTEIN, E. G., Translator. *A Journal of the First Voyage of Vasco da Gama, 1497-1499.* London.

RAWLINSON, PROFESSOR GEORGE. *History of Ancient Egypt.* 2 vols. 1881.

Red Sea and Gulf of Aden Pilot. London, 1921.

RIDLEY, H. N. *Spices.* London, 1912.

RIGBY, LIEUTENANT-COLONEL P. *Report on the Zanzibar Dominions.* 1860.

RODD, SIR J. RENNELL. *Social and Diplomatic Memories, 1884-1893.* London, 1922.

SACLEUX, CH. *Dictionnaire. Français-Swahili.* Zanzibar-Paris, 1891.

SALIL-IBN-RAZIK. *Imams and Seyyids of Oman.* Ed. G. P. Badger. London, 1871.

SAYCE, REV. A. H. *The Archæology of the Cuneiform Inscriptions.* S.P.C.K. London, 1908.

SCHOFF, W. H. *The Periplus of the Erythræan Sea.* London, 1912.

SKEAT, W. W. *Malay Magic.* London, 1900.

STEERE, E. *Handbook of the Swahili Language.* Ed. A. C. Madan. 1918.

STIGAND, CAPTAIN C. H. *The Land of Zinj.* London, 1913.

STRANDES, JUSTUS VON. *Die Portugiesenziet von Deutsch und English-Ostafrika.* Berlin, 1899.

STRONG, A. S. *History of Kilwa.* J.R.A.S. 1895.

STUHLMANN, F. *Beiträge zur Kulturgeschichte von Ostafrika.* Berlin, 1909.

STUHLMANN, F. *Handwerk und Industrie in Ostafrika.* Hamburg, 1910.

SYKES, P. *The Glory of the Shia World.* London.

THEAL, GEO. MCCALL. *Records of South Eastern Africa.* London, 1898-1903.

THOMPSON, R. CAMPBELL. *Semitic Magic.* London, 1908.

TORREND, J. *A Comparative Grammar of the South African Bantu Languages.* London, 1891.

VAUX, DE. *Les Penseurs de l'Islam.* 5 vols. Paris, 1921.
WAYLAND, E. J. *Report on the Geology of Zanzibar.*
WELLS, H. G. *The Outline of History.* London, 1920.
WERNER, A. *A Swahili History of Pate.* J.A.S. 1915.
WERNER, A. *The Wahadimu of Zanzibar.* J.A.S. 1916.
Zanzibar and East Africa, Gazette for. Various dates.
Zanzibar Official Gazette. Various dates.

INDEX

H

I

J

K

L

M

N

O

P

R

S